Exchange Rate Dynamics

T0295649

Are exchange rates determined by economic fundamentals or are they a prey to random speculative forces? Some economists assert that economic theory has so far performed poorly in explaining the dramatic increase in exchange rate volatility in the recent floating rate period. This book argues that modern macroeconomic theory does provide guidelines for understanding exchange rate fluctuations.

Since the mid-1990s, there has been an outpouring of research that aims at laying new foundations for open-macroeconomic theory. The so-called "New Open Economy Macroeconomics" (NOEM) approach embeds microfounded behavior into dynamic general equilibrium models. This provides a rich framework for thinking about exchange rate behavior and lays the groundwork for credible policy evaluation. This book shows how the most recent analytical tools proposed in this literature improve our understanding of exchange rate fluctuations.

With contributions from an international array of thinkers, this impressive book shall interest both students and researchers involved with macroeconomics, money and banking, as well as all those interested in international finance, including financial institutions.

Jean-Olivier Hairault is Professor of Economics at the University of Paris 1, Panthéon-Sorbonne, France.

Thepthida Sopraseuth is Assistant Professor at the University of Évry Val d'Essonne, France.

Routledge International Studies in Money and Banking

Exchange Rate Dynamics

A new open economy macroeconomics
perspective

**Edited by Jean-Olivier Hairault
and Thepthida Sopraseuth**

Routledge
Taylor & Francis Group

LONDON AND NEW YORK

First published 2004
by Routledge
11 New Fetter Lane, London EC4P 4EE

Simultaneously published in the USA and Canada
by Routledge
29 West 35th Street, New York, NY 10001

Routledge is an imprint of the Taylor & Francis Group

First issued in paperback 2016

© 2004 Jean-Olivier Hairault and Thepthida Sopraseuth;
individual chapters © individual contributors

British Library Cataloguing in Publication Data
A catalogue record for this book is available
from the British Library

Library of Congress Cataloging in Publication Data
A catalog record for this book has been requested

ISBN 0–415–29877–6

ISBN13: 978-0-415-29877-3 (hbk)
ISBN13: 978-1-138-96922-3 (pbk)

Contents

x   *Contents*

10   Price setting and optimal monetary cooperation: a New Keynesian perspective   **248**
MATTHIEU DARRACQ-PARIÈS

Figures

Tables

Contributors

Steve Ambler, CIRPEE and Université du Québec à Montréal, Canada.

Philippe Andrade, THEMA, Université de Cergy Pontoise, France.

Michele Cavallo, Federal Reserve Bank of San Francisco, USA.

Fabrice Collard, Université de Toulouse (GREMAQ-CNRS and IDEI), France.

Matthieu Darracq-Pariès, Ministère de l'économie, des finances et de l'industrie, France.

Luca Dedola, Banca d'Italia, Italy.

Patrick Fève, Université de Toulouse (GREMAQ and IDEI), France.

Fabio Ghironi, Boston College, USA.

Jean-Olivier Hairault, EUREQua, Université de Paris I, France.

Emmanuel Hakizimana, Université du Québec à Montréal, Canada.

Sylvain Leduc, Federal Reserve Bank of Philadelphia, USA.

Tommaso Monacelli, IGIER, Universita' Bocconi, Italy.

Lise Patureau, EUREQua, Université de Paris I, France.

Thepthida Sopraseuth, EPEE, CEPREMAP and Université d'Evry Val d'Essonne, France.

Preface

Following Obstfeld and Rogoff's (1995) seminal paper, the last decade has seen an outpouring of research aimed at laying new foundations for open-macroeconomic theory. This "New Open Economy Macroeconomics" (NOEM) addresses the core international issues within microfounded general equilibrium models. The intertemporal nature of this approach allows the dynamic effects to be tracked while the presentation of explicit utility and profit maximization problems lays the groundwork for credible policy evaluation.

The salient feature of Obstfeld and Rogoff's (1995) influential paper lies in the attempt to bridge the gap between two strands of the international macroeconomic theory: the agent optimizing framework developed by the "intertemporal approach to the current account" (Frenkel and Razin, 1987) and the Mundell (1963)–Fleming (1962)–Dornbusch (1976) sticky-price setting. Nesting nominal rigidities and imperfect competition within microfounded dynamic general equilibrium models echoes the emergence of the "neo-classical synthesis" (Goodfriend and King, 1997) or the "neo-monetarism" (Kimball, 1995a) in closed-economy macroeconomics. Moreover, the NOEM partakes of the International Real Business Cycle literature (Backus *et al.*, 1994, 1995).

This theoretical framework has spurred a profusion of developments that allow us to revisit the major issues in international macroeconomics. Obstfeld and Rogoff (2000b) recall that the theory is challenged by six empirical puzzles. How can we rationalize the bias for home goods in households' preferences (the home bias in trade puzzle)? Can the high correlation between investment and saving be reconciled with capital mobility (Feldstein and Horioka, 1980)? Why do households not fully take advantage of the international portfolio diversification (the home bias portfolio puzzle and the low consumption correlations puzzle)? Why do deviations from purchasing power parity (PPP), captured by real exchange rate fluctuations, exhibit a very persistent behavior (the PPP puzzle)? Finally, the extreme exchange rate volatility has no corresponding counterpart in macroeconomic fundamentals (the exchange rate disconnect puzzle). The latter empirical observation leads Flood and Rose (1995) to assert that

> There is remarkably little evidence that macroeconomic variables have consistent strong effects on floating rates [...]. Such negative findings have led the profession to a certain degree of pessimism *vis-à-vis* the exchange rate research.

The role of economic fundamentals in explaining exchange rate behavior is undoubtedly controversial. This book intends to propose studies that rely on macroeconomic dynamic models to shed light on exchange rate dynamics. In the first part of the book, we focus, in particular, on the last two puzzles, namely the PPP puzzle and the exchange rate disconnect puzzle. In addition, since NOEM models are far more equipped than the traditional Mundell–Fleming–Dornbusch framework to analyze policy design, the second part of the book examines the impact of alternative exchange rate regimes and policy rules. This book illustrates how NOEM models revisit positive and normative issues that are currently at the heart of the international macroeconomic research.

Some papers (Lane, 2001; Sarno, 2001) have surveyed the recent developments in this literature. However, the book format gives an insight to the heart of the renewal of theoretical open macroeconomics by displaying a full presentation of the models, the analytical solutions and the quantitative implications of the mechanisms at work. This book describes the empirical and theoretical contribution of this "NOEM" to the understanding of exchange rate dynamics and economic policy. Our purpose is to improve our understanding of fluctuations in the exchange rate. Furthermore, we aim to shed light on the choice of exchange rate regimes and monetary policy design in open economies. The partition of the book mirrors this double issue. In Part I, Chapters 1–6 are all concerned with exchange rate volatility and persistence. We present models of the NOEM that examine essential features of exchange rate fluctuations. In Part II, Chapters 8–10 provide guidelines for thinking about the choice of exchange rate regimes and monetary policy. Each chapter is self-contained and can be used independently of the others.

More specifically, Chapter 1 returns to the original intent of Obstfeld and Rogoff's (1995) paper by examining how net foreign assets affect exchange rate dynamics. Michele Cavallo and Fabio Ghironi develop a two-country, flexible-price model of exchange rate determination with incomplete asset markets and stationary net foreign assets. They compare exchange rate dynamics in the traditional case of exogenous money supplies and under endogenous interest rate setting. The nominal exchange rate then depends on the stock of real net foreign assets in both cases. Thus, shocks that cause holdings of net foreign assets to change generate movements of the exchange rate over time. The exchange rate exhibits a unit root when central banks set interest rates to react to inflation. Endogenous monetary policy and asset dynamics have consequences for exchange rate overshooting while a persistent relative productivity shock results in delayed overshooting.

The course of the book then mimics the evolution of the literature by de-emphasizing the role of current account dynamics in accounting for exchange rate fluctuations. Chapter 2 revisits the exchange rate overshooting phenomenon put forward by Dornbusch (1976). Since the end of the fixed exchange rate period in 1971, nominal and real exchange rates of the G7-countries have become extremely volatile, while no corresponding changes have appeared in the distribution of macroeconomic fundamentals. In the spirit of Dornbusch (1976), with

Lise Patureau, we assess whether nominal exchange rate overshooting is responsible for the exchange rate disconnect puzzle. As long as uncovered interest rate parity holds, nominal exchange rate overshooting is linked to a persistent fall in the spread between domestic and foreign nominal interest rates. Given nominal price rigidity, the over-reaction of the nominal exchange rate then translates into an exacerbated response of the real exchange rate. We thus develop a limited participation model in a small open economy setting, with monopolistic competition and price sluggishness. Introducing adjustment costs on money holdings in the model substantially raises the magnitude of the overshooting dynamics and the theoretical nominal and real exchange rate volatilities. Overshooting indeed plays a key role in explaining a substantial part of the exchange rate disconnect puzzle.

While Chapter 2 explores the implication of price stickiness along with credit market frictions, Chapter 3 investigates the role of nominal wage rigidities in the understanding of exchange rate behavior. Steve Ambler and Emmanuel Hakizimana build a dynamic general equilibrium model of a semi-small open economy in which staggered wages are the only source of nominal rigidity. The model is capable of generating highly variable real and nominal exchange rates while predicting relative variabilities of prices and consumption that are broadly compatible with the data. The real and nominal exchange rates predicted by the model are both highly persistent and highly correlated with one another, as in the data.

In Chapter 4, we explore the exchange rate behavior by focusing on two competing explanations to the exchange rate disconnect puzzle. The first one relies on the failure of the law of one price among internationally traded goods. Firms tend to set prices in the buyer's currency (pricing-to-market, PTM) and do not adjust prices to changes in the nominal exchange rate (Betts and Devereux, 1996). This explanation to exchange rate volatility is based on the behavior of traded good prices. In contrast, according to Hau (2000), large nominal exchange rate fluctuations are attributable to the presence of non-traded goods. Chapter 4 proposes a unified theoretical framework including PTM behavior and non-tradables in a two-country sticky-price model. The purpose of this work is twofold. First, we shed light on the way PTM and non-tradables interact in the exchange rate determination. It is shown that, on the one hand, since PTM affects the behavior of tradable prices, local currency pricing matters especially when the share of tradables is not negligible, that is, the economy is open. On the other hand, the degree of openness does not matter if import prices do not respond to exchange rate changes because of PTM behavior. Second, the model helps determine which effect is likely to be the key ingredient to the high exchange rate volatility. Is PTM, more than non-tradables, responsible for the extreme exchange rate variability observed since the fall of the Bretton Woods system? This chapter reveals that the answer is a qualified yes.

In Chapter 5, Philippe Andrade aims at providing empirical evidence on the sources of real exchange rates fluctuations since the collapse of the Bretton Woods system. Structural economic a priori required by such an analysis is drawn from a theoretical framework which can match the long lasting PPP deviations observed in the data. More precisely, Chapter 5 relies on a two-country dynamic general equilibrium model with monopolistic firms which face translog households demand. The long-run properties of this model allow him to identify structural supply, demand and money supply shocks from the empirical study of a three-dimensional system composed of (the logarithm of) the output and price-level differentials between a home and a foreign country and their real exchange rate. He shows that the money supply shock has a non-significant effect (at the 20 percent level) on the real exchange rate after roughly 20 months, which mitigates the PPP puzzle. Indeed, once the real yen/dollar exchange rate data are corrected from their long-run components, (conditional) business-cycles frequencies PPP deviations after a monetary shock are much less persistent than has been previously documented.

In contrast to the previous chapters, Chapter 6 adopts a different approach to exchange rate dynamics by developing a theoretical framework deprived of any kind of market frictions. Fabrice Collard and Patrick Fève rely on real indeterminacy that generates self-fulfilling prophecies. They introduce habit persistence in consumption decisions in an open economy monetary model with a cash-in-advance constraint. They first show that high enough – but still reasonable – values for habit persistence yield indeterminate equilibria. They however establish that real indeterminacy is not *per se* sufficient to generate volatile and persistent fluctuations in exchange rate dynamics. The form of the beliefs matters. When beliefs are purely extrinsic, the nominal exchange rate essentially mimics the dynamics of money supply growth and never overshoots. Conversely, when beliefs are sufficiently positively correlated with money supply shock, the model is capable of generating overshooting and therefore volatility and persistence in exchange rate dynamics.

The second part of the book uses the general equilibrium frameworks developed in the previous chapters to provide guidelines for the choice of exchange rate regimes and monetary policies. In Chapter 7, Thepthida Sopraseuth documents business cycle properties across exchange rate regimes in order to identify the specific impact of exchange rate arrangements on macroeconomic fluctuations. She finds that the consequences of exchange rate arrangements are twofold. Business cycle properties confirm that the volatility puzzle uncovered by Baxter and Stockman (1989) and Flood and Rose (1995) is robust: nominal and real exchange rate volatilities are stabilized by the fixed exchange rate regime with no corresponding changes in the variability of the macroeconomic aggregates. There is no apparent systematic relationship between the exchange rate regime and the volatility of quantities. This conclusion applies to the Bretton Woods System as well as to the European exchange rate arrangement. The second empirical salient feature deals with interdependence. Her conclusion is consistent with Baxter and Stockman's (1989) conclusion about the lack of systematic relationship between the fall of the Bretton Woods System and international comovement. However, this feature is not a stylized fact since the analysis of EMS does not yield the same conclusion. Indeed, during the EMS period, EMS countries are more synchronized with the German cycle than with the US cycle. In that sense, since Germany can be considered as an "anchor" to participating countries, the EMS seems to favor a greater degree of synchronization among EMS countries.

In order to rationalize the empirical findings stressed in Chapter 7, Luca Dedola and Sylvain Leduc construct a general equilibrium model featuring nominal rigidities and deviations from the law of one price, due to firms pricing to market. In Chapter 8, they first document that this framework is consistent with an important business cycle finding: but for the real exchange rate, the currency regime does not affect the volatility of macroeconomic variables. They then explore the welfare cost of pegging the exchange rate and find that a flexible exchange-rate system is preferred to a currency peg. Their result is driven by the fact that, under the flexible exchange-rate system, the central bank, via its interest-rate policy, is able to dampen the movements in output and, therefore, the volatility of employment.

In Chapter 9, Tommaso Monacelli discusses the interest rate rule-based approach to the conduct of monetary policy and the exchange rate regime management in a small open economy. A tractable framework for the analysis of both the optimal policy design problem as well as of simple feedback rules is provided. The relative price channel is specific to the open economy dimension of monetary policy. As such, flexibility in the nominal exchange rate enhances this channel. He shows that the optimal policy under commitment, unlike the time consistent one, entails a stationary nominal exchange rate. Such a feature is shared by a regime of fixed exchange rates. He also shows that under certain conditions, fixed exchange rates can dominate the optimal discretionary policy when the economy is sufficiently open. Tommaso Monacelli also sheds light on a new type of trade-off that a small economy may face when choosing to participate to a currency area, namely a trade-off between the cost of relinquishing exchange rate flexibility and the benefit of designing a monetary regime which allows to implement in practice some of the features of the optimal commitment policy.

Finally, Chapter 10 is another illustration of how the NOEM framework allows monetary policy analysis. Matthieu Darracq-Pariès investigates the implications of different price setting rules for optimal monetary cooperation. He presents a two-country dynamic general equilibrium model with imperfect competition, nominal price rigidities in which the export prices can be denominated either in the producer currency (producer currency pricing, PCP) or in the consumer currency (local currency pricing, LCP). In addition, the model can account both for efficient and inefficient shocks. He first determines the optimal policy rule under alternative price setting. Under LCP, the monetary authorities should target the consumer price index. A pure CPI inflation targeting strategy implements the optimal outcome when shocks are efficient. An analogous result holds under PCP concerning the optimality of PPI inflation targeting. Furthermore, the optimal discretionary policy can be implemented by Taylor style reaction functions. Under LCP the monetary authority adjusts the national nominal interest rate to domestic expected CPI inflation rate with semi-elasticity above one. Under PCP, nominal interest rate is a function of both domestic and foreign PPI inflation rate with a weight higher than one on domestic inflation. Besides, a fixed exchange rate regime may be optimal under LCP in order to alleviate distortions associated with failures of the law of one price. Under PCP, a flexible exchange rate regime is optimal following efficient shocks. However, the presence of cost-push shocks implies some kind of exchange rate management. Finally, in contrast to Chapter 9, Chapter 10 adopts a two-country setting, which allows to gauge gains from cooperation. Such gains are more likely to arise in a model incorporating cost-push shocks and incomplete exchange rate pass-through. Matthieu Darracq-Pariès' results stress the importance of correctly modeling international price settings when studying monetary policy.

Obstfeld and Rogoff (1995) launched a renewed interest in international macroeconomics by providing a workhorse model for thinking about exchange rate dynamics and economic policies. This book overviews the recent developments in this literature, thereby showing how the NOEM perspective allows for a fruitful study of exchange rate dynamics and policy analysis.

Jean-Olivier Hairault and
Thepthida Sopraseuth

Acknowledgments

We are grateful to the anonymous referees who reviewed the draft of this book and provided numerous helpful comments. We are also indebted to our editor, Robert Langham, who looked after this project and gave us complete support. His efficiency in dealing with the various stages of the project contributed to the quality of this book. Finally, we owe thanks to Terry Clague, Routledge editorial assistant, for guiding us during the preparation of the manuscript.

Part I
Exchange rate volatility and persistence

1 Net foreign assets and exchange rate dynamics

The monetary model revisited

Michele Cavallo and Fabio Ghironi

1.1 Introduction

Exchange rate determination has been the "holy grail" of international finance and macroeconomics ever since the collapse of the Bretton Woods regime in 1971 and the ensuing period of high exchange rate volatility. The work by Obstfeld and Stockman (1985) is an excellent survey of models put forth in the 1970s and early 1980s. Of these, perhaps the most successful was Dornbusch's (1976) overshooting model, centered on the assumptions of uncovered interest parity (UIP) and sticky prices. Dornbusch clarified how exchange rate volatility was indeed consistent with rational behavior in the presence of sticky prices, which would cause the short-run response of the exchange rate to shocks to overshoot the new long-run equilibrium level.

Sadly for a generation of promising theoretical work, Meese and Rogoff (1983) documented evidence that the assumption that the exchange rate is simply described by a random walk process would perform better than the theoretical competitors at predicting the path of the exchange rate at business cycle frequencies. Since then, Meese and Rogoff's (1983) result has been among the major hurdles that theoretical work in search of the "exchange rate grail" has had to overcome. Another major stumbling bloc has been the evidence in favor of delayed overshooting in Clarida and Gali (1994) and Eichenbaum and Evans (1995). Dornbusch's overshooting model predicts that the exchange rate should overshoot its new long-run position on impact in response to a monetary shock. But empirical evidence suggested that overshooting actually takes place several periods after shocks, a finding that was interpreted as evidence against the importance of UIP in exchange rate determination.

Theoretical research on exchange rates developed renewed momentum with the publication of Obstfeld and Rogoff's (1995) seminal article, "Exchange Rate Dynamics Redux." There, Obstfeld and Rogoff put forth a fully microfounded, general equilibrium model of international interdependence and exchange rate determination with an explicit role for current account imbalances.[1] Nevertheless, the non-stationarity of the Redux model led most of the subsequent literature in the so-called "new open economy macroeconomics" to develop in different directions and "forget" the insights of the model on the dynamic relation between the exchange rate and net foreign asset accumulation by de-emphasizing the role of the latter.[2] (The assumption of purchasing power parity (PPP) was admittedly another weakness of the Obstfeld and Rogoff (1995) model on empirical grounds, addressed by several subsequent contributions. Yet, it was *not* PPP that motivated most scholars to de-emphasize the role of net foreign asset dynamics.)

US data show a growing and persistent current account deficit over the 1990s, that is, capital inflow and accumulation of a large foreign debt. During the same period, the dollar has appreciated steadily. It is a commonly held view that the advent of the "new economy" has been the most significant exogenous shock to affect the position of the US economy relative to the rest of the world in recent years. We can interpret this shock as a (persistent) favorable relative productivity shock. A story that one could tell about the behavior of the dollar and US net foreign assets in the 1990s is that the shock caused the United States to borrow from the rest of the world and the capital inflow generated exchange rate appreciation. This story could be reconciled with models of exchange rate determination developed in the 1970s and early 1980s.[3] If the shock is taken as permanent, the story can also be reconciled with Obstfeld and Rogoff's model. Nevertheless, the argument cannot be reconciled with the overwhelming majority of new generation models that followed.

We returned to the original intent of Obstfeld and Rogoff's work in Cavallo and Ghironi (2002). In that article, we developed a two-country model of exchange rate determination in which stationary net foreign asset dynamics play an explicit role. We dealt with indeterminacy of the steady state and non-stationarity of the original incomplete markets setup by adopting the overlapping generations framework illustrated in Ghironi (2000). If exogenous shocks are stationary, the departure from Ricardian equivalence generated by the birth of new households with no assets in all periods is sufficient to ensure existence of a determinate steady-state distribution of assets between countries and stationarity of real variables. Unexpected temporary shocks cause countries to run current account imbalances, which are re-absorbed over time as the world economy returns to the original steady state.[4]

In this chapter, we illustrate the model put forth in our previous article and compare its results for the traditional case in which monetary policy is conducted through exogenous changes in money supply and the case of endogenous interest rate setting. Exogenous monetary policy has been at the center of the traditional approach to exchange rate determination from the 1970s until very recently, including Obstfeld and Rogoff's Redux model. Yet, the publication of Taylor's (1993) seminal article has shifted the focus of research and the policy debate on endogenous monetary policy through interest rate setting. In an open economy world, this tends to de-emphasize the role of relative money demand in exchange rate determination and, as we argued and we shall review, has important consequences for the dynamics of the exchange rate implied by the model.

We focus on the case of flexible prices in this chapter. The reason is that the flexible price assumption allows us to solve the model analytically, delve into its mechanics, and discuss intuitions clearly. The main mechanisms of the model as far as the role of net foreign asset dynamics is concerned are unchanged with the introduction of price stickiness, and we refer to our 2002 article for that case. Given the focus on flexible price dynamics, we see this chapter as a revisitation of the traditional monetary model of exchange rate determination reviewed in Obstfeld and Stockman (1985) in the light of modern, microfounded international economics and the progress in understanding monetary policy of the last few years.

We start from the traditional setup of Obstfeld and Rogoff's Redux model in which monetary policy is conducted through exogenous changes in money supply in both countries. To facilitate comparison of results and the understanding of model dynamics in a simple case, we retain the PPP assumption. As in Obstfeld and Rogoff (1995), UIP emerges as the outcome of optimizing behavior in our setup. As standard in the literature, we show that the exchange rate can be expressed in terms of the present discounted value of fundamentals: relative money supply and the cross-country consumption differential. A higher consumption differential causes the exchange rate to appreciate by increasing the demand for home currency relative to foreign. We then show that the present discounted value of the consumption differential is, in turn, a function of the stock of net foreign assets entering the current period and of current relative productivity in the two countries.[5] Thus, when monetary policy is conducted through exogenous money injections, the exchange rate depends on the stock of net foreign assets through the effect of the latter on the consumption differential. Accumulation of net foreign assets has a positive effect on the expected relative consumption path and allows the home country to sustain higher consumption than foreign. Hence, the demand for home currency is above foreign, and the exchange rate appreciates. Conversely, a worsening of the relative asset position, that is, a capital inflow is associated with a depreciation. Therefore, the exogenous money supply monetary model cannot deliver the combination of capital inflow and appreciation often observed in the data in terms of a causal linkage from the net foreign asset position to the exchange rate. Also, unless monetary and productivity shocks are non-stationary, this version of the model cannot reproduce the unit root in exchange rate behavior found in Meese and Rogoff (1983).

The exchange rate appreciates in response to a favorable shock to home productivity, because the expected path of the consumption differential is positive in response to the shock, which raises the demand for home currency above foreign. Even if the relative productivity shock is transitory, the exchange rate returns slowly to its pre-shock level. Asset dynamics and their effects through the consumption differential and relative money demand keep the exchange rate stronger than its pre-shock level for several periods.

The exchange rate depreciates following a positive relative money supply shock. The channel is the traditional one through a decrease in the interest rate differential. Not surprisingly, the results after monetary shocks are as in the traditional flexible-price, monetary model of exchange rate determination of the 1970s. The reason is that the exchange rate is ultimately determined by the same ingredients as in the old-fashioned, non-microfounded setup: PPP, UIP, relative money demand, and the assumption about money supply.

When we formulate monetary policy in terms of interest rate feedback rules for the two countries, we assume that interest rates react to the deviations of consumption-based price index (CPI) inflation and GDP from their steady-state levels. Interest rates are also subject to exogenous shocks to allow for the possibility of exogenous changes in monetary policy. Our specification is consistent with Taylor (1993) and allows us to obtain a rich set of implications in a transparent setting.[6]

With endogenous interest rate setting, the solution for the nominal exchange rate exhibits a unit root, consistent with the empirical findings of Meese and Rogoff (1983). However, as in the case of exogenous monetary policy, today's exchange rate also depends on the stock of real net foreign assets accumulated in the previous period. The mechanism here is different though, owing to the fact that money demand plays no active role in exchange rate determination when interest rates are set endogenously. The intuition for the role of asset dynamics in this case is as follows: absence of unexploited arbitrage opportunities implies that UIP holds in our model: expected exchange rate depreciation equals the nominal interest rate differential. To the extent that interest rates react to variables that are affected by net foreign assets (namely GDP, through the wealth effect on labor supply), net foreign assets too affect the exchange rate. As in the previous case, the model implies that asset holdings help predict the nominal exchange rate. A key difference is that now, consistent with the evidence for the United States, *ceteris paribus*, a decrease in asset holdings – a current account deficit/capital inflow – generates an appreciation of the domestic currency for reasonable parameter values. Also, we show that the response of the exchange rate to shocks is more different from that of a simple random walk – the slower the convergence of net foreign assets to the steady state and the higher the degree of substitutability between domestic and foreign goods in consumption.

In this case, the exchange rate overshoots its new long-run level following a temporary (relative) productivity shock. If the shock is persistent, endogenous monetary policy and asset dynamics generate delayed overshooting. Endogenous monetary policy is responsible for exchange rate *undershooting* after persistent (relative) interest rate shocks. ("Persistent" does *not* mean "permanent" throughout the chapter. When we consider permanent shocks, we say so explicitly.)

Our results on exchange rate overshooting contrast with those of Obstfeld and Rogoff (1995), who obtain no overshooting following monetary and/or productivity shocks in their benchmark setup. We show that price stickiness is not necessary to generate overshooting once asset dynamics and endogenous monetary policy are accounted for. This brings a new perspective to bear on a topic that has been at the center of theoretical and empirical research on exchange rates since Dornbusch's (1976) seminal paper. Our model has the potential to reconcile the evidence in favor of delayed overshooting in Clarida and Gali (1994) and Eichenbaum and Evans (1995) with rational behavior and UIP.

As far as the empirical performance is concerned, the model with endogenous monetary policy delivers exchange rate appreciation following a favorable shock to relative productivity in an environment in which monetary policy obeys the Taylor principle. However, the model does not generate accumulation of net foreign debt following the shock. The reason is that consumption smoothing is the only motive for asset accumulation, and a favorable productivity shock induces home agents to lend rather than borrow to smooth the effect of the shock on consumption. We show in Cavallo and Ghironi (2002) that a sticky-price version of the model delivers debt accumulation and appreciation when the relative productivity shock is permanent. This is a consequence of slow terms of trade dynamics, which cause the short-run response of the GDP differential to the shock to be smaller than the long-run effect, thus motivating home agents to borrow rather than lend. Nevertheless, if one believes that the relative productivity shock of the 1990s has been persistent, but not permanent, the model can explain only part of the dynamics in US data. Along with price stickiness, inclusion of physical capital accumulation and PPP deviations appears a promising way of completing the theory illustrated here. On more rigorous grounds, the model with endogenous interest rate setting yields straightforward, empirically testable implications for exchange rate dynamics. The result that exchange rate dynamics may coincide with those of a random walk or be sufficiently close that the difference is hard to detect in short series is no longer an a-theoretical, data-driven finding. It emerges from a fully specified, microfounded, general equilibrium model if central banks do not react to GDP movements in interest rate setting or if substitutability between home and foreign goods is low. Whether this has brought us closer to finding the "exchange rate grail," only more empirical work on the longer series now available will tell.

The rest of the chapter is organized as follows. Section 1.2 presents the model. Section 1.3 illustrates the log-linear equations that determine domestic and foreign variables and presents the solution for real variables. Section 1.4 studies exchange rate determination when monetary policy is conducted through exogenous changes in money supply. Section 1.5 discusses the relation between net foreign assets and the exchange rate with endogenous interest rate setting. Section 1.6 concludes.

1.2 The model

The model is a monetary version of the setup in Ghironi (2000). The world consists of two countries, *home* and *foreign*. In each period t, the world economy is populated by a continuum of infinitely lived households between 0 and N_t^W. Each household consumes, supplies labor, and holds financial assets. As in Weil (1989), we assume that households are born on different dates *owning no assets*, but they own the present discounted value of their labor income.[7] The number of households in the home economy, N_t, grows over time at the exogenous rate $n > 0$, that is, $N_{t+1} = (1 + n)N_t$. We normalize the size of a household to 1, so that the number of households alive at each point in time is the economy's population. Foreign population (N_t^*) grows at the same rate as home population. The world economy has existed since the infinite past. It is useful to normalize world population at time 0 to the continuum between 0 and 1, so that $N_0^W = 1$.

A continuum of goods $i \in [0, 1]$ is produced in the world by monopolistically competitive, infinitely lived firms, each producing a single differentiated good. Firms have existed since the infinite past. At time 0, the number of goods that are supplied in the world economy is equal to the number of households. The latter grows over time, but the commodity space remains unchanged. Thus, as time goes by, the ownership of firms spreads across a larger number of households. Profits are distributed to consumers via dividends, and the structure of the market for each good is taken as given. We assume that the domestic economy produces goods in the interval $[0, a]$, which is also the size of the home population at time 0, whereas the foreign economy produces goods in the range $[a, 1]$.

The asset menu includes nominal bonds denominated in units of domestic and foreign currency, money balances, and shares in firms. Private agents in both countries trade the bonds domestically and internationally. Shares in home (foreign) firms and domestic (foreign) currency balances are held only by home (foreign) residents.

1.2.1 Households

Agents have perfect foresight, though they can be surprised by initial unexpected shocks. Consumers have identical preferences over a real consumption index (C), leisure (LE), and real money balances (M/P, where M denotes nominal money holdings and P is the consumption-based price index (CPI)). At any time t_0, the representative home consumer j born in period $\upsilon \in [-\infty, t_0]$ maximizes the intertemporal utility function

$$U_{t_0}^{\upsilon^j} = \sum_{t=t_0}^{\infty} \beta^{t-t_0} \left[\rho \log C_t^{\upsilon^j} + (1 - \rho) \log \mathrm{LE}_t^{\upsilon^j} + \chi \log \frac{M_t^{\upsilon^j}}{P_t} \right], \quad (1.1)$$

with $0 < \rho < 1$.[8]

The consumption index for the representative domestic consumer is

$$C_t^{\upsilon^j} = \left[a^{1/\omega}(C_{Ht}^{\upsilon^j})^{(\omega-1)/\omega} + (1-a)^{1/\omega}(C_{Ft}^{\upsilon^j})^{(\omega-1)/\omega} \right]^{\omega/(\omega-1)},$$

where $\omega > 0$ is the intratemporal elasticity of substitution between domestic and foreign goods. The consumption sub-indexes that aggregate individual domestic and foreign goods are, respectively:

$$C_{Ht}^{\upsilon^j} = \left[\left(\frac{1}{a}\right)^{1/\theta} \int_0^a c_t^{\upsilon^j}(i)^{(\theta-1)/\theta} di \right]^{\theta/(\theta-1)},$$

and

$$C_{Ft}^{\upsilon^j} = \left[\left(\frac{1}{1-a}\right)^{1/\theta} \int_a^1 c_{*t}^{\upsilon^j}(i)^{(\theta-1)/\theta} di \right]^{\theta/(\theta-1)},$$

where $c_{*t}^{\upsilon j}(i)$ denotes time t consumption of good i produced in the foreign country, and $\theta > 1$ is the elasticity of substitution between goods produced inside each country.

The CPI is

$$P_t = \left[a P_{Ht}^{1-\omega} + (1-a) P_{Ft}^{1-\omega} \right]^{1/(1-\omega)},$$

where P_H (P_F) is the price sub-index for home (foreign)-produced goods – both expressed in units of the home currency. Letting $p_t(i)$ be the home currency price of good i, we have

$$P_{Ht} = \left(\frac{1}{a} \int_0^a p_t(i)^{1-\theta}\, di \right)^{1/(1-\theta)}, \quad P_{Ft} = \left(\frac{1}{1-a} \int_a^1 p_t(i)^{1-\theta}\, di \right)^{1/(1-\theta)}.$$

We assume that there are no impediments to trade and that firms do not engage in local currency pricing (i.e. pricing in the currency of the economy where goods are sold). Hence, the law of one price holds for each individual good and $p_t(i) = \varepsilon_t p_t^*(i)$, where ε_t is the exchange rate (units of domestic currency per unit of foreign) and $p_t^*(i)$ is the foreign currency price of good i. This hypothesis and identical intratemporal consumer preferences across countries ensure that consumption-based PPP holds, that is, $P_t = \varepsilon_t P_t^*$.

Workers supply labor (L) in competitive labor markets. The total amount of time available in each period is normalized to 1, so that[9]

$$\mathrm{LE}_t^{\upsilon j} = 1 - L_t^{\upsilon j}. \tag{1.2}$$

The representative consumer enters a period holding nominal bonds, nominal money balances, and shares purchased in the previous period. She or he receives interest and dividends on these assets, may earn capital gains or incur losses on shares, earns labor income, is taxed, and consumes.

Denote the date t price (in units of domestic currency) of a claim to the representative domestic firm i's entire future profits (starting on date $t+1$) by V_t^i. Let $x_{t+1}^{\upsilon ji}$ be the share of the representative domestic firm i owned by the representative domestic consumer j born in period υ at the end of period t. D_t^i denotes the nominal dividends firm i issues on date t. Then, letting $A_{t+1}^{\upsilon j}$ ($A_{t+1}^{*\upsilon j}$) be the home consumer's holdings of domestic (foreign) currency denominated bonds entering time $t+1$, the period budget constraint expressed in units of domestic currency is

$$A_{t+1}^{\upsilon j} + \varepsilon_t A_{t+1}^{*\upsilon j} + \int_0^a \left(V_t^i x_{t+1}^{\upsilon ji} - V_{t-1}^i x_t^{\upsilon ji} \right) di + M_t^{\upsilon j}$$

$$= (1+i_t) A_t^{\upsilon j} + \varepsilon_t (1+i_t^*) A_t^{*\upsilon j} + \int_0^a D_t^i x_t^{\upsilon ji}\, di$$

$$+ \int_0^a (V_t^i - V_{t-1}^i) x_t^{\upsilon ji}\, di + M_{t-1}^{\upsilon j} + W_t L_t^{\upsilon j} - P_t C_t^{\upsilon j} - P_t T_t^{\upsilon}, \tag{1.3}$$

where i_t (i_t^*) is the nominal interest rate on holdings of domestic (foreign) bonds between $t-1$ and t, W_t is the nominal wage, $M_{t-1}^{\upsilon j}$ denotes the agent's holdings of nominal money balances entering period t, and T_t^υ is a lump-sum net real transfer, which is identical across members of generation υ.[10]

The representative domestic consumer born in period υ maximizes the intertemporal utility function (1.1) subject to the constraints (1.2) and (1.3). Dropping the superscript j (because symmetric agents make identical choices in equilibrium), optimal labor supply is given by

$$L_t^\upsilon = 1 - LE_t^\upsilon = 1 - \frac{1-\rho}{\rho}\frac{C_t^\upsilon}{w_t}, \tag{1.4}$$

which equates the marginal cost of supplying labor with the marginal utility of consumption generated by the corresponding increase in labor income (w_t denotes the real wage, W_t/P_t).

Making use of this equation, the first-order condition for optimal holdings of domestic currency bonds yields the Euler equation:

$$C_t^\upsilon = \left[\beta(1+i_{t+1})\left(\frac{P_t}{P_{t+1}}\right)\right]^{-1} C_{t+1}^\upsilon \tag{1.5}$$

for all $\upsilon \leq t$.

Demand for home currency real balances is

$$\frac{M_t^\upsilon}{P_t} = \frac{\chi}{\rho}\frac{1+i_{t+1}}{i_{t+1}}C_t^\upsilon. \tag{1.6}$$

Real domestic currency balances increase with consumption and decrease with the opportunity cost of holding money.

Condition (1.5) can be combined with the first-order condition for holdings of foreign bonds to yield a no-arbitrage condition between domestic and foreign currency bonds for domestic agents. Absence of unexploited arbitrage opportunities requires

$$1+i_{t+1} = (1+i_{t+1}^*)\frac{\varepsilon_{t+1}}{\varepsilon_t}. \tag{1.7}$$

The consumption-based real interest rate between t and $t+1$ is defined by the familiar Fisher parity condition:

$$1+r_{t+1} = (1+i_{t+1})\frac{P_t}{P_{t+1}} = \frac{1+i_{t+1}}{1+\pi_{t+1}^{CPI}}, \tag{1.8}$$

where π_{t+1}^{CPI} is CPI inflation ($\pi_{t+1}^{CPI} \equiv (P_{t+1}/P_t)-1$). PPP ensures that $1+\pi_t^{CPI} = (1+e_t)(1+\pi_t^{CPI*})$, where $1+\pi_t^{CPI*} \equiv (P_t^*/P_{t-1}^*)$ and $1+e_t \equiv (\varepsilon_t/\varepsilon_{t-1})$. Combining (1.8) with (1.7) and making use of PPP shows that $1+r_{t+1} = 1+r_{t+1}^* = (1+i_{t+1}^*)P_t^*/P_{t+1}^*$: real interest rates are equal across countries in the absence of unexpected shocks that may cause no-arbitrage conditions to fail *ex post*.

Absence of arbitrage opportunities between bonds and shares in the domestic economy requires

$$1 + i_{t+1} = \frac{D_{t+1}^i + V_{t+1}^i}{V_t^i}. \tag{1.9}$$

Letting $d_t^i \equiv D_t^i / P_t$ and $v_t^i \equiv V_t^i / P_t$, we can re-write the no-arbitrage condition between bonds and shares as

$$1 + r_{t+1} = \frac{d_{t+1}^i + v_{t+1}^i}{v_t^i}. \tag{1.10}$$

As usual, first-order conditions and the period budget constraint must be combined with appropriate transversality conditions to ensure optimality.[11]

1.2.2 Firms

Output supplied at time t by the representative domestic firm i is a linear function of labor demanded by the firm

$$Y_t^{Si} = Z_t L_t^i. \tag{1.11}$$

Z_t is exogenous, economy-wide productivity. Production by the representative foreign firm is a linear function of L_t^{i*}, with productivity Z_t^*.[12]

Output demand comes from domestic and foreign consumers. The demand for home good i by the representative home consumer born in period v is

$$c_t^v(i) = \left(\frac{p_t(i)}{P_{Ht}}\right)^{-\theta} \left(\frac{P_{Ht}}{P_t}\right)^{-\omega} C_t^v,$$

obtained by maximizing C^v subject to a spending constraint. *Total demand* for home good i coming from domestic consumers is

$$c_t(i) = a\left[\cdots \frac{n}{(1+n)^{t+1}} c_t^{-t}(i) + \cdots + \frac{n}{(1+n)^2} c_t^{-1}(i) + \frac{n}{1+n} c_t^0(i)\right.$$
$$\left. + nc_t^1(i) + n(1+n)c_t^2(i) + \cdots + n(1+n)^{t-1} c_t^t(i)\right]$$
$$= \left(\frac{p_t(i)}{P_{Ht}}\right)^{-\theta} \left(\frac{P_{Ht}}{P_t}\right)^{-\omega} a(1+n)^t c_t,$$

where

$$c_t \equiv a\left[\cdots \frac{n}{(1+n)^{t+1}} C_t^{-t} + \cdots + \frac{n}{(1+n)^2} C_t^{-1} + \frac{n}{1+n} C_t^0\right.$$
$$\left. + nC_t^1 + n(1+n)C_t^2 + \cdots + n(1+n)^{t-1} C_t^t\right] \bigg/ a(1+n)^t$$

is aggregate per capita home consumption.[13]

Given the identity of intratemporal preferences, the expression for the demand of home good i from foreign consumers born in period v is analogous, and *total* demand for the same good by foreign consumers is

$$c_t^*(i) = \left(\frac{p_t(i)}{P_{\mathrm{H}t}}\right)^{-\theta} \left(\frac{P_{\mathrm{H}t}}{P_t}\right)^{-\omega} (1-a)(1+n)^t c_t^*,$$

where

$$c_t^* \equiv (1-a)\left[\cdots \frac{n}{(1+n)^{t+1}}C_t^{-t^*} + \cdots + \frac{n}{(1+n)^2}C_t^{-1^*} + \frac{n}{1+n}C_t^{0^*}\right.$$

$$\left. + nC_t^{1^*} + n(1+n)C_t^{2^*} + \cdots + n(1+n)^{t-1}C_t^{t^*}\right] \Big/ (1-a)(1+n)^t$$

is aggregate per capita foreign consumption.

Total demand for good i produced in the home country is obtained by adding the demands for that good originating in the two countries. Making use of the results above, it is

$$Y_t^{\mathrm{D}i} = \left(\frac{p_t(i)}{P_{\mathrm{H}t}}\right)^{-\theta} \left(\frac{P_{\mathrm{H}t}}{P_t}\right)^{-\omega} Y_t^{\mathrm{DW}}. \tag{1.12}$$

Y_t^{DW} is the aggregate world demand for the composite good, defined as $Y_t^{\mathrm{DW}} \equiv C_t^{\mathrm{W}}$. $C_t^{\mathrm{W}} \equiv (1+n)^t \left[ac_t + (1-a)c_t^*\right]$ denotes aggregate world consumption.

Given the no-arbitrage condition between bonds and shares (1.10) and a no-speculative bubble condition, the real price of firm i's shares at time t_0 is given by the present discounted value of the real dividends paid by the firm from $t_0 + 1$ on

$$v_{t_0}^i = \sum_{s=t_0+1}^{\infty} R_{t_0,s} d_s^i,$$

where

$$R_{t_0,s} \equiv \frac{1}{\prod_{u=t_0+1}^{s}(1+r_u)}, \quad R_{t_0,t_0} = 1.$$

At time t_0, firm i maximizes

$$v_{t_0}^i + d_{t_0}^i = \sum_{s=t_0}^{\infty} R_{t_0,s} d_s^i,$$

that is, the present discounted value of dividends to be paid from t_0 onwards. At each point in time, dividends are given by net real revenues, $(1-\tau)(p_t(i)/P_t)Y_t^i$, plus a lump-sum transfer (or tax) from the government, T_t^{fi}, minus costs, $(W_t/P_t)L_t^i$. The firm chooses the price of its product and the amount of labor demanded in order to maximize the present discounted value of its current and future profits subject to the constraints (1.11) and (1.12), and the market clearing condition $Y_t^{Si} = Y_t^{Di}(= Y_t^i)$. Firm i takes the aggregate price indexes, the wage rate, Z_t, world aggregates, and taxes and transfers as given.

Let λ_t^i denote the Lagrange multiplier on the constraint $Y_t^{Si} = Y_t^{Di}$. Then, λ_t^i is the shadow price of an extra unit of output to be sold in period t, or the marginal cost of time t sales. The first-order condition with respect to $p_t(i)$ yields the pricing equation

$$p_t(i) = \frac{\theta}{(\theta - 1)(1 - \tau)} P_t \lambda_t^i, \tag{1.13}$$

which equates the price charged by firm i to the product of the (nominal) shadow value of one extra unit of output – the (nominal) marginal cost $(P_t \lambda_t^i)$ – and a familiar, constant-elasticity markup $(\theta / [(\theta - 1)(1 - \tau)])$.

The first-order condition for the optimal choice of L_t^i yields

$$\frac{W_t}{P_t} = \lambda_t^i Z_t. \tag{1.14}$$

Today's real wage must equal the shadow value of an extra unit of labor in production.

Making use of the market clearing conditions $Y_t^{Si} = Y_t^{Di}$ and $Y_t^{DW} = Y_t^{SW} = Y_t^W$, of the expressions for supply and demand of good i, and recalling that symmetric firms make identical equilibrium choices (so that $p_t(i) = P_{Ht}$) yields

$$L_t^i = \left(\frac{p_t(i)}{P_t} \right)^{-\omega} \frac{Y_t^W}{Z_t}. \tag{1.15}$$

1.2.3 The government

We assume that governments in both countries run balanced budgets. The government taxes firm revenues at a rate that compensates for monopoly power in a zero-inflation steady state and removes the markup over marginal cost charged by firms in a flexible-price world. The tax rate is determined by $1 - \tau = \theta/(\theta - 1)$, which yields $\tau = -1/(\theta - 1)$. Because the tax rate is negative, firms receive a subsidy on their revenues and pay lump-sum taxes determined by $T_t^{fi} = \tau R P_t^i Y_t^i$. In addition, the government injects money into the economy through lump-sum transfers of seigniorage revenues to households: $P_t T_t^v = -(M_t^{vj} - M_{t-1}^{vj})$. Similarly for the foreign government.

1.2.4 Aggregation and equilibrium

Households

Aggregate per capita consumption and labor supply are obtained by aggregating consumption and labor supply across generations and dividing by total population at each point in time. The aggregate per capita labor–leisure trade-offs in the two economies are

$$L_t = 1 - \frac{1-\rho}{\rho}\frac{c_t}{w_t}, \quad L_t^* = 1 - \frac{1-\rho}{\rho}\frac{c_t^*}{w_t^*}.$$

Labor supply rises with the real wage and decreases with consumption.

Consumption Euler equations in aggregate per capita terms contain an adjustment for consumption by the newborn generation at time $t+1$:[14]

$$c_t = \frac{1+n}{\beta(1+r_{t+1})}\left(c_{t+1} - \frac{n}{1+n}C_{t+1}^{t+1}\right),$$

$$c_t^* = \frac{1+n}{\beta(1+r_{t+1})}\left(c_{t+1}^* - \frac{n}{1+n}C_{t+1}^{t+1*}\right). \tag{1.16}$$

Newborn households hold no assets, but they own the present discounted value of their labor income. We define human wealth, h_t, as the present discounted value of the household's lifetime endowment of time in terms of the real wage[15]

$$h_t \equiv \sum_{s=t}^{\infty} R_{t,s}w_s, \quad h_t^* \equiv \sum_{s=t}^{\infty} R_{t,s}w_s^*.$$

The dynamics of h and h^* are described by the following forward-looking difference equations:

$$h_t = \frac{h_{t+1}}{1+r_{t+1}} + w_t, \quad h_t^* = \frac{h_{t+1}^*}{1+r_{t+1}} + w_t^*. \tag{1.17}$$

Using the labor–leisure trade-off (1.4), the Euler equation (1.5), and a newborn household's intertemporal budget constraint, it is possible to show that the household's consumption in the first period of its life is a fraction of the household's human wealth at birth

$$C_{t+1}^{t+1} = \rho(1-\beta)h_{t+1}, \quad C_{t+1}^{t+1*} = \rho(1-\beta)h_{t+1}^*. \tag{1.18}$$

Aggregate per capita real money demands in the two economies are

$$m_t \equiv \frac{M_t}{P_t} = \frac{\chi}{\rho}\frac{1+i_{t+1}}{i_{t+1}}c_t, \quad m_t^* \equiv \frac{M_t^*}{P_t^*} = \frac{\chi}{\rho}\frac{1+i_{t+1}^*}{i_{t+1}^*}c_t^*. \tag{1.19}$$

In the absence of arbitrage opportunities between bonds and shares, the aggregate per capita equity values of the home and foreign economies entering period $t+1$ must evolve according to

$$v_t = \frac{1+n}{1+r_{t+1}}v_{t+1} + \frac{d_{t+1}}{1+r_{t+1}}, \quad v_t^* = \frac{1+n}{1+r_{t+1}}v_{t+1}^* + \frac{d_{t+1}^*}{1+r_{t+1}}. \tag{1.20}$$

where $v_t \equiv aV_t^i/(P_t N_{t+1})$, $v_t^* \equiv (l-a)V_t^{*i}/(P_t^* N_{t+1}^*)$, and d_t and d_t^* denote aggregate per capita real dividends, equal to $(1-\tau)y_t + T_t^f - w_t L_t$ and $(1-\tau^*)y_t^* + T_t^{f*} - w_t^* L_t^*$, respectively (note that $\tau = \tau^*$).

The law of motion of aggregate per capita net foreign assets is obtained by aggregating an equilibrium version of the budget constraint (1.3) across generations alive at each point in time.[16] It is

$$(1+n)B_{t+1} = (1+r_t)B_t + w_t L_t + d_t - c_t,$$
$$(1+n)B_{t+1}^* = (1+r_t)B_t^* + w_t^* L_t^* + d_t^* - c_t^*. \tag{1.21}$$

where

$$B_{t+1} \equiv \frac{A_{t+1} + \varepsilon_t A_{t+1}^*}{P_t} \quad \text{and} \quad B_{t+1}^* \equiv \frac{(A_{*t+1})/\varepsilon_t + A_{*t+1}^*}{P_t^*}$$

(A_* denotes foreign households' holdings of home bonds, A_*^* denotes their holdings of foreign bonds). A country's net foreign assets and net foreign bond holdings coincide in a world in which all shares are held domestically.[17]

Because $d_t = y_t - w_t L_t = 0$ and $d_t^* = y_t^* - w_t^* L_t^* = 0$ in equilibrium in a world of flexible prices in which revenue subsidies are chosen to offset markup distortions, equations (1.21) become

$$(1+n)B_{t+1} = (1+r_t)B_t + y_t - c_t,$$
$$(1+n)B_{t+1}^* = (1+r_t)B_t^* + y_t^* - c_t^*. \tag{1.22}$$

Firms

Aggregate per capita real GDP in each economy is obtained by expressing production of each differentiated good in units of the composite basket, multiplying by the number of firms, and dividing by population. It is

$$y_t = RP_t Z_t L_t, \quad y_t^* = RP_t^* Z_t^* L_t^*. \tag{1.23}$$

For given employment and productivity, real GDP rises with the relative price of the representative good produced, as this is worth more units of the consumption basket.

Aggregate per capita labor demand is

$$L_t = RP_t^{-\omega} \frac{y_t^W}{Z_t}, \quad L_t^* = RP_t^{*-\omega} \frac{y_t^W}{Z_t^*}, \tag{1.24}$$

where y_t^W is aggregate per capita world production of the composite good equal to aggregate per capita world consumption, c_t^W. It is $y_t^W = a y_t + (1-a) y_t^*$ and $c_t^W = a c_t + (1-a) c_t^*$. Market clearing requires $y_t^W = c_t^W$.

Domestic and foreign relative prices are equal to marginal costs

$$RP_t = \frac{w_t}{Z_t}, \quad RP_t^* = \frac{w_t^*}{Z_t^*} \tag{1.25}$$

International equilibrium

For international asset markets to be in equilibrium, aggregate home assets (liabilities) must equal aggregate foreign liabilities (assets), that is, it must be $\widehat{B}_t + \widehat{B}_t^* = 0$. In terms of aggregates per capita, it must be

$$a B_t + (1 - a) B_t^* = 0. \tag{1.26}$$

Using (1.26), the equations in (1.22) reduce to $y_t^W = c_t^W$: consistent with Walras' Law, asset market equilibrium implies goods market equilibrium, and vice versa.

1.2.5   The steady state

Real variables

The procedure for finding the steady-state levels of real variables follows the same steps as in Ghironi (2000). As described there, the departure from Ricardian equivalence caused by entry of new households with no assets in each period generates dependence of aggregate per capita consumption growth on the stock of aggregate per capita net foreign assets. This yields determinacy of steady-state real net foreign asset holdings, and thus of the steady-state levels of other real variables in the model.

We denote steady-state levels of variables with overbars. A subscript -1 indicates that the steady state described below is going to be the position of the economy up to and including period $t = -1$ in our exercise.[18] Unexpected shocks can surprise agents at the beginning of period 0, generating the dynamics we describe in the following sections.

Given initial steady-state levels of productivity ($\overline{Z}_{-1} = \overline{Z}_{-1}^* = 1$) and inflation ($\pi_{-1}^{PPI} = \pi_{-1}^{PPI^*} = \overline{\pi}_{-1}^{CPI} = \overline{\pi}_{-1}^{CPI^*} = 0$, where $\pi_t^{PPI} \equiv (p_t(i) - p_{t-1}(i))/p_{t-1}(i)$ and $\overline{\pi}_t^{PPI^*}$ is defined similarly), real variables are stationary, in the sense that they return to the initial position determined below following non-permanent productivity shocks.

To see the mechanism that determines the steady state at work, consider the home economy, and set aggregate per capita consumption to be constant. It is

$$\overline{c}_{-1} \left[1 - \frac{\beta(1 + \overline{r}_{-1})}{1 + n} \right] = \frac{n}{1 + n} \overline{C}_{v_{-1}}^v, \tag{1.27}$$

where $\overline{C}_v^v$ is steady-state consumption by a newborn generation in the first period of its life. We assume $\beta(1 + \overline{r}_{-1})/(1 + n) < 1$ to ensure that steady-state consumption is positive. As we shall see, this assumption is automatically satisfied as long as $n > 0$.

From equation (1.18) and the definition of h, $\overline{C}^v_{v_{-1}}$ is

$$\overline{C}^v_{v_{-1}} = \rho(1-\beta)\frac{1+\overline{r}_{-1}}{\overline{r}_{-1}}\overline{w}_{-1}. \tag{1.28}$$

Hence, aggregate per capita consumption as a function of the steady-state real wage and interest rate is

$$\overline{c}_{-1} = \frac{n\rho(1-\beta)(1+\overline{r}_{-1})}{\overline{r}_{-1}[1+n-\beta(1+\overline{r}_{-1})]}\overline{w}_{-1}. \tag{1.29}$$

Under the assumption that $\overline{Z}_{-1} = 1$, steady-state GDP is

$$\overline{y}_{-1} = \overline{RP}_{-1}\overline{L}_{-1}. \tag{1.30}$$

From the pricing equation,

$$\overline{RP}_{-1} = \overline{w}_{-1}, \tag{1.31}$$

because the monopolistic distortion is removed by the subsidy τ. It follows that

$$\overline{y}_{-1} = \overline{w}_{-1}\overline{L}_{-1}. \tag{1.32}$$

The labor–leisure trade-off implies

$$\overline{L}_{-1} = 1 - \frac{1-\rho}{\rho}\frac{\overline{c}_{-1}}{\overline{w}_{-1}}. \tag{1.33}$$

Using equations (1.29), (1.32), (1.33), and a steady-state version of the law of motion for home's net foreign assets yields[19]

$$\overline{B}_0 = \frac{1}{\overline{r}_{-1}-n}\left\{\frac{n(1-\beta)(1+\overline{r}_{-1})-\overline{r}_{-1}[1+n-\beta(1+\overline{r}_{-1})]}{\overline{r}_{-1}[1+n-\beta(1+\overline{r}_{-1})]}\right\}\overline{w}_{-1}. \tag{1.34}$$

Similarly, foreign steady-state assets are given by

$$\overline{B}^*_0 = \frac{1}{\overline{r}_{-1}-n}\left\{\frac{n(1-\beta)(1+\overline{r}_{-1})-\overline{r}_{-1}[1+n-\beta(1+\overline{r}_{-1})]}{\overline{r}_{-1}[1+n-\beta(1+\overline{r}_{-1})]}\right\}\overline{w}^*_{-1}. \tag{1.35}$$

Substituting equations (1.34) and (1.35) in the asset market equilibrium condition, $a\overline{B}_0 + (1-a)\overline{B}^*_0 = 0$, yields

$$\frac{1}{\overline{r}_{-1}-n}\left\{\frac{n(1-\beta)(1+\overline{r}_{-1})-\overline{r}_{-1}[1+n-\beta(1+\overline{r}_{-1})]}{\overline{r}_{-1}[1+n-\beta(1+\overline{r}_{-1})]}\right\}$$
$$\times\left[a\overline{w}_{-1} + (1-a)\overline{w}^*_{-1}\right] = 0.$$

Given non-zero real wages at home and abroad, the only admissible level of the interest rate that satisfies the market clearing condition is such that $\beta(1 + \bar{r}_{-1}) = 1$, or

$$\bar{r}_{-1} = \frac{1 - \beta}{\beta}. \tag{1.36}$$

Substituting this result into equations (1.34) and (1.35) yields steady-state levels of domestic and foreign net foreign assets $\bar{B}_0 = \bar{B}_0^* = 0$. Consistent with the fact that the two economies are structurally symmetric in per capita terms, the long-run net foreign asset position is a zero equilibrium. Differently from Obstfeld and Rogoff (1995), this position is pinned down *endogenously* by the model.

Given these results, it is easy to verify that steady-state levels of endogenous variables other than real balances are[20]

$$\bar{w}_{-1} = \overline{RP}_{-1} = \bar{w}_{-1}^* = \overline{RP}_{-1}^* = 1, \quad \bar{h}_{-1} = \bar{h}_{-1}^* = \frac{1}{1 - \beta},$$

$$\bar{y}_{-1} = \bar{c}_{-1} = \overline{C}_{\upsilon_{-1}}^\upsilon = \overline{L}_{-1} = \bar{y}_{-1}^* = \bar{c}_{-1}^* = \overline{C}_{\upsilon_{-1}}^{\upsilon*} = \overline{L}_{-1}^* = \bar{y}_{-1}^W = \bar{c}_{-1}^W = \rho.$$

Real money balances and nominal variables

Given steady-state consumption, domestic steady-state real balances are determined by

$$\bar{m}_{-1} = \chi \frac{1 + \bar{i}_{-1}}{\bar{i}_{-1}}.$$

Similarly for foreign.

In a zero-inflation steady state, nominal interest rates at home and abroad are equal to the steady-state real interest rate: $\bar{i}_{-1} = \bar{i}_{-1}^* = (1 - \beta)/\beta$. It follows that real balances are

$$\bar{m}_{-1} = \bar{m}_{-1}^* = \frac{\chi}{1 - \beta}.$$

Nominal money balances at home and abroad are determined by, respectively

$$\overline{M}_{-1} = \frac{\chi}{1 - \beta} \overline{P}_{-1}, \quad \overline{M}_{-1}^* = \frac{\chi}{1 - \beta} \overline{P}_{-1}^*. \tag{1.37}$$

Taking the ratio of $\overline{M}_{-1}$ to $\overline{M}_{-1}^*$ and using PPP yields

$$\bar{\varepsilon}_{-1} = \frac{\overline{M}_{-1}}{\overline{M}_{-1}^*}. \tag{1.38}$$

The steady-state exchange rate is determined by the ratio of money supplies. In the analysis below, we assume that monetary policy is conducted either through exogenous changes in money supply or by setting the nominal interest rate. In order to pin down the initial steady-state level of the exchange rate, we assume that the initial level of money supplies was set by the domestic and foreign central banks at $\overline{M}_{-1} = \overline{M}^*_{-1} = \chi/(1-\beta)$. Structural symmetry of the two economies implies that the central banks' optimal choice of steady-state money supplies would satisfy $\overline{M}_{-1} = \overline{M}^*_{-1}$ if the two authorities had identical objectives. The level $\chi/(1-\beta)$ conveniently implies $\overline{\varepsilon}_{-1} = \overline{P}_{-1} = \overline{P}^*_{-1} = \overline{p}_{-1}(h) = \overline{p}^*_{-1}(f) = 1$ ($\overline{p}_{-1}(h)$ and $\overline{p}^*_{-1}(f)$ are the steady-state levels of the domestic and foreign PPIs, respectively, which follow from $\overline{RP}_{-1} = \overline{p}_{-1}(h)/\overline{P}_{-1} = \overline{RP}^*_{-1} = \overline{p}^*_{-1}(f)/\overline{P}^*_{-1} = 1$). Because the model does not pin down the steady-state levels of all nominal variables endogenously as functions of the structural parameters only, monetary policy may generate the presence of a unit root in the dynamics of price levels, the exchange rate, and nominal money balances. In this case, steady-state levels of nominal variables will change as a consequence of temporary shocks depending on the nature of monetary policy.

1.3   The log-linear model

The equations that determine domestic and foreign variables can be log-linearized around the steady state. We use sans serif fonts to denote percentage deviations from the steady state.[21] As usual, it is convenient to solve the model for cross-country differences ($x_t^D \equiv x_t - x_t^*$ for any variable x) and world aggregates ($x_t^W \equiv ax_t + (1-a)x_t^*$). The levels of individual country variables can be recovered easily given solutions for differences and world aggregates. Because this chapter focuses on exchange rate dynamics, which are determined by cross-country differences in our setup, we report only the log-linear equations for the cross-country differences between the main variables in this section.

1.3.1   No-arbitrage conditions

PPP implies that the CPI inflation differential equals exchange rate depreciation:

$$\pi_t^{CPI^D} = e_t, \tag{1.39}$$

where $e_t \equiv \epsilon_t - \epsilon_{t-1}$ and ϵ denotes the percentage deviation of ε from the steady state.

UIP implies

$$i_{t+1}^D = \epsilon_{t+1} - \epsilon_t. \tag{1.40}$$

1.3.2   Households

The relative labor–leisure trade-off is

$$w_t^D = c_t^D + \frac{\rho}{1-\rho}L_t^D. \tag{1.41}$$

Log-linear Euler equations imply that the consumption differential obeys

$$c_t^D = (1 + n)c_{t+1}^D - nC_{t+1}^{t+1\,D}. \tag{1.42}$$

The *ex ante* real interest rate has no effect, because agents in both countries face identical real rates. The random walk result of the standard Obstfeld and Rogoff (1995) model for real variables is transparent here: if $n = 0$, that is, if no new agents with zero assets enter the economy, the consumption differential between the two countries follows a random walk. Any shock that causes a consumption differential today has permanent consequences on the relative level of consumption. When $n > 0$, the Euler equation is adjusted for consumption of a newborn generation in the first period of its life. It is

$$C_t^{tD} = h_t^D, \tag{1.43}$$

where h is the deviation from the steady state of a household's human wealth. The Euler equation for the consumption differential can thus be rewritten as

$$c_t^D = (1 + n)c_{t+1}^D - nh_{t+1}^D, \tag{1.44}$$

where h^D is determined by

$$h_t^D = \beta h_{t+1}^D + (1 - \beta)w_t^D. \tag{1.45}$$

Relative real balances depend on the consumption and nominal interest rate differential

$$m_t^D = c_t^D - \frac{\beta}{1 - \beta}i_{t+1}^D, \tag{1.46}$$

where $m_t^D \equiv M_t^D - P_t^D = M_t^D - \epsilon_t$.

1.3.3 Firms

The GDP differential obeys

$$y_t^D = RP_t^D + L_t^D + Z_t^D. \tag{1.47}$$

The relative price differential reflects relative marginal cost dynamics[22]

$$RP_t^D = w_t^D - Z_t^D. \tag{1.48}$$

The difference between domestic and foreign labor demands depends on relative marginal cost and productivity

$$L_t^D = -\omega(w_t^D - Z_t^D) - Z_t^D. \tag{1.49}$$

Substituting equations (1.48) and (1.49) into (1.47) yields an expression for the GDP differential as a function of relative cost dynamics

$$y_t^D = -(\omega - 1)(w_t^D - Z_t^D). \tag{1.50}$$

From firms' optimal pricing (equation (1.13) for domestic firms and the analogous equation for foreign), the PPI inflation differential depends positively on the

CPI inflation differential and on relative marginal cost growth

$$\pi_t^{\text{PPI}^D} = \pi_t^{\text{CPI}^D} + w_t^D - w_{t-1}^D - (Z_t^D - Z_{t-1}^D). \tag{1.51}$$

Alternatively, the PPI inflation differential can be written as a function of nominal depreciation and relative real GDP growth, if $\omega \neq 1$:

$$\pi_t^{\text{PPI}^D} = \epsilon_t - \epsilon_{t-1} - \frac{1}{\omega - 1}(y_t^D - y_{t-1}^D). \tag{1.52}$$

1.3.4 Asset accumulation

Log-linearizing the laws of motion for the real net foreign bond holdings of domestic and foreign households yields

$$B_{t+1} = \frac{1}{1+n}\left(\frac{1}{\beta}B_t + y_t - c_t\right), \tag{1.53}$$

$$B_{t+1}^* = \frac{1}{1+n}\left(\frac{1}{\beta}B_t^* + y_t^* - c_t^*\right). \tag{1.54}$$

Because $\overline{B}_0 = \overline{B}_0^* = 0$, B and B* are defined as percentage deviations of B and B^* from the steady-state level of domestic and foreign consumption, respectively. As steady-state asset holdings are zero, changes in the real interest rate have no impact on asset accumulation. Bond market equilibrium requires $aB_t + (1-a)B_t^* = 0$. Thus, taking the difference of (1.53) and (1.54) yields

$$B_{t+1} = \frac{1}{1+n}\left[\frac{1}{\beta}B_t + (1-a)\left(y_t^D - c_t^D\right)\right]. \tag{1.55}$$

Accumulation of aggregate per capita domestic net foreign assets is faster (slower) the larger the GDP (consumption) differential.

   Flexible prices and revenue subsidies that offset the steady-state monopolistic distortion imply that dividends at home and abroad are zero in all periods, and so are the equilibrium equity values of the two economies. Hence, $d_t^D = v_t^D = 0 \ \forall t$.

1.3.5 Solution: real variables

Flexible prices imply that a dichotomy exists between nominal and real variables in the model. Real variables affect nominal ones, but the converse is not true.[23] The solution for real variables other than real balances follows the same steps as in Ghironi (2000).

Combining labor demand (1.49) with the labor–leisure trade-off (1.41) yields the equilibrium real wage differential:

$$w_t^D = \frac{1}{1 + \rho(\omega - 1)} \left[(1 - \rho)c_t^D + \rho(\omega - 1)Z_t^D \right]. \tag{1.56}$$

Substituting equations (1.50) and (1.56) into (1.55), we obtain

$$B_{t+1} = \frac{1}{\beta(1 + n)}B_t - \frac{1 - a}{(1 + n)[1 + \rho(\omega - 1)]} \left[\omega c_t^D - (\omega - 1)Z_t^D \right]. \tag{1.57}$$

Human wealth can be written as

$$h_t^D = \beta h_{t+1}^D + \frac{(1 - \beta)(1 - \rho)}{1 + \rho(\omega - 1)}c_t^D + \frac{\rho(1 - \beta)(\omega - 1)}{1 + \rho(\omega - 1)}Z_t^D. \tag{1.58}$$

Aggregating the consumption functions for individual domestic and foreign households and log-linearizing yields the following expression for the consumption differential:

$$c_t^D = \frac{\rho(1 - \beta)}{\beta(1 - a)}B_t + h_t^D. \tag{1.59}$$

The consumption differential in each period reflects the net foreign asset position of the two economies and the differential between the expected real wage paths from that period on.

It is easy to show that $c_t^D = w_t^D = L_t^D = y_t^D = 0$, if $\omega = 1$.[24] Unitary intratemporal elasticity of substitution ensures that domestic and foreign consumption, the real wage, employment, and GDP are equal regardless of productivity. Hence, to preserve bond market equilibrium, it must be $B_t = B_t^* = 0$, if $\omega = 1$. This is the result first obtained by Cole and Obstfeld (1991), and generalized to the case of sticky prices by Corsetti and Pesenti (2001b). If the elasticity of substitution between domestic and foreign goods is one, accumulation of net foreign assets plays no role in the transmission of shocks, and current accounts are always zero: $y_t = c_t$ and $y_t^* = c_t^*$. The same result would arise with complete asset markets and $\omega = 1$. Assuming complete markets in one-period, contingent bonds with $\omega \neq 1$ would yield $c_t^D = 0$ through perfect "risk-sharing" between the domestic and the foreign economy. Net foreign assets would respond to relative GDP movements, but they would be determined residually.

Equation (1.59) can be substituted into equations (1.57) and (1.58) to obtain

$$
B_{t+1} = \frac{1 + \rho(\omega\beta - 1)}{\beta(1 + n)\,[1 + \rho(\omega - 1)]}\,B_t - \frac{\omega(1 - a)}{(1 + n)\,[1 + \rho(\omega - 1)]}\,h_t^D
$$

$$
+ \frac{(\omega - 1)(1 - a)}{(1 + n)\,[1 + \rho(\omega - 1)]}\,Z_t^D,
$$

(1.60)

$$
h_t^D = \frac{\beta\,[1 + \rho(\omega - 1)]}{\rho\omega + \beta(1 - \rho)}\,h_{t+1}^D + \frac{\rho(1 - \rho)(1 - \beta)^2}{\beta(1 - a)\,[\rho\omega + \beta(1 - \rho)]}\,B_t
$$

$$
+ \frac{\rho(1 - \beta)(\omega - 1)}{\rho\omega + \beta(1 - \rho)}\,Z_t^D.
$$

(1.61)

Equations (1.60) and (1.61) constitute a system of two equations in two unknowns (the endogenous state variable B and the forward-looking variable h^D) plus the exogenous relative productivity term Z^D. We assume

$$
Z_t = \phi Z_{t-1}, \quad Z_t^* = \phi Z_{t-1}^*,
$$

$\forall t > 0$ ($t = 0$ is the time of initial impulses in the exercises below), $0 \le \phi \le 1$. Hence, $Z_t^D = \phi Z_{t-1}^D$. The stock of net foreign assets and the levels of exogenous productivities describe the state of the (real) economy in each period. Ghironi (2000) shows that the solution of the system (1.60)–(1.61) exists and is unique. The solution can be written as:

$$
B_{t+1} = \eta_{BB} B_t + \eta_{BZ^D} Z_t^D,
$$

(1.62)

$$
h_t^D = \eta_{h^D B} B_t + \eta_{h^D Z^D} Z_t^D,
$$

(1.63)

where η_{BB} is the elasticity of time-$t+1$ assets to their time-t level, η_{BZ^D} is the elasticity of time-$t + 1$ assets to the time-t productivity differential between home and foreign (Z^D), $\eta_{h^D B}$ is the elasticity of h_t^D to time-t assets, and $\eta_{h^D Z^D}$ is the elasticity of h_t^D to Z_t^D. The values of the elasticities η as functions of the structural parameters of the model can be obtained with the method of undetermined coefficients as in Campbell (1994).[25] Given any pair of domestic and foreign endogenous, non-state, real variables x_t and x_t^* other than real money balances, the solution for their difference can be written similarly to (1.63):

$$
x_t^D = \eta_{x^D B} B_t + \eta_{x^D Z^D} Z_t^D.
$$

1.3.6 Impulse responses

Figures 1.1–1.5 show the responses of net foreign assets; the terms of trade (RP^D); and the labor effort, GDP, and consumption differentials to a 1 percent increase in relative home productivity for a plausible parameterization of the model. Periods are interpreted as quarters. We use the following parameter values: $\beta = 0.99$, $\rho = 0.33$, $\omega = 3$, $a = 0.5$, and $n = 0.01$. Our choice of n is higher than realistic, at least if one has developed economies in mind and n is interpreted strictly as the rate of growth of population.[26] However, we could reproduce the same speed of return to the steady state with slower population growth in a version of the model that incorporates probability of not surviving as in Blanchard (1985). We take $n = 0.01$ as a proxy for that situation. The value of ω is in the range of estimates from the trade literature.[27] We consider three values of the persistence parameter ϕ in the figures (0, 0.5, and 0.75) and omit (but mention) the responses for $\phi = 1$.

When $\phi < 1$, the home economy accumulates net foreign assets following the shock (Figure 1.1) to smooth its favorable effect on consumption over time. When the shock is temporary ($\phi = 0$), net foreign assets decrease monotonically in the periods after the initial one. A persistent increase in productivity ($0 < \phi < 1$) causes the home economy to continue accumulating assets for several quarters before settling on the downward path to the steady state. (The home economy accumulates no assets if the shock is permanent, $\phi = 1$. In this case, domestic GDP and consumption rise permanently above foreign exactly by the same amount in the period of the shock.) Net foreign asset dynamics triggered by non-permanent shocks are extremely persistent. This is consistent with the evidence in favor of persistence in net foreign assets in Kraay *et al.* (2000), whose regression results support an elasticity of net foreign assets at time $t + 1$ to the time-t value that is very close to 1.[28]

A favorable productivity shock at home increases the supply of home goods for any given amount of labor effort. Hence, the terms of trade worsen in Figure 1.2. (The terms of trade are permanently lower in the case $\phi = 1$.) In turn, a lower

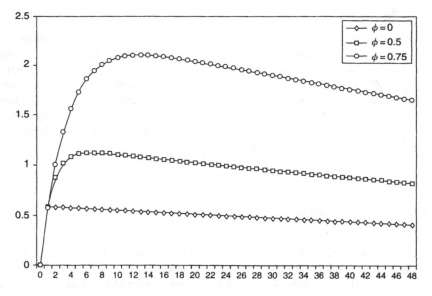

Figure 1.1 Net foreign assets.

relative price of domestic goods generates more demand for the latter, and an expansion in home labor effort above foreign on impact in Figure 1.3.

Other things given, positive net foreign assets allow home agents to sustain a given level of consumption with lower labor effort (in other words, it is $\eta_{c^D B} > 0$ and $\eta_{L^D B} < 0$ for most plausible parameter values, including those in our exercise). For this reason, once RP^D returns sufficiently close to the steady state that its effect on relative labor demand becomes very small, home labor effort falls slightly below foreign and L^D returns to 0 from below. (If $\phi = 1$, then labor effort does not move: agents simply consume the real value of the permanent increase in productivity in all periods without altering their labor supply relative to the steady state.)

The dynamics of relative GDP are similar to those of labor effort when $\phi < 1$ (Figure 1.4). The increase in labor employed in production and higher productivity more than offset the depreciation of the terms of trade, so that y^D rises above 0 on impact, and remains there until the wealth effect of net foreign assets on labor supply is sufficiently large to lower y^D below 0, from where it returns to the steady state over time.

Finally, higher productivity at home than abroad causes home consumption to rise above foreign (Figure 1.5). Consistent with intertemporal optimization, the dynamics of consumption are smoother than those of GDP. A more persistent shock has a larger effect on consumption at $t = 0$, as agents anticipate the fact that the shock will persist in the future. The consumption differential returns to zero slowly over time as the stock of aggregate per capita net foreign assets accumulated in the periods of high productivity decreases toward zero.

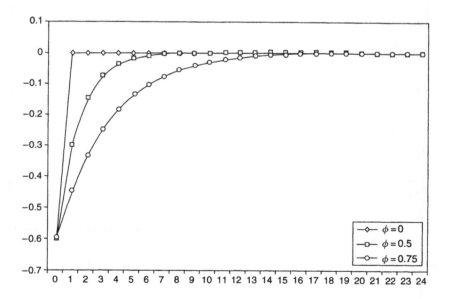

Figure 1.2 The terms of trade.

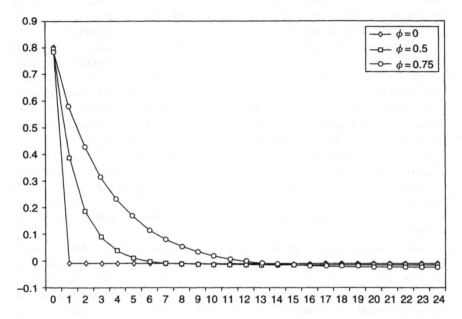

Figure 1.3 Labor effort.

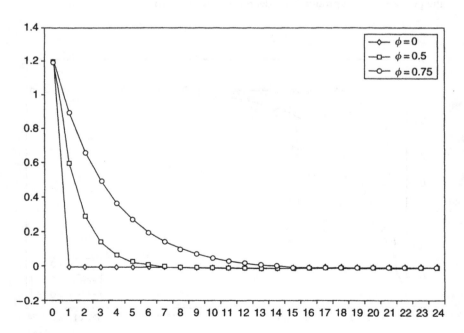

Figure 1.4 GDP.

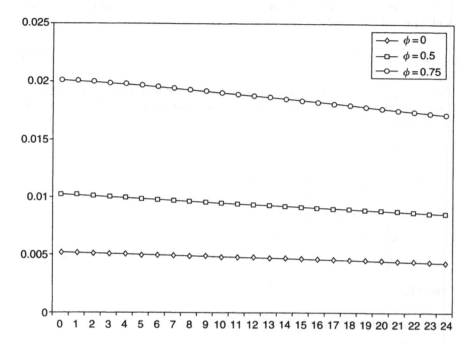

Figure 1.5 Consumption.

1.4 The exchange rate and net foreign assets with exogenous money supplies

We begin by analyzing exchange rate determination in a setup in which monetary policy is conducted through exogenous changes in money supply in both countries. This is the traditional framework for monetary policy and exchange rate determination of the Dornbusch (1976) and Obstfeld and Rogoff (1995) sticky-price models, and for the flexible-price models reviewed in Obstfeld and Rogoff (1996) and Obstfeld and Stockman (1985), among others.

We assume that the deviations of aggregate per capita money supplies from their steady-state levels at home and abroad follow autoregressive processes after initial impulses at time $t = 0$

$$M_t = \mu M_{t-1}, \quad M_t^* = \mu M_{t-1}^*, \quad \forall t > 0, \quad 0 \le \mu \le 1.$$

Then, of course,

$$M_t^D = \mu M_{t-1}^D. \tag{1.64}$$

The difference between nominal money demands at home and abroad, together with PPP and UIP, implies

$$M_t^D - \epsilon_t = c_t^D - \frac{\beta}{1-\beta}(\epsilon_{t+1} - \epsilon_t). \tag{1.65}$$

Combining (1.64) and (1.65) with the solutions for net foreign assets and the consumption differential and with our assumption about relative productivity yields the system

$$M_t^D = \mu M_{t-1}^D,$$

$$M_t^D - \epsilon_t = c_t^D - \frac{\beta}{1-\beta}(\epsilon_{t+1} - \epsilon_t),$$

$$B_{t+1} = \eta_{BB} B_t + \eta_{BZ^D} Z_t^D,$$

$$c_t^D = \eta_{c^D B} B_t + \eta_{c^D Z^D} Z_t^D,$$

$$Z_t^D = \phi Z_{t-1}^D, \tag{1.66}$$

where the first and last equations hold for all $t > 0$.

1.4.1   Solving for the exchange rate: brute force

The traditional way to look at the exchange rate solution is to express the exchange rate in terms of the present discounted value of its determinants. This is done as follows. Rewrite equation (1.65) as

$$\epsilon_t = \beta \epsilon_{t+1} + (1 - \beta)(M_t^D - c_t^D). \tag{1.67}$$

We assume that bubbles in prices and the exchange rate are ruled out by fractional backing mechanisms as in Obstfeld and Rogoff (1983) at home and abroad. (Appendix B discusses fractional backing in more detail for the case of endogenous interest rate policy.) Forward iteration of equation (1.67) yields

$$\epsilon_t = (1 - \beta) \sum_{s=t}^{\infty} \beta^{s-t}(M_s^D - c_s^D). \tag{1.68}$$

The exchange rate is proportional to the present discounted value of the money supply and consumption differentials.

If we make use of $M_t^D = \mu M_{t-1}^D$, equation (1.68) can be rewritten as

$$\epsilon_t = \frac{1-\beta}{1-\beta\mu} M_t^D - (1 - \beta) \sum_{s=t}^{\infty} \beta^{s-t} c_s^D. \tag{1.69}$$

In case of a permanent change in relative money supply ($\mu = 1$), the exchange rate responds to the monetary shock in a one-for-one fashion. Higher consumption

at home than abroad increases the demand for home currency relative to that for
foreign currency. Thus, it leads to appreciation.

Now, given the solution for the consumption differential and net foreign assets
and our assumption about the relative productivity process in system (1.66), we
can progress further by observing that the following equalities hold

$$
\sum_{s=t}^{\infty} \beta^{s-t} c_s^D = \frac{\eta_{c^D B}}{1 - \beta \eta_{BB}} B_t + \left[\frac{\eta_{c^D Z^D}}{1 - \beta \phi} + \frac{\beta \eta_{c^D B} \eta_{BZ^D}}{(1 - \beta \eta_{BB})(1 - \beta \phi)} \right] Z_t^D
$$

$$
= \frac{\eta_{c^D B}}{1 - \beta \eta_{BB}} B_t + \frac{\eta_{c^D Z^D}(1 - \beta \eta_{BB}) + \beta \eta_{c^D B} \eta_{BZ^D}}{(1 - \beta \eta_{BB})(1 - \beta \phi)} Z_t^D
$$

$$
= \eta_{\Sigma c^D B} B_t + \eta_{\Sigma c^D Z^D} Z_t^D. \tag{1.70}
$$

The present discounted value of the consumption differential is a function of the
stock of net foreign assets entering the current period and of the current level of
relative productivity. The elasticities of the present discounted value of the con-
sumption differential relative to these variables, $\eta_{\Sigma c^D B}$ and $\eta_{\Sigma c^D Z^D}$, depend on the
elasticities in the solution for relative consumption and net foreign assets and on the
persistence of productivity shocks. The denominators of both $\eta_{\Sigma c^D B}$ and $\eta_{\Sigma c^D Z^D}$
are positive under our assumptions. $\eta_{c^D B} > 0$ ensures $\eta_{\Sigma c^D B} > 0$: consistent with
the impulse responses above, accumulation of net foreign assets has a positive
effect on the expected relative consumption path. $\eta_{c^D Z^D} > 0$ and $\eta_{BZ^D} \geq 0$, in
conjunction with $\eta_{c^D B} > 0$, yield $\eta_{\Sigma c^D Z^D} > 0$: if domestic productivity is above
foreign, the expected path of domestic consumption is above foreign.

The equalities in (1.70) imply that the solution for the exchange rate in (1.69)
can be rewritten as

$$
\epsilon_t = \eta_{\varepsilon B} B_t + \eta_{\varepsilon M^D} M_t^D + \eta_{\varepsilon Z^D} Z_t^D, \tag{1.71}
$$

with

$$
\eta_{\varepsilon B} = -\frac{(1 - \beta) \eta_{c^D B}}{1 - \beta \eta_{BB}}, \quad \eta_{\varepsilon M^D} = \frac{1 - \beta}{1 - \beta \mu},
$$

and

$$
\eta_{\varepsilon Z^D} = -(1 - \beta) \frac{\eta_{c^D Z^D}(1 - \beta \eta_{BB}) + \beta \eta_{c^D B} \eta_{BZ^D}}{(1 - \beta \eta_{BB})(1 - \beta \phi)}.
$$

The advantage of writing the exchange rate solution as in equation (1.71) is that
it expresses today's exchange rate as a function of variables that are observable in
the current period (relative money supply, net foreign assets, relative productivity)
rather than as the (unobservable) present discounted value of the future paths of
relative money supply and consumption.

Equation (1.71) shows that, when monetary policy is conducted through exogenous money injections, the exchange rate depends on net foreign assets through
the effect of the latter on the consumption differential. $\eta_{c^D B} > 0$ implies $\eta_{\varepsilon B} < 0$.

Accumulation of net foreign assets allows the home country to sustain higher consumption than foreign. Hence, the demand for the home currency rises relative to that for the foreign currency, and the exchange rate appreciates. A negative elasticity of the exchange rate to net foreign assets implies that a capital inflow ($B_t < 0$) results in exchange rate depreciation, other things given. Thus, the monetary policy framework of this section cannot explain the observed connection between capital inflow and appreciation in the context of the model of this chapter.

Another implication of equation (1.71) is that the exchange rate is stationary if relative money supply and productivity are ($\mu < 1$ and $\phi < 1$). Unless shocks are permanent, the monetary policy framework of this section does not reproduce the unit root in exchange rate behavior that is observed in the data (Meese and Rogoff, 1983).

1.4.2   Solving for the exchange rate: sensitivity

We now show that it is possible to obtain the solution for the exchange rate that is implied by the traditional approach of forward solution of a difference equation by making use of the method of undetermined coefficients. Suppose we return to system (1.66). Conjecture a solution for the exchange rate as a function of the current state of the home economy relative to foreign, summarized by current relative money supply, net foreign assets entering the current period, and current relative productivity

$$\epsilon_t = \eta_{\varepsilon B} B_t + \eta_{\varepsilon M^D} M_t^D + \eta_{\varepsilon Z^D} Z_t^D.$$

Substitute this guess and its $t + 1$ version into (1.67). Taking the solutions for net foreign assets and the consumption differential and our assumptions on the relative money supply and productivity processes into account yields

$$\begin{aligned}
&\eta_{\varepsilon B} B_t + \eta_{\varepsilon M^D} M_t^D + \eta_{\varepsilon Z^D} Z_t^D \\
&= \beta[\eta_{\varepsilon B}(\eta_{BB} B_t + \eta_{BZ^D} Z_t^D) + \eta_{\varepsilon M^D} \mu M_t^D + \eta_{\varepsilon Z^D} \phi Z_t^D] \\
&\quad + (1 - \beta)[M_t^D - (\eta_{c^D B} B_t + \eta_{c^D Z^D} Z_t^D)].
\end{aligned} \qquad (1.72)$$

Equating coefficients on B_t, we find

$$\eta_{\varepsilon B} = -\frac{(1 - \beta)\eta_{c^D B}}{1 - \beta\eta_{BB}}.$$

Equating the coefficients on M_t^D yields

$$\eta_{\varepsilon M^D} = \frac{1 - \beta}{1 - \beta\mu}.$$

Finally, equating the coefficients on Z_t^D,

$$\eta_{\varepsilon Z^D} = \frac{\beta\eta_{\varepsilon B}\eta_{BZ^D} - (1 - \beta)\eta_{c^D Z^D}}{1 - \beta\phi}.$$

Substituting the solution for $\eta_{\varepsilon B}$ into this expression, we have

$$\eta_{\varepsilon Z^D} = -(1-\beta)\frac{\eta_{c^D Z^D}(1-\beta\eta_{BB}) + \beta\eta_{c^D B}\eta_{BZ^D}}{(1-\beta\eta_{BB})(1-\beta\phi)}.$$

The undetermined coefficients solution is the same as equation (1.71), with the same elasticities of the exchange rate to money supply, net foreign assets, and relative productivity. As thoroughly explained in Campbell (1994), given the uniqueness of the equilibrium, the undetermined coefficients solution for the exchange rate in terms of the minimum number of state variables (the endogenous state, B_t, and the exogenous states, M_t^D and Z_t^D) fully reflects the optimizing features of the model and the forward-looking nature of exchange rate determination. At the same time, the method of undetermined coefficients returns equation (1.71) in a much more efficient fashion.

1.4.3 Impulse responses

Productivity shock

Figures 1.6 and 1.7 show the responses of the exchange rate and the rate of depreciation to the same productivity shock in Figures 1.1–1.5 (a 1-percent increase in relative home productivity) and for the same values of structural parameters.

The exchange rate appreciates on impact in response to a favorable shock to home productivity. The shock causes home consumption to rise above foreign (Figure 1.5), which raises the relative demand for home currency and results in

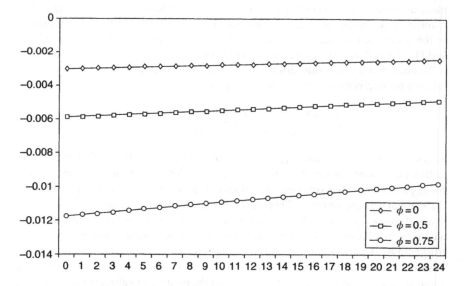

Figure 1.6 Exchange rate, productivity shock, exogenous money supplies.

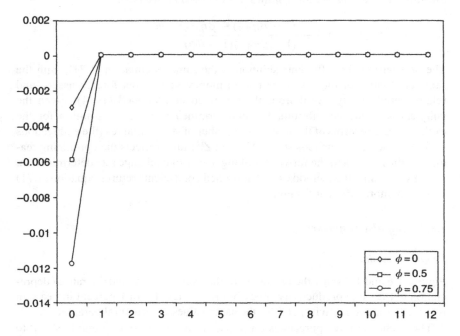

Figure 1.7 Depreciation, productivity shock, exogenous money supplies.

appreciation. The intuition is simple. Given money supplies at home and abroad, more demand for home currency relative to foreign widens the interest rate differential between home and foreign. This translates into expected future depreciation in the uncovered interest parity condition (1.40) (embedded in equations (1.65) and (1.68)) and triggers appreciation on impact.

To understand this result further, rearrange the elasticity of the exchange rate to relative productivity (which determines the impact reaction) as follows:

$$\eta_{\varepsilon Z^D} = -(1-\beta)\frac{\eta_{c^D Z^D}}{1-\beta\phi} - \frac{\beta(1-\beta)\eta_{c^D B}\eta_{B Z^D}}{(1-\beta\eta_{BB})(1-\beta\phi)}.$$

$\eta_{c^D Z^D} > 0$, $\eta_{c^D B} > 0$, and $\eta_{B Z^D} \geq 0$ ($= 0$ when $\phi = 1$) ensure that both terms in this expression are negative, so that $\eta_{\varepsilon Z^D} < 0$. The first term in the expression for $\eta_{\varepsilon Z^D}$ captures the exchange rate impact of the direct effect of the productivity differential on consumption. This term is larger in absolute value if ϕ increases. It is equal to $-\eta_{c^D Z^D}$ if $\phi = 1$. The second term captures the exchange rate effect of a change in relative productivity via the impact of net foreign asset accumulation triggered by the shock on the consumption differential. Also this term is larger in absolute value if ϕ increases, as long as $\phi < 1$. If the shock is permanent ($\phi = 1$), $\eta_{B Z^D} = 0$, and $\eta_{\varepsilon Z^D} = -\eta_{c^D Z^D}$ ($= -0.67$ for the parameter values in our exercise). Therefore, the absolute value of $\eta_{\varepsilon Z^D}$ increases with ϕ. The intuition is simple: as the relative productivity shock becomes more persistent, home consumption rises relative to foreign (Figure 1.5) due to the fact that agents anticipate the persistent effect of the shock. This puts more pressure on the relative demand for home currency, thus resulting in a larger appreciation.

Even when the productivity shock displays no persistence ($\phi = 0$), the exchange rate does not return immediately to its pre-shock level. This happens because the exchange rate depends also on net foreign assets via the effect of the latter on the consumption differential: $\eta_{\varepsilon B} = -(1-\beta)\eta_{c^D B}/(1-\beta\eta_{BB}) < 0$. In all periods after the initial one, positive net foreign assets (Figure 1.1) sustain a positive consumption differential (Figure 1.5) that translates into a persistently appreciated exchange rate (Figure 1.6) even if $\phi = 0$. As home net foreign assets return to zero over time, the consumption differential shrinks, and so does the extent of the appreciation (i.e. in all periods after $t = 0$ there is a small, positive depreciation rate in Figure 1.7). When ϕ increases, the persistence of exchange rate appreciation originates both in the persistence of the relative productivity shock itself and in slow net foreign asset dynamics. Home agents accumulate more assets during period 0 in anticipation of the persistence of the shock. When the latter dies out, slow decumulation of aggregate per capita net foreign assets causes the deviation of the exchange rate to shrink back to zero over time. A permanent productivity shock ($\phi = 1$) appreciates the exchange rate permanently by $-\eta_{c^D Z^D}$ as net foreign assets do not move in response to the shock.

Money supply shock

Figures 1.8 and 1.9 show the responses of the exchange rate and the rate of depreciation to a 1-percent increase in relative home money supply. In this case, the dynamics of the exchange rate are simply determined by $\epsilon_t = [(1-\beta)/(1-\beta\mu)]M_t^D$, $M_t^D = \mu M_{t-1}^D \cdot \eta_{\varepsilon M^D} = (1-\beta)/(1-\beta\mu) > 0$ ensures that the exchange rate depreciates in response to a monetary expansion, and it does so in a one-for-one fashion if the expansion is permanent ($\mu = 1$).

The intuition is familiar. An increase in relative money supply (which has no effect on the consumption differential and net foreign assets under flexible prices) causes the interest rate differential between home and foreign to fall, which results in expected appreciation in the uncovered interest parity condition (1.40), and thus in depreciation in the period of the shock, as in Figures 1.8 and 1.9. Both the initial jump of the exchange rate and its persistence are larger the higher the persistence of the money supply shock. If the shock has no persistence ($\mu = 0$), the exchange rate depreciates on impact by the amount $1 - \beta$ and then returns immediately to its pre-shock level. If the shock is more persistent, anticipation of this persistence results in a larger initial jump (higher $\eta_{\varepsilon M^D}$) and the speed of return to the steady state is the same as that of relative money supply. If $\mu = 1$, the exchange rate depreciates permanently by the full amount of the money supply shock. The expected rate of appreciation in all periods after the shock is zero in this case.

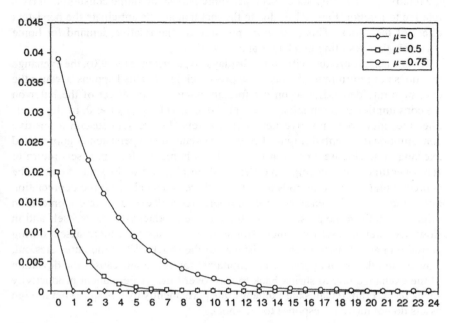

Figure 1.8 Exchange rate, money supply shock, exogenous money supplies.

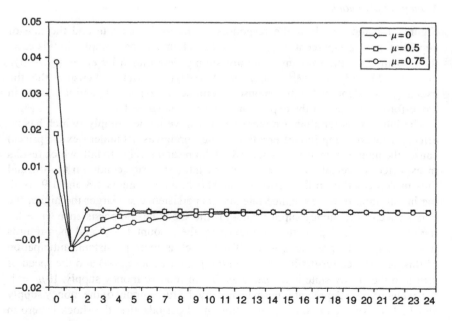

Figure 1.9 Depreciation, money supply shock, exogenous money supplies.

The results following money supply shocks are exactly as one would expect from knowledge of the standard, flexible-price, monetary model of the exchange rate. The focus on the elasticities $\eta_{\varepsilon M^D}$, $\eta_{\varepsilon Z^D}$, and $\eta_{\varepsilon B}$ in this subsection and the previous one allowed us to provide a fresh perspective on the mechanics behind the results of this benchmark approach to exchange rate determination.

1.5 Net foreign assets and exchange rate dynamics with endogenous interest rate setting

After Taylor's (1993) seminal article, a voluminous literature has developed that focuses on the conduct of monetary policy through endogenous interest rate setting. Woodford (2003) provides the most comprehensive treatment of this topic in a closed economy setting. Endogenous interest rate setting in microfounded, open economy models has been explored in a number of papers, including Benigno and Benigno (2001b) and Cavallo and Ghironi (2002). In particular, we demonstrated in our 2002 article that endogenous interest rate setting and net foreign asset dynamics have important consequences for exchange rate behavior under flexible and sticky prices. Here, we review the argument of that paper for the case of flexible prices and compare the results with those of the traditional monetary model with exogenous money.

1.5.1 Solving for the exchange rate

As in our 2002 paper, we assume here that central banks set interest rates according to simple Taylor-type rules of the form

$$i_{t+1} = \alpha_1 y_t + \alpha_2 \pi_t^{CPI} + \xi_t, \tag{1.73}$$

$$i_{t+1}^* = \alpha_1 y_t^* + \alpha_2 \pi_t^{CPI*} + \xi_t^*, \tag{1.74}$$

with $\alpha_1 \geq 0$, $\alpha_2 > 1$. (Recall that i_{t+1} and i_{t+1}^* are set at time t.) The reaction coefficients to GDP and inflation are identical at home and abroad. Because the two economies are identical in all structural features, if central banks with identical objectives independently chose the optimal values of α_1 and α_2, they would choose identical reaction coefficients. ξ and ξ^* are exogenous interest rate shocks. We assume

$$\xi_t = \mu \xi_{t-1}, \quad \xi_t^* = \mu \xi_{t-1}^*,$$

$\forall t > 0$ ($t = 0$ being the time of initial, surprise impulses), $0 \leq \mu \leq 1$ (μ now denotes the persistence of interest rate shocks). Hence, $\xi_t^D = \mu \xi_{t-1}^D$.

Equations (1.73) and (1.74) yield

$$i_{t+1}^D = \alpha_1 y_t^D + \alpha_2 \pi_t^{CPI^D} + \xi_t^D.$$

Because PPP implies $\pi_t^{CPI^D} = \epsilon_t - \epsilon_{t-1}$, it is

$$i_{t+1}^D = \alpha_1 y_t^D + \alpha_2 (\epsilon_t - \epsilon_{t-1}) + \xi_t^D. \tag{1.75}$$

Before moving on, we stress that nominal interest rates react to the deviations of GDP from the steady state rather than to the output gap – the deviation of GDP from the flexible price equilibrium – in our benchmark policy specification. This is consistent with Taylor's (1993) original analysis. But a reaction to the output gap is the standard in the recent normative literature on monetary policy. We stick to the Taylor benchmark for essentially two reasons. First, this is a positive, rather than normative, chapter, and the Taylor-specification fits the US data fairly well.[29] Second, the normative claim that central banks should react to the output gap is borne out of representative agent models subject to rather stringent assumptions. It is not clear that the same result would hold in a sticky-price version of our model.

In addition to the assumptions about interest rate setting, we retain the assumption that speculative bubbles in prices or the exchange rate are ruled out by the commitment to fractional backing mechanisms as in Obstfeld and Rogoff (1983).

Given the solutions for real variables obtained in Section 1.3 (which are not affected by a change in the monetary policymaking regime due to price flexibility), the path of the nominal exchange rate can be determined by using the UIP condition (1.40) in conjunction with the interest setting rules for the domestic and foreign economy. Combining equation (1.75) with UIP and rearranging, we obtain

$$\epsilon_{t+1} - (1 + \alpha_2)\epsilon_t + \alpha_2\epsilon_{t-1} = \alpha_1 y_t^D + \xi_t^D. \tag{1.76}$$

Now, the solution for the GDP differential is

$$y_t^D = \eta_{y^D B} B_t + \eta_{y^D Z^D} Z_t^D, \tag{1.77}$$

where $\eta_{y^D B}$ ($\eta_{y^D Z^D}$) is the elasticity of the GDP differential to the net foreign asset position (productivity differential).

Hence, the dynamics of real net foreign assets and the exchange rate are now determined by the system

$$\epsilon_{t+1} - (1 + \alpha_2)\epsilon_t + \alpha_2\epsilon_{t-1} = \alpha_1 y_t^D + \xi_t^D,$$
$$y_t^D = \eta_{y^D B} B_t + \eta_{y^D Z^D} Z_t^D,$$
$$B_{t+1} = \eta_{BB} B_t + \eta_{BZ^D} Z_t^D, \tag{1.78}$$
$$Z_t^D = \phi Z_{t-1}^D,$$
$$\xi_t^D = \mu \xi_{t-1}^D,$$

where the last two equations hold for all $t > 0$.

The roots of the characteristic polynomial for the exchange rate equation are 1 and α_2. The assumption that $\alpha_2 > 1$ is thus sufficient to ensure determinacy. Appendix B shows that the presence of a root on the unit circle does not pose problems for determinacy of the solution given our assumptions on fractional backing. We conjecture a solution for the exchange rate of the form:

$$\epsilon_t = \eta_{\epsilon\epsilon}\epsilon_{t-1} + \eta_{\epsilon B} B_t + \eta_{\epsilon Z^D} Z_t^D + \eta_{\epsilon\xi^D}\xi_t^D, \tag{1.79}$$

with elasticities $\eta_{\epsilon\epsilon}$, $\eta_{\epsilon B}$, $\eta_{\epsilon Z^D}$, and $\eta_{\epsilon\xi^D}$.

The conjectured solution and the equations in (1.78) can be used to obtain expressions for the exchange rate elasticities with the method of undetermined coefficients as we did in the case of exogenous money supplies. The following equation must hold

$$
\begin{aligned}
&\eta_{\varepsilon\varepsilon}(\eta_{\varepsilon\varepsilon}\epsilon_{t-1} + \eta_{\varepsilon B}B_t + \eta_{\varepsilon Z^{\mathrm{D}}}Z_t^{\mathrm{D}} + \eta_{\varepsilon\xi^{\mathrm{D}}}\xi_t^{\mathrm{D}}) \\
&+ \eta_{\varepsilon B}(\eta_{BB}B_t + \eta_{BZ^{\mathrm{D}}}Z_t^{\mathrm{D}}) + \eta_{\varepsilon Z^{\mathrm{D}}}\phi Z_t^{\mathrm{D}} + \eta_{\varepsilon\xi^{\mathrm{D}}}\mu\xi_t^{\mathrm{D}} \\
&- (1 + \alpha_2)(\eta_{\varepsilon\varepsilon}\epsilon_{t-1} + \eta_{\varepsilon B}B_t + \eta_{\varepsilon Z^{\mathrm{D}}}Z_t^{\mathrm{D}} + \eta_{\varepsilon\xi^{\mathrm{D}}}\xi_t^{\mathrm{D}}) + \alpha_2\epsilon_{t-1} \\
&= \alpha_1(\eta_{y^{\mathrm{D}}B}B_t + \eta_{y^{\mathrm{D}}Z^{\mathrm{D}}}Z_t^{\mathrm{D}}) + \xi_t^{\mathrm{D}}.
\end{aligned}
\tag{1.80}
$$

Equating coefficients on ϵ_{t-1} on the left-hand side and on the right-hand side of (1.80) yields

$$
\eta_{\varepsilon\varepsilon}^2 - (1 + \alpha_2)\eta_{\varepsilon\varepsilon} + \alpha_2 = 0.
$$

This polynomial has roots 1 and α_2. Because $\alpha_2 > 1$, this root would yield unambiguously unstable dynamics for the exchange rate. Hence, we select $\eta_{\varepsilon\varepsilon} = 1$: the exchange rate exhibits a unit root. The intuition is simple: the reaction of interest rates to CPI inflation in an environment in which PPP holds at all points in time (including when an unexpected shock happens) causes today's interest setting to depend also on yesterday's level of the exchange rate. (At time 0, it is $i_1^{\mathrm{D}} = \alpha_1 y_0^{\mathrm{D}} + \alpha_2\epsilon_0 + \xi_0^{\mathrm{D}}$, because the economy is assumed to be in steady state up to and including $t = -1$.) In turn, this causes today's exchange rate to depend on its past value. Stability imposes that the relevant root be 1.[30]

It is important to note that validity of the Taylor principle ($\alpha_2 > 1$) is not necessary for the exchange rate to exhibit a unit root. When the Taylor principle holds, the solution we are describing is unique. If the Taylor principle does not hold, it is possible to prove that there exists a solution in which the exchange rate does not contain a unit root. However, indeterminacy of the solution when α_2 is smaller than 1 causes the existence of sunspot equilibria that may well exhibit a unit root, including the solution described here.

Equating coefficients on B_t in (1.80) and using $\eta_{\varepsilon\varepsilon} = 1$ yields

$$
\eta_{\varepsilon B} + \eta_{\varepsilon B}\eta_{BB} - (1 + \alpha_2)\eta_{\varepsilon B} = \alpha_1\eta_{y^{\mathrm{D}}B},
$$

from which

$$
\eta_{\varepsilon B} = -\frac{\alpha_1\eta_{y^{\mathrm{D}}B}}{\alpha_2 - \eta_{BB}}.
$$

As $\alpha_2 > 1$ and $\eta_{BB} < 1$ (assets are stationary), $\alpha_2 - \eta_{BB} > 0$. Thus, the sign of $\eta_{\varepsilon B}$ – the elasticity of the exchange rate to net foreign assets – is the opposite of that of $\eta_{y^{\mathrm{D}}B}$ – the elasticity of the GDP differential to net foreign assets. If this elasticity is negative, accumulation of foreign debt (a capital inflow, $B_t < 0$)

results in an appreciation of the exchange rate below its steady-state level. The sign of $\eta_{y^D B}$ is the opposite of the sign of $\eta_{c^D B}$.[31] As we observed before, $\eta_{c^D B} > 0$ for most plausible combinations of parameter values. (Intuitively, accumulation of net foreign assets allows the home economy to sustain a higher consumption path than foreign.) It follows that $\eta_{y^D B} < 0$: *ceteris paribus*, accumulation of net foreign assets causes domestic agents to supply less labor than foreign, the domestic real wage is higher than abroad ($\eta_{w^D B} > 0$), the domestic terms of trade improve ($\eta_{RP^D B} > 0$), and domestic GDP falls relative to foreign. Hence, $\eta_{\varepsilon B} \geq 0$.

If central banks do not react to GDP movements ($\alpha_1 = 0$), the exchange rate is not affected by asset accumulation ($\eta_{\varepsilon B} = 0$). The latter matters for the exchange rate because it generates a GDP differential across countries. If this differential has no impact on interest rate setting, it has no effect on the exchange rate either.

Equating coefficients on Z_t^D in (1.80) and using the previous results yields the elasticity of the exchange rate to productivity

$$\eta_{\varepsilon Z^D} = -\frac{\alpha_1 \left[(\alpha_2 - \eta_{BB})\eta_{y^D Z^D} + \eta_{y^D B}\eta_{BZ^D}\right]}{(\alpha_2 - \phi)(\alpha_2 - \eta_{BB})}.$$

Our assumptions ensure that it is $\alpha_2 - \phi > 0$. The sign of $\eta_{\varepsilon Z^D}$ depends on that of $(\alpha_2 - \eta_{BB})\eta_{y^D Z^D} + \eta_{y^D B}\eta_{BZ^D}$. A favorable shock to relative domestic productivity causes domestic agents to accumulate net foreign assets to smooth consumption dynamics for plausible parameter values if $\phi < 1$. Hence, $\eta_{BZ^D} > 0$ and $\eta_{y^D B}\eta_{BZ^D} < 0$ if $\phi < 1$. Because $\eta_{y^D Z^D} > 0$ for the same combinations of parameters, a sufficiently aggressive reaction of the central banks to inflation (α_2 large) ensures $\eta_{\varepsilon Z^D} \leq 0$: *ceteris paribus*, a positive shock to relative domestic productivity generates an appreciation of the exchange rate.[32] If $\alpha_1 = 0$, the exchange rate does not react to relative productivity shocks ($\eta_{\varepsilon Z^D} = 0$). The intuition is similar to that for $\eta_{\varepsilon B}$.

Finally, equating coefficients on ξ_t^D in (1.80) and solving yields

$$\eta_{\varepsilon \xi^D} = -\frac{1}{\alpha_2 - \mu}.$$

Because $\alpha_2 - \mu > 0$ under our assumptions, the elasticity of the exchange rate to the relative interest rate shock is negative: $\eta_{\varepsilon \xi^D} < 0$. An exogenous increase in the domestic interest rate relative to foreign causes the domestic currency to appreciate. The appreciation is larger the smaller $\alpha_2 - \mu$. If central banks react aggressively to inflation (α_2 large), the appreciation triggered by the shock is smaller. To understand the mechanism, suppose $\mu = 0$. In this case, the exchange rate jumps instantly to its new long-run level. The depreciation rate ($\mathbf{e}_t = \epsilon_t - \epsilon_{t-1}$) is zero in all periods after the time of the shock ($t = 0$, during which the depreciation rate equals the initial jump of the exchange rate – $\mathbf{e}_0 = \epsilon_0$). On impact, domestic inflation falls relative to foreign by the extent of the initial appreciation. This causes the interest differential to fall endogenously by α_2 times the initial appreciation. In equilibrium, the interest rate differential must be zero at all points in time, because it must equal expected depreciation in the following period. (At time 0 agents expect no further exchange rate movement in future periods.) Given a 1-percent exogenous impulse to the interest rate differential, it follows that the initial appreciation that is required to keep the interest differential at zero at the time of the shock is smaller the larger α_2. If the interest rate shock is more persistent ($\mu \in (0, 1)$), the exchange rate appreciates by more: a persistent shock generates expectations of continuing appreciation that are incorporated in the initial movement of the exchange rate.

A permanent shock to the interest rate differential ($\mu = 1$) would cause the percentage deviation of the exchange rate from the steady state to increase (in absolute value) by a constant amount in all periods. This implies that the percentage deviation of the exchange rate from the steady state reaches -100 percent in finite time. But a constant deviation of the rate of depreciation from its steady-state level (zero) amounts to a constant, non-zero rate of depreciation (appreciation in this case). An exchange rate that appreciates at a constant rate becomes arbitrarily small, but never actually reaches zero. Thus, the case of a permanent shock raises the issue of the reliability of the log-linear approximation, which becomes less and less informative on the actual path of the exchange rate as its deviation from the steady state becomes larger. The zero bound on the exchange rate is indeed a non-issue in the case of a constant rate of appreciation. The conclusion of the log-linear model for long-run exchange rate behavior in the case of permanent shocks should be taken with caution.[33]

To summarize, a flexible price world yields the following exchange rate equation:

$$\epsilon_t = \epsilon_{t-1} - \frac{\alpha_1 \eta_{y^D B}}{\alpha_2 - \eta_{BB}} \mathbf{B}_t - \frac{\alpha_1 \left[(\alpha_2 - \eta_{BB}) \eta_{y^D Z^D} + \eta_{y^D B} \eta_{BZ^D} \right]}{(\alpha_2 - \phi)(\alpha_2 - \eta_{BB})} Z_t^D - \frac{1}{\alpha_2 - \mu} \xi_t^D .$$
$$(1.81)$$

The nominal exchange rate contains a unit root, but the stock of aggregate per capita real net foreign assets helps predict the exchange rate if central banks react to GDP movements in setting the interest rate. If there is no such reaction (or if there are no productivity shocks that generate movements in real variables), the process for the exchange rate simplifies to:

$$\epsilon_t = \epsilon_{t-1} - \frac{1}{\alpha_2 - \mu} \xi_t^D ,$$
$$(1.82)$$

which is exactly the random walk result of Meese and Rogoff (1983) if $\mu = 0$.

Equation (1.82) describes the exchange rate process also if $\omega = 1$. In this case, it is $\eta_{y^D B} = \eta_{y^D Z^D} = \eta_{BZ^D} = 0$, so that $\eta_{\epsilon B} = \eta_{\epsilon Z^D} = 0$ (and $\mathbf{B}_t = 0 \ \forall t$). If the intratemporal elasticity of substitution is equal to 1, productivity shocks do not affect the exchange rate regardless of whether or not interest rate setting is reacting to GDP movements. This suggests that models that assume $\omega = 1$ may be poorly suited to analyze the relation between the exchange rate and productivity.

Finally, a unit root in the exchange rate is associated with unit roots in price levels and nominal money balances. Taylor rules of the form (1.73) and (1.74) do not generate stationary levels of nominal variables. This is consistent with the empirical evidence in favor of unit roots in these variables.

1.5.2   Impulse responses

Productivity shock

Figures 1.10 and 1.11 show the responses of the exchange rate and the rate of depreciation to a 1-percent increase in relative home productivity for the same parameter values used in the impulse responses of Figures 1.1–1.9.

The exchange rate appreciates on impact, the more so the more persistent the shock (Figure 1.10). The initial jump equals the elasticity $\eta_{\varepsilon Z^D}$

$$\epsilon_0 = -\frac{\alpha_1 \eta_{y^D Z^D}}{\alpha_2 - \phi} - \frac{\alpha_1 \eta_{y^D B} \eta_{B Z^D}}{(\alpha_2 - \phi)(\alpha_2 - \eta_{BB})}. \tag{1.83}$$

The first part of this expression is negative and originates in the reaction of interest rates to the immediate change in relative GDP caused by the relative productivity shock (in Figure 1.4, domestic GDP is initially above foreign, more significantly the more persistent the shock). This component of the initial appreciation is larger the smaller the α_2 because the reaction of interest rates to inflation causes the

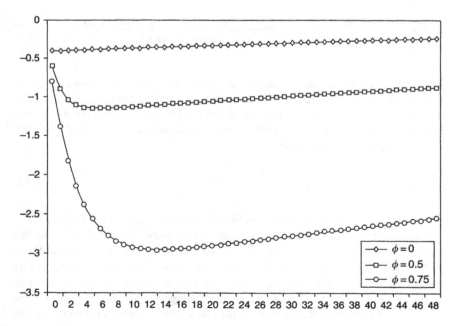

Figure 1.10 Exchange rate, productivity shock, endogenous interest rate setting.

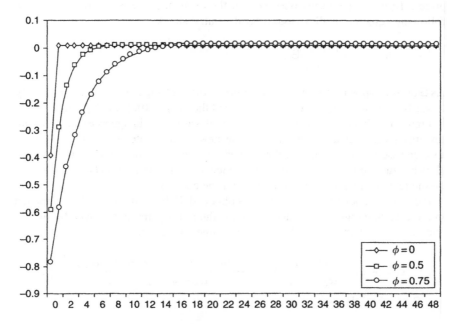

Figure 1.11 Depreciation, productivity shock, endogenous interest rate setting.

exchange rate to move in a direction opposite to the reaction to GDP movements (in Figure 1.11, the inflation differential falls on impact, the more so the more persistent the shock).[34] If $\eta_{y^D Z^D}/(\alpha_2 - \phi) > -\partial \eta_{y^D Z^D}/\partial \phi$, the first term in (1.83) is also larger the higher ϕ (because agents anticipate the effects of a persistent shock, which prolongs the time during which domestic GDP is above foreign and the exchange rate appreciates). The second part of (1.83) is positive, because $\eta_{y^D B} < 0$ and $\eta_{B Z^D} \geq 0$, and reflects the anticipated reaction of future interest rates to the persistent negative GDP differential generated by real asset accumulation (indeed, the GDP differential in Figure 1.4 becomes slightly negative during the second part of the transition dynamics, as assets slowly return to the steady state). For the same reasons as before, this component of the initial exchange rate jump is larger the less aggressive the reaction of policy to inflation and the more persistent the shock (the latter if $\eta_{B Z^D}/(\alpha_2 - \phi) > -\partial \eta_{B Z^D}/\partial \phi$.[35] The exchange rate movement caused by anticipated asset accumulation is larger the closer η_{BB} to 1. Slow convergence of assets to the steady state ensures a more persistent GDP differential, the effect of which on future interest setting is anticipated by the agents. For realistic parameter values, the effect of the first term in (1.83) dominates and the exchange rate appreciates on impact.

If $\phi = 0$, the path of the exchange rate is monotonic after the initial downward jump. The exchange rate overshoots its long-run level. Endogeneity of interest rate setting with $\alpha_1 > 0$ and asset dynamics generate overshooting with flexible prices. To understand this, observe that the exchange rate is determined by the following equation in all periods after the initial shock:

$$\epsilon_t = \epsilon_{t-1} - \frac{\alpha_1 \eta_{y^D B}}{\alpha_2 - \eta_{BB}} B_t.$$

As B becomes positive after the initial period, the exchange rate climbs very slowly towards the new steady-state position (recall that $\eta_{\epsilon B} > 0$). (The depreciation rate in Figure 1.11 becomes positive – albeit small – as the exchange rate starts moving towards its new steady-state level.) The new steady state is reached when net foreign assets have completed their transition back to zero. The transition is very slow because so is the speed of convergence of net foreign assets (which depends on the rate at which new households enter the economy).

If $\phi \in (0, 1)$, delayed overshooting is obtained. Differently from what happened in the case of exogenous monetary policy, the initial jump is followed by further appreciation. After the initial period, exchange rate and net assets obey

$$\epsilon_t = \epsilon_{t-1} - \frac{\alpha_1 \eta_{y^D B}}{\alpha_2 - \eta_{BB}} B_t - \frac{\alpha_1 \left[(\alpha_2 - \eta_{BB})\eta_{y^D Z^D} + \eta_{y^D B}\eta_{BZ^D} \right]}{(\alpha_2 - \phi)(\alpha_2 - \eta_{BB})} Z_t^D,$$

$$B_{t+1} = \eta_{BB} B_t + \eta_{BZ^D} Z_t^D.$$

A persistent (but not permanent) shock causes the stock of assets to increase until the shock has died out. That puts upward pressure on the exchange rate. However, the shock generates appreciation beyond the initial jump as long as the productivity differential remains positive. As the shock dies out, the dynamics of asset holdings drive the exchange rate to its new long-run level, between the initial response and the peak appreciation.

A permanent relative productivity shock ($\phi = 1$) causes no change in net foreign assets. The percentage deviation of the exchange rate from the steady state increases (in absolute value) by the same amount in all periods. The caveat we mentioned above about the reliability of the log-linearization for the path of the exchange rate following permanent shocks applies here.

Meese and Rogoff (1983) argued that the dynamic behavior of the exchange rate is essentially indistinguishable from a random walk. As Figure 1.12 shows, the extent to which the response of the exchange rate to a productivity shock with $\phi = 0$ differs from that of a random walk is significantly affected by the speed at which net foreign assets return to the steady state, and thus by the rate at which new households with no assets are born, n.[36] The intuition is simple. If net foreign assets return to the steady state quickly (n is high), the component $-[\alpha_1\eta_{y^D B}/(\alpha_2 - \eta_{BB})]B_t$ of the exchange rate equation dies out quickly. (To highlight this, we set n at an extremely unrealistic value of 0.5 in Figure 1.12.) In this case, the dynamic behavior of the exchange rate is entirely dominated by the unit root in the exchange rate itself when $\phi = 0$. If n is realistically small, even if the elasticity of the exchange rate to net foreign assets remains very small for the parameter values we use ($\eta_{\epsilon B} = 0.007$ [0.003] when $n = 0.01$ [0.5]), near

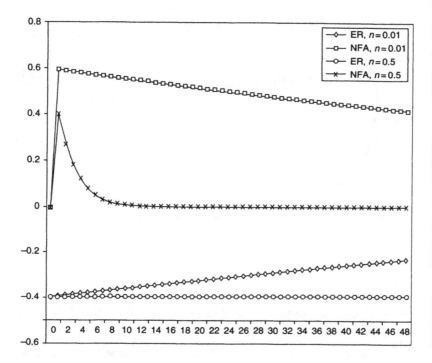

Figure 1.12 The role of *n*.

non-stationary net foreign assets generate exchange rate dynamics that can be quite different from those of a random walk.

Figure 1.13 shows that the difference between a random walk exchange rate response and the model response is larger if ω is significantly away from 1 by repeating the exercise of Figure 1.12 with $\omega = 1.2$. The range of variation of net foreign assets and the exchange rate is an order of magnitude smaller when ω is close to 1. Put differently, cross-country differences caused by asymmetric shocks are bigger if goods are more highly substitutable across countries. The difference between the $n = 0.01$ and $n = 0.5$ cases is more pronounced with the value of ω in line with the results of the trade literature used in Figure 1.12. (The exchange rate actually depreciates in the long run when $\omega = 3$ and $n = 0.01$.) Hence, the extent to which slow convergence to the steady state causes net foreign assets to affect exchange rate dynamics is more relevant the higher the degree of substitutability between domestic and foreign goods in consumption.

Interest rate shock

Figures 1.14 and 1.15 illustrate the reaction to a 1-percent domestic interest rate shock. Equation (1.82) determines the exchange rate. As expected, the

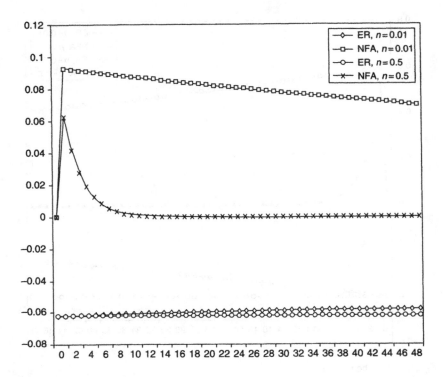

Figure 1.13 The role of ω.

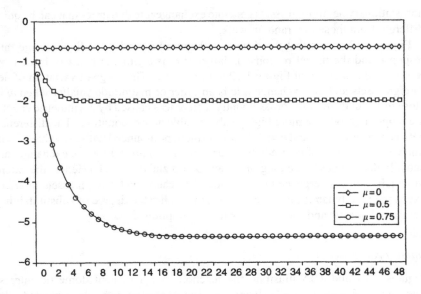

Figure 1.14 Exchange rate, interest rate shock.

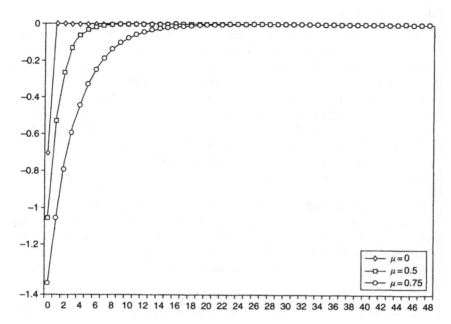

Figure 1.15 Depreciation, interest rate shock.

response to the shock is non-stationary (Figure 1.14) and no overshooting takes place. The cases $\mu = 0$ and $\mu = 1$ have been discussed before. When $\mu \in (0, 1)$, the exchange rate *under*shoots its new long-run level on impact. It continues to appreciate as the shock dies out and eventually settles at its new steady state. The depreciation rate/inflation differential falls and returns to the steady state at a speed that is inversely related to the persistence of the shock.[37]

To summarize our analysis of exchange rate dynamics with stationary net foreign assets and endogenous interest rate setting, the unit root in (1.81), combined with stationary real net foreign assets and shock processes, unambiguously delivers a non-stationary process for the nominal exchange rate. Because the deviation of net foreign assets from the steady state becomes negligible in finite time following a non-permanent shock, the exchange rate eventually settles on a new long-run position if shocks are not permanent.[38] Notwithstanding the presence of a unit root in the exchange rate, impulse response analysis supports the idea that net foreign asset dynamics help predict the path of the nominal exchange rate to the extent that the elasticity of the latter to net foreign assets is different from zero. The effect of net foreign assets on exchange rate dynamics is strengthened if their law of motion is near non-stationary and if the elasticity of substitution between domestic and foreign goods is significantly above 1. Finally, the exercise of this section shows that price stickiness is not necessary to obtain exchange rate over- or undershooting following exogenous impulses. Endogenous interest rate setting and asset dynamics are sufficient.

1.6   Conclusion

We presented a theory of exchange rate determination that highlights the relation between the exchange rate and net foreign assets. Our model builds on a flexible-price version of Obstfeld and Rogoff's (1995) seminal contribution with stationary asset positions. We showed how the method of undetermined coefficients illustrated in Campbell (1994) makes it possible to recover a solution for the exchange rate in terms of currently observable variables (rather than an infinite summation of future variables) that is fully consistent with the forward-looking nature of the model. The technique delivers a process equation for the exchange rate that facilitates interpretation and quantitative work.

We started from a version of the model with exogenous money supplies. As in the standard monetary approach to exchange rate determination, the exchange rate depends on the path of relative money supply and consumption. In turn, this can be rewritten as a function of the current levels of relative money supply and productivity and of the stock of net foreign assets entering the current period. Accumulation of assets leads to an increase in home consumption relative to foreign and this causes an appreciation of the home currency through its effect on relative money demand.

Next, as in Cavallo and Ghironi (2002), we formulated monetary policy in terms of endogenous interest rate feedback rules of the type made popular by Taylor (1993). Interest rates are set to react to CPI inflation and real GDP movements. The solution for the nominal exchange rate exhibits a unit root, consistent with Meese and Rogoff (1983). As in the previous case, today's exchange rate depends also on the stock of real net foreign assets accumulated in the previous period. Yet, this now happens through a different channel, which hinges on endogenous interest rate setting rather than money demand. For plausible parameter values, a capital inflow (accumulation of net foreign debt) generates appreciation of the exchange rate when monetary policy is endogenous. The predictive power of net foreign assets for the exchange rate is stronger the slower their convergence to the steady state following shocks and the higher the degree of substitutability between domestic and foreign goods in consumption.

The version of the model with endogenous interest rate setting yields a number of results on exchange rate overshooting. The exchange rate overshoots its new long-run level following a temporary (relative) productivity shock. If the shock is persistent, endogenous monetary policy and asset dynamics generate delayed overshooting. Endogenous monetary policy is responsible for exchange rate undershooting after persistent (relative) interest rate shocks. Our model has the potential for reconciling rational behavior and UIP with the empirical results in Clarida and Gali (1994) and Eichenbaum and Evans (1995) through a central role for endogenous, state variable dynamics. Also, we showed that a unit root in the exchange rate and responses to shocks that may coincide with those of a random walk or be hard to distinguish from those of a random walk in short data series is *not* a defeat for theory. It is what theory predicts if the nominal interest rates, the policy instruments of central banks, do not react to GDP, or if foreign goods substitute relatively poorly for domestic goods. Ultimately, it will be the task of further empirical analysis on the longer data series now available to determine whether these results lead research on exchange rates closer to the "holy grail" of exchange rate determination.

As for evidence from stylized facts of the 1990s, the model of this chapter delivers exchange rate appreciation after a favorable relative productivity shock under Taylor-type monetary policy. This is one side of the story that one would like to capture formally when trying to explain the recent behavior of the US economy and the dollar exchange rate. However, the model does not deliver appreciation *cum* accumulation of net foreign debt. Because consumption smoothing is the only motive for asset accumulation, the home economy accumulates assets rather than debt (unless the model is extended to allow for sticky prices and the shock is permanent, as shown in our 2002 article). Adding accumulation of physical capital to the scene appears a promising way of generating the dynamics we observe in the data for non-permanent changes in relative productivity. This is a direction for future work, along with empirical testing of the model's implications and exploring the consequences of deviations from PPP.[39]

Appendix A: aggregate per capita net foreign assets in the initial period

Aggregating the period budget constraint (1.3) across generations, dividing by population size, and imposing money market equilibrium and the seigniorage rebate yields

$$(1+n)\frac{A_{t+1} + \varepsilon_t A_{t+1}^*}{P_t} = \frac{1+i_t}{1+\pi_t^{\text{CPI}}}\frac{A_t}{P_{t-1}} + \frac{(1+i_t^*)(1+e_t)}{1+\pi_t^{\text{CPI}}}\frac{\varepsilon_{t-1} A_t^*}{P_{t-1}}$$
$$+ d_t + w_t L_t - c_t,$$

where it is understood that all variables are in levels rather than deviations from the steady state. Equilibrium aggregate per capita real dividends are $d_t = y_t - w_t L_t = 0$. Hence, domestic aggregate per capita net foreign assets obey

$$(1+n)\frac{A_{t+1} + \varepsilon_t A_{t+1}^*}{P_t} = \frac{1+i_t}{1+\pi_t^{\text{CPI}}}\frac{A_t}{P_{t-1}} + \frac{(1+i_t^*)(1+e_t)}{1+\pi_t^{\text{CPI}}}\frac{\varepsilon_{t-1} A_t^*}{P_{t-1}}$$
$$+ y_t - c_t. \tag{1.84}$$

Note that we have not used any no-arbitrage condition to obtain this equation. If we impose uncovered interest parity, the Fisher parity relation, and we define $B_{t+1} \equiv (A_{t+1} + \varepsilon_t A_{t+1}^*)/P_t$, it is immediate to recover

$$(1+n)B_{t+1} = (1+r_t)B_t + y_t - c_t, \tag{1.85}$$

which we used along with its foreign counterpart to solve for the model's initial steady state in Section 1.2. Log-linearization of this equation around the initial steady state yields equation (1.53). In general, it is not appropriate to use equation (1.85) (or its log-linear counterpart) to determine asset holdings in the period of an unexpected shock, which generally causes no-arbitrage conditions to be violated *ex post*. Asset dynamics in the initial period must be described by equation (1.84), which does not incorporate any no-arbitrage condition. However, the initial steady state is such that $\overline{B}_0 = 0$. If we assume that it is also $\overline{A}_0/\overline{P}_{-1} = \overline{\varepsilon}_{-1}\overline{A}_0^*/\overline{P}_{-1} = 0$ (i.e. not only their sum is zero), equation (1.84) at the time of the shock reduces to

$$(1+n)\frac{A_1 + \varepsilon_0 A_1^*}{P_0} = (1+n)B_1 = y_0 - c_0,$$

with log-linear version

$$(1+n)\mathsf{B}_1 = \mathsf{y}_0 - \mathsf{c}_0,$$

which is exactly what follows from using (1.53) directly for the initial period. The same holds for the foreign economy.

Appendix B: determinacy of the exchange rate under endogenous interest rate setting

The domestic and foreign interest rate rules can be written in anti-log form as

$$1 + i_{t+1} = y_t^{\alpha_1}(1 + \pi_t^{\text{CPI}})^{\alpha_2}\xi_t,$$

$$1 + i_{t+1}^* = y_t^{*\alpha_1}(1 + \pi_t^{\text{CPI}^*})^{\alpha_2}\xi_t^*, \quad \xi_t, \xi_t^* > 0.$$

(It is understood than that ξ and ξ^* now denote levels rather than percentage deviations from the steady state. Note that, for the interest rate rules to be consistent with the initial steady-state levels of GDP, inflation, and the interest rate in both countries, it must be $\overline{\xi}_{-1} = \overline{\xi}_{-1}^* = 1/\beta\rho^{\alpha_1}$, which we assume satisfied.) It follows that the ratio of domestic to foreign interest rate must obey

$$\frac{1 + i_{t+1}}{1 + i_{t+1}^*} = \left(\frac{y_t}{y_t^*}\right)^{\alpha_1}\left(\frac{1 + \pi_t^{\text{CPI}}}{1 + \pi_t^{\text{CPI}^*}}\right)^{\alpha_2}\frac{\xi_t}{\xi_t^*}$$

$$= \left(\frac{y_t}{y_t^*}\right)^{\alpha_1}(1 + e_t)^{\alpha_2}\frac{\xi_t}{\xi_t^*}, \qquad (1.86)$$

where the second equality follows from purchasing power parity.

Under flexible prices, the real GDP ratio is exogenous to nominal exchange rate dynamics. Define $u_t^D \equiv (y_t/y_t^*)^{\alpha_1}\xi_t/\xi_t^* > 0$. Combining (1.86) with UIP and making use of this definition yields the equation for the rate of depreciation

$$1 + e_{t+1} = (1 + e_t)^{\alpha_2} u_t^D,$$

or

$$1 + e_t = (1 + e_{t+1})^{1/\alpha_2} \left(u_t^D\right)^{-1/\alpha_2}.$$

Taking logs of both sides, it is

$$\log(1 + e_t) = \frac{1}{\alpha_2} \log(1 + e_{t+1}) - \frac{1}{\alpha_2} \log u_t^D. \tag{1.87}$$

We stress that equation (1.87) holds exactly. No approximation has been taken. Equation (1.87) is a linear, forward-looking difference equation for the rate of depreciation of the domestic currency. Given the initial level of the exchange rate $\bar{\varepsilon}_{-1}$, uniqueness of the solution for the rate of depreciation at all points in time is sufficient to ensure uniqueness of the solution for the level of the exchange rate. Solving equation (1.87) forward yields

$$\log(1 + e_t) = \lim_{T \to \infty} \left(\frac{1}{\alpha_2}\right)^T \log(1 + e_{t+T}) - \sum_{s=0}^{\infty} \left(\frac{1}{\alpha_2}\right)^{s+1} \log u_{t+s}^D. \tag{1.88}$$

Assuming a well-behaved forcing function $\log u_t^D$, $\alpha_2 > 1$ is sufficient to ensure that the summation term in (1.88) is well defined. Nevertheless, the condition $\alpha_2 > 1$ alone is not sufficient to ensure that $\lim_{T \to \infty} (1/\alpha_2)^T \log(1 + e_{t+T})$ is uniquely determined (in particular, that it is equal to zero).

For the limit in (1.88) to be indeterminate, it must be the case that either $e_{t+T} \to -1$ (the domestic currency is expected to appreciate by 100 percent between $t + T - 1$ and $t + T$) or that $e_{t+T} \to \infty$ (the domestic currency is expected to depreciate at an explosive rate).[40] Would these be rational equilibria under the interest rules we consider? If the domestic currency is expected to appreciate by 100 percent, UIP implies a ratio of domestic to foreign gross interest rates equal to zero. Equation (1.86) implies that the expectation would be validated by the interest rules, and it would actually be $e_{t+T-1} \to -1$, and so on. Similarly for the case of an explosive depreciation rate. In sum, $\alpha_2 > 1$ alone is not sufficient to rule out self-fulfilling, speculative movements of the exchange rate.

Now recall PPP: $P_t = \varepsilon_t P_t^*$. Assume that the foreign price level is well behaved (it is not approaching zero, it is not exploding to infinity). If the domestic currency depreciates at an explosive rate, it follows that the domestic price level is diverging to infinity at an explosive rate for any foreign price level. Similarly for the case of an explosive depreciation of the foreign currency under the assumption that the home price level is well behaved. We eliminate explosive solutions such as these by imposing that each monetary authority and government can back the nominal liabilities issued by domestic agents (currency and bonds) with goods, when the currency becomes too devalued. This is the solution proposed by Obstfeld and

Rogoff (1983). Focus on currency for simplicity. If the price level shoots to infinity, the real value of the currency $(1/P)$ falls to zero. But now suppose that the central bank is committed to redeeming money for goods at some strictly positive rate $(1/P)^{\text{MIN}}$. (The implicit assumption is that the resources for this are generated by tax revenues made available to the central bank by the government when need be.) This fractional backing imposes a strictly positive lower bound on the real value of nominal liabilities and causes the explosive equilibrium in which $P \to \infty$ to unravel, thus ruling it out. Similar fractional backing abroad rules out the situation in which the foreign currency is depreciating at an explosive rate.

Thus, the assumption that authorities are committed to fractional backing of nominal liabilities ensures that $\lim_{T\to\infty}(1/\alpha_2)^T \log(1 + e_{t+T}) = 0$, and the solution for the rate of depreciation (with no approximation) is uniquely determined by

$$\log(1 + e_t) = -\sum_{s=0}^{\infty}\left(\frac{1}{\alpha_2}\right)^{s+1} \log u_{t+s}^{D}. \tag{1.89}$$

Because $\bar{e}_{-1} = 0$ and $\bar{u}_{-1}^{D} = 1$, equation (1.89) is identical to

$$\log(1 + e_t) - \log(1 + \bar{e}_{-1}) = -\sum_{s=0}^{\infty}\left(\frac{1}{\alpha_2}\right)^{s+1} (\log u_{t+s}^{D} - \log \bar{u}_{-1}^{D}).$$

But $\log(1 + e_t) - \log(1 + \bar{e}_{-1}) = d\log(1 + e_t) = d(1 + e_t)/1 + \bar{e}_{-1} = de_t = \epsilon_t - \epsilon_{t-1}$ for sufficiently small deviations from the initial steady state. Also, $\log u_{t+s}^{D} - \log \bar{u}_{-1}^{D} = d\log u_{t+s}^{D} = \alpha_1 y_{t+s}^{D} + \xi_{t+s}^{D}$ (where ξ^{D} is now in percentage deviations from the steady state). Thus, given the initial level $\bar{\epsilon}_{-1}$ the path of the exchange rate is uniquely determined by

$$\epsilon_t = \epsilon_{t-1} - \sum_{s=0}^{\infty}\left(\frac{1}{\alpha_2}\right)^{s+1} (\alpha_1 y_{t+s}^{D} + \xi_{t+s}^{D}). \tag{1.90}$$

The root on the unit circle in the characteristic equation for (1.76) shows up in the presence of a unit root in the level of the exchange rate. We can verify that making use of the assumption $\xi_{t+s}^{D} = \mu\xi_{t+s-1}^{D}$, $0 \le \mu \le 1$, and the results for y_{t+s}^{D} into (1.90) returns the undetermined coefficients solution of Section 1.5 for the exchange rate.

Start by considering the term $\sum_{s=0}^{\infty}(1/\alpha_2)^{s+1}\xi_{t+s}^{D}$. Using $\xi_{t+s}^{D} = \mu\xi_{t+s-1}^{D}$, we obtain

$$\sum_{s=0}^{\infty}\left(\frac{1}{\alpha_2}\right)^{s+1} \xi_{t+s}^{D} = \frac{1}{\alpha_2}\xi_t^{D} \sum_{s=0}^{\infty}\left(\frac{\mu}{\alpha_2}\right)^{s} = \frac{1}{\alpha_2 - \mu}\xi_t^{D}. \tag{1.91}$$

Now consider the term $\sum_{s=0}^{\infty}(1/\alpha_2)^{s+1}\alpha_1 y_{t+s}^D$. It is

$$y_{t+s}^D = \eta_{y^D B} B_{t+s} + \eta_{y^D Z^D} Z_{t+s}^D,$$

$$B_{t+s} = \eta_{BB} B_{t+s-1} + \eta_{BZ^D} Z_{t+s-1}^D,$$

$$Z_{t+s}^D = \phi Z_{t+s-1}^D.$$

Given an initial level B_t, the equation for B_{t+s} implies

$$B_{t+s} = \eta_{BB}^s B_t + \eta_{BZ^D} \sum_{v=0}^{s-1} \eta_{BB}^{s-1-v} Z_{t+v}^D.$$

Hence, using $Z_{t+v}^D = \phi Z_{t+v-1}^D$ and the result

$$\sum_{v=0}^{s-1} \left(\frac{\phi}{\eta_{BB}}\right)^v = \frac{1 - (\phi/\eta_{BB})^s}{1 - \phi/\eta_{BB}}$$

in the general case in which $\phi \neq \eta_{BB}$, we obtain

$$B_{t+s} = \eta_{BB}^s B_t + \eta_{BZ^D} Z_t^D \sum_{v=0}^{s-1} \eta_{BB}^{s-1-v} \phi^v$$

$$= \eta_{BB}^s B_t + \eta_{BZ^D} \eta_{BB}^{s-1} Z_t^D \sum_{v=0}^{s-1} \left(\frac{\phi}{\eta_{BB}}\right)^v$$

$$= \eta_{BB}^s B_t + \eta_{BZ^D} \frac{\eta_{BB}^s - \phi^s}{\eta_{BB} - \phi} Z_t^D.$$

Thus, we can write

$$\sum_{s=0}^{\infty} \left(\frac{1}{\alpha_2}\right)^{s+1} \alpha_1 y_{t+s}^D$$

$$= \frac{\alpha_1}{\alpha_2} \left[\eta_{y^D B} \sum_{s=0}^{\infty} \left(\frac{1}{\alpha_2}\right)^s B_{t+s} + \eta_{y^D Z^D} Z_t^D \sum_{s=0}^{\infty} \left(\frac{\phi}{\alpha_2}\right)^s \right]$$

$$= \frac{\alpha_1}{\alpha_2} \left\{ \eta_{y^D B} B_t \sum_{s=0}^{\infty} \left(\frac{\eta_{BB}}{\alpha_2}\right)^s \right.$$

$$\left. + \left[\frac{\eta_{y^D B} \eta_{BZ^D}}{\eta_{BB} - \phi} \sum_{s=0}^{\infty} \left(\frac{1}{\alpha_2}\right)^s (\eta_{BB}^s - \phi^s) + \eta_{y^D Z^D} \sum_{s=0}^{\infty} \left(\frac{\phi}{\alpha_2}\right)^s \right] Z_t^D \right\}$$

$$= \frac{\alpha_1 \eta_{y^D B}}{\alpha_2 - \eta_{BB}} B_t + \frac{\alpha_1 \left[(\alpha_2 - \eta_{BB}) \eta_{y^D Z^D} + \eta_{y^D B} \eta_{BZ^D} \right]}{(\alpha_2 - \phi)(\alpha_2 - \eta_{BB})} Z_t^D. \tag{1.92}$$

Combining equation (1.90) with the results of (1.91) and (1.92) returns equation (1.81).

Notes

1 See also Chapter 10 of Obstfeld and Rogoff (1996).
2 This is achieved either by assuming unitary intratemporal elasticity of substitution between domestic and foreign goods in consumption as in Corsetti and Pesenti (2001b), or by combining the assumptions of complete markets and power utility. Tille (2000) provides a clear exposition of the consequences of complete markets. Kollmann (2001) is a recent exception to the trend, although he uses a non-stationary model. For a survey of the literature see Lane (2001).
3 Among others, examples are Dornbusch and Fischer (1980) and Branson and Henderson (1985).
4 Benigno (2001) achieves stationarity in an incomplete markets, open economy model by introducing the costs of bond holdings (see also Kollmann (2002); Schmitt-Grohé and Uribe (2003)). Mendoza (1991) deals with the stationarity issue by assuming an endogenous discount factor as in Uzawa (1968). Schmitt-Grohé and Uribe (2003) compare the quantitative performance of these approaches in a small open economy setup. Ghironi (2000) provides a detailed discussion of these and other approaches to the non-stationarity issue that have been explored thus far. Net foreign asset dynamics do not hinge on assumptions about a bond holding cost function or a non-standard discount factor in our model. Each individual household in the economy behaves as the representative agent of the original Obstfeld and Rogoff (1995) setup. Aggregate per capita assets are stationary, individual household's are not. Devereux (2003) and Smets and Wouters (2002) are other recent studies that use a setup similar to ours. Hau and Rey (2003) explore the relation between capital flows and the exchange rate in a continuous-time model, focusing on the information content of different financial assets.
5 Put differently, we show how to rewrite the solution for the exchange rate in terms of currently observable variables (and how to obtain the same solution through the method of undetermined coefficients).
6 Benigno and Benigno (2001b) studied the consequences of endogenous interest setting for exchange rate dynamics in a sticky-price model with no net foreign asset accumulation.
7 Blanchard (1985) combines this assumption with a positive probability of not surviving until the next period. This is advantageous for calibration purposes (see text), besides being plausible. We adopt the Weil (1989) setup here because it is relatively simpler to illustrate.
8 We focus on domestic households. Foreign agents maximize an identical utility function. They consume the same basket of goods as home agents, with identical parameters, and they are subject to similar constraints. We will sometimes refer to the representative consumer of generation υ simply as the "representative consumer" in the text. It is understood that consumers of different generations can behave differently in our model.
9 A similar constraint holds for foreign agents.
10 Given that individuals are born owning no financial wealth, because not linked by altruism to individuals born in previous periods, $A_{\upsilon}^{\upsilon^j} = A_{\upsilon}^{*\upsilon^j} = x_{\upsilon}^{\upsilon^{ji}} = M_{\upsilon-1}^{\upsilon^j} = 0$.
11 Similar labor–leisure trade-off, Euler equation, no-arbitrage, and transversality conditions hold for foreign agents.
12 Because all firms in the world economy are born at $t = -\infty$, after which no new goods appear, it is not necessary to index output and factor demands by the firm's date of birth. As for consumers, we focus on domestic firms in the text. Foreign firms are similar in all respects.
13 At time 0, home population is equal to a. At time 1, it is $a(1 + n)$. Hence, generation 1 consists of an households. Population at time 2 is $a(1 + n)^2$. It follows that generation 2 consists of $an(1 + n)$ households. Continuing with this reasoning shows

that generation t consists of $an(1 + n)^{t-1}$ households. Going back in time from $t = 0$, population at time -1 is $a/(1 + n)$. Hence, generation 0 consists of $an/(1 + n)$ households. Population at time -2 is $a/(1 + n)^2$. It follows that generation -1 consists of $an/(1 + n)^2$ households. Continuing with this reasoning makes it possible to show that generation $-t$ consists of $an/(1 + n)^{t+1}$ households.

14 To understand the presence of C_{t+1}^{t+1} in the aggregate Euler equation, apply the aggregation procedure to both sides of the Euler equation $C_t^v = [1/(\beta(1 + r_{t+1}))]C_{t+1}^v$. It is:

$$\frac{a\left[\cdots \dfrac{n}{(1+n)^{t+1}}C_t^{-t} + \cdots + \dfrac{n}{1+n}C_t^0 + nC_t^1 + \cdots + n(1+n)^{t-1}C_t^t\right]}{a(1+n)^t}$$

$$= \frac{1}{\beta(1+r_{t+1})}\frac{a\left[\cdots \dfrac{n}{(1+n)^{t+1}}C_{t+1}^{-t} + \cdots + \dfrac{n}{1+n}C_{t+1}^0 + nC_{t+1}^1 + \cdots + n(1+n)^{t-1}C_{t+1}^t\right]}{a(1+n)^t}.$$

The left-hand side of this equation is equal to c_t. The right-hand side is

$$[1/(\beta(1 + r_{t+1}))][(1 + n)c_{t+1} - nC_{t+1}^{t+1}].$$

15 Blanchard (1985) defines human wealth as the present discounted value of future, exogenous non-interest income. Weil (1989) defines human wealth as the present discounted value of after-tax endowment income. Labor income is endogenous in our model. Our definition of human wealth as the present discounted value of an agent's exogenous endowment of time parallels those of Blanchard (1985) and Weil (1989).

16 See Ghironi (2000) for details.

17 Strictly speaking, these equations hold in all periods *after* the initial one. No-arbitrage conditions may be violated between time $t_0 - 1$ and t_0 if an unexpected shock surprises agents at the beginning of period t_0. In Appendix A, we show that using log-linear versions of these equations to determine asset accumulation in the initial period is harmless if one is willing to assume that the steady-state levels of A, A^*, A_*, and A_*^* are all zero. (As we show in the text, the model pins down the steady-state levels of B and B^* endogenously. Because domestic and foreign bonds are perfect substitutes once no-arbitrage conditions are met, the model does not pin down the levels of A, A^*, A_*, and A_*^*.)

18 There are two reasons for time indexes for steady-state levels of variables. On the one hand, when we consider non-stationary exogenous shocks, these will cause the economy to settle at a new long-run position. On the other hand, we shall see that the levels of nominal variables may exhibit a unit root regardless of the stationarity of the exogenous shocks.

19 The subscript for initial steady-state asset holdings is 0 rather than -1 because time-0 asset holdings are determined at time -1.

20 See Ghironi (2000) for details.

21 Percentage deviations of inflation, depreciation, and interest rates from the steady state refer to gross rates. From now on, π denotes the percentage deviation of the corresponding (gross) inflation rate from the steady state.

22 We define the domestic terms of trade (following Obstfeld and Rogoff (1995, 1996); Ch. 10) as $p(h)/\varepsilon p^*(f)$, where $p(h)(p^*(f))$ is the producer currency price of the representative home (foreign) good. It is easy to verify that RP^D is the percentage deviation of the terms of trade from the steady state.

23 Except for real balances, which are a function of the nominal interest rate.

24 See Ghironi (2000).

25 See Ghironi (2000).

26 The average rate of quarterly population growth for the United States between 1973:1 and 2000:3 has been 0.0025.

27 See Feenstra (1994), Hummels (1999), and Shiells *et al.* (1986). $\omega = 3$ is in the lower portion of the range of estimates in these papers. See Cavallo and Ghironi (2002) for an analysis of alternative values of ω, including the standard assumption of the international RBC literature that ω is close to 1.

28 See also Ghironi (2000).

29 See Clarida and Gertler (1997) and Clarida *et al.* (1998) for evidence from other countries.

30 Taylor rules that allow for interest rate smoothing such that $i^D_{t+1} = \alpha_1 y^D_t + \alpha_2 \pi^{CPID}_t + \alpha_3 i^D_t + \xi^D_t$ ($0 \leq \alpha_3 < 1$) would still induce the presence of a unit root in the level of the exchange rate through the same channel. There would be no unit root in the exchange rate if central banks were setting interest rates to react to the level of the CPI rather than to CPI inflation.

31 See Ghironi (2000).

32 All the results in this paragraph hold for the values of structural parameters in the previous section and with the standard Taylor reaction of the interest rates to inflation, $\alpha_2 = 1.5$.

33 Perhaps less justifiably, we do not impose the zero bound on nominal interest rates. See Benhabib *et al.* (2002) and references therein for analyses of the consequences of this zero bound in (closed economy) environments in which monetary policy follows Taylor-type rules.

34 Figure 1.11 provides information also on the actual behavior of interest rates following the shock. Because of UIP, the realized interest rate differential at each date equals the rate of depreciation in the following period.

35 Note that changes in the persistence of shocks have no impact on the elasticity of other endogenous variables to asset holdings.

36 In Figures 1.12 and 1.13, ER denotes the exchange rate and NFA denotes net foreign assets.

37 The value of ω has of course no impact on the effect of interest rate shocks under flexible prices.

38 It should be noted that $n = 0$, which delivers non-stationary real assets, will not necessarily generate a stationary exchange rate. Keeping the other parameter values as the benchmark, a favorable shock to home productivity with $\phi = 0$ causes domestic net foreign assets to settle at a new (higher) steady-state level by the beginning of the period after the shock. The exchange rate appreciates on impact. But permanently higher assets from $t = 1$ on imply that expected exchange rate depreciation (and the interest rate differential) must be constant in all periods (including that of the shock). (At time 0, expected depreciation between time 0 and time 1 equals $\eta_{\varepsilon B} \bar{B}$, where $\bar{B}$ is the permanent deviation of asset holdings from the steady state.) A constant rate of depreciation in all periods following the initial one causes the exchange rate to eventually shoot to infinity.

39 There is a fast growing empirical literature on the relation between net foreign assets and the real exchange rate (Gagnon (1996); Lane and Milesi-Ferretti (2000, 2002a,b); Leonard and Stockman (2002)). See Obstfeld and Rogoff (2001) on the issues this may pose for the United States.

40 From $1 + e_t = \varepsilon_t/\varepsilon_{t-1}$, it follows that $1/(1 + e_t) = (1/\varepsilon_t)/(1/\varepsilon_{t-1})$. Thus, the case of an expected 100 percent appreciation of the home currency corresponds to an explosive depreciation of the foreign currency.

2 Dornbusch revisited

Jean-Olivier Hairault, Lise Patureau and Thepthida Spraseuth

2.1 Introduction

The emergence of the real business cycle literature in the beginning of the 1980s has induced substantial progress in macroeconomic theory and technical modelling, allowing economic research to tackle new or older questions with a renewed focus. Attention has thus been drawn to the quantitative properties of the business cycles in terms of first- and second-order moments. In the field of international macroeconomics, the focus is set on matching the volatilities and the co-movements of international time series data. In a seminal paper, Backus *et al.* (1995) recall that the international real business cycle literature has been able to account for some salient features of international data, such as the correlation between saving and investment rates (Cardia, 1991; Baxter and Crucini, 1993), or the counter-cyclical movements of the trade balance (Mendoza, 1991; Backus *et al.*, 1994).

Yet they identify one major long lasting discrepancy. Since the beginning of the flexible exchange rate period in 1971, nominal and real exchange rates have become extremely volatile and much more than macroeconomic fundamentals such as outputs or monetary growth factors. This puzzling behavior of relative international prices, the "price anomaly" in the Backus *et al.*'s (1995) terminology, has been one of the leading issues in international macroeconomics. Table 2.1 taken from Backus *et al.* (1995) presents evidence of the high volatility of terms of trade for the G7-countries group. Table 2.2 displays larger evidence of the price anomaly: for the median of the G7 countries vis-à-vis the United States, the nominal and real exchange rates are around seven times more volatile than output.

Backus *et al.* (1995) therefore identify the so-called "exchange rate disconnect puzzle" (Obstfeld and Rogoff, 2000b) that numerous papers have since been attempting to solve. Particular attention has been drawn to the role of monetary factors and nominal rigidity in line with the traditional Mundell (1963)–Fleming (1962)–Dornbusch (1976) theory. Recent research in the so-called new open-economy macroeconomics framework has thus been producing a significant renewal of old sticky-price models by introducing nominal rigidity into intertemporal general equilibrium models based on optimizing and rational agents. The seminal paper by Obstfeld and Rogoff (1995) first explores the determination of exchange rates and the international monetary transmission mechanism in a

Table 2.1 Terms of trade cyclical behavior

Volatility (s.d. in %)	Terms of trade σ_{TOT}	Output σ_Y	σ_{TOT}/σ_Y
Canada	2.99	1.50	1.99
France	3.52	0.90	3.91
Germany	2.66	1.51	1.76
Italy	3.50	1.69	2.07
Japan	7.24	1.35	5.36
United Kingdom	3.14	1.61	1.95
USA	3.68	1.92	1.91

Sources: Backus *et al.* (1995). Period 1970 to mid-1990. Statistics are based on Hodrick–Prescott filtered data OECD and IMF database sources.

Table 2.2 Stylized facts

Volatility (s.d. in %)	Nominal exchange rate σ_e	Real exchange rate σ_Γ	Output σ_Y	Relative σ_e/σ_Y	To output σ_Γ/σ_Y
Canada	2.861	2.959	1.539	1.859	1.922
France	8.619	8.003	0.975	8.837	8.237
Germany	8.208	7.842	1.833	4.478	4.278
Italy	8.421	7.619	1.420	5.928	5.364
Japan	9.198	8.966	1.556	5.911	5.762
Great Britain	8.082	7.743	1.692	4.777	4.576
Mean	7.565	7.194	1.503	5.034	4.787
Median	8.314	7.792	1.548	5.372	5.038

Source: OECD BSDB database. All series are quarterly and have previously been HP-filtered. Period 1971:1 to 1999:4, except exchange rates for France (1971:1–1997:4) and Canada (1971:1–1999:3).

purely analytical framework. Kollmann (2001) quantitatively assesses the story in an intertemporal, stochastic and small open economy model. Kollmann (2001) focuses on the role of imperfections on the good and labor market in the exchange rate disconnect puzzle by studying the combined role of deviations from the law of one price, staggered wage, and price setting. He derives promising results since monetary shocks generate amplified movements of nominal and real exchange rates.

The present chapter shares Kollmann's (2001) approach since we derive quantitative results from a dynamic general equilibrium model, in an attempt to explain the exchange rate disconnect puzzle. We also adopt the small open economy assumption; abstracting from movements in foreign variables allows us to identify the domestic propagation mechanisms in a very transparent way. Yet this chapter departs from Kollmann's (2001) paper by investigating a route other than the role for nominal rigidities. We focus on the role of credit market imperfections in order to assess the relevance of the nominal exchange rate overshooting in the exchange rate disconnect puzzle.

We therefore come back to the traditional overshooting explanation given by Dornbusch (1976) who builds "a theory that is suggestive of the observed large fluctuations in exchange rates." In a small open economy framework Dornbusch (1976) analytically demonstrates that a home monetary injection generates an over-reaction of the nominal exchange rate beyond its steady-state level. The overshooting phenomenon is thought as a key factor for the observed exacerbated exchange rate movements.[1] The objective of the chapter is to quantitatively assess the role of the overshooting dynamics in explaining the exchange rate disconnect puzzle.

The framework we adopt builds on nominal price rigidity. Furthermore, as in Dornbusch (1976), the nominal exchange rate overshooting is linked to imperfections on the market where the nominal interest rate is determined. A limited participation international business cycle model is then developed. Indeed, the limited participation assumption pioneered by Christiano (1991) and Fuerst (1992), aims at reproducing the persistent fall in the nominal interest rate following a monetary expansion in a closed economy setting: this assumption states that the household decides the amount of money she wants to put into the banks before the occurrence of the monetary injection. Furthermore, it is well known that a convenient way to generate a large and persistent liquidity effect consists in assuming adjustment costs on money holdings (Christiano and Eichenbaum, 1992a; King and Watson, 1996).

The liquidity effect has been already analyzed in an open economy setting by Schlagenhauf and Wrase (1995). Yet the focus of their paper is quite different from ours. The authors aim at reproducing the dynamic responses of the interest rate, the nominal exchange rate and the output given by a structural VAR model, following a monetary expansion. By using a two-country framework, Schlagenhauf and Wrase (1995) also measure the role played by the liquidity effect in the international transmission of economic fluctuations. In contrast, our chapter highlights the crucial role played by the overshooting phenomenon in explaining the exchange rate volatility. Hairault *et al.* (2001) recently investigated the role of credit market imperfections in a small open economy setting. They show that given the limited participation assumption, monetary shocks generate a nominal exchange rate overshooting that accounts for a substantial part of the huge observed nominal exchange rate fluctuations. Nevertheless, throughout their paper the law of one price and the purchasing parity power hold such that the real exchange rate equals one. The study of the real exchange rate behavior is consequently beyond their scope. Moreover, they adopt a flexible price framework. The present chapter extends Hairault *et al.*'s (2001) approach by introducing price stickiness and real exchange rate dynamics. In line with Dornbusch's (1976) seminal paper, the theoretical framework that we retain enables us to further analyze the role of monopolistic competition and nominal rigidity together with credit market imperfections in nominal and real exchange rate fluctuations.

The intuition behind our results is straightforward. Given credit market frictions, a home monetary injection translates into a decrease in the home nominal interest rate. The model is thus able to account for the liquidity effect. As a result, the foreign interest rate being constant uncovered interest rate parity requires an expected *appreciation* of the domestic currency. The nominal exchange rate displays an overshooting dynamics. Given sluggish price adjustment, the large nominal exchange rate response translates into a large real exchange rate depreciation. Combining rigidities on the credit market and the goods market might improve our understanding of the exchange rate disconnect puzzle.

The chapter proceeds as follows. Section 2.2 presents the building blocks of the model while Section 2.3 derives the results. Sections 2.3.1 and 2.3.2 analyze the properties of a version of the model based only on good market imperfections absent adjustment costs on the credit market side. Section 2.3.1 checks that technological shocks cannot be considered as serious candidates for explaining exchange rates movements. Section 2.3.2 therefore evaluates the role of monetary shocks. Even if the introduction of monetary perturbations improves the theoretical results, the model does not display any exacerbated response for exchange rates. The model lacks amplification mechanisms of monetary innovations. In Section 2.3.3, we consider the role of credit market frictions. In a model based on both credit market frictions and nominal price rigidities, monetary shocks generate a nominal exchange rate overshooting and we show that the model is able to account for a substantial part of the exchange rate fluctuations. Section 2.4 concludes.

2.2   The model

The model consists of four types of economic agents (the consumer-household, the good-producing firms, the financial intermediary and the central bank) and five markets (goods, labor, loanable funds, foreign assets and money markets) in a small open economy framework. We model both types of frictions, nominal rigidities and frictions on the credit market.

- *Credit market frictions*: In the spirit of Lucas (1990) and Christiano (1991), the limited participation assumption consists in modelling information asymmetries, in order to generate a liquidity effect after a money shock. Besides holding money for consumption purchases (M_t^c), the household uses some amount of money as bank deposits (M_t^b). Information asymmetries are introduced through the limited participation assumption: when choosing her amount of bank deposits the household does not know the realization of the monetary shock.

  Furthermore, following Christiano and Eichenbaum (1992a) and King and Watson (1996), we introduce adjustment costs on money holdings. Indeed, if the standard limited participation model generates a liquidity effect following a positive monetary shock, the decrease in the interest rate is not strong and persistent enough as compared to the stylized facts. As modelled by Christiano and Eichenbaum (1992a), one way to improve the liquidity effect is to modify the environment so that the financial sector remains more "liquid" than the real sector for several periods after the monetary shock. We model this intuition by assuming that adjusting the money-cash M_t^c is costly. If, after the shock, the household increases her money-cash by only a small amount, it implies that the withdrawal from her deposits is reduced. Then, in the following period the firm has to absorb a larger share of the economy's funds and the liquidity effect persists over time. In our setting, given uncovered interest rate parity, a large and lasting fall in the interest rate differential implies a significant overshooting of the nominal exchange rate. Thus our model can generate a large exchange rate overshooting which allows us to quantitatively evaluate its role in the exchange rate fluctuations.

- *Good market frictions*: In line with Dornbusch (1976), excessive exchange rate movements have long been thought as resulting from price rigidities. We thus model real and nominal price rigidities on the goods market. The domestic household consumes two varieties of goods. One is produced by the home country and the second is imported from the rest of the world. Each variety is produced by a continuum of firms entitled by some market power as we allow for monopolistic competition. We only consider the behavior of the domestics firms which sell part of their production on the domestic market, the other part being exported to the foreign country. In line with the menu costs literature, we introduce nominal price rigidity by assuming quadratic adjustment costs on prices.

2.2.1 Timing of decisions

As in Andolfatto and Gomme (2000), the limited participation assumption is modelled the following way: in the current period the household chooses the amount of deposits she wants to put into the bank the next period. Hence the timing of decisions within a period can be separated into five steps.

- At the beginning of period t, the monetary shock occurs: the monetary authorities inject liquidity into the loanable funds market, while the household's bank deposit choice has been made at the end of period $t - 1$.
- Then the credit market opens. The firms determine their demand for labor and capital so as to produce goods. As in Christiano (1991), they have to borrow to pay the labor revenues.
- In the third step, the good markets open and production and purchasing decisions are made. Each monopolistic firm optimally decides which price to set and which amount of good to produce, knowing the demand functions for its own good from domestic and foreign agents.
- At the end of the period, the foreign asset market opens. The representative household decides to buy or to sell foreign assets whose return is given by the exogenous foreign interest rate. Loans are repaid to the financial intermediary. Moreover, as the owner of the firm and the bank, the household receives dividend payments from them.

- At the end of the period, the household decides the amount of money to put into the banks for the next period, and consequently the amount of money-cash.

2.2.2   The agents

The household

PREFERENCES

At the end of period t, the household chooses the amount M_{t+1}^c of money available for consumption purchases (money-cash) in period $t+1$ and the amount M_{t+1}^b of money put into the bank (money-deposit) in period $t+1$. We assume that the time spent on reorganizing the flow of funds Ω_t is given by

$$\Omega_t = \frac{\xi}{2} \left(\frac{M_{t+1}^c}{M_t^c} - g \right)^2.$$

In the long-run steady state, M_{t+1}^c/M_t^c is equal to g. Then both the level of Ω_t and its derivative with respect to M_{t+1}^c/M_t^c equal zero in steady state. Changing M_t^c is costly (in terms of time) with a marginal cost being an increasing function of the parameter ξ.

Leisure is defined as

$$L_t = 1 - H_t - \Omega_t.$$

We retain a simple form for the instantaneous utility function

$$U(C_t^c, L_t) = \log C_t^c + \psi_L \log L_t.$$

As the domestic agent consumes goods from both countries, her bundle of goods is defined as

$$C_t^c = \left[\omega^{1/\theta} C_{Ht}^{(\theta-1)/\theta} + (1-\omega)^{1/\theta} C_{Ft}^{(\theta-1)/\theta} \right]^{\theta/(\theta-1)}, \quad 0 < \gamma < 1, \ \theta > 1,$$

$$(2.1)$$

where $\theta > 1$ represents the elasticity of substitution between domestic and foreign goods, and ω the relative weight of domestic goods in the consumption index.

STATIC PROGRAM

As in Blanchard and Kiyotaki (1987) we first solve for the within-a-period program of the household. She minimizes her consumption purchases given a certain amount of resources. We thus get the demand functions for each type of good

i ($i = H, F$) and the domestic consumption price index P_t^c

$$C_{Ht} = \omega \left[\frac{P_{Ht}}{P_t^c} \right]^{-\theta} C_t^c,$$ (2.2)

$$C_{Ft} = (1 - \omega) \left[\frac{P_{Ft}}{P_t^c} \right]^{-\theta} C_t^c,$$ (2.3)

$$P_t^c = \left[\omega P_{Ht}^{1-\theta} + (1 - \omega) P_{Ft}^{1-\theta} \right]^{1/(1-\theta)}$$ (2.4)

with P_{Ht} the price index for domestic goods and P_{Ft} the price index for foreign goods both being expressed in domestic currency. As we assume that the law of one price holds for each good, it can be said that

$$P_{Ft} = e_t P_{Ft}^*$$ (2.5)

with P_{Ft}^* the price of exported foreign goods in foreign currency. As we model a small open economy, we consider that the amount of goods exported by the foreign country is small enough so that the price index of the exported goods is equal to the exogenous foreign consumption price index

$$P_{Ft}^* = P_t^{c*}.$$

Each type of good (domestic or foreign) is composed of a continuum of differentiated goods given by the following equation

$$C_{Ht} = \left[\int_0^1 c_{Ht}^{(\eta-1)/\eta}(z) \, dz \right]^{\eta/(\eta-1)}$$

with $\eta > 1$ the elasticity of substitution between goods of the same variety. According to the same reasoning, the household's optimal allocation between goods of one variety leads to the domestic demand for the home good

$$c_{Ht}(i) = \left[\frac{p_{Ht}(i)}{P_{Ht}} \right]^{-\eta} C_{Ht}.$$

INTERTEMPORAL PROGRAM

The representative household maximizes the expected intertemporal flow of utility

$$U_0 = E_t \sum_{t=0}^{\infty} \beta^t U(C_t^c, L_t)$$ (2.6)

with C_t^c the consumption index and L_t leisure. In each period the household faces three constraints, a cash-in-advance constraint (equation (2.7)) and a budget constraint (equation (2.8)) and the law of motion for physical capital (equation (2.9)).

$$P_t^c C_t^c \leq M_t^c, \tag{2.7}$$

$$M_{t+1}^c + M_{t+1}^b + e_t B_{t+1} + P_t^c C_t^c + P_t \frac{\phi_I}{2} \frac{(K_{t+1} - K_t)^2}{K_t}$$

$$\leq M_t^c + P_t^c w_t (1 - L_t - \Omega_t) + P_t^c r_t K_t + (1 + R_t) M_t^b$$

$$+ e_t (1 + i_t^*) B_t + \int_0^1 D_t^f (z)\, dz + D_t^b, \tag{2.8}$$

$$K_{t+1} = (1 - \delta) K_t + I_t^c. \tag{2.9}$$

M_t^c denotes the amount of money-cash hold by the household for consumption purchases in period t and M_t^b the amount of money holdings put into the bank (both chosen at the end of period $t - 1$). The return on the bank deposits is given by the nominal interest rate R_t. The household also saves by holding foreign assets. International financial markets are incomplete and, in each period, the household buys B_{t+1} (in foreign currency) of assets issued by the rest of the world. The foreign financial asset yields an exogenous (small open economy assumption) no-risk nominal interest rate i^* tomorrow. As the foreign assets are issued in foreign currency, the nominal exchange rate is a key variable in the portfolio decisions.

In period t, the household decides the amount of domestic holdings for consumption purchases M_{t+1}^c and the amount of foreign assets B_{t+1} she wants to accumulate. Because of adjustment costs on money-holdings, at period t when the household chooses her amount of money-cash M_{t+1}^c and her complement (the amount of money-deposit M_{t+1}^b), she takes into account the fact that changing her money holdings M_{t+1}^c is costly: it takes time to reorganize the flow of funds. She also determines her consumption of good C_t, her labor supply H_t. w_t denotes the real wage, $\int_0^1 D_t^f (z)\, dz$ and D_t^b the profits of the firms and of the banks respectively, which are returned as dividends to the household at the end of the period. The household also decides to invest in physical capital, facing adjustment costs scaled by the parameter $\phi_I > 0$. The real rate of return on capital is r_t. In order to simplify the derivation of the demands for goods, we assume that the investment index and adjustment costs on capital have the same structure as the consumption one

$$I_t^c = \left[\omega^{1/\theta} I_{Ht}^{(\theta-1)/\theta} + (1 - \omega) I_{Ft}^{(\theta-1)/\theta} \right]^{\theta/(\theta-1)},$$

$$CK_t^c = \frac{\phi_I}{2} \frac{(K_{t+1} - K_t)^2}{K_t} = \left[\omega^{1/\theta} CK_{Ht}^{(\theta-1)/\theta} + (1 - \omega) CK_{Ft}^{(\theta-1)/\theta} \right]^{\theta/(\theta-1)},$$

implying a demand function similar to equations (2.2) and (2.3).

With λ_t the multiplier associated with the budget constraint and ϑ_t the one with the cash-in-advance constraint, the first-order conditions are

$$U'_{Ct} = P^c_t(\lambda_t + \vartheta_t), \tag{2.10}$$

$$U'_{Lt} = w_t P^c_t \lambda_t, \tag{2.11}$$

$$\lambda_t = \beta E_t[(1 + R_{t+1})\lambda_{t+1}], \tag{2.12}$$

$$e_t\lambda_t = \beta E_t\{e_{t+1}(1 + i^*_{t+1})\lambda_{t+1}\}, \tag{2.13}$$

$$q_t = \beta E_t \left\{ \frac{P^c_{t+1}\lambda_{t+1}}{P^c_t \lambda_t} \left[r_{t+1} + q_{t+1} - \delta + \frac{\phi_I}{2} \left(\frac{I_{t+1} - \delta K_{t+1}}{K_{t+1}} \right)^2 \right] \right\}, \tag{2.14}$$

with $q_t \equiv 1 + \phi_K((I_t - \delta K_t)/K_t)$. The first-order condition relative to money-holdings yields

$$P_t w_t \lambda_t \frac{\partial \Omega_t}{\partial M^c_{t+1}} + \lambda_t = \beta E_t \left[\frac{U'_{Ct+1}}{P_{t+1}} \right] + \beta E_t \left[P_{t+1} w_{t+1} \lambda_{t+1} \frac{\partial \Omega_{t+1}}{\partial M^c_{t+1}} \right]. \tag{2.15}$$

Equation (2.10) equates the marginal utility of consumption and the cost of consumption, composed by the shadow price associated with the household real wealth ($P^c_t \lambda_t$) plus the cost of having money-cash to hold. Equation (2.11) states the equality between the marginal utility and the opportunity cost of leisure. Equation (2.13) is related to the choice of foreign assets and equates the current marginal cost of buying foreign assets ($e_t\lambda_t$) to its expected return the next period. Equation (2.12) equates costs to benefits of a bank deposit. Putting one unit of money in the bank in the current period costs the shadow price λ_t but yields the expected return $(1+R_{t+1})$ which increases the household's wealth by $\lambda_{t+1}(1+R_{t+1})$. Equation (2.14) equates the shadow price for capital to its expected return given adjustment costs on capital. Equation (2.15) equates the costs (the left-hand side) to the benefits (the right-hand side) related to the choice in period t of the amount of money holdings available for consumption in $t + 1$. With $\xi = 0$, that is, without adjustment costs, the benefit of money holdings is simply to allow for consumption in $t + 1$. When $\xi \neq 0$, the household compares the cost of changing M^c_{t+1} today (time available to work is reduced) to the advantages such a decision will generate tomorrow: in terms of purchasing power and of time saved. Increasing M^c_{t+1} costs some fraction of time today $((\partial \Omega_t/\partial M^c_{t+1}) > 0)$ but it also implies saving time tomorrow $((\partial \Omega_{t+1}/\partial M^c_{t+1}) < 0)$.

The production sector

The good market structure relies on the monopolistic competition setting as in Blanchard and Kiyotaki (1987). Each firm produces a differentiated good, and sets price and quantity taking aggregate prices and aggregate demand functions as given. Domestic firms sell their goods both to domestic agents and foreigners. As domestic households consume both domestic and foreign goods, we assume that imported goods are brought to foreign firms by perfectly competitive importers, which re-sell it to domestic consumers.

DOMESTIC PRODUCERS

The production technology of a domestic firm i is given by a Cobb–Douglas function

$$y_t(i) = A_t k_t^\alpha(i) h_t^{1-\alpha}(i), \quad 0 < \alpha < 1, \tag{2.16}$$

where $k_t(i)$ and $h_t(i)$ represent the factors inputs for the firm i. A_t designs the aggregate domestic technology level assumed to follow an autoregressive process of order 1:

$$\ln A_{t+1} = \rho_a \ln A_t + (1 - \rho_a) \ln \overline{A} + \varepsilon_{at+1}$$

with $0 < \rho_a < 1$, ε_a is a i.i.d. white noise and $\overline{A}$ is the mean of the process.

Total individual output is sold on both domestic and foreign markets. Domestic export only depends on the relative price of exported goods:[2]

$$X_t = \left[\frac{P_{Xt}}{P_{Ft}^*} \right]^{-\theta}$$

and the specific foreign demand for good i is

$$x_t(i) = \left[\frac{p_{Xt}(i)}{P_{Xt}} \right]^{-\eta} X_t.$$

We suppose that domestic firms do not price to market, that is, they set one single price in domestic currency whatever market the good is sold on, hence $p_{Xt}(i) = p_{Ht}(i)/e_t$.

Nominal rigidities are introduced in the model as quadratic adjustment costs on prices. As in Hairault and Portier (1993a), price adjustment costs are given by

$$CP_t(i) = \frac{\phi_P}{2} \left(\frac{p_{Ht}(i)}{p_{Ht-1}(i)} - \overline{\pi} \right)^2.$$

As $\overline{\pi}$ represents the steady-state price growth rate, adjustment costs are null at the long-run equilibrium. These costs are paid in terms of composite good

$$CP_t(i) = \left[\omega^{1/\theta} CP_{Ht}^{(\theta-1)/\theta}(i) + (1 - \omega) CP_{Ft}^{(\theta-1)/\theta}(i) \right]^{\theta/(\theta-1)}$$

with

$$CP_{Ht}(i) = \left[\frac{P_{Ht}}{P_t^c} \right]^{-\theta} CP_t(i) \quad \text{and} \quad CP_{Ft}(i) = \left[\frac{P_{Ft}}{P_t^c} \right]^{-\theta} CP_t(i).$$

The domestic firm i maximizes the discounted stream of dividend payments where the dividends are discounted by its value to the owner of the firm (the consumer). The discounted rate that captures this decision is the ratio of the multipliers associated with the budget constraint of the household, since that ratio reflects the consumer's variation in wealth. The program of the firm is then

$$V(p_{Ht-1}(i)) = \text{Max} \left\{ D_t^f(i) + E_t \left[\beta \frac{\lambda_{t+1}}{\lambda_t} \right] V(p_{Ht}(i)) \right\} \tag{2.17}$$

with the instantaneous profit given by

$$D_t^f(i) = p_{Ht}(i)y_t(i) - P_t^c(1 + R_t)w_t h_t(i)$$
$$- P_t^c r_t k_t(i) - P_t^c \frac{\phi_P}{2} \left(\frac{p_{Ht}(i)}{p_{Ht-1}(i)} - \overline{\pi} \right)^2 \tag{2.18}$$

subject to the sequence of constraints

$$y_t(i) \leq \left[\frac{p_{Ht}(i)}{P_{Ht}} \right]^{-\eta} (D_{Ht} + X_t), \tag{2.19}$$

$$y_t(i) = A_t k_t^\alpha(i) h_t^{1-\alpha}(i) \tag{2.20}$$

with $D_{Ht} = C_{Ht} + I_{Ht} + CK_{Ht} + CP_{Ht}$ the aggregate demand for domestic goods given by

$$D_{Ht} = \omega \left[\frac{P_{Ht}}{P_t^c} \right]^{-\theta} D_t^c$$

with $D_t^c = C_t^c + I_t^c + CK_t^c + CP_t^c$ the domestic aggregate demand.

With ζ_t the multiplier associated to the demand constraint (2.19), the first-order conditions are

$$P_t^c(1 + R_t)w_t = (1 - \alpha)(p_{Ht}(i) - \zeta_t) \frac{y_t(i)}{h_t(i)} \tag{2.21}$$

$$P_t^c r_t w_t = \alpha(p_{Ht}(i) - \zeta_t) \frac{y_t(i)}{k_t(i)} \tag{2.22}$$

and the optimal price setting rule gives

$$y_t(i) + \beta E_t \left\{ \frac{\lambda_{t+1}}{\lambda_t} P_{t+1}^c \phi_P \frac{p_{Ht+1}(i)}{p_{Ht}^2(i)} \left(\frac{p_{Ht+1}(i)}{p_{Ht}(i)} - \overline{\pi} \right) \right\}$$
$$= \eta \frac{\zeta_t}{p_{Ht}} y_t(i) + \phi_P \frac{P_t^c}{p_{Ht-1}(i)} \left(\frac{p_{Ht}(i)}{p_{Ht-1}(i)} - \overline{\pi} \right). \tag{2.23}$$

Equations (2.21) and (2.22) represent the optimal demand for labor and capital, respectively. In the presence of monopolistic competition, the usual equality between marginal cost and marginal productivity does not hold since firms set their prices such as the marginal productivity of labor is above real wage. Their market power induces them to pay the workforce below its marginal productivity thus extracting positive rents. The same result applies for the demand for capital. Expression (2.21) (for instance) can therefore be written to make the mark-up rate explicit

$$(P_t^c(1 + R_t)w_t)(1 + \mu_t(i)) = (1 - \alpha)p_{Ht}(i)\frac{y_t(i)}{h_t(i)}$$

with

$$\mu_t(i) = \frac{\zeta_t}{p_{Ht}(i) - \zeta_t}.$$

Equation (2.23) shows that, absent any nominal price rigidity ($\phi_P = 0$), the mark-up is constant and equals $\mu = 1/(\eta - 1)$: when firms face adjustment costs on prices ($\phi_P > 0$), the mark-up rate is endogenous. Besides, as firms have to borrow cash to pay the labor salaries, the nominal interest rate is part of the marginal cost of labor.

IMPORTING FIRMS

We model the import sector in a very simple way: perfectly competitive firms import goods from the foreign country, for the foreign price P_t^* and they resell them to domestic consumers. As they perfectly compete with each other, we get that the import price for home consumers P_{Ft} expressed in domestic currency, equals the cost of imports (equation (2.5)).

The central bank

Each period, an amount of money Ψ_t is injected into the loanable funds market. The money stock evolves according to

$$M_{t+1} = M_t + \Psi_t \tag{2.24}$$

with the monetary injection defined as

$$\Psi_t = (g_t - 1)M_t. \tag{2.25}$$

The money growth factor g_t evolves according to a first-order autoregressive process

$$\log g_{t+1} = (1 - \rho_g)\log \overline{g} + \rho_g \log g_t + \varepsilon_{gt+1} \tag{2.26}$$

with ε_{gt+1} a white noise.

The financial intermediary

In the model, the financial intermediary accepts deposits from the household (M_t^b) which are repaid at the end of the period at the interest rate R_t. The bank also receives cash injections Ψ_t from the economy's monetary authorities. The bank's resources are loaned to the firm. The end-of-period profit is redistributed to the household in the form of dividends. The asset balance of the bank leads to

$$P_t^c w_t \int h_t(i)\, \mathrm{d}i = M_t^b + \Psi_t. \tag{2.27}$$

At the end of the period, the dividends of the bank are

$$D_t^b = (1 + R_t) P_t^c w_t \int h_t(i)\, \mathrm{d}i - (1 + R_t) M_t^b. \tag{2.28}$$

Using equations (2.27) and (2.28) we get the profit of the bank

$$D_t^b = (1 + R_t) \Psi_t. \tag{2.29}$$

2.2.3 Equilibrium

Market equilibria

We consider symmetric equilibria where all firms set the same price: $p_{Ht}(i) = p_{Ht}(j) = P_{Ht}$ and the same amount of production: $y_t(i) = y_t(j) = Y_t$, $y_{Ht}(i) = y_{Ht}(j) = Y_{Ht}$ and $x_t(i) = x_t(j) = X_t$. The expression for the domestic consumption price index becomes

$$P_t^c = \left[\omega P_{Ht}^{1-\theta} + (1 - \omega)(e_t P_t^{c*})^{1-\theta} \right]^{1/(1-\theta)}.$$

The different markets are on equilibrium:

- labor market

$$H_t = \int_0^1 h_t(i)\, \mathrm{d}i,$$

- physical capital market

$$K_t = \int_0^1 k_t(i)\, \mathrm{d}i,$$

- money market

$$M_t^s = M_t^c + M_t^b,$$

- domestic good market

$$Y_t = \omega \left[\frac{P_{Ht}}{P_t^c} \right]^{-\theta} D_t^c + X_t.$$

Since we model a small open economy, aggregate quantities are equilibrium quantities at the given foreign price level P^* and the given nominal foreign interest rate i^*. That is, on the foreign assets market the domestic household can carry out any foreign asset she is willing to hold given the foreign interest rate, being only constrained by her budget constraint. We thus infer from the budget constraint (2.8) and the market equilibria that the household's foreign asset holdings evolve as

$$e_t B_{t+1} - e_t (1 + i^*) B_t = P_{Ht} Y_t - P_t^c D_t^c. \tag{2.30}$$

This equation reflects the equilibrium of the balance of payments of the home economy. The small country trades with the rest of the world, depending on the levels of the home production and absorption, as shown in equation (2.30). If domestic production exceeds absorption, the trade balance is positive while the capital account is negative: the household sells the production surplus abroad and increases her holding of foreign assets. In contrast, if domestic production cannot satisfy the domestic demand for good, the economy has to import goods from the rest of the world and finance its trade deficit by borrowing from abroad.

2.2.4   Calibration and steady-state equilibrium

The period in the model is assumed to be a quarter. The calibration of the parameters $\{\alpha, \beta, \delta, H, \omega, \theta\}$ is standard. The steady-state mark-up rate comes from Morrison (1990). The parameter ν stands for the average of the trade balance to GDP ratio for the G7-countries except the United States,[3] for the period 1973:1–1998:3. We use this ratio to determine the long-run real debt to GDP ratio as shown below. The long-run inflation factor π is based on the average inflation factor on G7-countries between 1973:1 and 1997:4 (OECD sources). Calibration for the structural parameters is summarized in Table 2.3.

To determine the persistence coefficient of the monetary shock ρ_g and the standard deviation of the monetary innovations $\sigma_{\varepsilon g}$, we run regressions on the monetary base of G7-countries except the United States. Estimates are reported in Table 2.4. The median value of our estimates is our benchmark calibration for the small open economy monetary process.

Calibration for the technological process displayed in Table 2.5 comes from Prescott (1986).

Table 2.3 Calibration

α	β	δ	H	ς	π	ω	θ	μ
0.36	0.988	0.025	0.33	0.00061	1.014	0.85	1.5	0.19

Table 2.4 Calibration of the monetary shock

Country	ρ_g	$\sigma_{\varepsilon g}$
Canada	0.223	0.00807
France	0.162	0.00753
Germany	0.127	0.00897
Italy	0.339	0.00924
Japan	0.502	0.00663
United Kingdom	0.017	0.00600
Median	0.19	0.0078

Source: OECD Main Economic Indicators. Period 1973:1–1998:4. Quarterly series previously HP-filtered.

Table 2.5 Calibration of the technological process

ρ_a	σ_a
0.906	0.00852

The calibration of the structural parameters allows us to further derive the long-run values for aggregate variables. The first step consists in redefining the equations for the system to become stationary (see Appendix A). We then derive the steady-state equilibrium (see Appendix B).

The set of first-order conditions, the market equilibrium equations as well as the law of motion for physical capital, home money supply, foreign assets, technology level and monetary growth factor constitute a non-linear dynamic system. Following King *et al.* (1988), this dynamic system is log-linearized around the steady state. Decision rules are determined through Farmer's (1993) methodology.

2.3 What drives exchange rate fluctuations?

In line with Backus *et al.*'s (1995) paper, we first investigate the effects of real perturbations on exchange rates. In a first step, we check that a model based on technology shocks, even if monopolistic competition and nominal rigidities are included, cannot be considered as a consistent explanation for exchange rates movements. Section 2.3.1 makes this point clear. As we want to abstract from credit market frictions, we simply set the parameter for adjustment costs on money holdings ξ equal to 0.

2.3.1 Are technological shocks good candidates?

Our analysis focuses both on the dynamics for key variables that real shocks generate, and the cyclical properties we get.

Absent any clear estimation of the price adjustment costs parameter in the literature, we arbitrarily set $\phi_P = 1.5$. A small value will be enough to get significative effects according to the menu cost literature. As in Hairault and Portier (1993a), we gauge this value by measuring the real cost of a 1 percent increase of the price growth rate as a percentage of the steady-state output. We get that $CP(0.01) = 0.007\%\ \overline{Y}$: we consider very small adjustment costs on prices.

Impulse response functions

Figures 2.1 and 2.2 present the impulse response functions for output, real exchange rate, nominal exchange rate and nominal interest rate following a 1 percent increase in the technological level. The shock occurs in period 1.

The increase in the technology level raises output on impact since production factors become more productive. The effect vanishes as time goes by, rather persistently, given the autoregressive technological process.

The real exchange rate response derives from the combined dynamics for the nominal exchange rate and the price index. On the one hand, the positive supply shock generates a decrease in the price for the home good and the price index (not displayed), which tends to make the real exchange rate depreciate. On the other hand the nominal exchange rate appreciates on impact, which tends to lower the real exchange rate. According to Figure 2.1, the first effect dominates and on impact the real exchange rate increases.

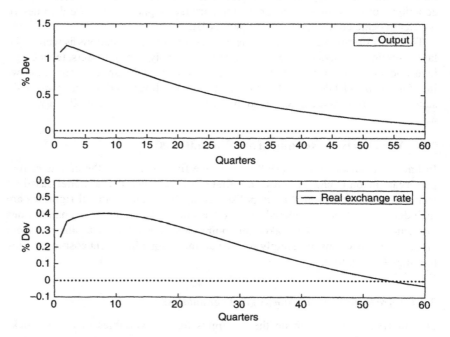

Figure 2.1 Technological shocks and real variables.

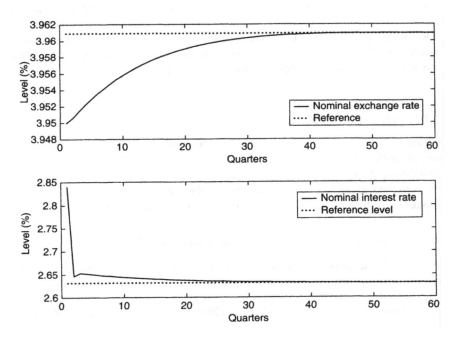

Figure 2.2 Technological shock and nominal variables.

Table 2.6 With technological shocks only

	σ_e(%)	σ_Γ(%)	σ_Y(%)	σ_e/σ_Y	σ_Γ/σ_Y
Model	0.4083	0.3165	1.0698	0.3822	0.2951
Median G7-group	8.314	7.792	1.548	5.372	5.038

Note
Theoretical volatilities are obtained through 500 simulations of the series. Series are filtered according to the Hodrick and Prescott's (1997) methodology.

The positive supply shock makes the home currency appreciate and the nominal interest rate increase on impact. The second period on, given uncovered interest rate parity, the positive interest rate differential requires the nominal exchange rate to depreciate. The technological shock thus implies a non-monotonic response for the nominal exchange rate. Nevertheless, the next section shows that the quantitative effects of real shocks are rather limited.

Quantitative properties

Table 2.6 displays the quantitative properties of the model.

The simulation results reported in Table 2.6 confirm the inability of the sticky-price model based on technology shocks to generate plausible exchange rates movements. As Backus *et al.* (1995) suggest and in line with Kollmann's (2001) paper, the next step consists in including monetary innovations in the sticky-price model. Given the monopolistic competition and price sluggishness, nominal shocks are likely to generate movements in the nominal exchange rate which translate into the real exchange rate, sufficient enough to bring the model closer to the data.

2.3.2   *With monetary shocks*

Given the failure of the model based only on real disturbances to explain the empirical exchange rate behaviors, we now introduce monetary perturbations. We first derive the dynamics of the key variables following a 1 percent increase in the home monetary factor growth to identify the transmission channel of a money shock before turning to the quantitative properties of the model.

The dynamic effects of a home expansionary monetary shock

Figures 2.3 and 2.4 present the dynamic effects of a 1 percent increase in the home monetary growth factor that occurs in period 1.

The positive home monetary injection now generates a decrease in the nominal interest rate on impact. As in Kollmann (2001), the sticky-price model correctly

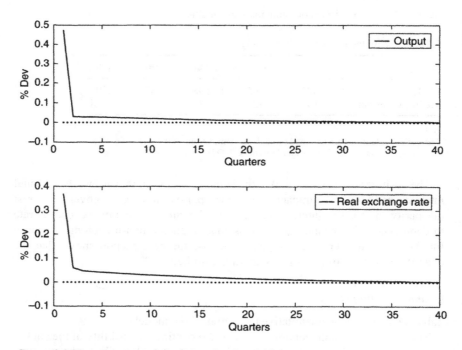

Figure 2.3 Home monetary injection and real variables.

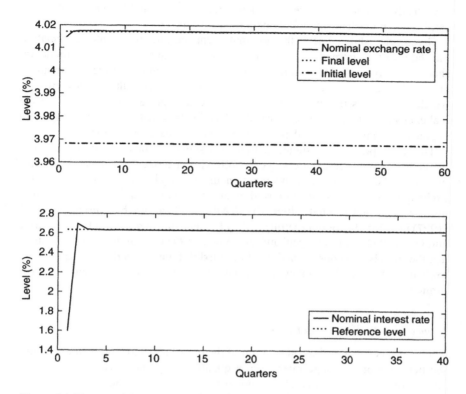

Figure 2.4 Home monetary injection and nominal variables.

accounts for the liquidity effect on impact. Given price sluggishness real money balances increase on impact and the monetary injection generates a decline in the interest rate. Yet, the liquidity effect is not persistent. Some periods after the shock the household is willing to reduce her bank deposits to preserve consumption from the expected inflation effect. The withdrawal of private deposits counteracts the persistent effects of the monetary injection. Furthermore, the monetary injection raises demand for the home good. Given monopolistic competition and price sluggishness, the home firms respond by adapting production. The raise in output implies an increase in labor demand hence the demand for loans. Both effects contribute to the increase in the nominal interest rate in the periods after the shock.

The nominal exchange rate response is linked to the interest rate dynamics. On impact the nominal exchange rate depreciates. As the interest rate stays below its steady-state level for some short period, agents expect an appreciation of the home currency to compensate for the relative low return of domestic assets. Yet, the nominal exchange rate response inherits the lack of persistence that the nominal interest rate exhibits. The nominal exchange rate almost immediately reaches its new steady-state level. Figure 2.4 makes clear that the model fundamentally lacks amplification mechanisms following a monetary injection.

Given price sluggishness, the nominal exchange rate immediate depreciation translates into an immediate increase in the real exchange rate. Yet the monetary shock has inflation effects on the price for the home good and the consumption price index. Even if sluggish the consumption price index ultimately increases, which counteracts the effect of the nominal exchange rate depreciation on the real exchange rate dynamics. Figure 2.3 thus displays that the real exchange rate depreciates on impact to further return to its steady-state value monotonically.

The sticky-price model subject to monetary shocks is consistent with the conditional features of the business cycles following a monetary shock. A positive monetary shock generates a decrease in the nominal interest rate, a nominal exchange rate depreciation (followed by an appreciation) and an increase in output, as identified through alternative VAR specifications by Christiano *et al.* (1997) in a closed-economy setting and by Eichenbaum and Evans (1995), Clarida and Gali (1994) and Schlagenhauf and Wrase (1995) in a multi-country setting. Yet the impulse response functions do not exhibit any exacerbated response for exchange rates, and this conveys the idea that the quantitative improvement is to be limited.

From a quantitative point of view

This section evaluates the contribution of the monetary innovations in explaining the behavior of exchange rates from a quantitative point of view. Do nominal shocks improve the ability of the model to match the second order moments? Table 2.7 displays the simulation results when the model is subject to both technological and monetary innovations.

If the introduction of monetary innovations undoubtedly improve the cyclical properties of the sticky-price model, the transmission channels to exchange rates are not sufficient enough to bring the model closer enough to the data. The model is unable to generate exchange rates more volatile than output. The results highlight the need for introducing a source of rigidity that amplify the effects of monetary shocks. On impact the implied dynamics is promising, yet the model lacks of consistent propagation mechanisms as shown by Figures 2.3 and 2.4. We thus modify the model to generate persistent effects of monetary shocks.

Table 2.7 With technological and monetary shocks

	$\sigma_e(\%)$	$\sigma_\Gamma(\%)$	$\sigma_Y(\%)$	σ_e/σ_Y	σ_Γ/σ_Y
Both shocks	1.2501	0.4097	1.113	1.1388	0.3694
Shock to technology	0.4083	0.3165	1.0698	0.3822	0.2951
Data	8.314	7.792	1.548	5.372	5.038

Note
Theoretical volatilities are obtained through 500 simulations of the series. Series are filtered according to the Hodrick and Prescott's (1997) methodology.

2.3.3 *With frictions on the credit market*

We now aim at evaluating the contribution of the credit market frictions, by relaxing the assumption that the money holdings adjustment cost parameter is equal to 0. We expect credit market frictions to deepen the propagation mechanisms in the model so as monetary shocks now have large and persistent effects.

Following the same approach as in the previous sections, we first derive the aggregate dynamics implied by a money shock before turning to the quantitative results.

The dynamics of a monetary shock

This section presents the aggregate dynamics following a 1 percent increase in the home monetary growth factor. As for the price adjustment cost parameter ϕ_P, absent any key value for ξ we arbitrarily set $\xi = 10$. In the same spirit as Christiano and Eichenbaum (1992b) and King and Watson (1996), we seek to analyze the consequences of very small adjustment costs on money-holdings: we thus evaluate the chosen value for ξ as regards to the corresponding cost of steady-state leisure and in terms of minutes per week. For $\xi = 10$, adjusting money-holdings 1 percent beyond the steady-state level costs 0.0625 percent of steady-state leisure, or around 4 minutes per week.[4]

Figure 2.5 displays the impulse response functions for output and the real exchange rate. A positive monetary injection generates a negative response for output on impact followed by a persistent increase in production some periods afterwards.

The real exchange rate response is similar to Figure 2.3 with a stronger depreciation on impact. This comes from the amplified response of the nominal exchange rate that the monetary shock now generates. Indeed, as shown by Figure 2.6, the nominal exchange rate depreciates on impact far beyond its new steady-state level, in close relation with the magnitude of the liquidity effect. An increase in the money supply now generates a strong and persistent decline in the nominal interest rate the second period on, even if on impact the nominal interest rate rises beyond its steady-state level.

To understand the aggregate dynamics, we adopt a partial equilibrium approach and consider first the effects on the loan market. The first period, the positive monetary injection translates into an increase in loan supply which, all other things being equal, tends to lower the nominal interest rate, the private supply for loans being fixed. Nevertheless the demand for loans increases, given that firms are willing to respond to the positive demand shock by adapting production rather than prices. All other things being equal, this should imply an increase in the nominal interest rate. Figure 2.6 reveals that the second effect dominates on impact, and the positive monetary shock generates an increasing the nominal interest rate.

On the labor market, it turns out that labor demand rises while labor supply vanishes. Indeed, given the expected inflation effect following the monetary shock, the household arbitrates in favor of leisure as compared to consumption, as leisure escapes the inflationist tax. The labor supply decrease dominates the

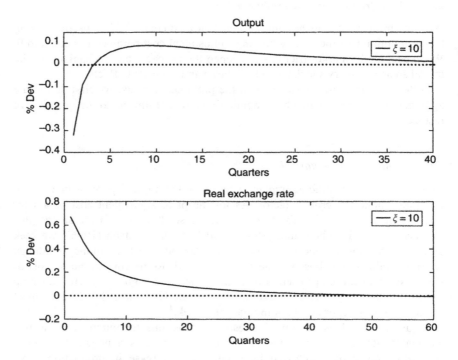

Figure 2.5 Adjustment costs on money holdings, monetary shock and real variables.

labor demand increase and on impact worked hours, hence aggregate production decreases below their steady-state levels. Nevertheless the model remains consistent with the empirical effects of monetary shocks since the positive money shock implies a longlasting positive response for output some short period after the shock.[5]

The nominal interest rate decreases below its steady-state level the second period on, before monotonically coming back to its long-run value. The model correctly accounts for a persistent liquidity effect (even if not on impact). The behavior for the supply for loans plays a crucial role in explaining the magnitude of the liquidity effect. In the period of the monetary shock, the household chooses the amount of money that she wants to consume tomorrow (M_{t+1}^c) and the amount of money that she will want to put into the bank tomorrow (M_{t+1}^b). After the occurrence of the money shock the agent anticipates inflation: she wants to preserve her future consumption by increasing today the amount of nominal money balances. However it is now costly for the household to raise the ratio M_{t+1}^c/M_t^c dramatically. Changing M_{t+1}^c deprives the agent from time available for leisure or labor. According to equation (2.15) with larger adjustment costs it is more expensive to modify money-holdings today and the household will rather wait. Hence the

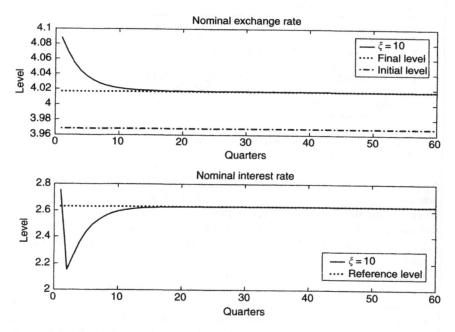

Figure 2.6 Adjustment costs on money holdings, monetary shock and nominal variables.

second period on the limited withdrawal of money deposits does not counteract the persistent increase in money supply coming from the monetary authorities. Regards loan demand, the persistent decrease in labor demand and the implied raise in the wage rate discourages firms to hire labor and reduces labor demand. The persistent increase in loan supply dominates the second period onwards and the nominal interest rate stays below its steady-state level long after the shock.

The nominal exchange rate overshooting results from the requirement that the persistent negative interest rate differential is equal to the expected rate of appreciation given uncovered interest rate parity. Beyond the qualitative responses of exchange rates our objective is to assess whether the model now accounts for the exchange rate fluctuations.

Quantitative properties

In this section we evaluate whether overshooting is responsible for the high volatility of exchange rates. To highlight the key role of frictions on the credit market, we derive the cyclical properties of exchange rates for increasing values of ξ. As before, we assess the chosen value for ξ with regard to the implied cost of leisure and in terms of minutes per week. For $\xi = 30$, a 1 percent increase in money-holdings beyond the steady-state value costs 1.875 percent of the steady-state leisure, or around 12 min per week. When $\xi = 50$, it costs 3.125 percent or

Table 2.8 The role of credit market frictions

	σ_e(%)	σ_Γ(%)	σ_Y(%)	σ_e/σ_Y	σ_Γ/σ_Y
$\xi = 10$	2.6985	0.6633	1.1369	2.4088	0.5921
$\xi = 30$	3.5032	0.8667	1.2639	2.8045	0.6971
$\xi = 50$	3.8848	0.9896	1.3447	2.9146	0.7453
$\xi = 100$	4.5774	1.2171	1.5187	3.0393	0.8119
$\xi = 300$	5.7903	1.6549	1.9241	3.023	0.8675

Note
Theoretical volatilities are obtained through 500 simulations of
the series. Series are previously HP-filtered.

equivalently 20 min per week to re-arrange deposits. For $\xi = 100$, it costs 6.25
percent or around 40 min per week and $\xi = 300$ a 1 percent increase costs 18.75
percent of the steady-state leisure, or equivalently around 2 h per week. We agree
that this last value might be extreme, nevertheless we consider the whole exercise
as giving a convincing and positive answer with regard to the role of credit market
frictions.

Quantitative results are displayed in Table 2.8.

The introduction of frictions in the credit market substantially improves the
predictions of the model with regard to the volatility of exchange rates. Indeed,
the nominal exchange rate is now more volatile than output. The higher the value of
ξ the more limited the withdrawal of private deposits. Hence the fall in the interest
rate and the depreciation of the nominal exchange rate are larger which implies
more exchange rate volatility. Yet, only small adjustment costs are needed for
the model to generate exacerbated movement of the nominal exchange rate. Given
price sluggishness the real exchange rate inherits the larger variance of the nominal
exchange rate. The model now generates a relative real exchange rate volatility
more than twice as high as a model lacking any credit market imperfections (for
$\xi = 100$, we get a relative real exchange rate volatility that amounts to 0.811
percent as compared with 0.36 percent for $\xi = 0$), even if the theoretical volatility
remains below the data.

2.4   Conclusion

The extremely volatile behavior of nominal and real exchange rates since the
collapse of the Bretton Woods system is a well-known stylized fact that a large
number of theoretical papers has tried to account for. Along the lines developed
by Dornbusch (1976), the chapter focuses on the role of the nominal exchange rate
overshooting in explaining the huge observed exchange rate fluctuations.

We therefore developed a small open economy model with nominal price rigidity and credit market frictions. First, we check that a model based only on real
perturbations is unable to account for the empirical behavior of exchange rate.
The introduction of monetary shocks in the sticky-price model improves the theoretical performances with regard to the exchange rates cyclical properties. Yet
the model does not generate any nominal exchange rate overshooting, and the

absence of any exacerbated response for nominal and real exchange rates results in theoretical volatilities far lower than these observed in the data.

Third, we consider the role for rigidities on the loan market by allowing for a positive degree of adjustment costs on money-holdings. We thus show that the presence of credit market frictions substantially improves the results both in terms of impulse response functions and quantitatively. Given both price sluggishness and credit market frictions, a positive monetary injection now generates a large nominal exchange rate overshooting. In accordance with Dornbusch (1976), over-shooting plays a key role in explaining the high volatility of exchange rates. Given nominal price rigidity, the real exchange rate inherits the nominal exchange rate behavior. Credit market frictions contribute to double the theoretical relative real exchange rate volatility, and we consider this result as encouraging. The chapter quantitatively highlights the vividness of the Dornbusch's (1976) overshooting demonstration in explaining a substantial part of the exchange rate disconnect puzzle. Yet results have to be improved regards the real exchange rate whose volatility remains too low compared to stylized facts. Further research is needed for a better understanding of the real exchange rate behavior.

Appendix A: stationarizing the model

As in Hairault and Portier (1993b), nominal variables are stationarized by dividing them by the past domestic price level. The nominal exchange rate is redefined as well. Let

$$m_t = M_t^s / P_{t-1}^c, \quad m_t^b = M_t^b / P_{t-1}^c, \quad m_t^c = M_t^c / P_{t-1}^c,$$

$$\pi_t = P_t / P_{t-1}, \quad b_t = e_{t-1} B_t / P_{t-1}, \quad \Delta e_t = e_t / e_{t-1},$$

$$\Delta M_t^c = M_{t+1}^c / M_t^c, \quad \Gamma_t = e_t P_t^* / P_t^c,$$

$$\gamma_{Ht} = P_{Ht} / P_t^c, \quad v_t = \zeta_t / P_t^c.$$

As foreign assets are expressed in foreign currency, we have to take into account the nominal exchange rate in the expression for b_t. The marginal utility of wealth is given by $\Lambda_t = P_t \lambda_t$. Finally, foreign inflation is defined as $\pi_t^* = P_t^* / P_{t-1}^*$.

The relevant equations in the cash-in-advance model are redefined in the following manner

$$\Gamma_t = \Delta e_t \frac{\pi_t^*}{\pi_t} \Gamma_{t-1}, \tag{2.31}$$

$$\pi_t C_t = m_t^c, \tag{2.32}$$

$$-U_{Ht}' = w_t \Lambda_t, \tag{2.33}$$

$$\Lambda_t = \beta E_t \left[(1 + i^*) \Delta e_{t+1} \frac{\Lambda_{t+1}}{\pi_{t+1}} \right], \tag{2.34}$$

$$\Lambda_t = \beta E_t \left[(1 + R_{t+1}) \frac{\Lambda_{t+1}}{\pi_{t+1}} \right], \tag{2.35}$$

$$\Lambda_t + \xi w_t \Lambda_t \frac{\pi_t}{m_t^c} (\Delta M_t^c - g)$$

$$= \beta E_t \left[\frac{U'_{Ct+1}}{\pi_{t+1}} + w_{t+1} \Lambda_{t+1} \xi \frac{\Delta M_{t+1}^c}{m_{t+1}^c} (\Delta M_{t+1}^c - g) \right], \tag{2.36}$$

$$q_t = \beta E_t \left[\frac{\Lambda_{t+1}}{\Lambda_t} \left\{ r_{t+1} + q_{t+1} - \delta + \frac{\phi_I}{2} \left[\frac{I_{t+1}^c - \delta K_{t+1}}{K_{t+1}} \right]^2 \right\} \right], \tag{2.37}$$

$$I_t^c = K_{t+1} - (1 - \delta) K_t, \tag{2.38}$$

$$w_t = (1 - \alpha)(\gamma_{Ht} - v_t) \frac{Y_t}{H_t}, \tag{2.39}$$

$$r_t = \alpha(\gamma_{Ht} - v_t) \frac{Y_t}{K_t}, \tag{2.40}$$

$$Y_t = A_t K_t^\alpha H_t^{1-\alpha}, \tag{2.41}$$

$$Y_t + \beta E_t \left\{ \frac{\Lambda_{t+1}}{\Lambda_t} \phi_P \frac{\pi_{t+1}\gamma_{t+1}}{\gamma_t^2} \left[\frac{\pi_{t+1}\gamma_{t+1}}{\gamma_t} - \pi \right] \right\}$$

$$= \eta \frac{v_t}{\gamma_{Ht}} Y_t + \phi_P \frac{\pi_t}{\gamma_{Ht-1}} \left[\frac{\pi_t \gamma_t}{\gamma_{t-1}} - \pi \right], \tag{2.42}$$

$$m_{t+1} = g_t \frac{m_t}{\pi_t}, \tag{2.43}$$

$$\Delta M_t^c = \frac{m_{t+1}^c \pi_t}{m_t^c}, \tag{2.44}$$

$$1 = \omega \gamma_{Ht}^{1-\theta} + (1 - \omega) \Gamma_t^{1-\theta}, \tag{2.45}$$

$$q_t = 1 + \phi_I \frac{I_t - \delta K_t}{K_t}, \tag{2.46}$$

$$X_t = \left[\frac{\gamma_{Ht}}{\Gamma_t} \right]^{-\theta}, \tag{2.47}$$

$$m_{t+1}^s = m_{t+1}^c + m_{t+1}^b, \tag{2.48}$$

$$\pi_t w_t H_t = m_t^b + (g_t - 1) m_t, \tag{2.49}$$

$$b_{t+1} - \Delta e_t (1 + i^*) \frac{b_t}{\pi_t} = \gamma_{Ht} Y_t - C_t - I_t, \tag{2.50}$$

$$\log g_{t+1} = (1 - \rho_g) \log \overline{g} + \rho_g \log g_t + \varepsilon_{gt+1}, \tag{2.51}$$

$$\log A_{t+1} = (1 - \rho_a) \log \overline{A} + \rho_a \log A_t + \varepsilon_{at+1}. \tag{2.52}$$

Appendix B: steady-state equilibrium

The steady-state equilibrium represents a situation where the agents' expectations are verified and, absent any trend in the model, real variables are constant.

We consider that the long-run inflation factor is equal between countries, that is, $\pi = \pi^*$. The steady-state monetary growth factor that supports long-run inflation is then

$$g = \pi.$$

We assume that all prices are equal to one, that is, $\gamma_H = \Gamma = 1$. Besides, the (stationary) purchasing power parity equation (2.31) yields that the nominal exchange rate change Δe is equal to π/π^*. Combining equations (2.34) and (2.35) expressed in log-deviation from steady state below yield to the uncovered interest rate parity (UIP). The UIP condition therefore implies that domestic and foreign interest rate are equal in the long run, that is, $R = i^*$. Combining equations (2.32) and (2.36) further gives the expression for nominal interest rates R and i^*

$$R = \frac{\pi}{\beta} - 1 \quad \text{and} \quad i^* = \frac{\pi^*}{\beta} - 1.$$

The first order condition on investment for firms determines the capital marginal productivity, hence the steady state capital/output ratio κ

$$\kappa \equiv \frac{K}{Y} = \frac{1}{\alpha}(1 + \mu) \left[\frac{1}{\beta} - (1 - \delta) \right].$$

Then, the equation for the production technology (equation (2.41)), given our calibration for H, yields to the long-run value for domestic output

$$Y = \kappa^{\alpha/(1-\alpha)} H^{1-\alpha}.$$

We then obtain the capital stock $K = \kappa Y$. The value for investment is derived through equation (2.38): $I = \delta K$.

The balance-of-payments equilibrium (equation (2.50)) allows us to determine the long-run real debt to GDP ratio. Indeed, consider equation (2.50) divided by output that gives

$$\frac{b}{Y}\left[1 - \left(\frac{1+i^*}{\pi} \right) \right] = \frac{Y - (C + I)}{Y} = \frac{BC}{Y},$$

where BC stands for domestic trade balance. This equation combined with our calibration for ς determines the real debt to GDP ratio

$$\frac{b}{Y} = \frac{1}{1 - (1 + i^*/\pi)} \varsigma.$$

We then derive the household stock of foreign asset in real terms

$$b = \frac{1}{1 - (1 + i^*/\pi)} \varsigma Y.$$

This allows us to get the steady-state consumption level through equation (2.50)

$$C = Y - I - b\left[1 - \frac{1 + i^*}{\pi}\right].$$

The cash-in-advance constraint gives the steady-state real balances

$$m^c = \pi C.$$

Hence, from equations (2.48) and (2.49), we get

$$m^s = wH + C, \quad m^b = m^s - m^c.$$

The first-order condition on labor demand gives the wage rate

$$w = \frac{1 - \alpha}{1 + R} \frac{1}{1 + \mu} \frac{Y}{H}$$

and the condition for consumption gives the marginal wealth utility

$$\Lambda = \beta \frac{1}{\pi C}.$$

Equation (2.44) gives $\Delta M^c = \pi$. Finally, the value for ψ_L is obtained through the condition for leisure (equation (2.33))

$$\psi_L = w\Lambda(1 - H).$$

Notes

1 The ongoing research on the VAR methodology has offered numerous works on the empirical relevance of the overshooting hypothesis. Eichenbaum and Evans (1995) have shown that, in response to a tighter US monetary policy, the US dollar exhibits a delayed overshooting pattern. However, some recent developments of the VAR methodology have led to reconcile the facts with the traditional overshooting story. Lack of accuracy in the measurement of monetary policy shocks may help explain why exchange rates do not exhibit any overshooting path. With more accurate monetary policy indicators, the overshooting hypothesis appears to be consistent with the data (Bonser-Neal *et al.* (1998); Kalyvitis and Michaelides (2001)). Besides, Faust and Rogers (2000) assert that the delayed overshooting result is quite sensitive to dubious identifying assumptions. Finally, Kim and Roubini's (2000) results go one-step further in favor of the overshooting story. Unlike Eichenbaum and Evans (1995), they use a structural VAR approach with non-recursive contemporaneous restrictions, in the lines of Sims and Zha (1998). They get that, initially the nominal exchange rate appreciates in response to a monetary contraction; after a few months, instead of the long and persistent appreciation found in Eichenbaum

and Evans (1995), it depreciates over time in accordance with the uncovered interest rate parity condition.

2 We simply assume that foreign demand is constant equal to 1.

3 The United States are excluded from our analysis because of our small open economy assumption.

4 These results are based on the Juster and Stafford's (1991) paper. The authors estimate time devoted to leisure or personal activities equal to 110 h per week for the men in the United States in 1981. The calculations are derived from this estimation.

5 Indeed, we consider that the key element here is the persistent and positive effect of the monetary shock on output, even if not immediate. This is consistent with the empirical effects of monetary shocks. Indeed as in Christiano *et al.* (1997), a positive monetary shock generates a persistent and positive output response, for a large number of OECD countries on short- and mid-term horizons. Nevertheless evidence is much more mixed with regard to the instantaneous response, allowing for positive or negative output responses depending on the countries. What seems important for us is that the model correctly reproduces the positive output response at short- and mid-term horizons following positive monetary shocks.

3 Nominal wage rigidities in an optimizing model of an open economy

Steve Ambler and Emmanuel Hakizimana

3.1 Introduction

Since the seminal articles of Kydland and Prescott (1982) and Long and Plosser (1983), researchers have attempted to put both closed- and open-economy macroeconomic models on firmer microfoundations. Dynamic general equilibrium (DGE) models have had some success in explaining the properties of business cycles in closed and open economies. Models which incorporate nominal wage and/or price rigidities have had success in explaining certain features of the data, such as the co-movements between nominal and real variables and the large and persistent responses of output and other real variables to monetary shocks.[1] The pioneering paper by Obstfeld and Rogoff (1995) developed an open-economy optimizing model with nominal price rigidities that was able to explain large fluctuations in real exchange rates in response to monetary shocks. Other recent papers such as Beaudry and Devereux (1995), Chari *et al.* (2002), and Kollmann (2001) have extended the analysis of Obstfeld and Rogoff (1995). In particular, the papers by Chari *et al.* (2002) and by Kollmann (2001) evaluate the quantitative impact of nominal rigidities on the persistence of real exchange rate fluctuations. Both papers construct dynamic open-economy models that are calibrated and subjected to stochastic simulations.[2] Chari *et al.* (2002) show that the observed degree of real exchange rate persistence can be explained only by supposing that firms change their prices at implausibly long intervals. Kollmann (2001) builds a model with both nominal price rigidities and nominal wage rigidities. He shows that if prices are adjusted by firms and wage contracts are renegotiated on average every 12.5 quarters, real exchange rate fluctuations are as persistent as in the data, as measured by the first-order autocorrelation coefficient. Kollmann (2001) cites evidence by Rotemberg (1982b) that this frequency of price adjustment is compatible with the data, but it falls in the range of what Chari *et al.* (2002) term "long stickiness," a frequency of price adjustment that is lower than their base-case scenario.

This chapter shows that of the two types of nominal rigidities, nominal wage rigidities are crucial in leading to persistent fluctuations of exchange rates and other real variables. We build a model in which wage setting by monopolistically competitive households is the only source of nominal rigidity. The model also includes additional dynamic propagation mechanisms such as capital accumulation and an endogenous domestic real interest rate. We show that if wages are adjusted by wage setters every four quarters on average, the model generates almost as much real exchange rate persistence as the Kollmann (2001) model, as much nominal exchange rate persistence, and output fluctuations that are slightly more persistent than in the data. Our model generates almost as much real exchange rate volatility as the Kollmann (2001) model, which is considerably higher than the real exchange rate volatility produced by the model of Backus *et al.* (1994), a model with flexible wages and prices. We interpret these results by examining the incentives for wage setters to adjust their nominal wages in our model, and comparing these to the incentives of firms to adjust their prices both in models with price rigidity alone and in models with both nominal wage and nominal price rigidity.

Our results confirm and extend results from closed-economy business cycle models on the relative roles of wage rigidity and price rigidity in explaining the persistent fluctuations of real variables. Chari *et al.* (2002) and Huang and Liu (2002) have questioned the ability of models with nominal price rigidities alone to explain persistence. They show that when firms are allowed to adjust their prices, they make large adjustments that rapidly neutralize the effects of shocks to aggregate demand. In order for monetary shocks to have persistent effects, either price adjustment must be very infrequent or the size of firms' price adjustment must be made small by introducing what are known as *real rigidities*, so that optimal prices are relatively insensitive to fluctuations in aggregate demand. Possible sources of real rigidities include increasing returns to scale and intermediate inputs that represent a significant fraction of production costs. Both of these features have the effect of flattening firms' marginal cost curves. Huang and Liu (2002) show that it is easier to generate persistence with a small degree of nominal wage stickiness, and without introducing real rigidities. Ambler (2002) shows that it is possible to support nominal wage rigidities as an equilibrium outcome in a standard business cycle model with modest and plausible fixed costs of adjusting wages.

The rest of the chapter is organized as follows. In Section 3.2, we present the details of the model. In Section 3.3, we discuss its solution. Section 3.4 deals with the calibration of the model's structural parameters. We present our main results in Section 3.5, and our conclusions in the last section.

3.2 The model

The economy is a semi-small open economy that produces a specialized output for which there is a downward-sloping demand curve on world markets. It is also semi-small in that it faces an imperfectly elastic supply curve for borrowing from abroad, so that the domestic real interest rate is endogenous. It does take as given the price of imports on world markets. The economy is composed of a collection of infinitely lived households that sell differentiated labor services to firms and set their nominal wages infrequently, a collection of perfectly competitive firms, and a government. There is a composite good made up of domestic output and imports which is used for consumption and investment by both households and the government. Domestic output is produced with labor and capital, with households accumulating capital (subject to convex adjustment costs) and renting it to firms.[3] The government finances its purchases of goods by lump-sum taxes and money creation. Its expenditures are subject to stochastic shocks.[4]

3.2.1   Households

There is a continuum of households on the unit interval, indexed by h. Each household chooses its consumption, investment and real money balances to maximize the utility function given by

$$
U(h) = E_0 \sum_{t=0}^{\infty} \beta^t \left\{ \alpha \ln(C_t(h)) + (1 - \alpha) \ln \left(\frac{M_t(h)}{P_t} \right) + \frac{\psi}{1 - \gamma} (1 - N_t(h))^{1-\gamma} \right\},
$$

$$(3.1)$$

where $C_t(h)$ is consumption, $N_t(h)$ denotes hours worked, $M_t(h)$ denotes nominal money balances, P_t is the price level of an aggregate of domestic and imported goods, E_0 is the conditional expectations operator based on information available at time 0, and β is the subjective discount factor. We also calculate households' optimal choice of hours worked, which is used to calculate *notional* labor supply. Because of the presence of wage contracts which fix the nominal wage, actual employment is determined by firms' labor demand. The difference between employment and notional labor supply measures labor market tightness, which affects wage contracts (see below). The presence of real balances in the utility function captures the transactions services provided by money. Individual households face the following budget constraint:

$$
C_t(h) + I_t(h) \left(1 + \frac{\varphi}{2} \frac{I_t(h)}{K_t(h)} \right) + \frac{T_t}{P_t} + \frac{M_t(h)}{P_t} + \frac{B_{t+1}(h)}{P_t}
$$
$$
= \frac{W_t}{P_t} N_t(h) + R_t(h) K_t(h) + \frac{B_t(h)}{P_t} (1 + r_t) + \frac{M_{t-1}(h)}{P_t}, \qquad (3.2)
$$

where $I_t(h)$, T_t, $B_t(h)$, P_t, $K_t(h)$, r_t and W_t are respectively investment, lump-sum taxes (which are identical across households), bond holdings (denominated in domestic currency), the price level, the capital stock, the real interest rate, and the average nominal wage. $M_{t-1}(h)$ gives money balances available at the *beginning* of period t, while $M_t(h)$ gives money balances accumulated during the current period which will be available at the beginning of the next period. The household's resources come from labor income,[5] the rental income from its holdings of capital, interest and principal on its holdings of financial assets, and previously accumulated real balances. The household allocates its resources to finance consumption, investment, payment of taxes to the government, and end-of-period holdings of real balances and financial assets. The term $(\varphi/2)(I_t(h)^2)/(K_t(h))$ captures capital adjustment costs, which are convex. Without capital adjustment costs, investment would be much too variable in the model.

The composite good used for consumption and investment by private households and the government is given by the following aggregator function, which follows Kollmann (2001):

$$D_t^{(1-\eta)} F_t^{\eta} = C_t + I_t \left(1 + \frac{\varphi}{2} \frac{I_t}{K_t}\right) + G_t, \tag{3.3}$$

where D_t is production of domestic output which is not exported, F_t is the volume of imports, and C_t, I_t and K_t are aggregate consumption, aggregate investment and the aggregate capital stock, respectively.[6] The η parameter gives the relative importance of the imported good in the composite good.

The law of motion for the aggregate capital stock is given by

$$K_{t+1} = (1 - \delta)K_t + I_t. \tag{3.4}$$

The Lagrangian for the maximization problem of household h is given by

$$\begin{aligned}
\mathcal{L}(h) = E_0 \sum_{t=0}^{\infty} \beta^t \Bigg\{ & \alpha \ln(C_t(h)) + (1 - \alpha) \ln\left(\frac{M_t(h)}{P_t}\right) \\
& + \frac{\psi}{1 - \gamma}(1 - N_t(h))^{(1-\gamma)} + \lambda_t(h)\left[\frac{W_t}{P_t}N_t(h) + R_t K_t(h)\right. \\
& + \frac{B_t(h)}{P_t}(1 + r_t) + \frac{M_{t-1}(h)}{P_t} - C_t(h) \\
& \left. - I_t(h)\left(1 + \frac{\varphi}{2}\frac{I_t(h)}{K_t(h)}\right) - \frac{T_t}{P_t} - \frac{M_t(h)}{P_t} - \frac{B_{t+1}(h)}{P_t}\right] \\
& + \lambda_t(h)q_t(h)\left[I_t(h) + (1 - \delta)K_t(h) - K_{t+1}(h)\right] \Bigg\}.
\end{aligned} \tag{3.5}$$

The first-order conditions of the household's problem with respect to choice variables at time t are as follows:

$$C_t(h): \frac{\alpha}{C_t(h)} = \lambda_t(h), \tag{3.6}$$

$$M_t(h): \frac{\lambda_t(h)}{P_t} = \frac{1 - \alpha}{M_t(h)} + \beta E_t \frac{\lambda_{t+1}(h)}{P_{t+1}}, \tag{3.7}$$

$$N_t(h): \psi(1 - N_t(h))^{-\gamma} = \lambda_t(h)\frac{W_t}{P_t}, \tag{3.8}$$

$$B_{t+1}(h): \frac{\lambda_t(h)}{P_t} = \beta E_t \frac{\lambda_{t+1}(h)}{P_{t+1}}(1 + r_{t+1}), \tag{3.9}$$

$K_{t+1}(h) : \lambda_t(h) q_t(h)$

$$= \beta E_t \lambda_{t+1}(h) \left[R_{t+1} + \frac{\varphi}{2} \left(\frac{I_{t+1}(h)}{K_{t+1}(h)} \right)^2 + (1 - \delta) q_{t+1}(h) \right], \qquad (3.10)$$

$$I_t(h) : q_t(h) = 1 + \varphi \frac{I_t(h)}{K_t(h)}, \qquad (3.11)$$

$$\lambda_t(h) : C_t(h) + I_t(h)(1 + \frac{\varphi}{2} \frac{I_t(h)}{K_t(h)}) + \frac{T_t}{P_t} + \frac{M_t(h)}{P_t} + \frac{B_{t+1}(h)}{P_t}$$

$$= \frac{W_t}{P_t} N_t(h) + R_t K_t(h) + \frac{B_t(h)}{P_t}(1 + r_t) + \frac{M_{t-1}(h)}{P_t}, \qquad (3.12)$$

$$q_t(h) : K_{t+1}(h) = (1 - \delta) K_t(h) + I_t(h). \qquad (3.13)$$

The interpretation of these conditions is straightforward. Equation (3.6) equates the marginal utility of consumption with the marginal value of an additional unit of the aggregate good at time t. The term on the left-hand side of equation (3.7) gives the marginal cost in terms of utility of increasing nominal balances by one unit of domestic currency. The right-hand side of the equation gives the marginal benefits. The first term captures the marginal utility from the trans-actions services provided by money at time t. The second term gives the expected marginal utility from carrying an additional unit of nominal balances into $t + 1$, weighted by the marginal utility of consumption in $t + 1$ given by $\lambda_{t+1}(h)$. The first-order condition with respect to hours equates the marginal utility of leisure to the marginal benefit of working an extra hour worked in terms of added consumption.[7]

The condition with respect to $B_{t+1}(h)$ gives a standard Euler equation. The term on the left-hand side gives the marginal cost of increasing foreign assets by one unit. The right-hand side gives the discounted expected marginal benefit, which depends on the rate of return on bonds and on the marginal utility of consumption.[8] The first-order condition with respect to $K_{t+1}(h)$ is an Euler equation which pins down the equilibrium rate of return on capital, and together with the preceding condition establishes a relationship between the rates of return on capital and financial assets. Equation (3.11) can be solved to give the equilibrium rate of investment, which depends only on the relative price of installed capital goods $q_t(h)$ and the size of adjustment costs given by the value of φ. The last two first-order conditions yield the budget constraint and the law of motion of capital.

3.2.2   Firms

Firms rent factors of production from households. Aggregate labor input is given by

$$N_t = \left(\int_0^1 N_t(i)^{(\theta-1)/\theta} \, di \right)^{\theta/(\theta-1)}, \qquad (3.14)$$

where i indexes different labor types. It follows that the demand for each individual type of labor is given by the following equation:

$$N_t(i) = \left(\frac{X_t(i)}{W_t} \right)^{-\theta} N_t, \tag{3.15}$$

where $X_t(i)$ is the wage for labor of type i. The elasticity of demand for each type of labor is given by the θ parameter, which also measures the elasticity of substitution across labor types. There is a continuum of different labor types on the unit interval. It also follows that the exact average nominal wage is given by the following aggregator function:

$$W_t = \left(\int_0^1 X_t(i)^{-(\theta-1)}\, di \right)^{-1/(\theta-1)}. \tag{3.16}$$

The aggregate production function is given by

$$Y_t = A_t N_t^{\phi} K_t^{(1-\phi)}, \tag{3.17}$$

where Y_t is total production of the domestic good, and A_t is the level of technology, whose natural logarithm follows a stationary $AR(1)$ process given by

$$\ln(A_t) = (1 - \rho_a)\ln(\overline{A}) + \rho_a \ln(A_{t-1}) + \varepsilon_{at}, \tag{3.18}$$

where, ρ_a is a parameter which affects the persistence of shocks to the level of technology, $\ln(\overline{A})$ is the unconditional mean of the level of technology and ε_{at} is a white noise shock with a standard deviation given by $\sigma_{\varepsilon at}$. Firms maximize profits, which are given by

$$\pi_t = P_{1t} A_t N_t^{\phi} K_t^{(1-\phi)} - W_t N_t - P_t R_t K_t, \tag{3.19}$$

where P_{1t} is the price of domestically produced goods.

The profit maximization problem of the representative firm is static. In addition to the conditional demand functions for individual types of labor i given by equation (3.15) above, it leads to the following first-order conditions, which in equilibrium determine the demand for aggregate labor (given the average nominal wage) and the rental rate of capital

$$N_t : \phi P_{1t} A_t N_t^{\phi-1} K_t^{1-\phi} = W_t, \tag{3.20}$$

$$K_t : (1 - \phi) P_{1t} A_t N_t^{\phi} K_t^{-\phi} = P_t R_t. \tag{3.21}$$

3.2.3   The government

The government finances its expenditures on the composite good by lump-sum taxation and by money creation. Its budget constraint is given by

$$G_t - \frac{T_t}{P_t} = \frac{M_t - M_{t-1}}{P_t}. \tag{3.22}$$

The law of motion for government spending is given by

$$\ln(G_t) = \rho_g \ln(G_{t-1}) + \varepsilon_{gt}. \tag{3.23}$$

Money balances follow the $AR(1)$ process[9] given by

$$M_t = (1 - \rho_M)M + \rho_M M_{t-1} + M\zeta_t, \tag{3.24}$$

where M is the unconditional mean of the money stock and ζ_t is the growth rate of the money stock, which is itself given by an $AR(1)$ process:

$$\zeta_t = \rho_m \zeta_{t-1} + \varepsilon_{mt}. \tag{3.25}$$

3.2.4   Foreign demand

Following Kollmann (2001), foreign demand for domestic goods is given by the following constant–elasticity demand function:

$$X_t = \left(\frac{e_t P_{2t}}{P_{1t}}\right)^{\mu}, \tag{3.26}$$

where μ gives the elasticity of export demand, P_{2t} is the price of imported foreign goods, and e_t is the nominal exchange rate defined as the price in domestic currency of a unit of foreign currency. The ratio of the domestic-currency price of imported goods to the price of domestic output is our measure of the real exchange rate, and is compatible with the definition of the real exchange rate used in studies such as Backus *et al.* (1994). Since it is expressed as a ratio of import prices to export prices, it is compatible with the standard definition of the terms of trade. We show in Section 3.2.7 that our real exchange rate variable is monotonically related to a real exchange rate defined using overall price levels.

3.2.5   Net foreign debt and domestic interest rates

Domestic agents can lend and borrow on international financial markets. Following Senhadji (1995), the rate of return on foreign bonds depends on the aggregate level of net foreign indebtedness according to the following equation:

$$r_t = r_t^* - \prod \frac{B_t}{P_t}, \tag{3.27}$$

where r_t, r_t^* and B_t are, respectively, the domestic real interest rate and the world real interest rate, which is exogenous, and the nominal value of net foreign assets in domestic currency. This specification captures the effects of default risk (on sovereign debt and other types of debt) on interest rates. It also has the consequence that the economy's steady state equilibrium is unique, with a domestic real interest that depends only on the subjective discount rate. In models with Π equal to zero, the domestic interest rate must equal the world real rate, independently of agents' subjective discount rates. In cases where $1/\beta \neq (1 + r_t^*)$, there is no stationary path for domestic consumption. Even when $1/\beta = (1 + r_t^*)$, there is hysteresis, and temporary shocks have permanent effects on the level of consumption and other macroeconomic aggregates.[10] Since we solve the model by approximating its dynamic equations around an initial steady state equilibrium, the approximation could break down if a sequence of small temporary shocks led to large changes in the steady state. This problem does not arise in our model since the steady state is unique.

3.2.6   Wage setting

Following Ambler *et al.* (2001) and Huang and Liu (2002), workers of labor type i set their own nominal wage acting as monopolistic competitors on the labor market. Following Calvo (1983), wage setters maintain a constant nominal wage unless they receive a signal to adjust the nominal wage at the beginning of the period, which happens with probability $(1 - d)$.[11] When setting the nominal wage, wage setters maximize their expected utility and take into account the elasticity of demand by firms for their type of labor. As shown in Ambler *et al.* (2001) and Huang and Liu (2002), this leads to a dynamic equation for the nominal wage set by workers in period t given by

$$x_t = dE_t x_{t+1} + (1 - d)w_t + (1 - d)\omega \left(n_t - n_t^o \right), \tag{3.28}$$

where we have dropped the i indices, where lower case variables are measured in proportional deviations from their steady state levels, and where n_{t+i}^o is *notional* labor supply at time $t + i$. The interpretation of x_t in this equation is the average wage set by households that receive a signal to adjust their wage at time t. The ω parameter measures the sensitivity of wage contracts to labor market tightness (the difference between employment and notional labor supply). It depends on the underlying structural parameters of the model as follows:

$$\omega \equiv \frac{\gamma(N/(1 - N))}{1 + \theta\gamma(N/(1 - N))},$$

where N is the aggregate per capita level of employment in the steady state. In the neighborhood of the steady state, the average wage follows the following law of motion:

$$w_t = dw_{t-1} + (1 - d)x_t. \tag{3.29}$$

The dynamics of the nominal wage in the neighborhood of the steady state collapse to two first-order difference equations. In models with staggered wage contracts of fixed duration, changing the duration of wage contracts alters the number of state variables, which is not the case here. We can easily conduct sensitivity analysis to variations in average contract length.

3.2.7 Prices

In order to derive the competitive price of the composite good (the price level), it is convenient to suppose the existence of a competitive import broker who aggregates domestic output and imports to form the composite final good. He solves the following cost minimization problem:

$$\min \left(\frac{P_{1t}}{P_t} D_t + \frac{e_t P_{2t}}{P_t} F_t \right), \tag{3.30}$$

subject to the constraint

$$D_t^{1-\eta} F_t^\eta \geq C_t + I_t \left(1 + \frac{\varphi}{2} \frac{I_t}{K_t} \right) + G_t. \tag{3.31}$$

The optimality conditions for cost minimization are given by

$$D_t : \frac{P_{1t}}{P_t} = \lambda_t^* (1 - \eta) D_t^{-\eta} F_t^\eta, \tag{3.32}$$

$$F_t : \frac{e_t P_{2t}}{P_t} = \lambda_t^* \eta D_t^{1-\eta} F_t^{\eta-1}, \tag{3.33}$$

$$\lambda_t^* : D_t^{1-\eta} F_t^\eta = C_t + I_t \left(1 + \frac{\varphi}{2} \frac{I_t}{K_t} \right) + G_t, \tag{3.34}$$

where λ_t^* is the Lagrange multiplier associated with the constraint. The optimality conditions can be used to solve for the cost-minimizing price of a unit of the composite good

$$P_t = \eta^{-\eta} (1 - \eta)^{(\eta-1)} P_{1t}^{(1-\eta)} (e_t P_{2t})^\eta. \tag{3.35}$$

Given this result, we have the following relation between the real exchange rate defined in terms of the ratio of import prices to export prices and the real exchange rate defined in terms of overall price levels

$$\frac{e_t P_{2t}}{P_t} = \frac{1}{\eta^{-\eta} (1 - \eta)^{(\eta-1)}} \left(\frac{e_t P_{2t}}{P_{1t}} \right)^{(1-\eta)}.$$

The price of foreign output obeys the following stochastic process:

$$\ln P_{2t} = (1 - \rho_{p2}) \ln P_2 + \rho_{p2} \ln P_{2t-1} + \varepsilon_{p2t}. \tag{3.36}$$

3.3 Model solution

3.3.1 Aggregation

Since households have a representative sample of labor types, the wage that is relevant for their decisions is the average wage. If the initial distribution of assets across households is homogeneous, each household h will make identical choices concerning consumption, investment and end-of-period asset holdings. It is possible to replace the household's choice variables indexed by the h argument in its first-order conditions by their aggregate per capita equivalents.

3.3.2 Equilibrium

Equilibrium in the model is defined in the standard way, except for the lack of labor market clearing in the short run. We require the following conditions:

1   Households', firms' and wage setters' first-order conditions are satisfied.
2   Individual households' choice variables are compatible with their aggregate per capita counterparts. Given the assumptions outlined in Section 3.3.1 on aggregation, this condition is automatically satisfied.
3   All markets clear except for the labor market. In the latter, aggregate employment is determined by firms' demand for labor.[12] Note that in the long run the nominal wage adjusts to equilibrate the labor market so that notional labor supply equals labor demand.

3.3.3 Numerical solution

To solve the model, we first assign numerical values to its parameters. The calibration of the model is discussed in detail in the next section. We then drop time subscripts from the equations and set the value of all white noise shocks equal to zero in order to calculate the model's deterministic steady state.

Once the deterministic steady state of the model has been calculated numerically, we solve the model using the methods developed by Blanchard and Kahn (1980) and King *et al.* (1987). The model is linearized around its deterministic steady state equilibrium, with variables measured as proportional deviations from their steady state values. We then group the variables of the model into a vector of state variables, a vector of control variables and a vector of shocks. The state variables of the model are the capital stock, the average wage, money balances in $t - 1$, the level of technology in $t - 1$, government expenditures in $t - 1$, the rate of growth of the money supply in $t - 1$, net foreign indebtedness, the price of foreign output in $t - 1$, the nominal exchange rate, the marginal utility of consumption, the relative price of installed capital goods, and the nominal wage set by wage setters who are allowed to adjust their wage at time t. Of these state variables, the first eight are predetermined at the beginning of period t. The last four variables are forward-looking or jump variables that can respond instantaneously to shocks at time t. The control variables include all variables that are related statically to state variables and shocks at time t. The vector of shocks is given by:

$$Z_t = \left\{ \varepsilon_{at}, \varepsilon_{gt}, \varepsilon_{mt}, \varepsilon_{p2,t} \right\}.$$

The state space form of the model can be written as follows:

$$E_t S_{t+1} = A_1 S_t + A_2 Z_t, \tag{3.37}$$

$$H_t = A_3 S_t + A_4 Z_t, \tag{3.38}$$

where S_t is the vector of state variables, H_t is the vector of controls, and the A_i are matrices of coefficients. The model is saddle-point stable for all the parameter values used in the numerical simulations, with eight stable roots (of absolute value less than unity) corresponding to the model's predetermined state variables and four unstable roots (of absolute value greater than unity) corresponding to the jump variables.

3.4   Model calibration and parameter values

The numerical values used for the parameters in our base-case simulations are summarized in Table 3.1. We calibrate the model with reference to recent studies in the literature on DGE business cycle models. The model is calibrated to quarterly data. Following Kollmann (2001), α is fixed so that monetary velocity is equal to unity. For US data, using M1 as the measure of the money stock, velocity is equal to 0.93. The subjective discount rate β is set equal to 0.99, which gives an annual steady state real interest rate equal to 4 percent. The γ parameter is set equal to 0.5, which gives an intertemporal elasticity of substitution equal to two, which is supported by recent empirical evidence by Dib and Phaneuf (1998). We restrict labor supply in the steady state to equal 0.33 (one third of the per-period

Table 3.1 Model calibration

Parameter	Value	Parameter	Value
α	0.99	ρ_a	0.95
β	0.99	ρ_g	0.94
γ	0.50	ρ_m	0.48
δ	0.025	ρ_M	0.99
Π	0.0014	ρ_{p2}	0.80
φ	0.50	r^*	0.01
ω	0.10	$\sigma_{\varepsilon at}$	0.007
η	0.19	$\sigma_{\varepsilon gt}$	0.0064
μ	0.78	$\sigma_{\varepsilon mt}$	0.0089
ϕ	0.64	$\sigma_{\varepsilon p2t}$	0.005
N	0.33	C/Y	0.59
G/Y	0.19	X/Y	0.20
d	0.75		

time endowment, which is normalized to equal one). This pins down the value of ψ, which is equal to 0.20.

Turning to technological parameters, the rate of capital depreciation δ is given a standard value of 0.025, which gives an annual depreciation rate of 10 percent. The parameter ϕ, which can be calibrated to labor's share of national income, is set equal to 0.64 (see Kydland and Prescott (1982); Prescott (1986), and many subsequent studies). The capital adjustment cost parameter φ is set in order to generate a relative volatility of investment which is plausible.[13]

The parameters of the contract wage equation are calibrated on the basis of recent empirical studies. Following Ambler *et al.* (2001) we set $d = 0.75$, which gives an average contract length equal to four quarters. The sensitivity of the contract wage to labor market tightness, ω, is set equal to 0.1 following Taylor (1980) and Ambler and Phaneuf (1994).[14]

We set the world interest rate equal to 0.01, as in Rebelo and Végh (1995), and the sensitivity of the domestic real interest rate to net indebtedness (Π) is set in order to yield a net foreign indebtedness equal to 10 percent of GDP in the steady state.

We calculate the average shares of consumption, gross exports, and government spending in output using OECD data for the G7 economies for the period 1972:1–1991:1, obtaining the values given in Table 3.1. The first two values allow us to solve endogenously for the values of η and μ, while the share of government spending in output allows us to calibrate the constant term in the law of motion for $\ln(G_t)$.

Finally, the other parameters of the forcing processes for technology, government spending, money and foreign prices are taken from other empirical studies. We set $\rho_a = 0.95$ following Prescott (1986), $\rho_g = 0.94$ and $\rho_m = 0.48$ following Cho and Phaneuf (1993), and $\rho_{p2} = 0.8$ as in Kollmann (2001). In order to avoid a unit root in nominal variables while remaining close to studies which specify a stochastic process for the *rate of growth* of nominal money balances, we set a high value for ρ_M, 0.99. Standard deviations of shocks come from Prescott (1986) and Kollmann (2001) for $\sigma_{\varepsilon at}$, Cho and Phaneuf (1993) for $\sigma_{\varepsilon gt}$, and Kollmann (2001) for $\sigma_{\varepsilon mt}$ and $\sigma_{\varepsilon at}$.

3.5 Numerical simulation results

The simulation results we present are designed to facilitate comparison with those of Kollmann (2001). We consider the relative variability of macroeconomic aggregates, persistence, the correlations of different aggregates with output, and impulse responses of different aggregates to the four different kinds of shocks in the model. In all cases, simulation results are averages across 1000 replications of samples of 89 periods in length. Volatility is measured by standard deviations in percent, relative volatilities are ratios of standard deviations, and persistence is measured by the first-order autocorrelation coefficient. All statistics are based on series that are filtered with the Hodrick and Prescott (1997) filter.[15] The results are presented in Table 3.2.

Table 3.2 Simulation results

	All shocks	Monetary shocks	Kollmann	Data
Absolute volatility				
Y	1.71	0.94	2.07	1.85
Relative volatility				
C	0.54	0.23	1.29	0.85
I	4.97	8.61	n/a	2.33/4.31[a]
N	0.64	1.11	1.04	0.78
P	0.54	0.22	0.29	0.87
e	2.13	2.39	2.97	2.59
eP_2/P_1	2.16	2.85	2.79	2.56
$(X - IM)$[b]	2.12	2.80	1.26	1.30
Autocorrelation				
Y	0.80	0.63	0.73	0.77
e	0.69	0.50	0.69	0.82
eP_2/P_1	0.62	0.49	0.66	0.79
Correlation w/ output				
C	0.44	0.76	0.95	0.75
I	0.95	0.97	n/a	0.44[c]
N	0.89	0.97	0.91	0.58
P	0.53	0.82	0.28	−0.63
e	0.87	0.95	0.80	−0.16
eP_2/P_1	0.87	0.93	0.87	−0.06
$(X - IM)$	−0.89	−0.97	−0.86	−0.24
Correlation				
$(e, eP_2/P_1)$	0.98	0.99	0.95	0.97

Source: Unless otherwise noted, statistics based on data are from Kollmann (2001).

Notes
a The smaller figure is based on calculations from OECD data (see text). The higher figure comes
   from Fairise and Langot (1995).
b $(X - IM)$ measures net exports.
c From OECD data.

3.5.1   Persistence

The third panel of Table 3.2 gives the first-order correlations of output and
exchange rates in our model, in Kollmann's model (2001), and in the data. Our
model generates substantial persistence in all three variables. Output persistence
is slightly higher than in Kollmann's model, while the persistence of the real
exchange rate is slightly lower. Our results are broadly compatible with the data,
as are Kollmann's model. In addition, the size of the nominal wage rigidity in
our model is significantly lower than in Kollmann's model: wages are adjusted
by wage setters on average every four quarters in our model as opposed to every
12.5 quarters in Kollmann's model. In this respect, we believe we have attained
our main objective, which was to elaborate a model with only wage rigidities
that is compatible with the observed persistence of exchange rate fluctuations.
The amount of persistence attributable to monetary shocks in our model is quite

modest. The first-order autocorrelations of output and both the nominal and real exchange rates are quite lower when only monetary shocks are present.

These results extend Huang and Liu's (2002) results for a closed economy. The relative importance of nominal wage rigidity in explaining persistence can be understood by considering wage setters' incentives to change wages when they are allowed to do so, and contrasting this with firms' incentives to change prices in models with monopolistic competition on the goods market. Wage setters' first-order condition for the choice of the optimal nominal wage equates the expected marginal revenue from adjusting the nominal wage, which depends on firms' elasticities of demand for individual labor types, to the expected marginal cost, which depends on foregone leisure, taking into account the probability that the wage set in period t will still be in effect at period $t + i$. The nominal marginal revenue in period t alone with respect to changes in hours worked is given by

$$X_t(i)\frac{(\theta - 1)}{\theta}.$$

The nominal marginal cost in period t is given by

$$-P_t\frac{\partial u(\cdot)}{\partial N_t(i)}\bigg/ \frac{\partial u(\cdot)}{\partial C_t(i)},$$

where $u(\cdot)$ gives period-t utility. Here, both marginal revenue and marginal cost are expressed in units of nominal value per hour. The price level P_t acts as a shift variable for wage setters' marginal cost curve. If there is an aggregate demand shock, this marginal cost curve will typically shift due to changes in the price level. However, if labor costs represent a substantial fraction of the total cost of production, the nominal marginal cost of domestic output changes only slowly. In our model, the price of domestic output is equal to marginal cost, so the price of domestic output changes only slowly. Finally, with $\eta = 0.19$, the cost of imported foreign good is a relatively small fraction of the cost of the composite final good. Even if the effect of a given shock on the nominal exchange rate is substantial, the impact on the domestic price level will be relatively small. This means that wage setters who are allowed to adjust their wages at time t make relatively small adjustments to their nominal wage. Since the price of domestic output depends to a large extent on wage costs, the price of domestic output changes slowly. Both domestic production and the real exchange rate inherit the persistence of the price of domestic output.

This can be contrasted with models with imperfectly competitive firms that set prices in advance. Without nominal wage rigidity, large changes in employment and output involve movements along the aggregate labor supply curve. If labor supply is relatively inelastic, as most empirical evidence would suggest, large changes in the equilibrium nominal wage are required to generate large changes in employment and output. Consider imperfectly competitive firms adjusting their price at time t. They equate the expected discounted value of marginal revenue to the expected discounted value of marginal costs, taking into account the probability that the price they set will still be in effect at time $t + i$. Nominal marginal revenue at time t as function of their output can be written as follows:

$$P_t(i)\frac{(\theta_d - 1)}{\theta_d},$$

where $P_t(i)$ is the output price of firm i, and θ_d is the elasticity of demand for the firm's output. With the Cobb–Douglas production function used in our model, its nominal marginal cost at time t as function of output can be written as follows:

$$\frac{W_t{}^\phi R_t{}^{(1-\phi)}}{A_t(1 - \phi)^{(1-\phi)}\phi^\phi}.$$

Wage costs represent a substantial fraction of total cost, and the nominal wage acts as a shift variable of the firm's marginal cost function. If the equilibrium nominal wage changes substantially in response to fluctuations in aggregate demand, the marginal cost curves of firms that are allowed to adjust their prices at time t are subject to large shifts in response to shocks that affect employment and output. This leads them to make large adjustments in their prices. These large adjustments by individual firms lead to a rapid adjustment of the price index of domestic output. This has the effect of reducing the persistence of the impact of shocks on both domestic output and on the real exchange rate.

Obviously, models with both nominal price and nominal wage rigidities should be capable of generating at least as much persistence as models with nominal wage rigidities alone. The nominal wage rigidity reduces substantially the shift in firms' marginal cost curves in response to aggregate demand shocks, thereby reducing the amount by which firms adjust their prices when they are allowed to do so. If models with either both types of rigidities or with nominal wage rigidities alone can generate substantial persistence, we need to compare the predictions of the two types of models along other dimensions in order to discriminate between the two. We show in the next section that our model with nominal wage rigidities alone is more successful in matching the volatility of the price level and of consumption than models with both nominal price and nominal wage rigidities such as Kollmann's model.

3.5.2   *Volatility*

As mentioned previously, given the presence of money in the utility function, introducing flexible output prices should lead to a higher relative volatility of prices in the model. This is confirmed by the results in Table 3.2. Simulation results with all shocks are given in the second column of the table. Compared to the Kollmann (2001) results, the relative volatility of prices is almost twice as high, going from 0.29 to 0.54, which is still slightly below the volatility of the price level in the data. The volatility of consumption also falls considerably (in fact our model slightly underpredicts the volatility of consumption). The variability of employment is lower than and is closer to the data in Kollmann's model. The variability of net exports in our model is too high. This arises mainly from our calibration of the investment adjustment cost parameter. A higher adjustment cost would bring both the volatility of investment and the volatility of net exports more in line with the data. Our model slightly underpredicts nominal and real exchange rate volatility, whereas Kollmann's model slightly overpredicts them. The predictions of both our model and Kollmann's model are much closer to the data than the flexible wage/price model of Backus *et al.* (1994), which underpredicts real exchange rate volatility by an order of magnitude.[16] Nominal rigidities are crucial in generating this result. Monetary shocks that affect the equilibrium nominal exchange rate have a strong impact on relative prices because of the sluggish response of the domestic price level. The effect is most pronounced in the case of a model with nominal price rigidity, leading Kollmann's model to slightly overpredict real exchange rate variability. In our model, with only nominal wage rigidity, the effect is still strong due to the fact that the major component of firms' marginal costs is the average wage, which responds slowly to a monetary shock.

The third column of Table 3.2 reports simulation results in response to monetary shocks only. With only monetary shocks, output is only about half as volatile as in the data. However, this brings out the importance of nominal rigidities in magnifying the impact of monetary shocks. In models without nominal rigidities, monetary shocks by themselves can account for only a small fraction of output volatility.[17] With only monetary shocks, consumption is excessively smooth and the relative volatility of investment is considerably higher than in the model with all shocks. The relative volatility of employment also increases.

3.5.3 Correlations

The model's predictions concerning correlations are shown in the lower panel of Table 3.2. The predictions of our model concerning correlations are quite similar to those of Kollmann's model. The main exception is consumption. Our model predicts a correlation of 0.44. Our model predicts the same large negative correlation between net exports and output as Kollmann's model. It does not appear that this correlation is dominated by the effect of technology shocks, with positive technology shocks boosting output and creating strong incentives to invest and import capital. Indeed, the correlation between net exports and output induced by monetary shocks is just as strongly negative. Our model predicts a slightly lower correlation between the nominal exchange rate and output than Kollmann's model, and a somewhat lower correlation between the real exchange rate and output. Despite eschewing nominal price rigidities, our model predicts a correlation between the nominal and real exchange rates that is just as high as in Kollmann's model and is very close to the correlation in the data.

3.5.4   *Impulse response functions*

Following Kollmann (2001), this section presents impulse responses to one-standard deviation shocks to all of the model's underlying shocks. The impulse responses are shown in Figures 3.1–3.4. In each case, we simulate the response to a positive innovation of 1 percent in the relevant forcing variable's process. This leads to persistent increases in the level of technology, the rate of growth of the money supply, the level of real government spending, and the level of foreign prices, with the degree of persistence depending on the $AR(1)$ coefficients of the relevant stochastic processes.

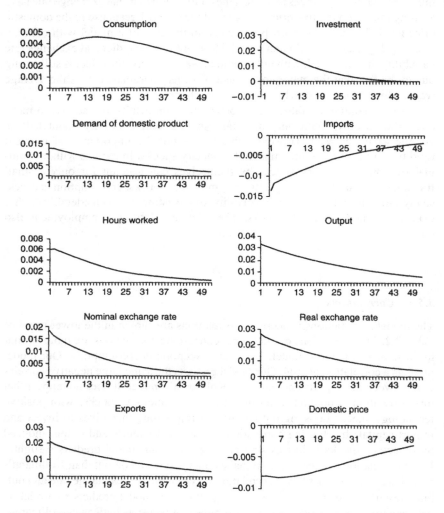

Figure 3.1 Technology shock. Each variable is measured as the deviation in logs from its steady-state value.

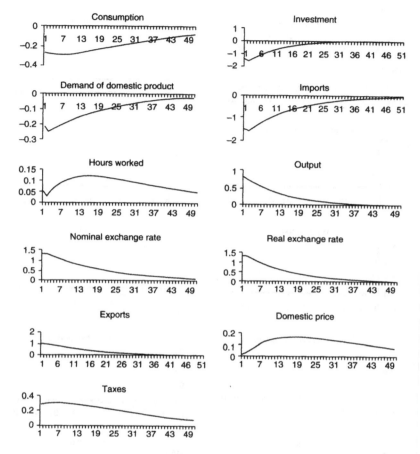

Figure 3.2 Government spending shock. Each variable is measured as the deviation in logs from its steady-state value.

Technology shocks

Figure 3.1 shows the response of variables to a positive technology shock. The shock leads to a depreciation of the real exchange rate as domestic output becomes relatively more abundant with respect to foreign output. The price level declines, as one would expect, and this means that the nominal exchange rate depreciates even more than the real rate. Employment, output, consumption, investment and exports all increase.

Monetary shocks

Because of equation (3.25), the increase in the rate of growth of money persists for several periods. The shock leads to a depreciation of the real exchange rate,

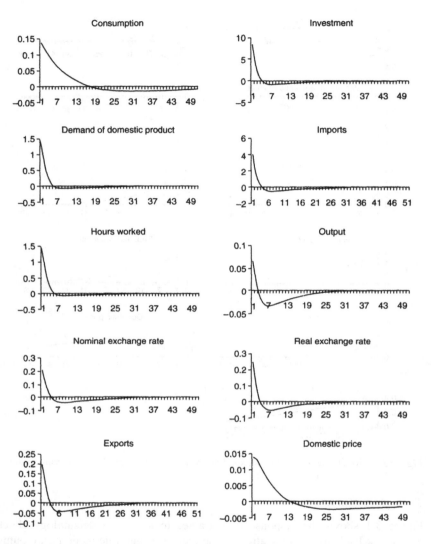

Figure 3.3 Monetary shock. Each variable is measured as the deviation in logs from its steady-state value.

and increases in prices, output, consumption, investment, employment and net exports.

Shocks to government spending

A positive shock to government spending leads to crowding out of both private consumption and investment, and overall domestic demand for domestic output

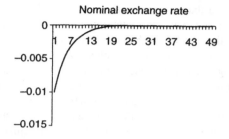

Nominal exchange rate

Figure 3.4 Foreign price shock. The variable is measured as the deviation in logs from its steady-state value.

declines. This can be explained by the endogenous increase in taxes in response to the shock. The fall in domestic demand leads to a fall in the demand for real money balances, which induces a nominal and real exchange rate depreciation and an increase in the domestic price level. The model of Obstfeld and Rogoff (1995) generates a similar response to government spending shocks.

Foreign price level shocks

A persistent increase in the price of foreign output leads to an immediate nominal exchange rate appreciation of the same magnitude. The effect on the real exchange rate and on other real variables is almost non-existent. Similar results are obtained by Kollmann (2001). The implication of this result is that the only role of foreign price shocks in the model is to boost the predicted volatility of the nominal exchange rate.

Summary

The model generates strong movements real variables in response to three of the four kinds of shocks. It is interesting to note that none of the shocks in the model leads to *hump-shaped* responses of output and other real variables. In the light of the results (in a closed-economy context) of Ambler *et al.* (2001), this should not come as a surprise. They show that it is necessary to combine nominal wage rigidities with other mechanisms (they focus on labor adjustment costs) in order to reproduce the hump-shaped responses that seem to characterize the data. We have not pursued this avenue here, since it would have made an already complicated model more complicated, and since this was not the focus of this chapter.

3.6 Conclusion

Our open-economy model with staggered wage setting and flexible prices generates a high degree of nominal and real exchange rate persistence with a modest degree of nominal wage rigidity. It generates a high degree of nominal and real exchange rate variability, while generating fluctuations in prices and consumption that are more compatible with the data than models with price as well as wage rigidities. We view our results as extending to an open-economy context the results of Huang and Liu (2002), who argue that models with nominal wage rigidities are better able to generate persistent responses of real variables than models with price rigidities alone. The results suggest that the use of open-economy models with nominal wage rigidities is a promising avenue of future research on explaining the size and persistence of fluctuations in nominal and real exchange rates. Given the results of Ambler (2002) that nominal wage rigidities can be more easily supported as an equilibrium outcome in the face of modest fixed costs in adjusting wages than can nominal price rigidities, this also suggests that introducing nominal wage rigidities may be a more promising way of building dynamic macroeconomic models with solid microfoundations.

Notes

1 See Ambler *et al.* (2001) for the closed-economy case.
2 Obstfeld and Rogoff (1995) use a model that is simple enough for an analytical solution, and contrast the qualitative response of nominal and real exchange rates to monetary shocks in the short run, with no price adjustment, to the long run, with full price adjustment.
3 Backus *et al.* (1994) show that the behavior of the trade balance is largely determined by capital formation. Consumption smoothing in response to temporary technology shocks would lead to a procyclical balance of trade, while the optimal response of investment to technology shocks leads to a countercyclical balance of trade, which is compatible with the data.
4 Cardia (1995) shows that nominal rigidities can magnify the impact of government spending shocks on real aggregates.
5 Because households sell differentiated labor types to firms and labor types adjust their wages in staggered fashion, different labor types receive different nominal wages. As is standard in the literature, we assume that each household has a representative sample of labor types, so the relevant wage for its decisions is the average wage.
6 Aggregation is considered in Section 3.3.1.
7 It is important to note that this first-order condition does not necessarily hold given the rigid nominal wage. Once contracts are signed, workers cede to firms the right to determine employment, which depends on labor demand. We use the condition in our numerical simulations in order to calculate *notional* labor supply, which affects the nominal contract wage via its effect on current and expected future labor market tightness.
8 Using the first-order condition with respect to consumption to substitute out $\lambda_t(h)$ and $\lambda_{t+1}(h)$, this condition yields an equation for the slope of the intertemporal consumption profile. When $1/\beta = 1 + r_t$ in the long run, steady state consumption is constant.
9 Using a stationary stochastic process for the level of the money stock simplifies the algebra of the model, since we do not have to use a stationarity-inducing normalization of the model's nominal variables. The results of the model are not affected.
10 See Giavazzi and Wysploz (1984) for an early discussion of this problem.
11 This gives an average contract length of $(1 - d)^{-1}$.
12 Technically, it is also necessary to impose an incentive compatibility condition on wage setters. Once the nominal wage is set, it must be the case that the marginal benefit from working an additional hour exceeds the marginal cost in terms of foregone leisure.

Because the nominal wage embeds a markup over wage setters' marginal costs, this condition will be satisfied unless there are large shocks to aggregate demand.

13 Fairise and Langot (1995) calculate a relative volatility of investment of 4.81 for the US economy, somewhat higher than in our data set.

14 As discussed in Ambler *et al.* (2001), it is generally not possible to obtain simultaneous econometric estimates of d and ω because of problems of identification. However, for a given value of d it is possible to recover estimates both of ω and the elasticity of substitution across labor types θ.

15 All variables other than net exports are measured in logs before filtering. Net exports are measured relative to output.

16 In their benchmark model, the standard deviation of the terms of trade is equal to 0.48 percent.

17 This result was first demonstrated by Cooley and Hansen (1989).

4 Sources of exchange rate fluctuations

Pricing-to-market versus non-tradables

Jean-Olivier Hairault and Thepthida Sopraseuth

4.1 Introduction

Since the fall of the Bretton Woods system, nominal and real exchange rate fluctuations exhibit large and persistent departures from purchasing power parity. The Betts and Devereux's (1996) interpretation of this phenomenon relies on the failure of the law of one price among internationally traded goods. Firms tend to set prices in the buyer's currency (pricing-to-market, PTM) and do not adjust prices to changes in the nominal exchange rate. As a consequence, following a money expansion, the money market equilibrium requires an increase in the consumption price level. With sticky-product prices and PTM, nominal exchange rate hardly affects import prices. For a given change in relative money supplies, a larger nominal exchange rate depreciation is needed to clear the money market. As a result, PTM magnifies exchange rate responses to monetary shocks. Chari *et al.* (2002) assess the empirical relevance of this mechanism by embedding PTM into a general equilibrium dynamic model. Chari *et al.* (2002) find that PTM behavior generates deviation from the law of one price whose volatility is somewhat consistent with the data.

Betts and Devereux's (1996) explanation of exchange rate volatility is based on the behavior of traded good prices. In contrast, according to Hau (2000), large nominal exchange rate fluctuations are attributable to the presence of non-traded goods. The more closed the economy, the larger the exchange rate fluctuations. Indeed, when the law of one price holds, non-tradables reduce the impact of import prices on the consumer price level. The money market equilibrium requires a larger exchange rate depreciation following the expansion in the money supply. The literature tends to discard this explanation to exchange rate fluctuations since Chari *et al.* (2002) and Engel (1999) assert that the relative price of non-traded goods play no role in accounting for real exchange rate fluctuations.

However, the non-tradable sector represents a sizeable part of any industrial country. Besides, taking into account the presence of non-traded goods, as suggested by Hau (2000), it may actually mitigate the impact of PTM on exchange rates through the effect of non-tradables on consumer price indices. This chapter therefore proposes a unified theoretical framework including PTM behavior and non-tradables in a two-country sticky-price model. The purpose of this work is twofold. First, we shed light on the way PTM and non-tradables interact in the exchange rate determination. It is shown that, on the one hand, since PTM affects the behavior of tradable prices, local currency pricing matters especially when the share of tradables is not negligible, that is, the economy is open. On the other hand, the degree of openness does not matter if import prices do not respond to exchange rate changes because of PTM behavior. Second, the model could help us determine which effect is likely to be the key ingredient in the understanding of the high exchange rate volatility. Is PTM, more than non-tradables, responsible for the extreme exchange rate variability observed since the fall of the Bretton Woods system? This chapter is an attempt to answer this question.

Section 4.2 presents the model. Section 4.3 deals with the exchange rate determination in this framework while Section 4.4 provides a quantitative discussion of the results. Section 4.5 concludes.

4.2 The model

The model can be viewed as a generalized version of the "new open macroeconomy" model with which the Obstfeld and Rogoff's (1995) model, Betts and Devereux's (1996) framework and Hau's (2000) paper correspond to extreme values for the key parameters.

The model consists of two equally sized countries: home and foreign. Foreign variables are denoted with a star. Home country (foreign country) is composed of households indexed on the interval $[0, \frac{1}{2}]$ ($[\frac{1}{2}, 1]$).

Following Blanchard and Kiyotaki's (1987) formulation, all firms face a monopolistic competition environment. Home produces an array of differentiated tradable goods indexed by the interval $[0, \frac{1}{2}]$. Foreign's tradables are indexed by the interval $[\frac{1}{2}, 1]$. In each country, a fraction s of goods cannot be traded freely across countries by consumers (due to high transportation costs or custom regulations). As a result, for these goods, the law of one price does not hold. Hence, a fraction s of firms can "price-to-market" (PTM) by setting different prices for the local and the foreign markets. Prices for these goods are set in the buyer's currency. The remaining $(1 - s)$ fraction of goods can be freely traded by households so the law of one price holds for those goods. Non-PTM firms set a unified price across countries in the seller's currency. In addition, each country produces a continuum of differentiated non-traded goods indexed by $[0, \frac{1}{2}]$.

4.2.1 Households

Agent i in the home economy has preferences over consumption, leisure and money given by

$$U^i = \log C^i + \frac{\gamma_M}{1 - \epsilon} \left(\frac{M^i}{P} \right)^{1-\epsilon} + \gamma_H \log(1 - h^i),$$

where

$$C^i = \left[(1-\xi)^{1/\theta}(C^{Ti})^{(\theta-1)/\theta} + \xi^{1/\theta}(C^{Ni})^{(\theta-1)/\theta}\right]^{\theta/(\theta-1)}, \tag{4.1}$$

where C^{Ti} (respectively C^{Ni}) is the quantity of tradable (non-tradable) consumed by the home household i, θ denotes the elasticity of substitution between tradables and non-tradables and ξ the share of non-traded goods in the consumption basket. When $\xi = 0$, the model boils down to Betts and Devereux's (1996) model. Consumption bundles in terms of tradables and non-tradables are defined as

$$C^{Ni} = \left[\int_0^{1/2} c^{Ni}(j)^{(\eta-1)/\eta}\,dj\right]^{\eta/(\eta-1)}, \tag{4.2}$$

$$C^{Ti} = \left[\int_0^1 c^{Ti}(j)^{(\eta-1)/\eta}\,dj\right]^{\eta/(\eta-1)}, \tag{4.3}$$

with $\eta > 1$ the elasticity of substitution between goods of the same category, $c^{Ni}(j)$ ($c^{Ti}(j)$) the consumption of the nontraded good j (traded good j).

Domestic-currency consumption indexed for the three preceding consumption baskets (4.1), (4.2) and (4.3) are respectively P, P^N and P^T. The consumption index for the consumption basket C is

$$P = \left[(1-\xi)(P^T)^{1-\theta} + \xi(P^N)^{1-\theta}\right]^{1/(1-\theta)}. \tag{4.4}$$

The first element of P is the price index for non-tradables, that is

$$P^N = \left[\int_0^{1/2} p^N(j)^{1-\eta}\,dj\right]^{1/(1-\eta)}. \tag{4.5}$$

The price index for tradable consumption C^T is given by

$$P^T = \left[\int_0^{1/2} p(j)^{1-\eta}dj + \int_{1/2}^{(1/2)+(s/2)} p^*(j)^{1-\eta}\,dj \right.$$
$$\left. + \int_{(1/2)+(s/2)}^1 (eq^*(j))^{1-\eta}\,dj\right]^{(1/1-\eta)}. \tag{4.6}$$

Let prices denoted by p represent home-currency prices while prices denoted by q represent foreign-currency prices. $p(j)$ is the home-currency price of the home-produced good j, $p^*(j)$ is the home-currency price of a foreign PTM good j while q^* is the foreign-currency price of a foreign non-PTM good. "e" denotes the nominal exchange rate.

The home household i receives income from wages Wh, profits on their ownership of domestic firms π and transfers from the government TR. Her budget constraint is then

$$PC^i + M^i = Wh^i + \pi^i + \text{TR}^i + M_0^i.$$

M_0^i is the money holding at the beginning of the period. The increase in money is transferred to households such that $\text{TR}^i = M^i - M_0^i$. The optimal allocation of consumption between each of the differentiated good is such that

$$c^{Ti}(j) = \left[\frac{v(j)}{P^T}\right]^{-\eta} C^{Ti} \tag{4.7}$$

with $v(j) = p(j)$ if $j \in \left[0, \frac{1}{2}\right]$, $p^*(j)$ if $j \in \left[\frac{1}{2}, \frac{1}{2} + \frac{s}{2}\right]$ or $eq^*(j)$ if $j \in \left[\frac{1}{2} + \frac{s}{2}, 1\right]$.

$$c^{Ni}(j) = \left[\frac{p^N(j)}{P^T}\right]^{-\eta} C^{Ni}, \tag{4.8}$$

$$C^{Ti} = (1 - \xi)\left[\frac{P^T}{P}\right]^{-\theta} C^i, \tag{4.9}$$

$$C^{Ni} = \xi\left[\frac{P^N}{P}\right]^{-\theta} C^i. \tag{4.10}$$

The household's decisions about labor supply and money demand are given by

$$\frac{M^j}{P} = (\gamma_M C^j)^{1/\epsilon},$$

$$\frac{\gamma_H}{1 - h^j} = \frac{W}{PC^j}.$$

4.2.2 Firms

Firms operate a linear technology

$$y(j) = Ah(j),$$

where A is a constant, $y(j)$ total output of the firm, $h(j)$ employment. The output of PTM firms is divided between the output sold locally $(x(j))$ and output sold abroad $(z(j))$. The output of the firm in the non-tradable sector is denoted by $y^N(j)$.

PTM firms choose prices $p(j)$ and $q(j)$ so as to maximize its profit

$$\Pi(j) = p(j)x(j) + eq(j)z(j) - \frac{W}{A}(x(j) + z(j))$$

subject to demand schedules given by (4.7) and its foreign counterpart. Firms in the non-tradable sector face an analogous program with profits written as

$$\Pi(j) = p^N(j)y^N(j) - \frac{W}{A}y^N(j)$$

subject to (4.8). All firms set their prices as a mark-up over marginal cost such that

$$p^N(j) = eq(j) = p(j) = \frac{\eta}{\eta-1}\frac{W}{A}.$$

4.3   Exchange rate determination

Under the symmetric equilibrium assumption, households and firm behavior are identical within a country. In a sticky-price economy, all product prices are pre-set. The equilibrium is defined by

$$\frac{M}{P} = (\gamma_M C)^{1/\epsilon}, \tag{4.11}$$

$$\frac{M^*}{P^*} = (\gamma_M C^*)^{1/\epsilon}, \tag{4.12}$$

$$PC = s(px + eqz) + (1-s)py + p^N y^N, \tag{4.13}$$

$$P^*C^* = s\left(\frac{p^*x^*}{e} + q^*z^*\right) + (1-s)p^*y^* + p^{N*}y^{N*}, \tag{4.14}$$

$$y = \left[\frac{p}{P^T}\right]^{-\eta}\frac{C^T}{2} + \left[\frac{p}{eP^{T*}}\right]^{-\eta}\frac{C^{T*}}{2}, \tag{4.15}$$

$$y^* = \left[\frac{eq^*}{P^T}\right]^{-\eta}\frac{C^T}{2} + \left[\frac{q^*}{eP^{T*}}\right]^{-\eta}\frac{C^{T*}}{2}, \tag{4.16}$$

$$x = \left[\frac{p}{P^T}\right]^{-\eta}\frac{C^T}{2}, \tag{4.17}$$

$$z = \left[\frac{q}{P^{T*}}\right]^{-\eta}\frac{C^{T*}}{2}, \tag{4.18}$$

$$x^* = \left[\frac{p^*}{P^T}\right]^{-\eta}\frac{C^T}{2}, \tag{4.19}$$

$$z^* = \left[\frac{q^*}{P^{T*}}\right]^{-\eta}\frac{C^{T*}}{2}, \tag{4.20}$$

$$y^N = C^N, \tag{4.21}$$

$$y^{N*} = C^{N*}. \tag{4.22}$$

The system is solved after linearizing the model around the steady state. Let $\hat{X}$ denote the deviation from the steady state $(X - \bar{X})/\bar{X}$.

From the definition of the price indices (equations (4.4)–(4.6) and their foreign counterparts), we get

$$\hat{P} = \frac{(1-\xi)(1-s)}{2}\hat{e}, \tag{4.23}$$

$$\hat{P}^* = -\frac{(1-\xi)(1-s)}{2}\hat{e}, \tag{4.24}$$

in a sticky-price environment (i.e. $\hat{p} = 0$, $\hat{q} = 0$, $\hat{p}^* = 0$, $\hat{q}^* = 0$, $\hat{p}^N = 0$, $\hat{p}^{N*} = 0$).

Equations (4.23) and (4.24) state that, since product prices are sticky, changes in consumer price indices only stem from changes in import prices. A nominal exchange rate depreciation increases (decreases) the price of imports in the home country (in the foreign country) as long as the law of one price holds for tradables (s low) providing that tradables represent a significant fraction of the consumption basket (ξ low). The larger the s or ξ, the more incomplete the exchange rate pass-through to consumer price indices.

The model can be viewed as a generalized version of the "new open macroeconomy" paradigm. The model boils down to the Obstfeld and Rogoff's (1995) framework with no PTM and no tradables ($s = 0$ and $\xi = 0$) and is consistent with Hau's (2000) setting if the law of one price holds for all goods ($s = 0$). Finally, Betts and Devereux's (1996) effects are captured in a completely open economy ($\xi = 0$).

In order to grasp intuition for the mechanisms at work in the model, the determination of the nominal exchange rate can be viewed as resulting from the equilibrium on the money market (Section 4.3.1).

4.3.1 Equilibrium nominal exchange rate

The equilibrium nominal exchange rate solves the system given by equations (4.11)–(4.22). Money market clearing requires that the money supply equals the money demand. The latter is given by (4.11) and (4.12):

$$(\hat{M} - \hat{M}^*) = (\hat{P} - \hat{P}^*) + \frac{1}{\epsilon}(\hat{C} - \hat{C}^*). \tag{4.25}$$

Equation (4.25) states that the expansion in the relative money supply is matched by an increase in the relative money demand that consists of two elements: inflation in the consumer price indices and a widening consumption gap. Using (4.23) and (4.24), changes in relative consumption price indices are

$$\hat{P} - \hat{P}^* = \hat{e}(1-\xi)(1-s), \tag{4.26}$$

while the consumption gap results from the linearization of (4.13) and (4.14). Using (4.15)–(4.22) and subtracting, the consumption differential is written as

$$\hat{C} - \hat{C}^* = \hat{e}(\xi\theta - 1)(1-s) + \hat{e}[s + (1-s)\eta]. \tag{4.27}$$

Combining (4.26) and (4.27) into (4.25), the equilibrium exchange rate is given by

$$(\hat{M} - \hat{M}^*) = \underbrace{\hat{e}(1-\xi)(1-s)}_{\substack{\text{exchange rate} \\ \text{magnification effect}}} + \underbrace{\hat{e}\frac{(1-s)(\eta+\xi\theta-1)}{\epsilon}}_{\substack{\text{home product} \\ \text{consumption bias}}} + \underbrace{\hat{e}\frac{s}{\epsilon}}_{\substack{\text{profits of} \\ \text{PTM firms}}}.$$

(4.28)

The monetary expansion is matched by a rise in the relative consumer price indices. Since product prices are sticky, only import prices of non PTM traded goods could contribute to the increase in the consumer price index. More PTM or more non-traded goods reduce the exchange rate pass-through to import prices, thus magnifying the exchange rate response to money shocks. This exchange rate magnification effect is supplemented by a home product consumption bias: the law of one price holds for a fraction $(1 - s)$ of non-PTM goods. As a result, a nominal exchange rate depreciation causes the relative price of foreign non-PTM goods to rise. The home demand shifts toward home goods whether tradables or non-tradables. The expenditure switching effect favors home production, thus home consumption, to the detriment of its foreign counterpart: the consumption gap $\hat{C} - \hat{C}^*$ increases. More home consumption results in more demand for home money, which favors an appreciation of the home currency. The increase in the consumption differential then limits the exchange rate depreciation. The term $(\hat{e}/\epsilon)s$ stems from the profits of PTM firms. The exchange rate depreciation increases the sale value of PTM firms, thereby creating a positive wealth effect: the home consumption rises relative to its foreign counterpart. In a nutshell, equation (4.28) captures Hau's (2000) as well as Betts and Devereux's (1996) effects.

Equation (4.28) can be rewritten as

$$\hat{e} = \frac{\epsilon(\hat{M} - \hat{M}^*)}{s + (1-s)[\eta - 1 + \epsilon + \xi(\theta - \epsilon)]}.$$

(4.29)

Thus, the exchange rate response to an expansion in the home money supply could be illustrated by Figure 4.1.

The change in the money demand is given by the upward sloping line (equation (4.29)) while the expansion in the home money supply shifts the vertical money supply differential to the right. As a result, the nominal exchange rate depreciates. How do PTM behavior and the share of non-tradables affect the exchange rate determination? How do both mechanisms interact in our integrated framework? The subsequent sections shed light on these issues.

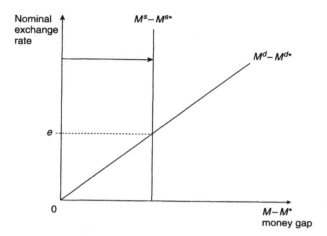

Figure 4.1 Exchange rate determination.

4.3.2 Impact of PTM on the exchange rate equilibrium

Betts and Devereux's (1996) magnification effect

Betts and Devereux's (1996) exchange rate magnification effect relies on the failure of the law of one price. Less non-PTM goods (an increase in s) reduces the impact of import prices on the domestic consumer price level. Given the relative consumption and the relative consumer price levels, the equilibrium on the money market thus requires a larger depreciation of the Home currency to compensate for the incomplete exchange rate pass-through.

The response of the consumption differential stems from the presence of the expenditure switching effect. The latter decreases the nominal exchange rate response. Under full PTM, relative prices are immune to changes in the nominal exchange rate. There is no expenditure switching effect. More PTM firms thus magnify the nominal exchange rate depreciation. Figure 4.2 illustrates the Betts and Devereux's (1996) effect. As the share of PTM firms expands, the money demand schedule shifts up. The nominal exchange rate depreciation is then larger ($e_B > e_A$).

The impact of PTM on the exchange rate is conditional on the share of non-tradables

How does PTM affect the response of the exchange rate? From equation (4.29), it is easily shown that PTM magnifies the nominal exchange rate response to monetary shocks so long as

$$-(1 - \xi) + \frac{2 - (\eta + \xi\theta)}{\epsilon} < 0. \tag{4.30}$$

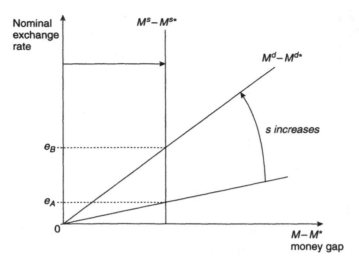

Figure 4.2 PTM magnification effect.

Equation (4.30) is a generalization of Betts and Devereux's (1996) condition. The first term of equation (4.30), $-(1 - \xi)$, refers to the exchange rate magnification effect associated with PTM. As in the Betts and Devereux's (1996) model, the second term of equation (4.30), $(2 - (\eta + \xi\theta))/\epsilon$, states that the larger the expenditure switching effect, the bigger the impact of PTM on the exchange rate. Indeed, the expenditure switching entices the demand to fall on home goods whether tradables or non-tradables. The increase in domestic income, thus domestic consumption in the home country relative to foreign consumption is proportional to the reallocation of the demand, which is determined by $(\eta + \xi\theta)$. Besides, ϵ appears in equation (4.30) since more home consumption results in more demand for home money. When the expenditure switching effect is potentially large because goods are highly substitutable, the share of PTM firms has an important impact on the exchange rate. More PTM reduces the expenditure switching effect.

In addition, nontraded goods has two contrasting effects on the responsiveness of the exchange rate to PTM. Through the second term of equation (4.30), more non-tradables, by enlarging the expenditure switching effect, increase the impact of PTM on the exchange rate. In contrast, in more closed economies, the exchange rate magnification effect due to PTM is reduced by the presence of nontraded goods. The latter mechanism gets the upper hand (i.e. PTM magnification effect is reduced in more closed economies) provided that $\theta < \epsilon$.[1] Notice that, Betts and Devereux (1996) set $\epsilon = 1$ while Stockman and Tesar (1995) argue that the elasticity of substitution between tradables and non-tradables θ equals 0.44. A realistic calibration suggests that $\theta < \epsilon$, implying that nontraded goods reduce the impact of PTM on the exchange rate.

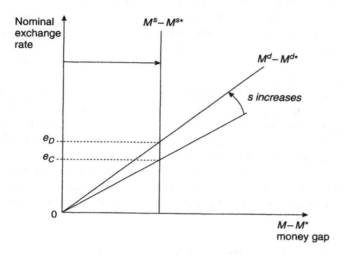

Figure 4.3 The PTM magnification effect is reduced in more closed economies.

Figure 4.2 actually exemplifies the Betts and Devereux's (1996) model and illustrates the nominal exchange rate response in the case of an open economy. However, in closed economies, more PTM does not result in a larger depreciation. Indeed, the increase in the share of PTM firms makes the demand schedule steeper. The magnitude of this effect as well as the slope of the relative money demand are parameterized by the share of non-tradables (ξ). The more the nontraded goods in the economy, the steeper the relative money demand schedule, thus the smaller the magnitude of the shift in the slope of the money demand following the change in PTM (s). As can be seen from Figure 4.3, the PTM magnification effect is reduced in more closed economies ($e_D - e_C$ on Figure 4.3 is lower than $e_B - e_A$ on Figure 4.2).

4.3.3 Impact of non-tradables on the exchange rate equilibrium

Hau's (2000) magnification effect

This section analyzes the impact of non-tradables on the equilibrium exchange rate by pointing at the two mechanisms mentioned above. As for the exchange rate magnification effect, the increase in the price level that clears the money market is achieved through an increase in import prices of non-PTM goods. However, more non-tradables reduce the impact of import prices on the domestic consumption price level. The equilibrium of the money market thus requires a larger depreciation of the home currency to compensate for fewer tradables in the consumer price index.

Equation (4.29) also characterizes the home product consumption bias in Hau's (2000) terminology and the Betts and Devereux's (1996) expenditure switching effect. More non-tradables imply that a domestic demand expansion is concentrated on domestic products. This fall in international demand spillover results in a larger increase in domestic income and therefore domestic consumption. This expansion in the home consumption increases the money demand, which creates a pressure towards the appreciation of the home currency. The exchange rate depreciation is thus reduced.

In a nutshell, as the share of non-tradables expands, the exchange rate magnification effect along with the expenditure switching effect produce opposite effects of the nominal exchange rate. While the exchange rate magnification effect magnifies the nominal exchange rate response, the expenditure switching effects tend to reduce the exchange rate depreciation.

Figure 4.4 illustrates the impact of the presence of non-tradables on the equilibrium exchange rate. The higher the ξ, the steeper the money demand schedule. More closed economies experience a larger exchange rate depreciation following an expansionary money shock.

The impact of non-tradables on the exchange rate is conditional on PTM

How do non-tradables affect the exchange rate response? From equation (4.29), non-traded goods magnify the exchange rate response to monetary shocks so long as

$$-(1-s) + \frac{\theta(1-s)}{\epsilon} < 0. \tag{4.31}$$

The first term stems from the exchange rate magnification effect due to the presence of non-traded goods. The second term of equation (4.31) refer to the expenditure

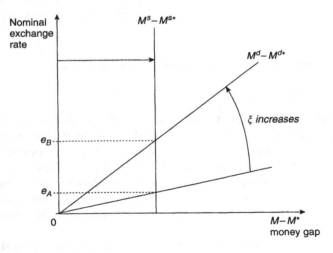

Figure 4.4 Magnification effect due to non-tradables.

switching effect. In more closed economies, the demand falls mainly on non-traded goods. Home income, thus home consumption and the demand for home money, increases, which mitigates the exchange rate depreciation.

Furthermore, PTM has two contrasting effects on the sensitiveness of the exchange rate to non-traded goods. First, more PTM enlarges the impact of non-traded goods on the exchange rate: PTM reduces the expenditure switching, thus the home consumption bias that limits the exchange rate depreciation. In contrast, PTM reduces the impact of non-traded goods on the nominal exchange rate. For, the magnification effect due to non-traded goods relies on the responsiveness of import prices to exchange rate changes. However, PTM reduces this exchange rate pass-through. In a nutshell, PTM lowers the responsiveness of exchange rates to non-traded goods as long as $\theta < \epsilon$, which is supported by a realistic calibration.

Figure 4.4 illustrates the Hau's (2000) framework in which the exchange rate response to a money shock is larger in more closed economies. However, as shown by Figure 4.5, when the deviation from the law of one price applies to a large number of goods, the impact of non-tradables on exchange rate volatility is reduced ($e_D - e_C$ on Figure 4.5 is lower than $e_B - e_A$ on Figure 4.4). For, the share of PTM firms affects the slope of the money demand schedule. The larger the deviation from the law of one price, the steeper the relative money demand line, thus the smaller the shift in the slope of the money demand schedule following a change in the share of non-tradables. As a result, the nominal exchange rate depreciation is less sensitive to the share of non-tradables (Figure 4.5).

The model proposes a generalized framework in which the Obstfeld and Rogoff's (1995) model, Betts and Devereux's (1996) framework and Hau's (2000) paper correspond to extreme values for the two key parameters, s and ξ. As in Betts and Devereux (1996), PTM actually magnifies the exchange rate response to the expansion in the money supply. Moreover, we show that this magnification effect

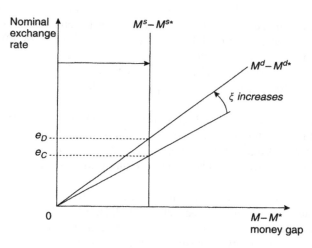

Figure 4.5 The magnification effect due to non-tradables is reduced with PTM.

is at work especially in open economies. Symmetrically, more closed economies experience more volatile exchange rates, which is consistent with Hau's (2000) findings. Besides, we underline that this mechanism does affect the exchange rate changes only if the law of one price holds for a large number of goods.

Is PTM more important than tradables in the nominal exchange rate determination? A preliminary analysis suggests a positive answer to this question. Indeed, PTM behavior and the presence of non-tradables seem to play an asymmetric role in the exchange rate determination. The impact of non-tradables on the nominal exchange rate response is diminished in countries that experience large deviation from the law of one price. In contrast, as the economy becomes more closed, PTM still matters in the nominal exchange rate determination.

4.3.4 Real exchange rate

Using the definition of CPIs (4.23) and (4.24), real exchange rate changes are given by

$$\hat{\Gamma} \equiv \hat{e} + \hat{P}^* - \hat{P} = \hat{e}[s + (1 - s)\xi]. \tag{4.32}$$

The real exchange rate actually consists of two components, the first one being the relative price of tradables that is given by the Betts and Devereux's (1996) PTM effect

$$\hat{\Gamma}^T \equiv \hat{e} + \hat{P}^{T*} - \hat{P}^T = s\hat{e}. \tag{4.33}$$

The presence of non-tradables implies that the relative price of tradables to non-tradables in both countries can be written as

$$\hat{\Gamma}^N \equiv \xi[\hat{P}^{N*} - \hat{P}^{T*} + \hat{P}^T - \hat{P}^N] = \hat{e}(1 - s)\xi. \tag{4.34}$$

The sum of (4.33) and (4.34) yields (4.32). As shown by equation (4.32), conclusions drawn for the nominal exchange rate applies to the real exchange rate. Both are affected by non-tradables as well as PTM. Besides, with $\theta < \epsilon$ and if (4.30) and (4.31) hold, PTM magnifies the real exchange rate response to monetary shocks especially in open economies while real exchange rate volatility is sensitive to the degree of openness as long as the law of one price holds for a large number of goods.

Furthermore, any increase in PTM enlarges the response of the relative price of tradables ($\hat{\Gamma}^T$) and reduces the relative price of tradables to non-tradables ($\hat{\Gamma}^N$), which is consistent with Engel's (1999) empirical findings about the dominant importance of the relative price of tradables in accounting for real exchange rate fluctuations.

Conclusions drawn for the nominal exchange rate applies to the real exchange rate. Both are affected by non-tradables as well as PTM. Besides, PTM magnifies the real exchange rate response to monetary shocks especially in open economies while real exchange rate volatility is sensitive to the degree of openness as long as the law of one price holds for a large number of goods.

4.4 A quantitative evaluation

The model predicts that both PTM and non-tradables account for exchange rate volatility. What element is the most important in understanding nominal exchange rate volatility? This section sheds light on this issue.

Our calibration is based on Betts and Devereux (1996) who suggest a unit money demand elasticity ($\epsilon = 1$). Hau (2000) sets the average mark-up to 1.2, which implies $\eta = 6$. Stockman and Tesar (1995) argue that the elasticity of substitution between tradables and non-tradables θ equals 0.44.[2] Figure 4.6 exhibits the percentage changes of the nominal rate as a function of non-tradables and PTM (equation (4.29)).

Our results qualify Hau's (2000) conclusions about the effect of non-tradables on the nominal exchange rate volatility. Indeed, it was shown in the previous section that the Hau's (2000) magnification effect associated with the presence of non-tradables is at work only when the law of one price holds for a large fraction of goods. Figure 4.6 provides an additional reason for qualifying Hau's (2000) results. Figure 4.6 reveals that, even under incomplete PTM ($s \leftarrow 0$), the impact of non-tradables on the nominal exchange rate response is quantitatively small: when the law of one price holds, country B that is a more closed economy than country A, exhibits a nominal exchange rate depreciation that is only slightly larger than the one observed in country A.

In contrast, PTM countries (point D on Figure 4.6) exhibit a higher exchange rate volatility than non PTM countries (point B), which illustrates the asymmetry between the effects of PTM and non-tradables on exchange rate determination.

Figure 4.7 displays the percentage changes of the real exchange rate as a function of non-tradables and PTM (equation (4.32)).

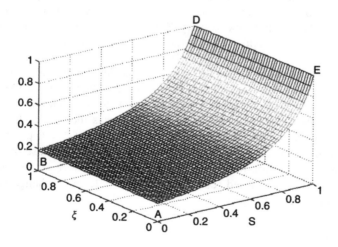

Figure 4.6 Nominal exchange rate response to the home money shock as a function of PTM (s) and non-tradables (ξ).

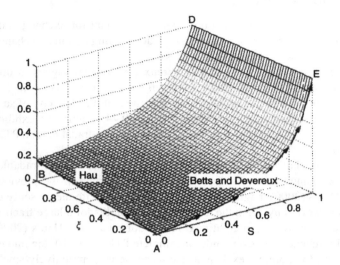

Figure 4.7 Real exchange rate response to the home money shock as a function of PTM (*s*) and non-tradables (ξ).

This figure suggests that, for the benchmark calibration, PTM is more important than non-tradables in accounting for exchange rate volatility. On Figure 4.7, country *A* is deprived of non-tradables and PTM firms (Obstfeld and Rogoff's (1995) model). PPP holds such that the real exchange rate is constant. Starting from point *A*, as underlined by Hau (2000), moving to a more closed economy (country *B*) increases the real exchange rate response from 0 to 0.2. Symmetrically, starting from point *A*, as uncovered by Betts and Devereux (1996), moving to a more complete PTM framework (country *E*) raises deviation from PPP from 0 to 1. The effect of PTM on real exchange rate volatility seems larger than that of non-tradables.

In addition, Figure 4.7 allows to quantify the effects underlined in the previous sections. As can be seen from Figure 4.7, non-tradables matter when PTM is low. Increasing the share of non-tradables raises exchange rate volatility from *A* to *B* when the law of one price holds (*s* = 0) whereas the real exchange rate remains unaffected by non-tradables under complete PTM (*s* = 1, point *D* to *E*). Symmetrically, enlarging the share of PTM results in an increase in the real exchange rate depreciation from *A* to *E* in open economies (ξ = 0). This depreciation is lower in more closed economies (when ξ = 1, real exchange rate depreciation goes up only from *B* to *D*).

4.5   Conclusion

The international macroeconomic literature attributes the nominal and real exchange rate volatility to two mechanisms. The first one, underlined by

Betts and Devereux (1996), lays stress on the deviation from the law of one price due to PTM behavior whereas the second mechanism uncovered by Hau (2000) relies on the presence of non-tradables. This chapter aims at studying the impact of both mechanisms on exchange rate determination. Indeed, the Betts and Devereux's (1996) framework is developed without non-tradables whereas the law of one price holds in Hau's (2000) model.

We have shown that both effects are deeply intertwined. PTM increases exchange rate volatility especially in open economies. Similarly, non-tradables magnify the exchange rate depreciation providing that the law of one price holds for a large share of tradables. Finally, the model suggests that PTM is more important than non-tradables in accounting for the high exchange rate volatility.

Notes

1 Notice that equation (4.30) can be rewritten as

$$\xi(\epsilon - \theta) < \eta - 2 + \epsilon,$$

when $\xi = 0$, we find Betts and Devereux (1996) condition. Besides, as long as $\theta < \epsilon$, equation (4.30) yields a more restrictive condition than Betts and Devereux (1996).
2 Note that, under this benchmark calibration, the conditions $2 - \eta - \xi\theta < 0$ and $\theta - \epsilon < 0$ hold.

5 Sources of non-stationary real exchange rate fluctuations

Elements of theory and some empirical evidence

Philippe Andrade

5.1 Introduction

This chapter aims at providing empirical evidence on the sources of real exchange rates fluctuations since the modern floating area by investigating the yen/dollar particular case. It is well established that real exchange rates have been substantially more variable after the fixed exchange rate system of Bretton Woods collapsed at the beginning of the 1970s. But whether this reflects an increase in the volatility of monetary policy combined with sluggish prices adjustments, as Mussa (1986) argues, or, as Stockman (1988) puts forth, a rise in the variability of real (supply and demand) shocks, is still debated.

Recently, two influential empirical studies by Clarida and Gali (1994) and Eichenbaum and Evans (1995) rely on structural vectorial auto regressive models (VARs) analysis to point out the importance of monetary policy shocks interacting with prices rigidities to account for real exchange rates fluctuations. They thus support Dornbusch's (1976) "overshooting" mechanism of real exchange rate fluctuations. They also echo recent theoretical works which, starting with Obstfeld and Rogoff (1995) and Beaudry and Devereux (1995), aim at extending Dornbusch's (1976) model into a dynamic general equilibrium framework (see Lane, 2001, for a survey).

However, the empirical evidence also questions the so-called "new open economy macroeconomics" (NOEM) research program. To date yet, even if it gives us models that are able to fit fairly well floating real exchange rates empirical volatility, it still lacks a mechanism that can replicate the high degree of persistence they also exhibit (see Chari *et al.* 2002). Indeed, at least over the post-Bretton Woods period, real exchange rates revert only very slowly to their (even relative) purchasing power parity (PPP) levels. According to most floating real exchange rate raw data, the hypothesis that they contain a unit-root cannot be rejected (see Froot and Rogoff, 1995 or Rogoff, 1996). Consequently, whenever one relies on price-rigidities as the central mechanism that precludes immediate adjustment to PPP, this strong persistence can be accounted for only if one is willing to accept incredibly long-lived price contracts.

We propose to reevaluate the real exchange rates fluctuations relative contributions of real sources – namely in this work supply and demand shocks – and nominal ones – namely here money supply shocks – by taking for granted the fact that one cannot reject the hypothesis that real exchange rate are non-stationary processes, integrated of order one. Moreover, rather than explaining the real exchange rate strong persistence by an internal specific transmission mechanism implied by a theoretical model we postulate the sources of non-stationarity to be exogenous. Most NOEM models consider that PPP holds once nominal rigidities are non-effective anymore. They aim at reproducing the pattern of low-frequencies filtered (but still highly persistent) real exchange rate data. Here instead we do not disentangle the short- and long-term analysis. We work on real exchange rate raw data and assess together the contributions of the different shocks at business and low-frequencies.

Even though we assume the presence of exogenous sources of non-stationarity, we cannot spare a theoretical analysis of real exchange rate dynamics since we need structural a priori to identify the three postulated structural shocks from the data. We draw them from a two-country model that shares the same analytical framework as NOEM models, that is, optimizing agents in a dynamic general equilibrium and imperfect competition setup, but which can also generate non-stationary real exchange rate. More precisely we rely on a slightly simplified version of Bergin and Feenstra (2001) model in which monopolistically competitive firms can charge different prices across segmented national markets and face non-constant elasticity demand curves due, in this model, to translog consumers preferences. In contrast to the more standard case where households demand is derived from constant elasticity of substitution (CES) preferences *à la* Dixit–Stiglitz, this framework allows for PPP deviations even once prices have fully adjusted and when all goods varieties are internationally traded. This latter feature of the model is important since it is also established that, as for price stickiness, non-traded goods and Balassa (1964) – Samuelson (1964) effects alone cannot account for the observed persistence in real exchange rates (see Engel, 1999).

This theoretical framework allows to recover supply, demand and money supply shocks from the investigation of a three-dimensional dynamic system consisting of the logarithms of the output, the cross-country difference in price levels and the real exchange rate. We also point out that the theoretical model allows for particular specifications of the system long-run dynamic properties. Namely it eventually yields cointegration relationships between its three components. A cointegration property implies that the transmission mechanism of the shocks to these three variables is such that this system admits a vectorial error correcting model (VECM) representation of its dynamics (see Engle and Granger, 1987). In other words, if cointegration holds, the induced error correcting mechanisms have to be taken into account to properly assess the transmission mechanism of the various impulses to the system.

Our empirical analysis therefore goes in two steps. First, we empirically identify whether the system dynamics is characterized by any cointegration constraint. Over the 1973–2001 period, and for the particular case of the yen/dollar, the cointegration hypothesis is rejected. However, we rely on recent works by Clarida *et al.* (1998, 2000), to motivate the presence of a structural modification of the system dynamics before and after the arrival of Paul Volcker at the Fed's head which, these author argue, corresponds to a modification of the monetary policy rules in most industrialized countries. We implement the test procedure built in Andrade *et al.* (2001) to show that indeed cointegration with a structural break at that particular date holds. Second, we use the associated VECM representation of the system dynamics to perform traditional impulse response function (IRF) and forecast error variance decomposition (FEVD) analysis.

Accounting for this long-run dynamic constraint significantly modifies the empirical evidence compared with related studies. IRF and FEVD analysis shows that (i) real shocks, in particular demand shocks, account for most of the yen/dollar real exchange rates fluctuations over the floating period. In contrast, the contribution of monetary policy shocks is of lower order, *even* for short horizons. Moreover, (ii) the length of the real exchange rate transitory deviations from its long-run equilibrium level in the wake of the shocks, in particular the money supply one, is also sensibly lower than in previous studies.

The rest of the chapter is organized as follows. Section 5.2 describes the theoretical model on which the empirical analysis will be based and in particular discusses its dynamic properties. Section 5.3 sets out the statistical approach and identification scheme of the structural shocks chosen. Section 5.4 provides the empirical results and comments. Lastly, Section 5.5 concludes.

5.2   An open economy with translog preferences

Our empirical analysis relies on a two-country dynamic general equilibrium model. Each country is fielded with monopolistically competitive firms that produce different varieties of goods, can price discriminate between segmented national markets and face non-constant elasticity demand curves. The motivation to study this model is to obtain structural economic a priori that could account for the low frequency or long-term behavior of real exchange rates dynamics. The theoretical model lays the groundwork for our empirical analysis. At first, we thus leave aside the description of short-term or business-cycle frequencies fluctuations. We therefore abstract from capital accumulation and also consider an economy where prices are fully flexible or have fully adjusted. However, a general description of short-term dynamic adjustment effects in this model, such as those produced by prices-rigidities or capital accumulation, for example, is given at the end of this section.

A word on notations. The two countries are named home and foreign. Superscripts h and f will respectively denote home and foreign variables or parameters. A number of symmetry assumptions between the home and the foreign country will be made. More precisely every parameters that are not marked by a h or f superscript are assumed to be identical in both countries. These assumptions will allow us to work on variables taken in cross-country difference, that is, difference between the home and the foreign one: $x \equiv x^h - x^f$. For sake of exposition parsimony, we will focus on the description of the home country. Otherwise stated, similar relationships hold in the foreign one. Lastly, lowercase letters denote the logarithm transformation of the corresponding capital letter variables, $x \equiv \ln X$.

5.2.1 Households

Intratemporal preferences

Most of the recent attempts to model open-economies in a general equilibrium framework with imperfect firms competition specify national consumption baskets of Dixit–Stiglitz type, that is, a CES index of the varieties of goods. This specification is easily tractable but implies a demand with constant elasticity. This has serious drawbacks for models that rely on nominal rigidities together with monetary policy to account for business fluctuations: they need to assume implausible exogenous nominal contract length in order to account for the observed persistent response of real variables to monetary shocks. This limit applies obviously to real exchange rate persistence (see Chari *et al.*, 2002). Kimball (1995b) or Bergin and Feenstra (2000) point out the importance of a demand with non-constant elasticity for generating significant real effects of monetary policy shocks. One way to do this in an open-economy framework is to follow Bergin and Feenstra (2001) and rely on translog household preferences. As shown in the following sections, another advantage of the translog preferences framework compared with the standard CES one is to allow for real exchange rate fluctuations (defined with consumer price indices) even when prices are fully flexible and without resorting to non-traded goods or to the home bias hypothesis. By contrast, CES preferences tie the real exchange rate to one once prices have adjusted.

Translog household preferences are defined by a unit-expenditure function that satisfies

$$p_t^h = \sum_{i=1}^{N} \left(\alpha_i^h + d_{it}^h \right) p_{it}^h + \frac{1}{2} \sum_{i=1}^{N} \sum_{j=1}^{N} \gamma_{ij}^h p_{it}^h p_{jt}^h, \tag{5.1}$$

where $p_t^h \equiv \ln P_t^h$, with P_t^h the home consumption price index, $p_{it}^h \equiv \ln P_{it}^h$, with P_{it}^h the variety i home-currency price, N the number of variety consumed by home households and d_{it}^h a demand random shock in favor of variety i. We postulate the following restrictions in order to get homogeneity of degree one of the price index:

$$\sum_{i=1}^{N} \alpha_i^h = 1, \quad \sum_{i=1}^{N} d_{it}^h = 0 \quad \forall t, \quad \gamma_{ij}^h = \gamma_{ji}^h \quad \text{and} \quad \sum_{i=1}^{N} \gamma_{ij}^h = \sum_{j=1}^{N} \gamma_{ij}^h = 0.$$

The two countries are supposed of equal size: Varieties $i = 1, \ldots, (N/2)$ are produced at home, while the remaining ones, $i = (N/2) + 1, \ldots, N$ are produced in the foreign country. Let C_{it}^h and C_t^h respectively denote the time t expenditure in good i and aggregate home expenditure. Let also θ_{it}^h and ϕ_{it}^h respectively denote the home households elasticity of demand for good i and expenditure share in good i which are defined by

$$\phi_{it}^h \equiv \frac{P_{it}^h C_{it}^h}{P_t^h C_t^h} = \frac{\partial P_t^h / P_t^h}{\partial P_{it}^h / P_{it}^h},$$

$$\theta_{it}^h \equiv -\frac{\partial (C_{it}^h / C_t^h) / (C_{it}^h / C_t^h)}{\partial (P_{it}^h / P_t^h) / (P_{it}^h / P_t^h)}.$$

The translog preference consumption price index (5.1) implies that the expenditure share in variety i satisfies

$$\phi_{it}^h = \alpha_i^h + d_{it}^h + \sum_{j=1}^{N} \gamma_{ij}^h p_{jt}^h, \tag{5.2}$$

so that the demand elasticity for that good follows

$$\theta_{it}^h = 1 - \frac{\partial \phi_{it}^h / \phi_{it}^h}{\partial P_{it}^h / P_{it}^h} = 1 - \frac{\gamma_{ii}^h}{\phi_{it}^h}, \tag{5.3}$$

where the condition $\gamma_{ii}^h < 0$ is required to ensure that demand is elastic. When good i price is raised while those of the other varieties remain constant, the elasticity of demand for that good increases so that consumers substitute more easily their consumption to others varieties. Moreover, the higher the prices, the stronger the competition between firms.

Intertemporal preferences and optimality conditions

Each country is populated with a continuum of identical households indexed by z on a set of mass one, $z \in [0, 1]$. A home representative household z has time-separable preferences and maximizes the expected discounted (at a constant rate) sum of current and future period utility function given by

$$U_t^h(z) = \frac{1}{1 - \sigma_1} (C_t^h(z))^{1 - \sigma_1} + \frac{1}{1 - \sigma_2} \left(\frac{M_t^h(z)}{P_t^h} \right)^{1 - \sigma_2},$$

where $C_t^h(z)$ denotes individual consumption of the aggregate basket of goods defined above, so that $C_t^h = \int_0^1 C_t^h(z) \, \mathrm{d}z$. Besides, $M_t^h(z) / P_t^h$ denotes individual real money balance. Each household is supposed to inelastically supply a constant amount of labor per period to national firms and to own an equal share of them. We also assume complete asset markets, zero government net transfers and exogenous monetary policy. The foreign representative agent has similar preferences.

The intertemporal utility maximization program of the home and foreign consumers under the individual budget constraint implied by the postulated framework produces[1] the following optimality conditions that we directly express in aggregate, log-linear and cross-country difference form

$$s_t - p_t = \sigma_1 c_t, \tag{5.4}$$

$$m_t - p_t = \frac{\sigma_1}{\sigma_2} c_t - \frac{1}{\sigma_2} i_t, \tag{5.5}$$

where s_t denotes the logarithm of the nominal exchange rate, S_t, that we express in home-currency units for one unit of foreign currency (so that when S_t rises the home currency depreciates against the foreign one) and i_t is the nominal interest rate differential. Equation (5.4) is the standard risk-sharing condition that results from the optimal intertemporal individual consumption plans and the complete asset markets assumption. Equation (5.5) is the optimal money demand condition. Home and foreign nominal interest rates, i_t^h and i_t^f, are defined as the state-contingent assets portfolio nominal rates of return in each national currency. Arbitrage opportunities are ruled out by the uncovered interest parity (UIP) condition

$$E_t\{\Delta s_{t+1}\} = i_t, \tag{5.6}$$

where $E_t\{\cdot\}$ is the expectation conditional on time t information operator.

5.2.2 Firms

For analytical tractability, we now restrict our analysis to the case where home and foreign households consume only two varieties of goods: $N = 2$. The home firm produces good $i = 1$, and the foreign one good $i = 2$. Therefore P_{1t}^f designates the foreign-currency price of a good produced at home and sold in the foreign country. Likewise, P_{2t}^h is the home-currency price of a good produced in the foreign country and sold at home.

Technology

Labor is the only production factor in this economy and the home firm produces its good according to

$$Y_t^h = A_t^h L_t^h, \tag{5.7}$$

where A_t^h is a home specific technology shock and L_t^h is a CES index of each home household labor unit employed by the home firm $L_t^h(z)$

$$L_t^h = \left[\int_0^1 \left(L_t^h(z) \right)^{1-\nu} dz \right]^{1/(1-\nu)}.$$

We define the value of one home output unit, $\widetilde{P}_{1t}$, as the maximum of domestic and foreign unit home revenue: $\widetilde{P}_{1t} \equiv \max\left[P_{1t}^h, S_t P_{1t}^f \right]$. Since all households are assumed to be identical, wages are equalized across workers. The production technology therefore induces the following home firm labor demand

$$L_t^h = \left(\frac{W_t^h}{\widetilde{P}_{1t}}\right)^{-1/\nu} Y_t^h, \tag{5.8}$$

where W_t^h designates the nominal wage and $1/\nu$ the elasticity of labor demand with respect to the factor price ($\nu < 1$ is required for the labor demand to be elastic). The production function also implies that the nominal marginal cost borne by the home firm is

$$MC_t^h = W_t^h \frac{\partial Y_t^h}{\partial L_t^h} = \frac{W_t^h}{A_t^h}. \tag{5.9}$$

Optimal price setting decisions

The objective of one firm is to maximize its intertemporal profit, which is equivalent to deal with a static problem as capital accumulation is left aside and one considers the state where nominal rigidities are no longer effective. The profit function of the home firm is given by

$$\prod_t^h = \left(P_{1t}^h - MC_t^h\right) C_{1t}^h + \left(S_t P_{1t}^f - MC_t^h\right) C_{1t}^f,$$

with S_t the nominal exchange rate. By definition of the expenditure share, this rewrites as

$$\prod_t^h = \left(1 - \frac{MC_t^h}{P_{1t}^h}\right) \phi_{1t}^h P_t^h C_t^h + \left(1 - \frac{MC_t^h}{S_t P_{1t}^f}\right) \phi_{1t}^f S_t P_t^f C_t^f.$$

Using the elasticity of demand expression (5.3), the home firm optimality conditions are

$$\frac{\partial \prod_t^h}{\partial P_{1t}^h} = -\gamma_{11}^h \frac{P_t^h C_t^h}{P_{1t}^h} \left[\left(1 - \frac{\phi_{1t}^h}{\gamma_{11}^h}\right) \frac{MC_t^h}{P_{1t}^h} - 1\right] = 0,$$

$$\frac{\partial \prod_t^h}{\partial P_{1t}^f} = -\gamma_{11}^f S_t \frac{P_t^f C_t^f}{P_{1t}^f} \left[\left(1 - \frac{\phi_{1t}^f}{\gamma_{11}^f}\right) \frac{MC_t^h}{S_t P_{1t}^f} - 1\right] = 0,$$

which can be approximated by

$$\ln\left(\frac{MC_t^h}{P_{1t}^h}\right) = \frac{\phi_{1t}^h}{\gamma_{11}^h}, \quad \ln\left(\frac{MC_t^h}{S_t P_{1t}^f}\right) = \frac{\phi_{1t}^f}{\gamma_{11}^f}.$$

Remark that with $N = 2$, the restrictions on the unit expenditure specification, $\gamma_{ij}^h = \gamma_{ji}^h$ and $\sum_{i=1}^N \gamma_{ij}^h = \sum_{j=1}^N \gamma_{ij}^h = 0$, imply that $\gamma_{11}^h = -\gamma_{12}^h = \gamma_{22}^h \equiv -\gamma^h < 0$. The same hold in the foreign country. The unit expenditure share expression (5.2) thus implies that this set of optimality conditions rewrites into (neglecting constant terms)

$$p_{1t}^h = \frac{1}{2}\left(mc_t^h + p_{2t}^h + \frac{d_{1t}^h}{\gamma^h}\right), \quad p_{1t}^f = \frac{1}{2}\left(mc_t^h - s_t + p_{2t}^f + \frac{d_{1t}^f}{\gamma^f}\right),$$

$$p_{2t}^f = \frac{1}{2}\left(mc_t^f + p_{1t}^f + \frac{d_{2t}^f}{\gamma^f}\right), \quad p_{2t}^h = \frac{1}{2}\left(mc_t^f + s_t + p_{1t}^h + \frac{d_{2t}^h}{\gamma^h}\right).$$

By contrast, in the standard CES case, optimal prices are fixed at a constant markup over marginal cost so that

$$p_{1t}^h = mc_t^h + \log\frac{\theta}{\theta - 1} = p_{1t}^f + s_t, \tag{5.10}$$

$$p_{2t}^f = mc_t^f + \log\frac{\theta}{\theta - 1} = p_{2t}^h - s_t, \tag{5.11}$$

with θ the constant demand elasticity. As in the standard CES case, when facing translog demand curves, each producer price setting decision depends on its marginal cost and the exchange rate when the product is exported. However, these influences are muted because of the demand elasticity reaction, which prompts each firm to react to the price decision of its competitors on each national market. Furthermore, each producer is encouraged to raise its local or export prices when he benefits from a positive demand shock for its good on each national market. This reaction is limited however by the γ's parameters that we can relate to the intensity of price competition on each market. In the sequel, we assume that the strength of price competition is the same in each country: $\gamma^h = \gamma^f = \gamma$. Yet, whatever the competition strength, the weight each type of firm assigns to its idiosyncratic production cost is greater than the one attributed to its competitors'. Indeed, from the preceding equations, it is straightforward to express each good national-currency prices in terms of the marginal cost, the exchange rate and demand shocks and get

$$p_{1t}^h = \frac{2mc_t^h}{3} + \frac{(mc_t^f + s_t)}{3} + \frac{d_{1t}^h}{3\gamma}, \quad p_{1t}^f = \frac{2\left(mc_t^h - s_t\right)}{3} + \frac{mc_t^f}{3} + \frac{d_{1t}^f}{3\gamma},$$
$$\tag{5.12}$$

$$p_{2t}^f = \frac{(mc_t^h - s_t)}{3} + \frac{2mc_t^f}{3} + \frac{d_{2t}^f}{3\gamma}, \quad p_{2t}^h = \frac{mc_t^h}{3} + \frac{2(mc_t^f + s_t)}{3} + \frac{d_{2t}^h}{3\gamma}.$$
$$\tag{5.13}$$

With flexible prices, CES preferences induce full exchange rate pass-through, as firms fully report exchange rate fluctuations into their exports prices, and no deviations from the law of one price. This is not the case with the translog specification adopted here. Because of pricing decision interactions induced by translog preferences, there is limited exchange rate pass-through phenomena: a 1 percent nominal depreciation of the home currency against the foreign one reduces the foreign-currency price of the home good (p_{1t}^f) and increases the home-currency price of the foreign good (p_{2t}^h) by only roughly 0.67 percent. This incomplete adjustment to nominal exchange rate variations is symmetric however and thus does not lead to deviations from the law of one price per se. Still those deviations can occur from asymmetric national demand shocks. Indeed one can easily check that for each type of goods home and foreign prices (5.12) and (5.13) lead to

$$p_{it}^h - p_{it}^f - s_t = \frac{1}{3\gamma} \left(d_{it}^h - d_{it}^f \right), \quad i = 1, 2.$$

These deviations from the law of one price thus generates PPP deviations in spite of price flexibility. However, as we show in the next section, these are not the only channel by which translog preferences can lead to such long-term non-zero real exchange rate.

Price index differential and real exchange rate

Remark that with $N = 2$, the restrictions on the unit expenditure specification, $\sum_{i=1}^N \alpha_i^h = 1$ and $\sum_{i=1}^N d_{it}^h = 0 \ \forall t$, imply that $\alpha_2^h = 1 - \alpha_1^h$ and $d_{1t}^h = -d_{2t}^h$. The same hold in the foreign country. The unit expenditure function (5.1) thus gives us the following home and foreign consumption price indices

$$p_t^h = \alpha_1^h p_{1t}^h + \left(1 - \alpha_1^h\right) p_{2t}^h + d_{1t}^h \left(p_{1t}^h - p_{2t}^h\right) - \frac{\gamma}{2} \left(p_{1t}^h - p_{2t}^h\right)^2,$$

$$p_t^f = \alpha_1^f p_{1t}^f + \left(1 - \alpha_1^f\right) p_{2t}^f + d_{1t}^f \left(p_{1t}^f - p_{2t}^f\right) - \frac{\gamma}{2} \left(p_{2t}^f - p_{1t}^f\right)^2.$$

Holding everything else constant, higher values of γ strengthens competition between home and foreign firms on each national markets and thus lowers national price indices. It should be noted that the translog setup does not impose that each good enters perfectly symmetrically into the price index. In other words, the specification does not require that $\alpha_1^h = (1 - \alpha_1^h) = \frac{1}{2}$. Symmetric preferences of the consumers in both countries can be postulated in a broader sense by letting the fixed fraction of aggregate expenditure in local and imported goods be the same in each country $\alpha_1^h = \alpha_2^f = \alpha$ and $\alpha_2^h = \alpha_1^f = 1 - \alpha$.

One should be cautious with the meaning of such preference restriction. For instance, $\alpha > \frac{1}{2}$ should not be interpreted as a home bias phenomena, that is, a situation where the local good expenditure share is greater than the imported good one while the elasticity of substitution between the two goods is constant. Rather here the elasticity of substitution between the two goods depends on their relative price. Therefore, $\alpha > \frac{1}{2}$ only implies that the demand for local goods is less elastic than the demand for imports when their prices are equalized.

The price index differential between the two countries stays log-linear if one further restricts the analysis to global, instead of country-specific, demand shocks for each type of good: $d_{it}^h = d_{it}^f$, $i = 1, 2.$[2] By definition of the home and the foreign price indices, we also have $d_{1t}^h = -d_{2t}^h$ and $d_{1t}^f = -d_{2t}^f$. Let $d_t \equiv d_{1t}^h - d_{2t}^f = 2d_{1t}^h$.

A positive demand shock cross-country differential, $d_t > 0$, thus corresponds to an exogenous reallocation of world demand from foreign products to home goods. Under this simplication it is easy to show from the preceding equations and the optimal price setting decisions, (5.12) and (5.13), that the price index cross-country differential follows:

$$p_t = \left(\frac{2\alpha - 1}{3} \right) mc_t + \left(\frac{4 - 2\alpha}{3} \right) s_t + \frac{1}{\gamma} \left(\frac{2\alpha - 1}{3} \right) d_t. \tag{5.14}$$

It is easier to interpret this price index equation after having rewritten it in terms of *real* marginal costs differential: $rmc_t \equiv mc_t - \widetilde{p}_t$, with $\widetilde{p}_t \equiv \ln \widetilde{P}_{1t} / \widetilde{P}_{2t}$, where $\widetilde{P}_{2t}$ is the value of one foreign output unit defined by $\widetilde{P}_{2t} \equiv \max \left[S_t^{-1} P_{2t}^h, P_{2t}^f \right]$. Under assumptions $\sum_i d_{it}^h = \sum_i d_{it}^f = 0$ and $d_{it}^h = d_{it}^f$, $i = 1, 2$, the optimal pricing decisions (5.12) and (5.13) imply that (5.14) rewrites as

$$p_t = \left(\alpha - \frac{1}{2} \right) rmc_t + s_t + \frac{1}{\gamma} \left(\alpha - \frac{1}{2} \right) d_t.$$

Let $q_t \equiv s_t - p_t$ denote the logarithm of the *real* exchange rate, it is direct to see that the preceding expression also implies that

$$q_t = \left(\frac{1}{2} - \alpha \right) rmc_t + \frac{1}{\gamma} \left(\frac{1}{2} - \alpha \right) d_t. \tag{5.15}$$

Holding everything else constant, a variation in the real marginal cost cross-country differential affects the price index differential. The sign of the effect depends on whether the fixed national expenditure share in local goods, α, exceeds or not the imported goods one. When $\alpha > \frac{1}{2}$, local firm pricing decisions dominate in the national price indices. A greater domestic real marginal cost inflates the domestic price index compared with the foreign one and the real exchange rate appreciates (q_t falls). The situation is reversed for $\alpha < \frac{1}{2}$. Whatever the sign of the effect, the price index under-reacts to real marginal cost variations because of the competition induced by the non-constant elasticity of demand. The same comments apply to the demand shock variation effects, holding everything else constant, on the price index cross-country differential and the real exchange rate. The only demand shock effects specificity is that their magnitude decreases with the intensity of competition between firms (γ). Finally, whatever the value of α, the price index differential always positively reacts to nominal exchange rate variations. A depreciation of the domestic currency compared with the foreign one prompts foreign firms to raise their export prices and domestic firms to lower theirs. The reaction is one-for-one so that nominal exchange rate variations do not imply real exchange rate ones.[3]

Note that equation (5.15) allows for non-zero real exchange rates even when prices have fully adjusted for $\forall \alpha \neq \frac{1}{2}$. This feature of the model is an essential difference with models that use the standard CES preferences specification. Indeed, the latter framework restricts the prices of the different goods varieties to enter national price index in a perfectly symmetric way.[4] In the two-country, two-product case dealt with here, national price CES index would be given by[5]

$$P_t^h = \left[\frac{1}{2}\left(P_{1t}^h\right)^{1-\theta} + \frac{1}{2}\left(P_{2t}^h\right)^{1-\theta}\right]^{1/(1-\theta)},$$

$$P_t^f = \left[\frac{1}{2}\left(P_{1t}^f\right)^{1-\theta} + \frac{1}{2}\left(P_{2t}^f\right)^{1-\theta}\right]^{1/(1-\theta)}.$$

Combining these equations together with optimal CES firms pricing decisions (5.10) and (5.11), one gets

$$P_t^h = \left[\frac{1}{2}\left(S_t P_{1t}^f\right)^{1-\theta} + \frac{1}{2}\left(S_t P_{2t}^f\right)^{1-\theta}\right]^{1/(1-\theta)} = S_t P_t^f.$$

In other words, when demand curves are CES and prices have fully adjusted, the real exchange rate equals unity, that is, in log form $q_t = 0 \forall t$.

5.2.3   Solving the model

In that flexible price economy, there is no unemployment. Let $\overline{L}^h$ denotes the constant labor amount (inelastically) supplied by home households. Using the labor demand function (5.8) and the production function (5.7), labor market equilibrium $L_t^h = \overline{L}^h$ requires that

$$\left(\frac{W_t^h}{\widetilde{P}_{1t}}\right) = \left(A_t^h\right)^\nu. \tag{5.16}$$

Good market equilibrium is supply determined. From the production function (5.7), the equilibrium (log) output cross-country differential is given by

$$y_t = a_t, \tag{5.17}$$

where we have assumed that home and foreign households supply the same number of labor units, $\overline{L}^h = \overline{L}^f$.

Using the nominal marginal cost (5.9), the labor market equilibrium condition (5.16) implies an equilibrium real marginal cost of

$$RMC_t^h = \frac{W_t^h}{A_t^h \widetilde{P}_{1t}} = \left(A_t^h\right)^{\nu-1}.$$

The same holds for the foreign firm with a price $\widetilde{P}_{2t} \equiv \max\left[S_t^{-1} P_{2t}^h, P_{2t}^f\right]$. In log and cross-country difference form we obtain

$$rmc_t = (\nu - 1)a_t.$$

Using (5.15), the equilibrium real exchange rate is then given by

$$q_t = (v-1)\left(\frac{1}{2} - \alpha\right) a_t + \frac{1}{\gamma}\left(\frac{1}{2} - \alpha\right) d_t. \tag{5.18}$$

Remember that labor demand is assumed to be elastic so that $v - 1 < 0$. Supply and demand shock thus have opposite effects on the real exchange rate. The sign of these effects is determined by the fixed expenditure share on national goods parameter, α. Consider an asymmetric supply shock in favor of the domestic country: $a_t > 0$. It reduces the home firm real marginal cost by a factor of $1 - v$ and thus prompts the home firm to reduce its local and export prices. Because of pricing interactions, the foreign firm also does, but to a lesser extent. When $\alpha > \frac{1}{2}$, local firms pricing decision dominates in national indices, so that p_t^h falls more than p_t^f. Thus p_t falls in the wake of that supply shock and the real exchange rate depreciates (q_t rises). The situation is reversed for $\alpha < \frac{1}{2}$. Similar comments apply for demand shocks effects on the real exchange rate, where now an asymmetric demand shock in favor of the domestic good prompts home firms to raise their prices compared with foreign firm's ones.

The money demand (5.5), UIP condition (10.27) and perfect risk-sharing condition (5.4) allow us to find the equilibrium nominal exchange rate

$$s_t = \left(\frac{1}{1+\sigma_2}\right) \sum_{j=0}^{\infty} \left(\frac{1}{1+\sigma_2}\right)^j E_t\{(\sigma_2 - 1)q_{t+j} + \sigma_2 m_{t+j}\}.$$

so that using (5.18) we have

$$s_t = \sum_{j=0}^{\infty} \left(\frac{1}{1+\sigma_2}\right)^{j+1} E_t\{(\sigma_2 - 1)(\kappa a_{t+j} + \lambda d_{t+j}) + \sigma_2 m_{t+j}\}, \tag{5.19}$$

with $\kappa \equiv (v-1)\left(\frac{1}{2} - \alpha\right)$, $\lambda \equiv \frac{1}{\gamma}\left(\frac{1}{2} - \alpha\right)$ two parameters of opposite sign. The nominal exchange rate solves the money market equilibrium. Relative inflation can be generated by monetary policy or aggregate demand differentials, m_t and c_t (the latter being directly related to the real exchange rate through the risk sharing condition (5.4)) and produces a relative money devaluation in the inflationary country. Expectation terms appear because of the role played by expected inflation on money demand through the nominal interest rate.

The associated equilibrium price level differential is finally obtained by taking the difference between (5.19) and (5.18) to get

$$p_t = \left(m_t - \frac{\kappa}{\sigma_2} a_t - \frac{\lambda}{\sigma_2} d_t\right) + \sum_{j=1}^{\infty} \left(\frac{1}{1+\sigma_2}\right)^{j+1}$$

$$\times E_t\left\{\sum_{k=1}^{j} [(\sigma_2 - 1)(\kappa \Delta a_{t+j} + \lambda \Delta d_{t+j}) + \sigma_2 \Delta m_{t+k}]\right\}.$$

Current supply and demand shocks affect aggregate demand c_t through the real exchange rate reaction. Given money supply and nominal interest rate cross-country differentials, the money market equilibrium associates these aggregate demand variations to an opposite sign reaction in the price index. These effects are compensated by the reversed effects of expected future supply and demand shocks on the nominal interest rate through the nominal exchange rate. Whether current or expected, money supply differentials always inflate the price level in the expansionary country.

So far we have postulated exogenous monetary supply without describing it. Yet monetary authorities may partly supply money in a systematic way, this systematic component aiming at stabilizing prices and attaining the full employment equilibrium by reacting to the state of the economy. Without discussing on the optimality of such a rule, a simple way of modeling this (without taking any stance on the optimality of such a behavior) is to assume that the money supply reacts positively to supply shocks (in order to compensate for the short-term rigidities that preclude an immediate adjustment to the new long-run output level) and negatively to demand shocks (in order to counteract the induced long-term inflation). We thus suppose that, in each country, monetary supply follows:

$$m_t = \pi_1 a_t - \pi_2 d_t + b_t, \tag{5.20}$$

with b_t a "pure" money supply shock. In the long-run, this monetary authorities behavior only influences nominal variables. In particular, combining the previous price index differential along with this particular exogenous monetary policy supply process (5.20), the long-term equilibrium price level differential becomes

$$p_t = \left[\left(\pi_1 - \frac{\kappa}{\sigma_2} \right) a_t - \left(\pi_2 + \frac{\lambda}{\sigma_2} \right) d_t + b_t \right]$$
$$+ \sum_{j=1}^{\infty} \left(\frac{1}{1+\sigma_2} \right)^{j+1} E_t \left\{ \sum_{k=1}^{j} \left[\mu \Delta a_{t+j} + \xi \Delta d_{t+j} + \sigma_2 \Delta b_{t+k} \right] \right\}. \tag{5.21}$$

with $\mu \equiv (\sigma_2(\pi_1 + \kappa) - \kappa)$ and $\xi \equiv (\sigma_2(\lambda - \pi_2) - \lambda)$.

Equations (5.17), (5.18) and (5.21) produce a three-dimensional dynamic system that we can express in a state-space form. Let $S_t \equiv (a_t \quad d_t \quad b_t)'$ denotes the state variable of the system and assume that this process has for law of motion:

$$\Delta S_t = (R - I)S_{t-1} + v_t, \tag{5.22}$$

with Δ the first-difference operator and

$$R \equiv \begin{pmatrix} \rho_a & 0 & 0 \\ 0 & \rho_d & 0 \\ 0 & 0 & \rho_b \end{pmatrix}, \quad v_t \equiv \begin{pmatrix} v_t^a \\ v_t^d \\ v_t^b \end{pmatrix},$$

where the autocorrelation of order one parameters, ρ_a, ρ_d and ρ_b, are assumed to be on or strictly inside the unit-circle. v_t^a, v_t^d and v_t^b are three independent white noises i.i.d. processes so that the optimal forecast at time t for the horizon j is given by

$$E_t\{\Delta S_{t+j}\} = (R - I)^j S_t.$$

The variables v_t^a, v_t^d and v_t^b thus represent unpredictable supply, demand and money supply shocks on the system at date t. Equations (5.17), (5.18) and (5.21) then rewrites in matrix form as

$$X_t = F S_t,$$ (5.23)

with $X_t \equiv (y_t \quad q_t \quad p_t)'$ and where F is a full rank matrix defined by $F \equiv G + H$ with

$$G \equiv \begin{pmatrix} 1 & 0 & 0 \\ \kappa & \lambda & 0 \\ \left(\pi_1 - \dfrac{\kappa}{\sigma_2}\right) & -\left(\pi_2 + \dfrac{\lambda}{\sigma_2}\right) & 1 \end{pmatrix}',$$

$$H \equiv \sum_{j=1}^{\infty} \left(\frac{1}{1+\sigma_2}\right)^{j+1} \left[\begin{pmatrix} 0 \\ 0 \\ 1 \end{pmatrix} \otimes \begin{pmatrix} \mu \\ \xi \\ \sigma_2 \end{pmatrix}'\right]^j \sum_{k=1}^{j} (R - I)^k.$$

This state-space form rewrites into a VECM: using the identity $\Delta X_t = F \Delta S_t$ and the law of motion for the state variable (5.22), we obtain

$$\Delta X_t = B X_{t-1} + F v_t$$ (5.24)

with

$$B \equiv F(R - I)F^{-1}.$$

When R has all its elements strictly on the unit-circle, B is equal to zero. The elements of X_t are non-stationary, integrated of order one, and the dynamics of the system expresses as a vectorial random walk. When all the elements of R are strictly inside the unit-circle, the elements of X_t are stationary, B is of full rank 3 and the dynamics of the system expresses as a VAR of order one. However this last parametric configuration rules out the possibility that the model generates non-stationary real exchange rate. Lastly, when $r < 3$ diagonal elements of R lie strictly inside the unit-circle and the others strictly on the unit-circle, the elements of X_t are non-stationary, integrated of order one, and B is of reduced rank r. In other words, there exist r cointegration relationships between the elements of X_t, that is, r linear combinations of the X_t components, $\beta' X_t$, with β' a $r \times 3$ matrix of r cointegrating vectors, that are stationary. For example, when the system is such that $\rho_a = \rho_d = 1$ and $|\rho_b| < 1$, that is, has two real stochastic trends (which is the particular configuration to which lead the empirical results that follows in

Section 5.4), there exists one cointegrating vector. One can check that in this particular case, letting

$$\beta' = \left(-\left(\pi_1 + \pi_2 \frac{\kappa}{\lambda} \right) \quad \left(\pi_2 \frac{1}{\lambda} + \frac{1}{\sigma_2} \right) \quad 1 \right), \tag{5.25}$$

gives $\beta' X_t = 1/(1 - \rho_b) b_t$ which is stationary since $b_t = \rho_b b_{t-1} + v_t^b$ with $|\rho_b| < 1$.

5.2.4   *Inserting short-term rigidities*

Nominal or real rigidities of whatsoever kind but transitory will prevent the adjustment of the system to the long-run level described in the preceding sections from being instantaneous. For sake of simplicity (but also generality), stickiness will be inserted here without resorting on a specific model. Assuming that these short-term rigidities do not influence the long-run equilibrium of the economy, they can be inserted in the model simply by replacing (5.23) with

$$\Phi(L) X_t = F S_t, \quad \Delta S_t = (R - I) S_{t-1} + v_t,$$

where $\Phi(\cdot)$ a stable matrix polynomial of finite order verifying $\Phi(0) = I$ and L the lag operator. $\Phi(L)$ thus conveys the gradual adjustment of the system to the long-run equilibrium in the wake of a state-variable variation. The state-space form of the model with short-term rigidities produces a VECM of higher order, but still finite, than previously, namely

$$\Delta X_t = \overline{B} X_{t-1} + B(L) \Delta X_{t-1} + F v_t, \tag{5.26}$$

with

$$\overline{B} \equiv F(R - I) F^{-1} \Phi(1), \quad B(L) \equiv F(R - I) F^{-1} \widetilde{\Phi}(L) - \widetilde{\Phi}_0(L),$$

where the decompositions $\Phi(L) = \Phi(1) + (1 - L) \widetilde{\Phi}(L) = \Phi(0) + L \widetilde{\Phi}_0(L)$ have been used. Note that from the stability of $\Phi(\cdot)$, $\Phi(1)$ is of full rank and thus $\overline{B}$ has the same rank than B in equation (5.24). Therefore, the long-run dynamic properties of the system, especially cointegration, are the same whether or not short-term rigidities are effective in the economy.

5.3   Statistical approach

Our final aim is to identify the qualitative and quantitative effects of the three structural shocks, $v_t \equiv \left(v_t^a \quad v_t^d \quad v_t^b \right)'$, on each of the system's three variables, $X_t \equiv (y_t \quad q_t \quad p_t)'$. We do this by relying on the standard exercises of IRF and FEVD analysis, conducted conditionally on the long-run characterization of the dynamics implied by our theoretical setup. Structural shocks are not directly observed however. Moreover our theoretical setup does not entirely specify the long-run dynamic properties (i.e. the rank of the matrix $\overline{B}$ in (5.26)) of the system since they depend on how many autoregressive unit-roots we have in the state variable law of motion (5.22). Yet a full characterization of the system dynamics can be identified from the empirical study of a statistical model describing the process of interest, X_t. This statistical model together with identification structural a priori also allow to recover the structural shocks from the data.

More precisely consider the process $\Delta X_t \equiv (\Delta y_t \quad \Delta q_t \quad \Delta p_t)'$ and assume, as will be confirmed by the data, that it is stationary. Let

$$\Delta X_t = C(L)\epsilon_t, \tag{5.27}$$

be its Wold decomposition with $C(L) \equiv \sum_{j=0}^{\infty} C_j L^j$, where the $\{C_j\}$ matrix sequence is absolutely summable and $C_0 = I$, the identity matrix, and with ϵ_t, the statistical innovation of the system, an i.i.d. white noise process with variance–covariance matrix Σ_ϵ satisfying $\epsilon_t = \Delta X_t - E\{\Delta X_t | \Omega_{t-1}\}$, $\Omega_{t-1} = \{\Delta X_{t-1}, \Delta X_{t-2}, \ldots\}$. This Wold decomposition inverts into a VECM model (see Engle and Granger, 1987):

$$\Delta X_t = \Pi X_{t-1} + \Pi(L)\Delta X_t + \epsilon_t, \tag{5.28}$$

where Π is a matrix of reduced rank r, with $0 \leq r < 3$ the number of cointegration relationships between the components of X_t, and $\Pi(L) \equiv \sum_{j=1}^{p} \Pi_j L^j$, with $\{\Pi_j\}$ an absolutely summable matrix sequence.

This statistical model can be related to the structural VECM form (5.26) derived in the preceding section. Identifying terms we have

$$\Pi = \overline{B}, \quad \Pi(L) = B(L), \quad \epsilon_t = F v_t.$$

Thus the long-run dynamics properties of the structural model can be recovered from a statistical identification procedure (namely cointegration tests) of the rank of Π. Likewise, as the structural matrix F is of full rank, we can define $S = F^{-1}$ a 3×3 invertible matrix, and directly recover structural shocks from statistical innovations through

$$v_t = S\epsilon_t, \tag{5.29}$$

once each of the S matrix parameters has been identified. This requires a number of 9 identifying assumptions.

We choose these identifying restrictions in accordance with the flexible price solution of our theoretical setup embodied in the state-space representation (5.23). Remark that all elements of the matrix H are equal to zero except those on its third line so that F is lower triangular. Equation (5.23) thus says that once prices have fully adjusted, that is, in the long-run, output is only influenced by supply (technology) shocks and the real exchange rate is only influenced by technology and demand shocks. Moreover, we have postulated independence between each structural shocks. The two-country model investigated above therefore implies the three identifying restrictions below:

- *Structural shocks are mutually uncorrelated.* This implies that $E(v_t v_t')$ is diagonal. Imposing furthermore that this variance–covariance matrix is the identity

$$E(v_t v_t') = I,$$

  is nothing but a matter of normalization. Remark that the structural shocks definition (5.29) together with this assumption implies that

$$S \Sigma_\epsilon S' = I \iff S^{-1} (S')^{-1} = \Sigma_\epsilon.$$

  This assumption thus produces 6 restrictions.
- *Only supply shocks have long-run effects on output.* Let $\Gamma(L) \equiv C(L)S^{-1}$, so that the Wold decomposition (5.27) rewrites as

$$\Delta X_t = C(L)S^{-1} S \epsilon_t = \Gamma(L)v_t. \tag{5.30}$$

  Then

$$\Gamma(1) = \begin{pmatrix} \Gamma_{11}(1) & \Gamma_{12}(1) & \Gamma_{13}(1) \\ \Gamma_{21}(1) & \Gamma_{22}(1) & \Gamma_{23}(1) \\ \Gamma_{31}(1) & \Gamma_{32}(1) & \Gamma_{33}(1) \end{pmatrix} \equiv \sum_{j=0}^{\infty} C_j S^{-1}$$

  denotes the long-run effects of the structural shocks on the system variables. This second assumption is equivalent to posit that

$$\Gamma_{12}(1) = \Gamma_{13}(1) = 0.$$

  This produces two additional restrictions.
- *Money supply shocks have no long-run effects on the real exchange rate.* This last identifying constraint amounts to assume that

$$\Gamma_{23}(1) = 0,$$

  which produces one more constraint.

  These three hypothesis are sufficient to identify the matrix S. To see this, note that

$$\Gamma(1) = C(1)S^{-1} \tag{5.31}$$

with $C(1) \equiv \sum_{j=0}^{\infty} C_j$ and thus the long-run covariance matrix of the system verifies

$$C(1)\Sigma_\epsilon C(1)' = \Gamma(1)\Gamma(1)'.$$

The chosen identification scheme implies that $\Gamma(1)$ is lower-triangular. This matrix can thus be obtained as the Choleski decomposition of the long-run covariance matrix $C(1)\Sigma_\epsilon C(1)'$. Let R be such a lower triangular matrix, then using (5.31), we have

$$S = R^{-1}C(1).$$

From an empirical point of view, once the cointegration rank r has been identified, consistent estimates of the variance–covariance matrix Σ_ϵ and of the long-run multiplier $C(1)$ are provided by estimation and inversion of the VECM model (5.28) (for details see, for example, Warne, 1993).

It should be stressed that the identification constraints retained are identical to the Blanchard and Quah (1989) type identification scheme used by Clarida and Gali (1994). As those authors also worked on the same system of variables as ours, this will allow direct comparisons of our results with their findings.

5.4 Empirical results

5.4.1 The data

The data come from the Datastream base. The home country is Japan and the foreign country the United States. The (log) real GDP differential, $y_t \equiv y_t^h - y_t^f$, is obtained by taking the difference between the logarithm of the real Japanese and the real American GDPs. We use the logarithm of the Japanese and American consumption prices indices to get the (log) price index differential, $p_t \equiv p_t^h - p_t^f$. Lastly, the real exchange rate is obtained from the nominal exchange rate and those price indices by applying the definition, $q_t \equiv s_t - p_t^h + p_t^f$, with s_t the logarithm of the nominal yen/dollar exchange rate. All these data are expressed in monthly frequency[6] and (except the real exchange rate) are seasonally adjusted. Our sample runs from March 1973 to March 2001. Figure 5.1 presents the joint evolution of these variables (taken in difference between the home and the foreign country) over the period of study.

Table 5.1 provides the results of unit-root and stationary tests applied to each three variables. One can check that they lead to the conclusion that y_t, q_t and p_t, are all integrated of order one,[7] as postulated in our statistical model above.

5.4.2 Cointegration tests

Once the integration degree of the data has been selected, the next step in the empirical analysis is to identify the long-run dynamic properties of the system, that is, the rank of $\overline{B}$ in (5.26) or equivalently the rank of Π in (5.28). The well-known Johansen procedure of test (Johansen, 1988, 1991) provides statistical devices to identify the number of cointegration relationships, that is, the rank of the Π matrix in the model (5.28). To apply this test, we must choose the lag length parameter, p, of the regression (5.28) such that the residual obtained from that estimation at least satisfy the non-autocorrelation and conditional homoskedasticity requirements (in which case Johansen's test rely on quasi maximum likelihood estimates). A multivariate portemanteau test and equation by equation ARCH

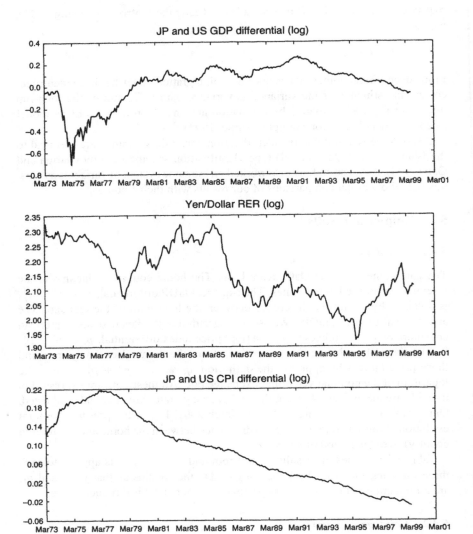

Figure 5.1 Time series of the variables.

effects LM tests (see Lütkepohl, 1991, chapter 4) shows that this is obtained for $p = 5$.

Table 5.2 shows that we cannot reject the null hypothesis that $n - r = 3$ against the alternative that $n - r < 3$ (with n the dimension of X_t), which means that there exists no cointegration relationship between y_t, q_t and p_t or equivalently that Π and thus $\overline{B}$ are of full rank 3. However before rejecting the cointegration hypothesis, we investigate whether this result is due to structural instability of

Table 5.1 Unit–root tests[a,b]

Series	MZ_t^0	MZ_t^μ	$DF-GLS^\mu$	η_μ	MZ_t^τ	$DF-GLS^\tau$	η_τ
y_t	−2.34	−1.72	0.67	2.17**	−2.56	−1.86	0.15*
q_t	−1.06	−2.08	0.26	3.19**	−2.14	−1.55	0.18*
p_t	−2.30	0.59	−0.18	1.93**	−0.72	1.09	0.36**
Δy_t	−6.84**	−8.77**	−11.72**	0.11	—	—	—
Δq_t	−7.46**	−8.06**	−6.02**	0.220	—	—	—
Δp_t	−2.26*	−2.04	−13.65**	0.74*	—	—	—
1%	−2.58	−3.45	−2.58	0.739	−3.99	−3.48	0.216
5%	−1.95	−2.87	−1.95	0.463	−3.43	−2.89	0.146
10%	−1.62	−2.57	−1.62	0.347	−3.13	−2.57	0.119

Notes

* (resp. **) indicates that the statistic is significant at the 5% level (resp. 1% level).

a The autocorrelation order, k, is determined using the specific optimal rules of these different tests. For the Perron and Ng (1996) test, $k = O(T^{1/3})$. For the Elliot *et al.* (1996) test, k is identified by use of an AIC criteria. Lastly for Kwiatkowski *et al.* (1992), $k = O(T^{1/2})$.

b Critical values are obtained from Fuller (1976) for the statistics MZ_t^0, MZ_t^μ, MZ_t^τ and $DF-GLS^\mu$, from Elliot *et al.* (1996) for the statistic $DF-GLS^\tau$ and from Kwiatkowski *et al.* (1992) for the statistics η_μ and η_τ.

Table 5.2 Johansen's test of cointegration whole sample: 1973–2001

$n-r$	Trace[a]	90%	95%
3	24.81	25.03	29.38
2	6.63	13.31	15.34
1	0.66	2.71	3.84

Note

a The test is performed from the estimation of the model (5.28) where the number of lag required to whiten the residuals is identified through a multivariate Portemanteau test and is equal to 5.

the cointegration space. Indeed, Gregory *et al.* (1996) showed that if a cointegrated system is subject to structural shifts which are not taken into account by the modeler, then the cointegrating rank should be strongly underestimated. Yet, as Clarida *et al.* (1998, 2000) recently enlightened, it turns out that most of industrialized countries experienced a major shift in the conduct of their monetary policy at the end of the 1970s, a date that coincides with the arrival of Paul Volcker at the head of the Fed. This modification could have influenced the long-term equilibrium of the economy through a shift in the exogenous monetary policy process, m_t given in (5.20) so that such empirical evidence should also be related to a structural shift in our model.

If we relate the potential structural break in our model with the beginning of Paul Volcker's tenure, that is, October 1979, we can perform a test of cointegration with a structural break (at this specific date) following the methodology

Table 5.3 Cointegration test with a structural break

$n - r$	$\xi_T(\tau_0)^a$	90%	95%
3	300.35*	87.42	94.44
2	44.24	41.71	46.61
1	10.41	9.62	12.64

Note
a The number of lag required to whiten the residuals is identified through a multivariate Portemanteau test and is equal
to 5. The date of the break is October 1979.

developed in Andrade *et al.* (2001). This statistical procedure aims at identifying the cointegrating rank of a system once one allows for a structural break at a
known date in the cointegrating vectors. As for Johansen's procedure, it proceeds
by testing for the null hypothesis that the cointegration rank equals r against the
alternative that it is greater than r. With October 1979 being the date of break, we
obtain the results reported in Table 5.3.

Table 5.3 shows that we reject the null hypothesis that $n - r = 3$ (i.e. $r = 0$). But
we cannot reject the null hypothesis that $n - r = 2$ (i.e. $r = 1$) at the 10 percent
level. We therefore conclude from this second cointegrating rank analysis that
the long-run dynamic properties of the system under study is characterized by
one cointegrating vector which shifts at the date of October 1979. Re-estimating
separately the VECM by (quasi) maximum likelihood over the two sub-regimes
gives us the results provided in Table 5.4 where the matrix Π is decomposed into
$\Pi = \delta\beta'$ and the cointegrating vector β is normalized to one with respect to the
price level differential.[8]

Once structural instability of the system has been recognized, one may ask
wether the long-run relationship identified over the two separate sub-regimes is
stable over each period. To answer that question, we implement Hansen's (1992)
tests of stability in a cointegration relationship for each sub-samples.[9] Table 5.5
gives the results. They show that the we cannot reject the hypothesis of stability of
the cointegration relationship over the pre- and post-Volcker periods. The evidence
is less conclusive for the pre-Volcker episode yet. According to the Mean F test
statistic, the null hypothesis of stability is rejected at the 10 percent significance
level (but not at the at the 5 percent one).

It is remarkable that, working on the same trivariate system (but with quarterly
data and over a 1975–1992 sample), Clarida and Gali (1994) found no statistical evidence of cointegration between these same three variables. We confirm
their result if we investigate the whole sample and do not introduce the case for
structural instability. However, long-run co-movements between output and price
differentials and the real exchange rate show up once the structural instability is
accounted for. One of Clarida and Gali's (1994) main result was that a substantial
part of real exchange rate fluctuations comes from money supply shocks. The next
section investigates whether their conclusion is preserved once the cointegration
property enlightened is taken into account in the empirical analysis.

Table 5.4 Estimation of the VECM model (5.28)

Pre-Volcker period: 1973–1979			
Variables are ordered into: (y_t, q_t, p_t)			
β'	-0.139	-1.139	1
δ'	0.010	-0.001	-0.020
Order of the VECM:			$p = 5$

Residuals autocorrelation (joint tests)

Stat.	LM(1)	LM(4)	LM(12)
Value	5.84	8.29	3.22
p-value	0.75	0.51	0.96

ARCH effects

Stat.	LM(4)	LM(4)	LM(4)
Value	6.25	5.26	4.39
p-value	0.18	0.26	0.35

Post-Volcker period: 1979–2001			
Variables are ordered into: (y_t, q_t, p_t)			
β'	-0.248	-0.408	1
δ'	-0.0010	-0.0014	-0.0003
Order of the VECM:			$p = 6$

Residuals autocorrelation(joint tests)

Stat.	LM(1)	LM(4)	LM(12)
Value	5.46	5.14	6.03
p-value	0.79	0.82	0.74

ARCH effects

Stat.	LM(4)	LM(4)	LM(4)
Value	1.32	4.32	1.06
p-value	0.86	0.36	0.90

Table 5.5 Stability of the cointegrating vector (Hansen, 1992)

Pre-Volcker period: 1973–1979			
Statistic	Sup$F$	Mean$F$	L_c
Value	8.67	5.37	0.30
p-value	>0.20	0.08	0.16
Post-Volcker period: 1979–2001			
Statistic	Sup$F$	Mean$F$	L_c
Value	2.23	0.68	0.06
p-value	>0.20	>0.20	>0.20

5.4.3 Shocks

The previous section identified the long-run dynamic properties of the system studied by means of cointegration tests. We now use the estimation of the associated VECM as the identification scheme described in Section 5.3 to assess the qualitative and quantitative effects of the three structural sources of shocks postulated – supply, demand and monetary policy – by the standard mean of IRFs and FEVDs analysis. We focus on the post-Volcker period of our sample, that is, 1979–2001.

Impulse response functions

Figure 5.2 displays the cumulated response (or level response) of each variable of the system to unpredictable supply, demand and monetary shocks along with their 80 percent confidence interval bands.

Let us start by the analysis of real shocks effects on the system, and in particular the real exchange rate. A positive one standard deviation supply shock (i.e. in favor of Japan) has a permanent positive impact on Japanese output compared with the United States. This shock also induces an immediate real appreciation of nearly 0.7 percent of the yen against the dollar (remember that when q_t falls, the yen appreciates against the dollar) and a long-run effect of 0.6 percent appreciation. The supply shock impact on prices differential is instantaneously negative but positive (or non-significant) in the long run. A positive one standard deviation demand shock (i.e. a demand shock in favor of Japan) temporarily increases output in Japan compared with the United States. It also induces a 0.9 percent impact and 0.4 percent permanent real devaluation of the yen against the dollar and a permanent positive reaction in the price index differential. Short-term rigidities preclude immediate adjustment of the economy to its long-run equilibrium and thus generate real exchange rate overshooting in the wake of these real shocks.

Those long-run real shocks effects can be interpreted in the light of the two-country model studied previously. They correspond to the configuration where the fixed part of the national expenditure shares in imported goods, $1 - \alpha$, is greater than $\frac{1}{2}$. A supply shock in favor of Japan prompts the Japanese firms to lower their prices to a greater extent than the American ones. As each domestic price index reaction is dominated by importers' pricing decisions, the Japanese price level rises relatively to the American one. This in turn produces a real appreciation of the yen compared with the dollar. The effects of a demand shock in favor of Japanese goods are symmetric with a positive demand shock in favor of the Japan inducing the Japanese firms to raise their prices to a greater extent than the American ones. Again, remember that this particular parametric configuration, $\alpha < \frac{1}{2}$, only implies that the demand elasticity for imported good is relatively lower than the one for domestic goods when their prices are equalized which implies that the import price reactions to real shocks dominate in national price indices. It thus does not mean that there is reversed home-bias (a bias in favor of imported goods) effect. Moreover, the fact that the domestic price indices reaction is dominated by imported prices variations only applies to the effects of asymmetric shocks which are analyzed here.

Now we turn to the monetary shock transmission to the system. An asymmetric expansionary monetary shock in Japan generates a transitory rise in Japan output relatively to the United States. In accordance with the classical overshooting mechanism, this expansionary monetary shock produces an immediate real depreciation of the yen against the dollar and then a steady appreciation until the

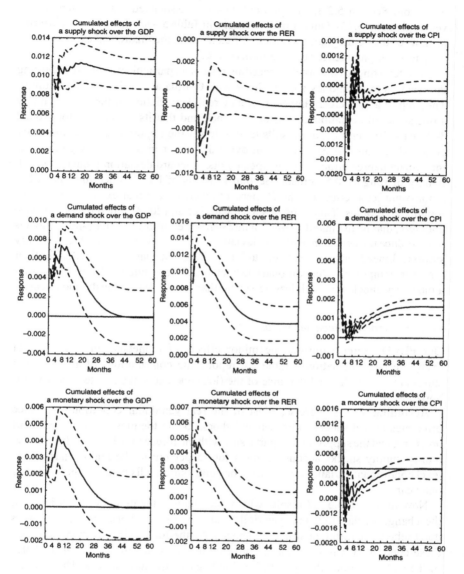

Figure 5.2 Cumulated IRF to structural shocks – post-Volcker period.

real exchange rate goes back to its initial value. The price differential reaction is positive at the impact and zero in the long run. Monetary policy differentials do not have any long-run component. This does not stem from our identification scheme but rather from the fact that there are only two sources of non-stationarity in this economy. The IRF analysis thus makes clear that both sources are real. Remark that, from Section 5.2.3, this particular case is associated with a cointegrating vector given in (5.25). Our estimation results in Table 5.4 are thus coherent in terms of signs of the cointegrating vector coefficients with the theoretical expression for the particular parametric configuration $\alpha < \frac{1}{2}$.

It is interesting to contrast the preceding results, in particular the ones concerning the reaction to the money supply shock with Clarida and Gali's (1994) findings. They report a 3.4 percent impact currency real depreciation of the country hit by a one standard deviation expansionary shock and that its effects last for around 3–4 years. By contrast, our results tend to lower the importance of the monetary policy shock on real exchange rate dynamics. First in terms of magnitude, as the impact depreciation to an unexpected one standard deviation monetary shock is only of roughly 0.5 percent. Second in terms of length since this shock has a non-significant effect (at the 20 percent level) on the real exchange rate after roughly 20 months. This mitigates what Chari *et al.* (2002) called the *persistence anomaly*, that is, the inability of dynamic general equilibrium sticky-price models to reproduce the persistence of PPP deviations that follow an asymmetric monetary surprise. Indeed, once the real yen/dollar exchange rate data are corrected for their long-run components, (conditional) business-cycle frequency PPP deviations after a monetary shock are much less persistent than has been previously documented.

Forecast error variance decomposition

Our FEVD exercise mirrors the minor effects of monetary surprises on real exchange rate fluctuations. Table 5.6 reports the contributions of all structural shocks to the conditional variance of the (log) real exchange rate level at various horizons.

According to this exercise, most of the real yen/dollar conditional variance originates in real shocks, with demand shocks being the most important at short horizons, and the supply shocks part rising with the forecasting horizon. In contrast, money supply shocks account at most for 15 percent of the real exchange rate level conditional variance on impact. The contribution falls below 10 percent after one year.

Now turn to Table 5.7 results which decomposes the conditional variance of the change in the (log) real yen/dollar rate for various horizons into fractions due to the three different structural shocks. As the forecasting horizon increases, these conditional variance shares converge to the unconditional variance shares of the real yen/dollar changes attributable to each structural shocks. This convergence is quite rapid. Again, the most important share is associated with demand shocks with more than 50 percent and the lowest to monetary shocks with less than 15 percent.

Let us again compare our results with Clarida and Gali's (1994) conclusions. Their similar FEVD exercises show that nearly 35 percent of the conditional forecast error variance in the real yen/dollar levels can be explained by nominal shocks on impact and at a 1 year horizon. They also provide evidence that the money supply shocks account for roughly 35 percent of the real yen/dollar variations

Table 5.6 Forecast error variance decomposition – post-Volcker period real exchange rate levels, q_t

Horizon	Contribution[a]		
	Supply shock	Demand shock	Monetary shock
Impact	0.325	0.529	0.146
1	0.338	0.556	0.105
	(0.301–0.375)	(0.500–0.611)	(0.087–0.125)
3	0.329	0.583	0.088
	(0.270–0.387)	(0.495–0.667)	(0.063–0.117)
9	0.259	0.655	0.086
	(0.156–0.377)	(0.468–0.808)	(0.038–0.154)
12	0.238	0.675	0.086
	(0.130–0.369)	(0.468–0.837)	(0.033–0.163)
24	0.249	0.675	0.075
	(0.116–0.413)	(0.422-0.861)	(0.023–0.164)
36	0.299	0.635	0.064
	(0.141–0.482)	(0.370–0.838)	(0.021–0.148)

Note
a The numbers in brackets give the 10% and 90% critical values of the different shocks contribution distribution, computed by bootstrapping method with 500 draws from the estimated asymptotic distribution of the VECM parameters.

Table 5.7 Forecast error variance decomposition – post-Volcker period real exchange rate changes, Δq_t

Horizon	Contribution[a]		
	Supply shock	Demand shock	Monetary shock
Impact	0.324	0.529	0.145
1	0.330	0.542	0.129
	(0.301–0.360)	(0.507–0.560)	(0.127–0.132)
3	0.330	0.539	0.130
	(0.303–0.356)	(0.499–0.560)	(0.127–0.132)
9	0.348	0.522	0.130
	(0.347–0.350)	(0.508–0.532)	(0.128–0.132)
12	0.348	0.522	0.130
	(0.347–0.349)	(0.511–528)	(0.129–0.132)
24	0.345	0.515	0.130
	(0.342–0.347)	(0.511–0.519)	(0.129–0.131)
36	0.345	0.515	0.130
	(0.342–0.347)	(0.511–0.519)	(0.129–0.131)

Note
a The numbers in brackets give the 10% and 90% critical values of the different shocks contribution distribution, computed by bootstrapping method with 500 draws from the estimated asymptotic distribution of the VECM parameters.

unconditional variance. Moreover almost none of these conditional or unconditional variances could be attributed to supply shocks. These results contrast sharply with our evidence. By leaving aside the cointegration property of the set of variables, these authors may have merged monetary shocks with demand and supply shocks components. Loosely speaking, setting $\Pi = 0$ in (5.28) while it is not the case actually reports the error-correcting influence on the system dynamics to the residuals and therefore to the identified structural shocks.

5.5   Conclusion

This chapter provides some new empirical results on real exchange rate fluctuations sources based on the analysis of the yen/dollar case. The constraints required to identify structural shocks from the data are motivated by the analysis of a two-country dynamic general equilibrium model with optimizing agents and where monopolistically competitive firms face translog households demand. This model allows for long-run (flexible prices) PPP deviations and also cointegration constraints on the system long-run dynamics. This cointegration property is not rejected by the data once potential structural instability is taken into account. Taking this long-run constraint and the associated error-correcting mechanism of the system's dynamics into account significantly modify previous results on real and nominal shocks relative contributions to the yen/dollar real exchange rate fluctuations. First, the contribution of monetary policy shocks is significantly reduced, even for short horizons. This result does not mean that monetary authorities are unable to manage exchange rate fluctuations but rather that the non-systematic component of monetary policy accounts for only a reduced part of the observed PPP deviations. Second, the length of the real exchange rate transitory deviations from its long-run equilibrium level in the wake of that nominal shock is also sensibly lower than in previous studies. PPP deviations appear to be much less persistent than previously documented if one takes into account the non-stationary real long-run determinants of the real exchange rate. Although they apply to a particular case, these results stress that theoretical models of real exchange rate dynamics should also focus on real determinants to account for both their business and low-frequencies fluctuations.

Notes

1 See, for example, Chari *et al.* (2002) for details.
2 It should be remarked that, from (5.12) and (5.13), this particular specification of demand shocks sets the deviations from the law of one price to zero. Still long-run PPP deviations may occur in that framework.
3 This would not hold if one relaxes the assumption on demand shocks: $d_{it}^{h} = d_{it}^{f}, i = 1, 2$. In that more general case, the price index differential would be a non-linear function of demand shocks, (log) marginal costs and the (log) exchange rate.
4 It is possible to modify the standard CES specification in a way that allows the weight of domestic and foreign prices to differ in the aggregate index (see Warnock, 1998). But this implies that there is an exogenous home bias effect: at any relative prices, consumption in domestic goods exceed consumption of imports. Rather, the translog specification with

$\alpha \neq \frac{1}{2}$ does not impose any systematic occurrence of such phenomena. If it holds, it stems from each good demand elasticity differences and firms' pricing interactions.

5 See, for example, chapter 10 in Obstfeld and Rogoff (1996) for details.

6 Quarterly GDP's data are transformed into monthly ones by use of a monthly industrial production index and the Chow–Lin method (Chow and Lin, 1976).

7 The decision is not obvious for the price index differential. We chose the integration order after computing the DF – GLS$^\mu$ test statistic with a deterministic trend in the price index differential (and a constant term into the inflation differential).

8 Implementing two separate Johansen's rank test procedures over these two separate sub-samples also led to the conclusion that $r = 1$ for each of them.

9 The author provides different procedures of test which corresponds to different formulations of the instability alternative: a unique break of unknown timing into the sample or drifting stochastic parameters over the whole sample.

6 Beliefs-based exchange rate dynamics

Fabrice Collard and Patrick Fève

6.1 Introduction

Obstfeld and Rogoff (2000b) identify six major puzzles in international macroeconomics, among which we think one of the most important is to explain *why are exchange rates so volatile and so apparently disconnected from fundamentals?* (Obstfeld and Rogoff, 2000b, p. 2). Indeed, the exchange rate is the key relative price in international transactions which exerts potential feedback in the whole real side of an open economy. Most existing models in international macroeconomics have difficulties accounting for the high volatility of the exchange rate. One explanation for this result lies in the fact that, in these models, the dynamics of the nominal exchange rate essentially depends on the domestic and foreign real consumption streams. It therefore inherits the excess smoothness of consumption. However, some recently developed models have proven to be helpful in accounting for the dynamics of the nominal exchange rate and explaining its high volatility (see Betts and Devereux, 1996; Engel, 1996; Hau, 2000; Chari *et al.*, 2002, among others). In these models, the nominal exchange rate dynamics is fully related to that of fundamentals and most of the successes in accounting for the nominal exchange rate volatility stem from assumptions imposed on the structure of international trade (pricing to market, price stickiness). Recently, Hairault *et al.* (2001) proposed a small open economy version of Fuerst (1992) or Christiano (1991). Their model generates a persistent liquidity effect, and therefore – through the uncovered interest rate parity – a persistent overshooting of the nominal exchange rate following a money supply injection for high enough adjustment costs on money holdings. This mechanism is sufficient to account for the nominal exchange rate volatility. Common to all these models is the fact that they assume the existence of frictions that either affect the price-setting behavior or the revelation of information to obtain a satisfying monetary transmission mechanism to account for high enough exchange rate volatility.

In this chapter, we follow another route and go back to the initial monetary models approach, keeping the full price flexibility and complete information assumptions. We introduce intertemporal complementarities in consumption decisions in an open economy monetary model where money is held because households face a cash-in-advance constraint. More important is the fact that households' preferences are characterized by habit persistence, introducing time non-separability in the model. Habit persistence has proven to be a relevant assumption for representing preferences, and helpful for understanding several puzzles (see e.g. Deaton, 1992; Lettau and Uhlig, 1995; Beaudry and Guay, 1996; Boldrin *et al.*, 2001), in particular asset pricing puzzles (see e.g. Constantidines, 1990; Campbell and Cochrane, 1999).

We first show that – in our model economy – high enough habit persistence generates real indeterminacy. It results from the interplay between habit persistence and the cash-in-advance constraint. Indeed, when individuals face the same positive belief on future inflation, higher expected inflation leads them to substitute current for future consumption, thereby increasing their habits. This translates into higher money demand for tomorrow when habit persistence is strong enough, putting upward pressure on prices. Then, inflation expectations become self-fulfilling. One interesting feature of this result lies in its ability to account for the disconnection of the nominal (and the real) exchange rate from the underlying fundamentals such as interest rates, output and money supply. Indeed, when the equilibrium paths are not determinate, beliefs matter. In other words, there exists an infinite number of beliefs functions which are consistent with the rational expectation equilibrium. Nevertheless, we show that real indeterminacy is not sufficient per se to account for the dynamics of the exchange rate. When beliefs are not correlated with money injection, the model generates perfect price flexibility and money is neutral. Then the nominal exchange rate behaves exactly as in the flexible price monetary model, and does not display enough volatility. Conversely, when beliefs are correlated with money injections, the model mimics price stickiness and magnifies the volatility of the nominal exchange rate. Moreover, in this case, the propagation mechanism at play in the model is strong enough to create persistence in the dynamics of the nominal exchange rate. Furthermore, it can lead to overshooting. The model therefore highlights the importance of beliefs in the determination of the nominal exchange rate.

The chapter is organized as follows. Section 6.2 presents our benchmark model economy, insisting on the individual's behavior. Section 6.3 characterizes the local dynamic properties of the model and discusses the conditions under which real indeterminacy occurs. After explaining the failure of the basic flexible prices cash-in-advance model, Section 6.4 discusses the role of beliefs in exchange rate dynamics. The last section offers some concluding remarks.

6.2 The model economy

This section presents a two-country monetary model in which preferences are characterized by habit persistence. Although we do not explicitly model the foreign economy, this is not a small open economy model as all prices are endogenously determined for the domestic economy. We first present the domestic economy, insisting on the modelling of preferences. We then present the rest of the world economy and finally characterize the equilibrium.

6.2.1   The domestic economy

The domestic economy is comprised of a unit mass continuum of identical infinitely lived agents, so that we will assume that there exists a representative household in the economy. Like in Backus *et al.* (1992), we assume that each country specializes in the production of an internationally traded local good, which is imperfectly substitutable with the goods produced abroad. The domestic good is traded on a perfectly competitive market and produced by means of labor according to a constant returns-to-scale technology, represented by the production function

$$y_t = h_t. \tag{6.1}$$

Profit maximization then implies that the real wage is given by $w_t = P_{h,t}/P_t$ in equilibrium, where $P_{h,t}$ is the price of the domestic good expressed in domestic currency and P_t is the aggregate price level that will be defined later.

The household then consumes a bundle of both goods (c_t) composed of both domestic ($c_{h,t}$) and foreign ($c_{f,t}$) produced goods, described by the following constant elasticity of substitution (CES) aggregator:

$$c_t = \left[\omega^{1/\rho} c_{h,t}^{(\rho-1)/\rho} + (1-\omega)^{1/\rho} c_{f,t}^{(\rho-1)/\rho}\right]^{\rho/(\rho-1)}, \tag{6.2}$$

where $\rho \in (0, \infty)$ is the elasticity of substitution between foreign and domestic goods. $(1 - \omega) \in [0; 1]$ is the import share. The optimal composition of the consumption basket is then determined by minimizing the overall expenditures, $P_{h,t}c_{h,t} + e_t P_{f,t}^\star c_{f,t}$, taking (6.2) into account. This yields the following demand functions:

$$c_{h,t} = \left(\frac{P_{h,t}}{P_t}\right)^{-\rho} \omega c_t \quad \text{and} \quad c_{f,t} = \left(\frac{e_t P_{f,t}^\star}{P_t}\right)^{-\rho} (1-\omega) c_t, \tag{6.3}$$

where $P_{h,t}$ and $P_{f,t}^\star$, respectively, denote the domestic and foreign production prices expressed in the currency of the producer. e_t is the nominal exchange rate and P_t is the consumption price level which is expressed as

$$P_t = [\omega P_{h,t}^{1-\rho} + (1-\omega)(e_t P_{f,t}^\star)^{1-\rho}]^{1/(1-\rho)}. \tag{6.4}$$

Given this intratemporal allocation of resources, the household takes her intertemporal decisions. She enters period t with nominal balances M_t brought into period t from the previous period and net real foreign assets (b_t), as a means to transfer wealth from one period to another. The household supplies her hours on the labor market at the real wage w_t. During the period, she also receives a lump-sum transfer from the monetary authorities in the form of cash equal to N_t and interest rate payments from bond holdings ($P_t r_{t-1} b_t$), where r_{t-1} is the real interest rate. All these revenues are then used to purchase a consumption bundle c_t, money balances and net foreign assets for the next period. Therefore, the budget constraint simply writes as:[1]

$$P_t b_{t+1} + M_{t+1} + P_t c_t \leqslant (1 + r_{t-1}) P_t b_t + P_t w_t h_t + M_t + N_t. \qquad (6.5)$$

Implicit in this budget constraint is that bonds are denominated in local currency.[2] Money is held because the household must carry cash – money acquired in the previous period and the money lump-sum transfer – in order to purchase goods. She therefore faces a standard cash-in-advance constraint of the form:

$$P_t c_t \leqslant M_t + N_t + (1 + r_{t-1}) P_t b_t - P_t b_{t+1}. \qquad (6.6)$$

Note that, we will focus next on equilibria where the gross nominal interest rate exceeds unity or equivalently where the inflation rate is strictly positive. The constraint will therefore bind in each and every period.[3]

Each household has preferences over consumption and leisure represented by the following intertemporal utility function:

$$E_t \sum_{\tau=t}^{\infty} \beta^{\tau-t} (\log(s_\tau) - \kappa h_\tau), \qquad (6.7)$$

where $\beta \in (0, 1)$ is the discount factor, h_t denotes the number of hours supplied by the household. As it will be made explicit later, s_t is a consumption index from which the household derives utility. E_t denotes the expectation operator conditional on the information set available in period t. The linearity of disutility in labor is assumed for simplicity[4] and corresponds to Hansen's (1985) labor indivisibility assumption. An attractive feature of this specification is that the model can be directly compared against the standard cash-in-advance economy considered by Cooley and Hansen (1989, 1995).

This specification of the utility function implicitly allows for habit persistence in the consumption behavior, through the s_t index, and therefore introduce time non-separability in the utility function. More precisely, following Constantidines and Ferson (1991) and Braun *et al.* (1993), we consider that s_t takes the form:

$$s_t = c_t - \theta c_{t-1} \quad \text{with } \theta \in (0, 1) \qquad (6.8)$$

such that the household values current and previous period consumption streams. In other words, preferences display internal habit persistence, which we assume to be specified in difference with one lag. Note that setting θ to zero, we retrieve a standard cash-in-advance model for an open economy.

The household then determines her optimal consumption/money/assets holdings and labor supply plans maximizing (6.7) subject to the budget (6.5) and cash-in-advance (6.6) constraints, yielding the following first-order optimality conditions:

$$\frac{1}{c_t - \theta c_{t-1}} - E_t \left[\frac{\beta \theta}{c_{t+1} - \theta c_t} \right] = \beta E_t \left[(1 + r_t) \left(\frac{1}{c_{t+1} - \theta c_t} - \frac{\beta \theta}{c_{t+2} - \theta c_{t+1}} \right) \right],$$
(6.9)

$$\frac{\kappa}{w_t} = \beta E_t \left[\frac{P_t}{P_{t+1}} \left(\frac{1}{c_{t+1} - \theta c_t} - \frac{\beta \theta}{c_{t+2} - \theta c_{t+1}} \right) \right].$$
(6.10)

The first equation furnishes the demand for bond holdings, while the second relationship is actually a demand for money.

Finally, money is exogenously supplied by the central bank according to the following money growth rule:

$$M_{t+1}^s = g_t M_t^s,$$
(6.11)

where $g_t \geqslant 1$ is the exogenous gross rate of growth of money, such that $N_t = M_{t+1}^s - M_t^s = (g_t - 1)M_t^s$. Hereafter, we will assume, following Cooley and Hansen (1989), that g_t evolves as an exogenous AR(1) process,

$$\widehat{g}_{t+1} = \rho_g \widehat{g}_t + \varepsilon_{t+1}^g,$$

where $\widehat{g}_t \equiv \log(g_t/\overline{g})$, $|\rho_g| < 1$ and ε^g is a centered Gaussian white noise with variance σ_ε^2.

6.2.2   The rest of the world

Following Cole and Ohanian (1999), we simplify the analysis and abstract from production and consumption/savings (including money holdings) decisions. At first glance, this assumption leads to consider a small open economy model in which the rest of the world is taken as given. However, our model economy departs from a small open economy as we allow for some feedback from the domestic economy to the rest of the world. Indeed, shock in the domestic economy will affect the price level in the rest of the world through the optimal intratemporal allocation of consumption between domestic and foreign goods. More precisely, the representative household in the rest of the world consumes a consumption bundle $(c_t^\star)$ composed of both domestic $(c_{h,t}^\star)$ and foreign $(c_{f,t}^\star)$ produced goods:

$$c_t^\star = \left[(1 - \omega)^{1/\rho} c_{h,t}^{\star(\rho-1)/\rho} + \omega^{1/\rho} c_{f,t}^{\star(\rho-1)/\rho} \right]^{\rho/(\rho-1)},$$
(6.12)

where the elasticity of substitution between goods ($\rho \in (0, \infty)$) and the import share ($(1 - \omega) \in [0; 1]$) are assumed to be the same as in the domestic economy. Since we leave aside the determination of the consumption behavior, the sequence $\{c_t^\star\}_{t=0}^\infty$ is an exogenous – possibly stochastic – sequence.[5] As in the domestic economy, the optimal composition of the consumption basket is determined by minimizing the overall expenditures, taking (6.12) into account. This yields the following demand functions:

$$c_{h,t}^* = \left(\frac{P_{h,t}}{e_t P_t^*}\right)^{-\rho} (1 - \omega) c_t^* \quad \text{and} \quad c_{f,t}^* = \left(\frac{P_{f,t}^*}{P_t^*}\right)^{-\rho} \omega c_t^*, \tag{6.13}$$

where P_t^* is the consumption price which is expressed as

$$P_t^* = \left[(1 - \omega)\left(\frac{P_{h,t}}{e_t}\right)^{1-\rho} + \omega P_{f,t}^{*1-\rho}\right]^{1/(1-\rho)}. \tag{6.14}$$

Output in the rest of the domestic economy is also given by an exogenous sequence $\{y_t^*\}_{t=0}^{\infty}$. This hypothesis amounts to imposing that production capacities in the rest of the world are left unaffected by a shock occurring in the domestic economy.

The exogeneity of the world demand and world production capacities does not imply that the rest of the world is totally nonresponsive to shocks in the domestic economy. Indeed, any domestic shock affects the relative price between foreign and domestic goods. This will translate into a reallocation of consumption purchases between goods produced in the domestic economy and in the rest of the world. Likewise, the consumption-based price index (CPI) will be affected. Therefore, this model does not represent a small open economy, since price effects still exert an impact in the rest of the world.[6] Note that although aggregate output and consumption are taken to be exogenous in the foreign economy, the intratemporal allocation of consumption between foreign and domestic goods is endogenous. A direct implication of the latter assumption is that all prices are determined by market clearing conditions and are therefore endogenous.

6.2.3 The equilibrium

An equilibrium[7] of this economy is a sequence of prices $\{P_t, P_t^*, P_{h,t}, P_{f,t}^*, e_t, w_t, r_t\}_{t=0}^{\infty}$ and a sequence of quantities $\{c_t, c_{h,t}, c_{f,t}, c_{h,t}^*, c_{f,t}^*, y_t, h_t, m_{t+1}, b_{t+1}\}_{t=0}^{\infty}$ such that

(i) Given a sequence of prices, the sequence of quantities solves the firm's and the household's problem;
(ii) Given a sequence of quantities, the sequence of prices clears the markets.

Goods market clearing condition implies:

$$y_t = c_{h,t} + c_{h,t}^*, \tag{6.15}$$

$$y_t^* = c_{f,t} + c_{f,t}^*. \tag{6.16}$$

The labor market clearing in the domestic economy imposes $y_t = h_t$ and the money market clearing requires

$$M_{t+1} = M_{t+1}^s = M_t^s + N_t. \tag{6.17}$$

The domestic current account is given by

$$P_t b_{t+1} = (1 + r_{t-1}) P_t b_t + P_{h,t} c^\star_{h,t} - e_t P^\star_{f,t} c_{f,t} \tag{6.18}$$

and the current account in the foreign economy then satisfies

$$P^\star_t b^\star_{t+1} = (1 + r_{t-1}) P^\star_t b^\star_t + P^\star_{f,t} c_{f,t} - \frac{P_{h,t}}{e_t} c^\star_{h,t}. \tag{6.19}$$

Asset market clearing finally imposes that $b_{t+1} + b^\star_{t+1} = 0$ in each and every period, which translates in the world aggregate resources constraint to

$$P_{h,t} y_t + e_t P^\star_{f,t} y^\star_t = P_t c_t + e_t P^\star_t c^\star_t.$$

In order to study the dynamic properties of the model, we deflate each nominal variable for nominal growth. We therefore define the set of variables $p_t = P_t/M_t$, $p^\star_t = e_{t-1} P^\star_t/M_t$, $p_{h,t} = P_{h,t}/M_t$, $\Delta e_t = e_t/e_{t-1}$ and $p^\star_{f,t} = e_{t-1} P^\star_{f,t}/M_t$. Note that one of the prices cannot be determined in this setting because we did not specify either producer price-setting behavior or any cash-in-advance constraint in the rest of the world, such that one equation is missing. Therefore, $p^\star_{f,t}$ will be assumed to be exogenous in the sequel.[8]

Hereafter, and to keep things simple, we will assume that all exogenous sequences will be set to constants such that $c^\star_t = c^\star$, $y^\star_t = y^\star$ and $p^\star_{f,t} = p^\star_f = 1$.

6.3   Dynamic properties

This section investigates the dynamic properties of our model economy, putting emphasis on the aggregate dynamics in the domestic economy. More precisely, it characterizes conditions on the level of habit persistence for real indeterminacy to occur and discuss these results.

6.3.1   Habit persistence and indeterminacy

The dynamic properties of output are strongly related to the perfect foresight version of the model economy. First of all, note that when the two economies are perfectly symmetric, we have

$$y = y^\star = h = h^\star = c = c^\star,$$

further, we have

$$p = p^\star = p_h = p^\star_f = \Delta e = 1.$$

Therefore, in the steady state, output is given by:

$$y^\star = \frac{\beta}{g} \frac{1 - \beta\theta}{\kappa(1 - \theta)}.$$

The local dynamic properties of our model economy may then be investigated taking a first order log-linear approximation[9] about the deterministic steady state, which yields the following linear second-order finite difference equation:

$$\widehat{y}_{t+2} - \left[\frac{1+\beta}{\beta} + \frac{(1-\omega)(1-\theta)(1-\beta\theta)}{2\omega\rho\beta\theta} \right] \widehat{y}_{t+1}$$

$$+ \left[\frac{1}{\beta} - \frac{(1-\theta)(1-\theta\beta)}{\beta\theta} \right] \widehat{y}_t = 0, \tag{6.20}$$

where $\widehat{y}_t = (y_t - y^\star)/y^\star$. Equation (6.20) can be expressed in the more compact form:

$$(1 - \lambda L)(1 - \mu L)\widehat{y}_{t+2} = 0,$$

where L denotes the lag operator. The position of λ and μ around the unit circle determines the local dynamic properties of the log-linear economy. The model satisfies a saddle path property if and only if both λ and μ lie outside the unit circle. Conversely, if at least one of the eigenvalues lies inside the unit circle the equilibrium is locally indeterminate – that is, there exists a continuum of equilibria in the neighborhood of the steady state. First of all, we can establish the following property.[10]

Proposition 1 *There exists $\theta^\star \in (0, 1)$ such that for all $\theta \geqslant \theta^\star$ one and only one eigenvalue lies inside the unit circle.*

Proposition 1 establishes that – for a given value of the discount factor (β) – there exists a value of the weight of habit persistence above which equilibria paths are indeterminate.

Figure 6.1 illustrates Proposition 1 and this discussion. The two curves represent the evolution of the two roots of the characteristic polynomial and show that one of the two roots always remains greater than unity. The shaded area corresponds to values of θ for which the equilibrium is totally determinate. Above $\theta^\star$ the equilibrium becomes indeterminate. It is worth noting that as θ tends to 1, the stable root tends to one. Further, as can be seen from Figure 6.1, the stable root is positive for high level of habit persistence. This leads to the following proposition.

Proposition 2 *There exists a threshold $\widetilde{\theta} \in (\theta^\star, 1)$ such that the stable root is strictly positive.*

An implication of this last result is that there exists values for the habit persistence parameter such that output is positively serially correlated, which is consistent with the observed persistence in aggregate data. This contrasts with the standard cash-in-advance model that generates no persistence, when the money growth process – if assumed to be exogenous – is serially uncorrelated. The latter proposition therefore establishes that the cash-in-advance model, when coupled with habit persistence, possesses internal propagation mechanisms strong enough to generate persistence. Beyond this, the proposition states that, in this model, persistence goes together with real indeterminacy, as $\widetilde{\theta} > \theta^\star$. Another interesting result is

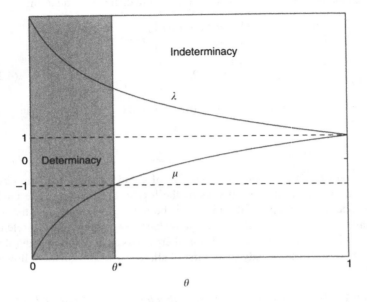

Figure 6.1 Roots of the characteristic polynomial.

that oscillatory sunspot equilibria may also occur as for values of $\theta \in (\theta^\star, \widetilde{\theta})$, the stable eigenvalue is strictly negative. It should however be noted, that, in this case, output is negatively serially correlated which is not empirically appealing.

6.3.2 Discussion

This section sheds light on the underlying mechanisms that are at work in the model. We first investigate the real indeterminacy result. Then, we characterize the behavior of all other aggregates of interest.

In an equilibrium, the dynamics of the economy may be rewritten as

$$\kappa = \beta E_t \vartheta_{t+1} \left[\frac{1}{c_{t+1} - \theta c_t} - \frac{\beta \theta}{c_{t+2} - \theta c_{t+1}} \right], \tag{6.21}$$

where ϑ_{t+1} denotes the inflation tax in the economy – taken as given by the individuals when determining their optimal plans. The inflation tax, expressed in terms of CPI, can be viewed as an increasing marginal tax function of future aggregate consumption – taken as given by individuals.

Let us assume that the utility function of the household is time separable ($\theta = 0$), the study of the dynamics of the economy reduces to the study of

$$\kappa = \beta E_t \left[\vartheta_{t+1} \frac{1}{c_{t+1}} \right]. \tag{6.22}$$

The latter equation makes it clear that the household makes an arbitrage between demanding more leisure in order to avoid the inflation tax (left-hand side of the Euler equation) and postponing consumption – by holding more money – that will deliver an after inflation tax expected utility in the next period (right-hand side of the Euler equation). Note that the linearity of preferences with respect to leisure simplifies the analysis as the problem reduces to the analysis of consumption decision in the presence of an inflation tax. Assume now that all individuals have the same positive belief on future inflation. This leads every individual to increase current consumption to escape the future inflation tax.[11] Since intertemporal substitution is high, individual consumption drops in the next period. Since all individuals are identical and face the same belief, aggregate consumption drops in the next period. Therefore, the inflation tax shall decrease, which cannot support inflation beliefs. Any change in beliefs can only be due to monetary policy, and is therefore related to fundamental shocks.

Let us now consider the case where habit persistence is large enough to weaken intertemporal substitution motives ($\theta \gg 0$) and that all individuals again face the same positive belief on future inflation. Like in the previous case, individuals consume more today. But, contrary to the preceding case, the irreversibility in consumption decisions associated with habit persistence leads the agents to increase their future individual consumption too. Since, they are all identical and face the same belief, aggregate future consumption eventually increases. It follows that the aggregate inflation tax increases, therefore supporting the initial individual beliefs. Note that these beliefs may now depart from fundamentals – even though they can be arbitrarily correlated to fundamentals.

We now turn to the analysis of the other aggregates of our model economy, given the consumption dynamics in response to a monetary shock. Let us first consider the domestic PPI. The log-linearized PPI is simply given by[12]

$$\widehat{p}_{h,t} = \widehat{g}_t - \widehat{c}_t. \tag{6.23}$$

Equation (6.23) enables us to understand the behavior of the production price index (PPI) over the Business Cycle in equilibrium. Indeed, let us first consider a situation where money is totally neutral in the economy – leaving unaffected the level of consumption – any money injection translates into a one for one increase in PPI. Let us now consider that equilibrium is indeterminate and agents have positive beliefs in the face of a money injection,[13] then consumption may rise sufficiently to weaken the inflationary effects of monetary policy. There may also be a situation where beliefs are strong enough to totally offset inflationary pressure, such that the PPI is rigid in the short-run.

Figure 6.2 illustrates such a situation. It makes clear that beliefs actually create a supply-side effect that makes the PPI nonresponsive in equilibrium. Indeed, following a monetary injection, demand shifts upward, which would solely trigger an increase in prices should supply be nonresponsive (this corresponds to the situation when money is neutral). If beliefs are positively correlated with the money injection, as already explained, labor supply shifts upward to sustain the increase

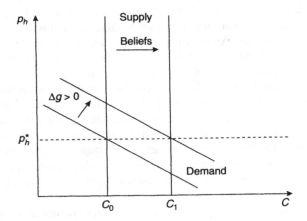

Figure 6.2 Beliefs and equilibrium PPI.

in consumption. This corresponds to a positive supply shock that shifts the supply, which may, in some cases, exactly offset the upward pressure on prices.

Since the CPI is given by

$$\widehat{p}_t = \widehat{g}_t - \left(1 - \frac{1-\omega}{2\omega\rho}\right)\widehat{c}_t, \tag{6.24}$$

it will respond to a money injection even if the PPI remains unchanged, when $\omega \in (0,1)$ and $\rho < \infty$. Indeed, the latter equation may be rewritten as

$$\widehat{p}_t = \widehat{p}_{h,t} + \frac{1-\omega}{2\omega\rho}\widehat{c}_t.$$

In other words, assuming that the PPI is rigid in the short run ($\widehat{p}_{h,t} \simeq 0$), the response of the CPI is essentially given by $(1-\omega)\widehat{c}_t/(2\omega\rho)$, which accounts for imported inflation. Indeed, the only way to break this effect is either to set $\omega = 1$, autarky, or to let $\rho \to \infty$, which corresponds to a perfect substitutability between goods, in which case any increase in foreign prices translates into a drop in the consumption of goods produced in the rest of the world. This imported effect can be found, with the opposite sign, in the CPI of the rest of the world which can be expressed as

$$\widehat{p}_t^\star = -\frac{1-\omega}{2\omega\rho}\widehat{c}_t. \tag{6.25}$$

Note that the absence of any PPI effect stems from our assumption that $p_{f,t}^\star = p_f^\star$. The observed decline in the CPI in the rest of world results from the depreciation of the nominal exchange rate following a money injection. Indeed, changes in the nominal exchange rate can be written as

$$\widehat{\Delta e_t} = \widehat{g}_t + \frac{1 - 2\omega\rho}{2\omega\rho}\widehat{c}_t,\tag{6.26}$$

which may be better understood as[14]

$$\widehat{\Delta e_t} = (\widehat{g}_t - \widehat{g}_t^\star) + \frac{1 - 2\omega\rho}{2\omega\rho}(\widehat{y}_t - \widehat{y}_t^\star),$$

where, from our assumptions $\widehat{g}_t^\star = 0$, no/or constant monetary policy in the rest of the world, and $\widehat{y}_t^\star = 0$, constant world production capacities. We therefore retrieve the standard monetary model of nominal exchange rate determination. Consider first a situation where money is neutral. A positive money injection yields a one for one depreciation of the exchange rate, which instantaneously shifts to its long-run level. If we now consider a situation where beliefs matter and are positively correlated with money injections, the response is ambiguous. It crucially depends on the elasticity of substitution between goods. When this elasticity is low enough ($\rho < 1/2\omega$), the nominal exchange rate depreciation is magnified. Indeed, if money leads individuals to increase their consumption purchases and if goods are complement, the increase in consumption yields an increase in the demand for both goods. This therefore creates an upward pressure on both $\widehat{p}_{h,t}$ and $\widehat{\Delta e_t} + \widehat{p}_f^\star$. Conversely, when goods are substitutable, substitution effects imply that nominal exchange rate depreciation is weakened and may even be totally offset in the short run.

Let us now consider the real exchange rate $Q_t = e_t P_t^\star / P_t$. It can be written as

$$\widehat{q}_t = \frac{2\omega - 1}{2\omega\rho}\widehat{c}_t\tag{6.27}$$

in equilibrium. Like many other variables, it does not react when money is neutral. When a money injection matters and yields an increase in consumption, the real exchange rate depreciates provided $\omega > 1/2$, the degree of openness is not too large. The limit case where $\omega = 1/2$ corresponds to a situation where

$$\widehat{\Delta e_t} = \widehat{p}_t - \widehat{p}_t^\star$$

or otherwise stated where purchasing power parity (PPP) holds as $\widehat{q}_t = 0$ or $Q_t = 1$. Also note that the PPP also holds when goods are perfect substitutes ($\rho \to 0$). Finally, terms of trade, $\tau_t = e_t P_{f,t}^\star / P_{h,t}$, are given by

$$\widehat{\tau}_t = \frac{1}{2\omega\rho}\widehat{c}_t.\tag{6.28}$$

Terms of trade vary in a similar way to the real exchange rate in response to a money injection, but the magnitude of their fluctuations differs.

6.4   Exchange rate dynamics

This section attempts to shed light on the nominal exchange rate dynamics. More precisely, we characterize the long-run and the short-run properties of nominal exchange rate, focusing on the so–called overshooting property. We first show how the standard cash-in-advance model fails in accounting for the main features of the nominal exchange rate dynamics, and then turn to our model economy.

6.4.1   The failure of the cash-in-advance economy

To provide with a better understanding of the major failures of the standard cash-in-advance open economy model, we set up a benchmark experiment where we set $\theta = 0$. Then the equilibrium consumption decision is determined by the arbitrage relation,

$$\kappa = \frac{\beta}{g_t} E_t \frac{p_{h,t}}{p_{t+1} c_{t+1}},$$

which admits, in general equilibrium, the log-linear representation:

$$\widehat{c}_t = -\rho_g \widehat{g}_t + \mu E_t \widehat{c}_{t+1} \quad \text{with } \mu = -\frac{1 - \omega}{2\omega\rho}.$$

The equilibrium path is locally unique when $-1 < \mu < 1$. First note that since $\omega \in [0, 1]$ and $\rho > 0$, the equilibrium is determinate provided $\rho > (1 - \omega)/(2\omega)$ – the economy has to display high enough substitutability between domestic and foreign goods.[15] The solution to the log-linear representation of the economy is then given by

$$\widehat{c}_t = -\frac{2\omega\rho\rho_g}{2\omega\rho + \rho_g(1 - \omega)} \widehat{g}_t \equiv \gamma_0 \widehat{g}_t.$$

When money displays positive serial correlation,[16] then consumption converges back to its steady state monotonically and so do changes in the nominal exchange rate:

$$\widehat{\Delta e_t} = \widehat{g}_t + \frac{1 - 2\omega\rho}{2\omega\rho} \widehat{c}_t = \left(1 + \frac{1 - 2\omega\rho}{2\omega\rho} \gamma\right) \widehat{g}_t \equiv \psi_0 \widehat{g}_t.$$

However, note that since ρ is positive, $\omega \in (0, 1)$ and $|\rho_g| < 1$, γ_0 will always be negative, such that consumption, and therefore output, drops following a monetary injection. The standard cash-in-advance economy cannot, as is well known, generate the monetary transmission mechanism.

Proposition 3   *The domestic currency depreciates following a monetary injection provided the elasticity of substitution between foreign and domestic goods satisfies*

$$\rho > \frac{\rho_g}{2(1 + \rho_g)}.$$

When money shocks are i.i.d., $\rho_g = 0$, the constraint of Proposition 3 always holds. When ρ_g is positive, then foreign and domestic goods have to display enough substitutability. The result may be understood recalling that consumption drops following a money injection. Therefore, an individual will demand less of the two goods. But, the domestic prices respond more than one to one following the money injection (see equation (6.23)). Since goods are substitutable enough, there is a shift away from domestic goods toward goods produced in the rest of the world. Hence, domestic households are willing to import more. Therefore, this puts upward pressure on the nominal exchange rate. Domestic currency depreciates. Note that when ρ_g is large the inflation tax displays more persistence, such that consumption drops to a larger extent as a result of which the demand for domestic bonds increases as bonds are a way to escape the inflation tax. Therefore, higher substitutability is needed to counter this effect and the constraint on ρ is more stringent.

Proposition 4   *The nominal exchange rate cannot overshoot its long term level – when it depreciates – when $\rho_g \geqslant 0$.*

In order to provide with some intuition, let us consider the case where the monetary shock is i.i.d. In this case, money is neutral and consumption does not react to a monetary injection. The shock is totally accommodated by changes in nominal variables:

$$\widehat{\Delta e_t} = \widehat{p}_{h,t} = \widehat{p}_t = \widehat{g}_t.$$

Furthermore, while the model implies that the domestic currency depreciates in the face of a positive monetary injection, it does not generate overshooting as the nominal exchange rate instantaneously shifts to its new level.

Figure 6.3 reports impulse response functions (IRF) to a positive money injection when $\rho_g = 0.5$. This illustrates our previous statements that output drops in the face of money supply shock, and the nominal exchange rate does not overshoot its long-run level when the inflation tax is persistent.

This analysis illustrates the well-known drawbacks of the standard cash-in-advance model for the analysis of exchange rate dynamics. In the next section we will show the potential of our augmented cash-in-advance model.

6.4.2   The role of beliefs

In this section, we go back to our specification and consider $\theta > 0$. Then, output dynamics is described by the second-order finite difference equation:

$$E_t \widehat{y}_{t+2} - \left[\frac{1+\beta}{\beta} + \frac{(1-\omega)(1-\theta)(1-\beta\theta)}{2\omega\rho\beta\theta} \right] E_t \widehat{y}_{t+1}$$
$$+ \left[\frac{1}{\beta} - \frac{(1-\theta)(1-\theta\beta)}{\beta\theta} \right] \widehat{y}_t = \frac{(1-\theta)(1-\theta\beta)}{\beta\theta} E_t \widehat{g}_{t+1}.$$

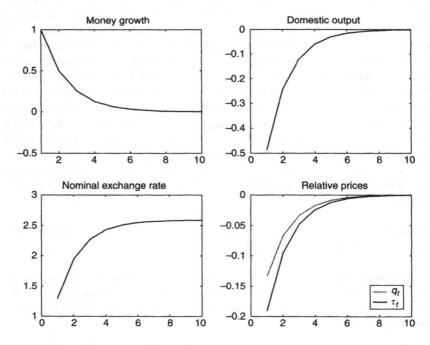

Figure 6.3 Impulse responses ($\rho_g = 0.5$).

In this case, the threshold values for θ, θ^* and $\widetilde{\theta}$, take the simple forms

$$\theta^* = \frac{3(1 + \beta) - \sqrt{9(1 + \beta)^2 - 4\beta}}{2\beta},$$

$$\widetilde{\theta} = \frac{2 + \beta - \sqrt{\beta^2 + 4}}{2\beta}.$$

Reasonable values for β (β close to unity) imply that $\theta^* \approx 0.17$ and $\widetilde{\theta} \approx 0.38$. Note that both θ^* and $\widetilde{\theta}$ are independent from ρ and ω, and are as a matter of fact identical to those that would be obtained in a close economy version of the model. Therefore, real indeterminacy occurs rather easily in this economy. More remarkable is that the model generates positive serial correlation in output dynamics with a value for θ which is not too high with respect to existing point estimates. Indeed, empirical studies suggest parameter estimates for θ that significantly exceed the minimal value that yields indeterminacy. For instance, Constantidines and Ferson (1991) and Braun *et al.* (1993) obtain an estimated value of θ that lies within $[0.5; 0.9]$ on macro data. Habit persistence appears to be lower but still significant on micro data. Naik and Moore (1996) report estimates for habit persistence on food consumption data of 0.486 which is far above the threshold value of θ yielding indeterminacy and exceeds that needed for positive persistence.

We now focus on solutions associated with indeterminate equilibrium. In such cases, we have

$$\widehat{y}_t = \mu \widehat{y}_{t-1} + \gamma \widehat{g}_{t-1} + \varepsilon_t^y \quad \text{where } \gamma = -\frac{\rho_g}{\lambda - \rho_g} \frac{(1-\theta)(1-\theta\beta)}{\beta\theta}, \quad (6.29)$$

where λ and μ are, respectively, the explosive and stable root of output dynamics, and ε_t^y is a martingale difference sequence that can be related to fundamental shocks (money shocks), depending on individual's beliefs about monetary policy, such that it can be written

$$\varepsilon_t^y = b(g_t - E_{t-1}g_t) + v_t$$
$$= b\varepsilon_t^g + v_t \quad (6.30)$$

with $E_{t-1}v_t = 0$ and $|b| < \infty$. v_t denotes pure extrinsic beliefs that are unrelated to fundamentals. The parameter b rules the dependency of agents' beliefs to fundamentals. It is worth noting that this parameter is an extrinsic characteristic of agents' beliefs, which will prove to be critical for the properties of the equilibrium. Then, the nominal exchange rate dynamics takes the simple ARIMA(2,1,1) form:

$$(1 - \mu L)(1 - \rho_g L)(1 - L)\widehat{e}_t = (1 + \psi b + (\psi(\gamma - \rho_g b) - \mu)L)\varepsilon_t$$

$$\text{where } \psi = \frac{1 - 2\omega\rho}{2\omega\rho}. \quad (6.31)$$

To keep the exposition simple, let us consider the case where $\rho_g = 0$ and $v_t = 0$, $\forall t$. Then, (6.29) and (6.31) are reduced to

$$\widehat{y}_t = \mu \widehat{y}_{t-1} + b\varepsilon_t^g,$$
$$\Delta\widehat{e}_t = \mu\Delta\widehat{e}_{t-1} + (1 + \psi b)\varepsilon_t - \mu\varepsilon_{t-1}.$$

Note that the two last equations just show that the model can generate persistence, provided $\mu > 0$. But they also show that real indeterminacy is not per se sufficient to generate the monetary transmission mechanism (output increases in face of a positive money injection) or the overshooting of nominal exchange rate; additional assumption are to be placed on individuals' beliefs – in particular how they co-move with money supply shocks – as we now illustrate.

Let us first consider the case where $b = 0$, such that the above system reduces to

$$\widehat{y}_t = \mu\widehat{y}_{t-1},$$
$$\Delta\widehat{e}_t = \varepsilon_t,$$

which implies that money is neutral. Indeed, following a money injection, output remains at its steady state level ($\widehat{y}_t = 0$) and $\widehat{y}_t$ is a degenerated stochastic variable. Conversely, changes in the nominal exchange rate respond one for one to a money injection. Hence, it fully absorbs the shock and so does all other nominal variables. This case corresponds to a full price flexibility situation where the nominal exchange instantaneously shifts to its new long-run level and cannot overshoot. We therefore retrieve the quantity theory of money, which can then be associated with a particular form of beliefs. This also implies that the volatility of changes in the nominal exchange rate is the same as the one of the money supply shock. The behavior of the model is then similar to the standard cash-in-advance model. Figure 6.4 reports IRF in the more general case $\rho_g = 0.5$.

As stated, the model resembles the standard cash-in-advance model, in that it fails to account for the monetary transmission mechanism and the exchange rate dynamics. The only notable difference stems from the higher persistence of adjustment dynamics.

We now investigate a situation where individuals' beliefs are sufficiently positively correlated with the money supply shock. We set $b = 1$. The output/changes in the nominal exchange rate dynamics can then be rewritten as

$$\widehat{y}_t = \mu \widehat{y}_{t-1} + \varepsilon_t^g,$$
$$\Delta \widehat{e}_t = \mu \Delta \widehat{e}_{t-1} + (1 + \psi)\varepsilon_t - \mu \varepsilon_{t-1}.$$

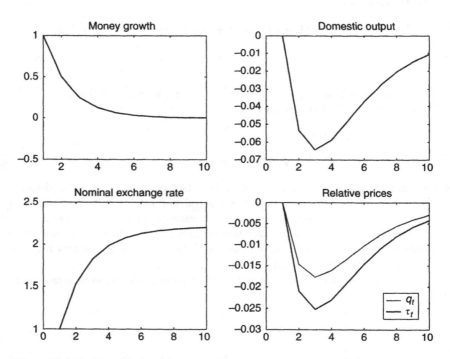

Figure 6.4 Impulse responses.

Note

These IRF are obtained with $\rho_g = 0.5$, $\beta = 0.99$, $\omega = 0.85$, $\rho = 1.5$ and $\theta = 0.75$.

Let us first analyze the impact effect of a positive money supply shock in the domestic economy ε_t on the nominal exchange rate. A positive money supply shock always yields a depreciation of the domestic currency as the impact effect is given by $1 + \psi = 1/(2\omega\rho) > 0$, which eventually corresponds to the change in the terms of trade. But the magnitude of the depreciation depends on the substitutability between goods. When goods are perfect substitutes, $\rho \to \infty$, changes in the nominal exchange rate essentially correct any change in the terms of trade arising from a money supply shock since the household is able to reallocate her consumption purchases between the two goods. But, on impact, production prices are left unaffected by a monetary injection since consumption responds one for one to a money injection and the domestic PPI is given by (6.23). Hence, the model is found to generate endogenous price rigidity. Suppose now that the nominal exchange rate depreciates (appreciates), given perfect substitutability between goods, there will be a perfect switch away toward domestic (rest of the world) goods. Therefore, in order to acquire domestic (rest of the world) goods, the rest of the world must instantaneously sell (purchase) bonds denominated in foreign currency which yields an appreciation (depreciation) that offsets the initial depreciation (appreciation). Therefore, the nominal exchange rate does not respond. Terms of trade and real exchange rate are left unaffected. Hence, besides PPI rigidity, this version may account for complete short-run nominal rigidity in an open economy. When goods are not perfect price substitutes, the initial increase in consumption is associated with an increase in the willingness to consume the two types of goods. This, in particular, leads the domestic household to sell bonds denominated in domestic currency in order to purchase goods produced in the rest of the world, yielding a depreciation of the nominal exchange rate. The lower the substitutability, the greater the willingness to consume both types of goods, and therefore the greater is this effect. The depreciation is therefore magnified.

A widely discussed question in the literature dealing with nominal exchange rate is the long-run effect of a money injection on its dynamics – the so-called $\mathcal{A}(1)$. Moreover, it provides a way to characterize the dynamic properties of the nominal exchange rate as it is related to the size of the unit root. In the case we investigate $\mathcal{A}(1)$ is simply given by

$$\mathcal{A}(1) = 1 + \frac{\psi}{(1 - \mu)}$$

and we can establish the following proposition.

Proposition 5 *When beliefs are correlated with monetary shocks, a positive money injection can yield either $\mathcal{A}(1) \geq 1$ when goods are complement enough or $\mathcal{A}(1) < 1$ when they display substitutability.*

A first implication of the last proposition is that when beliefs are sufficiently correlated with money injections ($b = 1$), the model may either generate a long-run effect of money greater than that obtained in the simple random walk model, or a long-run effect lower than 1 reflecting an anti-persistent property. It can eventually become negative when goods are substitute enough. In order to understand this result, let us consider the case of perfect substitutability. In the face of a positive money supply shock, the terms of trade are left unaffected so that

$$\widehat{\Delta e_t} = \widehat{p_{h,t}} = \widehat{g_t} - \widehat{c_t}.$$

Since the shock is i.i.d., the only effect that plays the following period is the effect transiting through consumption. Since consumption responds positively on impact and displays positive persistence (for $\theta > \widetilde{\theta}$), changes in the nominal exchange rate are negative from the second period on, such that the domestic currency appreciates in the long run. Conversely, when goods are complement, the increase in overall domestic consumption translates in higher demand for both domestic and foreign goods. Since, foreign production prices (deflated for domestic money) are left unaffected, the extra demand for foreign goods leads the domestic currency to depreciate, because of bonds trading. This effect being stronger as complementarity increases. Since consumption displays positive persistence (for $\theta > \widetilde{\theta}$), this effect too persists such that the $\mathcal{A}(1)$ is greater than 1.

Endowed with these preliminary results on short-run and long-run effects of money shocks, we now tackle the key question of overshooting.

Proposition 6   *When beliefs are positively correlated with monetary shocks, the nominal exchange rate overshoots its long-run value if (i) $\rho > 1/(2\omega)$ when $\theta < \widetilde{\theta}$, or (ii) $\rho < 1/(2\omega)$ when $\theta > \widetilde{\theta}$.*

Proposition 6 makes it explicit that overshooting is fundamentally related to goods substitution on the one hand, therefore appealing to intratemporal substitution effects, and habit persistence on the other hand, therefore reflecting the fundamental role of intertemporal motives in the determination of exchange rate properties. It may indeed either be obtained for high θ (positive persistence) and high substitution between foreign and domestic goods or low θ (negative persistence) and low elasticity of substitution. Intratemporal motives essentially have to do with the level of the $\mathcal{A}(1)$, and therefore with the long-run effect. Indeed, as established by Proposition 5, when ρ is high enough – when goods are sufficiently substitutable – the money shock can yield a long-run appreciation of the domestic currency when beliefs are correlated with money injections, while the domestic currency depreciates (appreciates) in the short run. Therefore, the nominal exchange rate overshoots. On the other hand, situations where goods are high substitutable are associated with negative persistence such that changes in the nominal exchange rate are necessarily negative in the second period.

This, however, leaves open the question of the coincidence between a positive (and higher than 1) $\mathcal{A}(1)$ and overshooting. This is reported in Figure 6.5 which characterizes pairs (θ, ρ) yielding both overshooting and a high value for the long-run effect of money on the nominal exchange rate. It is worth noting

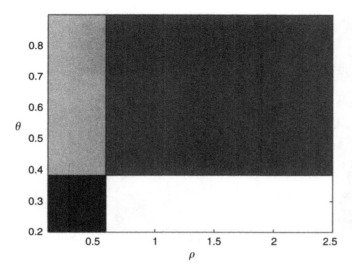

Figure 6.5 Zone of overshooting ($\rho_g = 0$).

Note
White, neither overshooting nor $\mathcal{A}(1) > 1$; Light gray; no overshooting, but $\mathcal{A}(1) > 1$; dark gray, overshooting but $\mathcal{A}(1) < 1$; black, both overshooting and $\mathcal{A}(1) > 1$.

that overshooting occurs for a wide range of values for habit persistence and substitutability parameters. For example, in Backus *et al.* (1992) calibration of $\rho = 1.5$, overshooting occurs for θ greater than 0.38, which is in accordance with empirical findings on habit persistence.

We also report in Figure 6.6, the overshooting area in the case of a persistent money injection ($\rho_g = 0.5$). At first glance, it appears that the region of overshooting is narrowed compared to the i.i.d. case. For instance, when goods are substitutable, the required values of habit persistence to get overshooting are much higher than in the i.i.d. case. The main reason for this result may be found in the greater persistence of the inflation tax.

Indeed, persistent inflation leads the household to reduce her consumption along the transition path if habit persistence is not sufficient – the inflation tax dominates intertemporal complementarity in consumption decisions. The demand for goods produced in the rest of the world shifts downward so that the relative demand for foreign assets decreases. Therefore, the depreciation is weakened. Conversely, when habit persistence is large enough with regard to the persistence of the inflation tax, households will be able to maintain their consumption plans and will therefore, among other, maintain their demand for goods produced in the rest of the world. Depreciation of the nominal exchange rate is therefore magnified.

Figure 6.7 reports IRF when money supply shocks are persistent ($\rho_g = 0.5$). Contrary to the standard cash-in-advance model and the model with no confidence

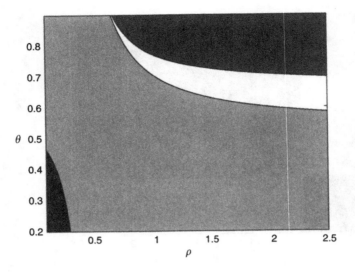

Figure 6.6 Zone of overshooting ($\rho_g = 0.5$).

Note
White, neither overshooting nor $\mathcal{A}(1) > 1$; Light gray, no overshooting, but $\mathcal{A}(1) > 1$; dark gray, overshooting but $\mathcal{A}(1) < 1$; black, both overshooting and $\mathcal{A}(1) > 1$.

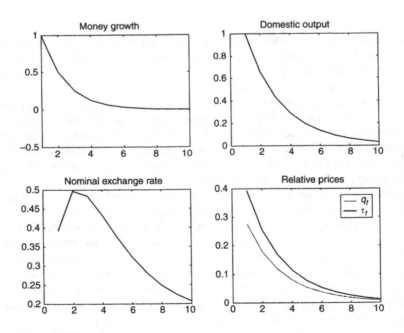

Figure 6.7 Impulse responses.

Note
These IRF are obtained with $\rho_g = 0.5$, $\beta = 0.99$, $\omega = 0.85$, $\rho = 1.5$ and $\theta = 0.75$.

in money, the model is capable of generating both the monetary transmission mechanism and overshooting.

Note that, in this case, even if the inflation is persistent, the effect of large habit is sufficient to offset its effect on consumption decision, as output is always above its steady-state value. Therefore, households are willing to consume more of each type of good, so that the demand for foreign currency rises such that the depreciation is magnified. Overshooting follows.

We finally investigate the volatility implications of the model for the nominal exchange rate. The MA(∞) representation of $\widehat{\Delta e_t}$ is given by

$$\widehat{\Delta e_t} = g_t + \psi \sum_{i=0}^{\infty} \mu^i g_{t-i},$$

such that its volatility can be written as

$$\sigma_{\Delta e} = \left(1 + 2\psi + \frac{\psi^2}{1 - \mu^2} \right)^{1/2} \sigma_g.$$

The model can endogenously amplify the volatility of the money supply shocks – that is, can generate a ratio of volatility of nominal exchange rate to volatility of monetary shocks greater than unity – when beliefs are positively related to money injections. This is established by the following proposition.

Proposition 7 *When beliefs are positively correlated with money shocks, $\zeta \equiv \sigma_{\Delta e}/\sigma_g > 1$ if*

(i) *domestic and foreign goods are complement enough, $\rho < 1/2\omega\rho$, or*
(ii) *domestic and foreign goods are substitute enough, $\rho > 1/2\omega\rho$, and the following inequality holds*

$$2 + \psi > 2\mu^2.$$

Note that condition (i) corresponds to the zone where the model generates a long-run effect of money supply shocks $\mathcal{A}(1)$ greater than 1 in the i.i.d. case. This suggests that most of the volatility in the nominal exchange rate dynamics may be found at low frequencies phenomena rather than high frequencies. In other words, the ability of the model to account for low frequency properties of the nominal exchange rate seems to be more important than its ability to generate an overshooting property. When goods are substitute enough (see condition (ii)), the amplification of money shocks only occurs for high enough persistence (μ). This corresponds to situations where the model, despite the fact that it generates a $\mathcal{A}(1)$ lower than 1, generates overshooting. In this case, most of the nominal exchange rate volatility is accounted for by high frequency phenomena.

Note that, in the latter analysis, we omitted the extrinsic uncertainty stemming from the pure extrinsic belief v_t. As soon as v_t is brought back into the model, the volatility of the exchange rate is given by

$$\sigma_{\Delta e} = \left(\left(1 + 2\psi + \frac{\psi^2}{1 - \mu^2} \right) \sigma_g^2 + \frac{\psi^2}{1 - \mu^2} \sigma_v^2 \right)^{1/2},$$

where $\sigma_v^2 = E(v_t^2)$. Therefore, the model can generate any level of nominal exchange rate volatility when agents have extrinsic beliefs. Note that the same level of volatility may be achieved with a particular degree of indexation, b, beliefs on money shocks ($v_t = b\varepsilon_t^g$), since

$$\sigma_{\Delta e} = \left(1 + 2b\psi + \frac{b^2\psi^2}{1 - \mu^2} \right)^{1/2} \sigma_g.$$

Hence for $b \gg 0$, the model can generate high volatility in the nominal exchange rate. Indeed, confidence in money is so high that it induces very strong amplification mechanisms of money shocks in the economy.

6.5   Concluding remarks

This chapter has shown that introducing time non-separability in consumption decisions, an infinitely lived agents monetary model with a cash-in-advance constraint may be helpful to understand nominal exchange rate dynamics. We assume that one period lagged consumption produces service flows, that are perfectly internalized by the representative household. We first show that high enough habit persistence yields self-fulfilling prophecies. Depending on the form of the beliefs, the model can account for greater volatility and persistence in the exchange rate dynamics. Implicit in this result is that real indeterminacy is not per se sufficient to explain exchange rate dynamics. Two conditions have to be fulfilled: (i) beliefs should matter and (ii) beliefs should be positively related to money injection.

Several issues may be worth considering. First of all, one may check the robustness of our results against other specifications for the money demand. Another issue would be to provide with a systematic quantitative evaluation of the time series implications of the mechanism we discussed. In particular, it may be interesting to assess the ability of this model to account quantitatively for observed volatility and persistence of both the nominal and real exchange rates.

Appendix A: equilibrium conditions

The deflated equilibrium is characterized by the following system of dynamic equations:

$$\kappa = \frac{\beta}{g_t} \frac{p_{h,t}}{p_{t+1}} E_t \left[\frac{1}{c_{t+1} - \theta c_t} - \frac{\beta\theta}{c_{t+2} - \theta c_{t+1}} \right], \tag{6.32}$$

$$\kappa(1 + i_t) = \frac{p_{h,t}}{p_t} E_t \left[\frac{1}{c_t - \theta c_{t-1}} - \frac{\beta\theta}{c_{t+1} - \theta c_t} \right], \tag{6.33}$$

$$h_t = \left(\frac{p_{h,t}}{p_t}\right)^{-\rho} \omega\, c_t + \left(\frac{p_{h,t}}{\Delta e_t\, p_t^\star}\right)^{-\rho}(1-\omega)\,c^\star, \tag{6.34}$$

$$y^\star = \left(\frac{\Delta e_t\, p_f^\star}{p_t}\right)^{-\rho}(1-\omega)\,c_t + \left(\frac{p_f^\star}{p_t^\star}\right)^{-\rho}\omega\,c^\star, \tag{6.35}$$

$$p_t c_t = g_t + (\Delta e_t\, p_f^\star)^{1-\rho} p_t^\rho (1-\omega)c_t - p_{h,t}^{1-\rho}(\Delta e_t\, p_t^\star)^\rho (1-\omega)c^\star, \tag{6.36}$$

$$p_t = \left[\omega p_{h,t}^{1-\rho} + (1-\omega)(\Delta e_t\, p_f^\star)^{1-\rho}\right]^{1/(1-\rho)} \tag{6.37}$$

$$p_t^\star = \left[(1-\omega)\left(\frac{p_{h,t}}{\Delta e_t}\right)^{1-\rho} + \omega p_f^{\star 1-\rho}\right]^{1/(1-\rho)} \tag{6.38}$$

$$1 + i_t = (1+r_t)g_t\,\frac{p_{t+1}}{p_t}. \tag{6.39}$$

Appendix B: log-linear representation

The log-linear representation of the previous system is

$$
\begin{aligned}
0 = \widehat{p}_{h,t} - \widehat{g}_t - \widehat{p}_{t+1} + {}&\frac{1}{(1-\theta)(1-\beta\theta)}E_t \\
&\times [\beta\theta\widehat{c}_{t+2} - (1+\beta\theta^2)\widehat{c}_{t+1} + \theta\widehat{c}_t],
\end{aligned} \tag{6.40}
$$

$$\widehat{i}_t = \widehat{p}_{h,t} - \widehat{p}_t + \frac{1}{(1-\theta)(1-\beta\theta)}E_t[\beta\theta\widehat{c}_{t+1} - (1+\beta\theta^2)\widehat{c}_t + \theta\widehat{c}_{t-1}], \tag{6.41}$$

$$\widehat{h}_t = \omega\rho\widehat{p}_t - \rho\widehat{p}_{h,t} + \omega\widehat{c}_t + \rho(1-\omega)(\widehat{p}_t^\star + \widehat{\Delta e}_t), \tag{6.42}$$

$$(1-\omega)\widehat{c}_t - \rho(1-\omega)(\widehat{\Delta e}_t - \widehat{p}_t) + \omega\rho\widehat{p}_t^\star = 0, \tag{6.43}$$

$$\widehat{p}_t + \omega\widehat{c}_t = \widehat{g}_t + (1-\rho)(1-\omega)(\widehat{\Delta e}_t - \widehat{p}_{h,t}) + \rho(1-\omega)(\widehat{p}_t - \widehat{p}_t^\star - \widehat{\Delta e}_t), \tag{6.44}$$

$$\widehat{p}_t = \omega\widehat{p}_{h,t} + (1-\omega)\widehat{\Delta e}_t, \tag{6.45}$$

$$\widehat{p}_t^\star = (1-\omega)(\widehat{p}_{h,t} - \widehat{\Delta e}_t), \tag{6.46}$$

$$\widehat{i}_t = \widehat{r}_t + \widehat{g}_t + \widehat{p}_{t+1} - \widehat{p}_t, \tag{6.47}$$

where $\widehat{x}_t = \log(x_t/x^\star)$ for any variable, and $\widehat{i}_t = \log((1+i_t)/(1+i^\star))$, $\widehat{r}_t = \log((1+r_t)/(1+r^\star))$.

Plugging (6.46) and (6.45) into (6.43), we get:

$$\widehat{\Delta e}_t = \widehat{p}_t + \frac{1}{2\rho}\widehat{c}_t. \tag{6.48}$$

Then, using the latter result in (6.45), we get

$$\widehat{p}_{h,t} = \widehat{p}_t - \frac{1-\omega}{2\omega\rho}\widehat{c}_t. \tag{6.49}$$

Now, note that using (6.45), (6.46) can be rewritten as

$$\widehat{p}_t^* = \widehat{p}_{h,t} - \widehat{p}_t, \tag{6.50}$$

from which we then get

$$\widehat{p}_t^* = -\frac{1-\omega}{2\omega\rho}\widehat{c}_t. \tag{6.51}$$

Plugging (6.48), (6.49) and (6.51) into (6.42), we get

$$\widehat{h}_t = \widehat{c}_t. \tag{6.52}$$

Likewise, using the same equation in (6.44) we get

$$\widehat{p}_t = \widehat{g}_t - \left(1 - \frac{1-\omega}{2\omega\rho}\right)\widehat{c}_t, \tag{6.53}$$

therefore

$$\widehat{\Delta e}_t = \widehat{g}_t + \frac{1-2\omega\rho}{2\omega\rho}\widehat{c}_t, \tag{6.54}$$

$$\widehat{p}_{h,t} = \widehat{g}_t - \widehat{c}_t, \tag{6.55}$$

$$\widehat{p}_t^* = -\frac{1-\omega}{2\omega\rho}\widehat{c}_t. \tag{6.56}$$

Then, using (6.52), (6.53) and (6.55) into (6.40) we get

$$E_t\widehat{c}_{t+2} + \frac{\varphi(1-\theta)(1-\beta\theta) - (1+\beta\theta^2)}{\beta\theta}E_t\widehat{c}_{t+1}$$

$$+ \left(\frac{1}{\beta} - \frac{(1-\theta)(1-\beta\theta)}{\beta\theta}\right)\widehat{c}_t = \frac{(1-\theta)(1-\beta\theta)}{\beta\theta}E_t\widehat{g}_{t+1}, \tag{6.57}$$

where $\varphi = 1 - (1-\omega)/2\omega\rho$. Finally, using (6.53) and (6.55) the nominal gross interest rate is given by

$$\widehat{i}_t = \frac{(\varphi-1)(1-\theta)(1-\beta\theta) - (1+\beta\theta^2)}{(1-\theta)(1-\beta\theta)}\widehat{c}_t$$

$$+ \frac{\beta\theta}{(1-\theta)(1-\beta\theta)}E_t\widehat{c}_{t+1} + \frac{\theta}{(1-\theta)(1-\beta\theta)}\widehat{c}_{t-1}. \tag{6.58}$$

Appendix C: proof of propositions

Proof of proposition 1   See Auray *et al.* (2000).   □

Proof of proposition 2   See Auray *et al.* (2000).   □

Proof of proposition 3   Recall that in equilibrium, we have

$$\Delta \widehat{e_t} = \widehat{g_t} + \frac{1 - 2\omega\rho}{2\omega\rho}\widehat{c_t} = \psi_0\widehat{g_t}.$$

The nominal exchange rate depreciates following a monetary injection iff $\psi_0 > 0$

$$1 - \frac{\rho_g(1 - 2\omega\rho)}{2\omega\rho + \rho_g(1 - \omega)} > 0$$

which is equivalent to

$$\frac{2\omega\rho + 2\omega\rho\rho_g - \rho_g\omega}{2\omega\rho + \rho_g(1 - \omega)} > 0$$

which reduces to

$$2\rho\left(1 + \rho_g\right) > \rho_g.$$ □

Proof of proposition 4   Recall that overshooting occurs following a monetary injection if the exchange rate is above its steady-state level on impact. Since the impact effect of a unitary money supply shock is equal to ψ_0, and the long-run effect of this shock is given by

$$\mathcal{A}(1) = \frac{\psi_0}{1 - \rho_g}.$$

Overshooting occurs if

$$\psi > \frac{\psi_0}{1 - \rho_g}.$$

Since we are restricting ourselves to situations where the domestic currency depreciates we necessarily have $\psi_0 > 0$, such that the last inequality holds iff $\rho_g < 0$.   □

Proof of proposition 5   Since $|\mu| < 1$, $1 - \mu > 0$ such that $\mathcal{A}(1) > 1$ as soon as $\psi > 0$, or otherwise stated when foreign and domestic goods do not display too much substitutability ($\rho < 1/2\omega$).   □

Proof of proposition 6   Note that when $\rho_g = 0$, $\gamma = 0$ such that $\widehat{e_0} - \mathcal{A}(1)$ reduces to

$$\widehat{e_0} - \mathcal{A}(1) = -\frac{\psi\mu}{1 - \mu}. \tag{6.59}$$

Two cases are then to be considered

1   $\theta < \widetilde{\theta}$, in which case $-1 < \mu < 0$. Therefore, (6.59) reduces to

$$\psi > 0 \iff \rho < \frac{1}{2\omega}.$$

2   $\theta > \widetilde{\theta}$, $\mu \in (0, 1)$, therefore the nominal exchange rate overshoots if

$$\psi < 0 \iff \rho > \frac{1}{2\omega}.$$ □

Proof of proposition 7 $\zeta > 1$ is equivalent to

$$2\psi + \frac{\psi^2}{1 - \mu^2} > 0 \iff \psi \left(2(1 - \mu^2) + \psi\right) > 0.$$

Two cases are then to be considered:

1   $\psi > 0 \iff \rho < 1/(2\omega)$, in which case the second term of the above inequality is also positive since $|\mu| < 1$.
2   $\psi < 0 \iff \rho > 1/(2\omega)$, in which case the second term of the above inequality has to be negative for the inequality to be satisfied, $2 + \psi > 2\mu^2$.

□

Notes

1   Note that throughout this chapter, lowercases will denote real variables and uppercase letters nominal variables.
2   Accordingly, the budget constraint reads $P_t^* b_{t+1}^* + M_{t+1}^* + P_t^* c_t^* \leqslant (1 + r_{t-1}) P_t^* b_t^* + P_t^* w_t^* h_t^* + M_t^* + N_t^*$ abroad.
3   This will turn out to be the case for the specification of the shock we will consider.
4   Auray *et al.* (2000) show that the main dynamic result is left unaffected by considering a more general utility function. It should, however, be stressed that Hansen's specification magnifies the labor supply effect and henceforth facilitates the emergence of indeterminacy.
5   Implicit in this assumption is that the aggregate demand in the rest of the world is a strong exogenous variable, which is therefore left unaffected by changes occurring in the domestic economy.
6   This also have the very attractive feature of not creating the unpleasant unit root property that small open economy models usually exhibit.
7   See Appendix A for the set of equilibrium conditions.
8   Note that by the homogeneity of degree one of the price indices, the choice of the price we decide to make exogenous does not matter, since what really determines the CPI is the terms of trade $P_{h,t}/(e_t P_{f,t}^*)$.
9   See Appendix B for the log-linear representation of equilibrium.
10   The interested reader is left to refer to Appendix C for the proof of the propositions.
11   Note that this increase in current consumption is possible because the labor supply responds positively and sufficiently. Conversely, should the labor supply be inelastic, output and aggregate consumption would be left unaffected by this change in beliefs.
12   See Appendix B for a detailed exposition of the log-linearization.
13   From a technical point of view, this would amount to the assumption that the extrinsic uncertainty that hits the economy is positively correlated with money injections. Denoting by ν_t a sunspot, this would just reflect that $\mathrm{corr}(\nu_t, \varepsilon_t^g) \geqslant 0$.

14 We made use of the fact that in the log-linearized equilibrium, $\widehat{c}_t = \widehat{y}_t$. See Appendix B.
15 Note that the converse situation is eventually of low interest since it is associated to a negative eigenvalue such that consumption displays negative serial correlation. This is highly counterfactual and we therefore do not investigate this situation any further.
16 We do not investigate the case of negative serial correlation, which is counterfactual.

Part II

Exchange rate regimes and monetary policy

7 Exchange rate regimes and international business cycles

Some stylized facts

Thepthida Sopraseuth

7.1 Introduction

This chapter aims at shedding light on the impact of exchange rate regime on business cycle properties. In the spirit of Mundell (1961) and Fleming (1962), open macroeconomics teaches us that the propagation of real and monetary impulses depends on the exchange rate regime. The short run dynamics of macroeconomic quantities should then be affected by the degree of flexibility of the nominal exchange rate. Do flexible exchange rates imply more volatile aggregates by introducing an additional source of uncertainty or, in contrast, do they generate more stabilized fluctuations? Does the exchange rate regime affect the international comovement? This chapter provides some answers to these questions by examining business cycle properties that are affected by the shift in the exchange rate regime. This empirical study is a prerequisite to the modelling exchange rate regimes.

This chapter draws on Flood and Rose (1995) and Baxter and Stockman (1989). The latter document the consequences of the fall of the Bretton Woods System by comparing business cycle properties under fixed exchange rates (1960–73) and under floating rates (1973–86). Flood and Rose (1995) as well as Baxter and Stockman (1989) conclude that, following the fall of the Bretton Woods System, transition to floating rates leads to sharp increases in the nominal and real exchange rate volatility with no corresponding changes in the distribution of macroeconomic quantities. This finding adds to the "exchange rate disconnect," that is, the discrepancy between exchange rate fluctuations and the behavior of its macroeconomic fundamentals (Obstfeld and Rogoff, 2000b). Furthermore, Baxter and Stockman (1989) do not uncover any systematic relationship between exchange rate regimes and cross-country interdependence.

The originality of this chapter compared to Baxter and Stockman's (1989) work is twofold. First, the robustness of Baxter and Stockman's (1989) findings is checked in this chapter since we abstract from the decade of oil shocks (1971–86). Since, Baxter and Stockman (1989) sample ends in 1985, the floating rate period coincides with major oil price changes so that one can hardly distinguish business cycle properties due to the common world disturbances from fluctuations inherent to the shift to the flexible exchange rate regime. This chapter overcomes this difficulty by neglecting the 1971–86 period in the sample. Furthermore, we check the relevance of Baxter and Stockman's (1989) conclusion with regard to another exchange rate regime, namely the European Monetary System (EMS). Are Flood and Rose (1995) and Baxter and Stockman's (1989) stylized facts still relevant when one measures the impact of the EMS on business cycle behavior? Artis and Zhang (1999) gauge the consequences of membership to the EMS on comovement of industrial production indices. We extend their analysis by investigating the impact of the EMS on comovement of output, consumption and investment. Moreover, the sample consists of EMS countries as well as non-EMS countries in order to distinguish EMS-specific phenomena from general tendencies in the business cycle. More specifically, in the EMS case, the flexible exchange rate period ranges from 1971 to 1979. Comparing business cycle properties of non-EMS vs EMS countries allows to control for the impact of these world disturbances. Should the oil prices play a major role in the shift in business cycle properties, this shift would be observed in EMS as well as non-EMS countries. Finally, the UK, Greece and Sweden have never been part of the European Exchange Rate arrangement. The analysis of business properties in these countries allows to distinguish between the impact of the European economic integration and the consequences of the EMS.

The second originality of this chapter lies in the statistical technique used to characterize business cycle changes. After characterizing the short run behavior of macroeconomic aggregates across exchange rate regimes, one has to assess the statistical significance of the evolution of business cycle statistics. Due to the uncertainty on the distribution of the variables under study, we resort to bootstrap techniques. This nonparametric method allows to measure the statistical significance of changes in business cycle properties observed under pegged and floating rates.

After presenting the methodology (in Section 7.2), we investigate the impact of the Bretton Woods System and the EMS on volatility (in Section 7.3) and international comovement (Section 7.4).

7.2   Methodology

The quarterly time series, except net exports, are logged. Appendix A provides a full description of the data. The sample consists of 17 countries: 15 members to the European Union (except Luxemburg) and 3 other G7 partners (the US, Japan and Canada). The chronology of membership to the EMS is recalled in Appendix B. The short run dynamics is identified with the Hodrick and Prescott (1997) filter.[1]

7.2.1   Sub-periods

Recent history of industrialized countries offers two opportunities to study the impact of exchange rate regimes on macroeconomic aggregates.

First, at the end of the Second World War, the Bretton Woods System established a fixed parity arrangement based on gold and the US dollar. Each country had to defend its own parity against the US dollar within a 1 percent margin around the reference value. On August 15th, 1971, president Nixon decided to suspend the convertibility between gold and the US dollar, thus putting an end to the Bretton Woods System. For want of a longer data set, Baxter and Stockman's (1989) floating exchange rate period is also the decade of oil shocks.

> Because the industrialized nations adopted floating exchange rates nearly simultaneously, and at roughly the same time as some major world macroeconomic disturbances such as the oil price change, it is difficult to discriminate between the effects of changes in the exchange-rate system and other real disturbances.
>
> (Baxter and Stockman, 1989, p. 378)

In order to overcome this difficulty, we compare business cycle properties observed under pegged rates (1960:1–1971:3) to those computed after the oil shocks (1987:1–1998:4).

Are Baxter and Stockman's (1989) findings robust to another exchange rate regime? By studying the impact of the EMS, we are able to provide a first answer to this question. In 1972, EMS countries try to tame exchange rate fluctuations by creating the "European Snake." However, France decided to leave the system, then joined again with Italy, before quitting again. The system failed to stabilize exchange rate fluctuations so that we consider the 1970s a flexible exchange rate regime.

In March 1979, eight European countries created the EMS. This agreement compelled the European central banks to keep their respective parities within a narrow band defined as some margin around the reference value. There is a consensus (Gros and Thygesen, 1998) that the EMS went through three periods marked by the breaks in 1983, 1987 and 1992. According to econometric studies, in the 1980s, the most significant break is 1987 (Bordes *et al.*, 1996; Uctum, 1999). Before 1987, the EMS went through a turbulent start with eleven realignments that affected all monies in the system. In contrast, in the post-1987 era, only five realignments occurred. Moreover, these realignments affected only four monies (the lira, the peseta, the escudo and the punt). Finally, the Basle–Nyborg agreements in September 1987 gave birth to a more stringent EMS by strengthening central bank interventions on exchange rate markets. As a result, the post-1987 era can be considered as a fixed exchange rate period. The volatility of nominal exchange rates should confirm this conclusion (Section 7.3.1).

We investigate the consequences of the EMS by comparing business cycle properties under floating rates (1971:3–1979:2) and under fixed rate (1987:1–1998:4). The sample consists of EMS countries as well as non-EMS countries in order to distinguish EMS-specific phenomena from general tendencies in the business cycle. More specifically, in the EMS case, the flexible exchange rate period ranges from 1971 to 1979, the decade of the first oil shock. Comparing business cycle properties of non-EMS vs EMS countries allows to control for the impact of these world disturbances. Should the oil prices play a major role in the shift in business cycle properties, this shift would be observed in EMS as well as non-EMS countries. Finally, the UK, Greece and Sweden have never been part of the European Exchange Rate arrangement. The analysis of business properties in these countries allows to distinguish between the impact of the European economic integration and the consequences of the EMS.

In the study of the impact of both exchange rate regimes on business cycle properties, the second sub-period begins in 1987, which allows to discard (i) the years of the oil shocks in the case of the Bretton Woods System (1973, 1979 and 1986) and (ii) the turbulent start of the European Monetary System (1979–86) characterized by numerous and sharp realignments.

7.2.2   Testing the significance of the modification in business cycle properties

The literature proposes different methodologies to measure the statistical significance of changes in business cycle statistics. Baxter and Stockman (1989) resort to a F test to gauge the magnitude of the change in the volatility of exchange rates, exports and imports. This test relies on assumptions on the underlying distribution of these variables. However, there is little consensus in the literature on the underlying distribution, especially for the exchange rate (Boothe and Glassman, 1987; Artis and Taylor, 1994). This entices us to be cautious about parametric methods used by Baxter and Stockman (1989).

Nonparametric approaches are developed in the literature. The first one is based on ARCH (Engle, 1982) that allows to assess the evolution of the variance conditional on past information. This technique applied by Artis and Taylor (1994) and Caporale and Pittis (1995) to the EMS case and the Bretton Woods System provides information about changes in the variability of shocks in the economy. However, this phenomenon, uncovered with monthly data, does not appear either on all countries or on all macroeconomic quantities when quarterly data are used.[2]

Finally, Gavin and Kydland (1999) tested the equality of correlations using a Wald test. In order to take into account the uncertainty about the relevance of the assumption underlying the Wald test, Gavin and Kydland (1999) resort to Monte Carlo simulation techniques to build the distribution of the test.

The literature stresses that little is known about the true distribution of the nominal exchange rate and that of macroeconomic quantities. We adopt an agnostic approach by discarding parametric methods and by choosing the nonparametric bootstrap technique.

One thousand replications of the HP-filtered time series observed under the flexible exchange rates are randomly drawn. For each replication, the statistical business cycle property $\hat{\theta}$ (for instance, standard deviation of nominal exchange rate or output cross-country correlation) is computed. The 1000 replications allow to build a distribution of $\hat{\theta}$. It is then possible to identify the bound values that encompass 95 percent of the $\hat{\theta}$ statistics. The experiment is repeated with the HP-filtered time series observed under the pegged rates. We then infer the 95 percent confidence interval of $\hat{\theta}'$, the business cycle statistic obtained under the

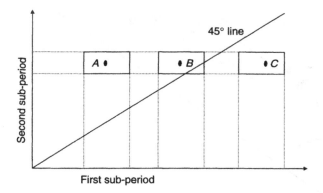

Figure 7.1 Bootstrap test.

alternative exchange rate regime. Both statistics are considered to be different when their 95 percent confidence interval do not overlap.

Figure 7.1 illustrates the bootstrap test. On the horizontal axis (respectively, on the vertical axis) is displayed, for country A, the mean value of $\hat{\theta}$ obtained under the first sub-period (the second sub-period). The 95 percent confidence interval under both sub-samples defines a rectangular era around country A. Around country B (around country A and C), the 45° line crosses the 95 percent confidence intervals. Business cycle properties in country B (in country A and C) are not significantly modified (are significantly modified) by the change in the exchange rate regime. In country A (respectively, in country C), the statistic is significantly higher (significantly lower) in the second sub-period.

7.3 Impact of exchange rate regimes on volatility

This section gauges the impact of exchange rate regime on the magnitude of exchange rate fluctuations. We then investigate whether the evolution of exchange rate volatility affected the variability of macroeconomic quantities.

7.3.1 Exchange rates

Nominal exchange rates

Were pegged rates successful in stabilizing nominal exchange rate fluctuations? In order to measure the ability of the Bretton Woods System to do so, we study the behavior of the nominal exchange rate *vis- à-vis* the US dollar in the 1960s vs in the post-1987 era.

As in Baxter and Stockman (1989), Figure 7.2 illustrates the impact of the post Second World War agreement to tame the exchange rate. On all figures, countries are Belgium (Bel), Denmark (Den), France (Fra), Germany (Ger), Greece (Gre),

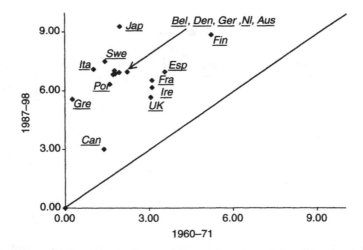

Figure 7.2 Standard deviation in percent of the HP-filtered nominal exchange rate *vis-à-vis* the US dollar.

Ireland (Ire), Italy (Ita), the Netherlands (NL), Portugal (Por), Spain (Spa), Austria (Aus), The United Kingdom (UK), Finland (Fin), Sweden (Swe), the US (US), Canada (Can) and Japan (Jap). For each country, Figure 7.2 reports the standard deviation of its nominal exchange rate against the US Dollar under pegged rates (on the horizontal axis) and under floating rates (on the vertical axis). Like on Figure 7.1, countries that are close to the diagonal do not display any significant change in their nominal exchange rate volatility. Countries that experience a significant fall (rise) in the nominal exchange rate volatility in the post-1987 era are located far below (far above) the 45° line. The country name is then underlined. On Figure 7.2, all countries are located far above the 45° line, suggesting that the shift to floating rates was associated with significantly higher exchange rate volatility.

A similar conclusion is drawn from the analysis of Figure 7.3 that displays nominal exchange rate volatility *vis-à-vis* the Deutschemark (DM). The location of each country is determined by the nominal exchange rate standard deviation *vis-à-vis* the DM under floating rates (1971:3–1979:2) on the horizontal axis and under fixed exchange rates (1987:1–1998:4) on the vertical axis. Countries that experience a significant fall (rise) in the nominal exchange rate volatility in the post-1987 era are located far below (far above) the 45° line. The country name is then underlined. The volatility of the French Franc, for instance, dropped from 4.65 percent in the 1970s to 0.94 percent in the post-1987 period, which is significantly lower than the volatility under the floating era.

For all EMS countries but Italy the creation of the EMS actually resulted in a significant drop in the nominal exchange rate volatility against the DM. In countries that are not part of the European arrangement (the US, Japan, Canada, the UK, Greece and Sweden) or a latecomer to the EMS (Finland), the nominal exchange

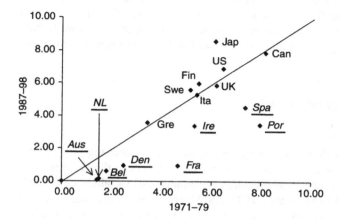

Figure 7.3 Standard deviation in percent of the HP-filtered nominal exchange rate *vis-à-vis* the DM.

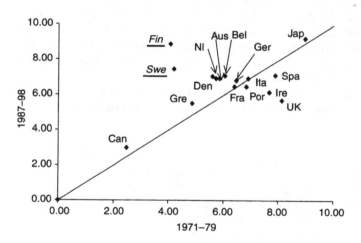

Figure 7.4 Standard deviation of the nominal exchange rate *vis-à-vis* the US dollar.

rate volatility is not altered by the change in the exchange rate regime. The statistics confirm that fixed-exchange rates do result in a lower variance in the nominal exchange rate.

This evolution is not observed when the nominal exchange rate is considered in relation to the US dollar (Figure 7.4). All countries but Finland and Sweden are scattered around the diagonal: they do not exhibit any significant volatility shift across exchange rate regimes. This evidence suggests that nominal exchange rate stabilization *vis-à-vis* the DM stems from membership to the European arrangement.

In line with Baxter and Stockman (1989) and Mussa's (1986) results, nominal exchange rate fluctuations are characterized by significantly lower volatility under pegged rates. This result is also observed for member countries to the EMS. Nominal exchange rate stabilization under fixed rates is a robust stylized fact.

Real exchange rates

The real exchange rate is defined as

$$q_t = e_t + p_t^* - p_t,$$

where q_t denotes the real exchange rate, e_t the nominal exchange rate (1 US dollar or 1 DM equals e units of local currency), p_t^* the US or the German consumer price index and p_t the local consumer price index. All variables are logged.

As mentioned by Stockman (1983) and Mussa (1986), real exchange rate fluctuations differ across exchange rate regimes. Stockman (1983) and Mussa's (1986) findings are robust to a longer data set.

Real exchange rate behavior exhibits a significant rise in volatility in the post-1987 period (Figure 7.5). The distribution of countries is similar to the one observed on Figure 7.2: All points are located above the 45° line, which exemplifies a significant upsurge in real exchange rate volatility after the fall of the Bretton Woods System. This result is consistent with Mussa's (1986) stylized fact that stresses the high correlation observed in the short run between the behavior of real and nominal exchange rates.

This similarity between nominal and real exchange rate is also obtained when one analyzes the effects of the EMS. On Figure 7.6, countries that undergo a lower

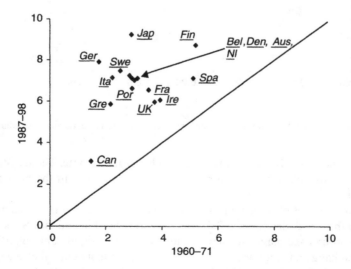

Figure 7.5 Bretton Woods – standard deviation in percent of the HP-filtered real exchange rate *vis-à-vis* the US dollar.

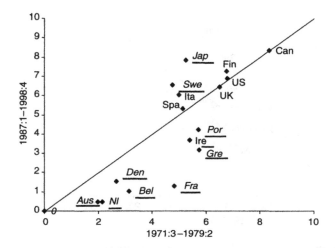

Figure 7.6 EMS – standard deviation in percent of the HP-filtered real exchange rate *vis-à-vis* the DM.

nominal exchange rate volatility *vis-à-vis* the DM in the post-1987 era, with the exception of Spain, also display the similar stabilization of their real exchange rate.

The fall of the Bretton Woods System was associated with higher nominal and real exchange rate volatility. This conclusion remains relevant when one analyzes the impact of the EMS on exchange rate short run behavior.

International macroeconomics considers the nominal exchange rate as a key adjustment variable. Under pegged rates, countries adjust to shocks through other channels, such as movements in macroeconomic aggregates. In that case, we would observe a "volatility transfer" under fixed rates: macroeconomic aggregates respond more to exogenous impulses, thereby exhibiting a higher volatility. The next section evaluates the relevance of this intuition.

7.3.2 Business cycle stabilization

Baxter and Stockman (1989), Eichengreen (1994) and Flood and Rose (1995) investigate the impact of the Bretton Woods System on business cycle volatility. However, in these studies, the specific impact of oil shocks is not identified. In order to remedy this drawback, we abstract from the 1971:4–1986:4 period that was characterized by major oil price changes. In addition, we assess the robustness of Baxter and Stockman's (1989) findings to an alternative exchange rate regime, namely the EMS.

GDP

Was this reduced volatility in exchange rates associated with a more volatile business cycle? Figure 7.7 summarizes the impact of the post-Second World War

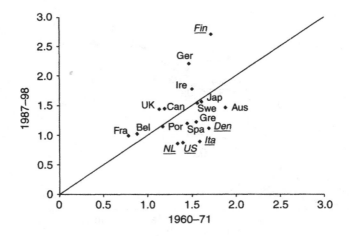

Figure 7.7 Bretton Woods – GDP volatility across exchange rate regimes.

exchange rate arrangement on GDP fluctuations. For each country, GDP standard deviation under pegged rates (under floating rates) is reported on the horizontal axis (on the vertical axis). Countries that display significant rise (significant decline) in GDP standard deviation are located above (below) the 45° line. Finland, for instance, experienced an increase in its GDP volatility from 1.72 percent in the 1960s to 2.71 percent, which is significantly higher than 1.72 percent.

All countries are scattered around the diagonal: GDP volatility is not significantly affected by the change to floating rates. Had the Bretton Woods System been responsible for any volatility shift, this change would have been observed for all countries. All points would have been concentrated in the lower right corner (in case of a fall in GDP volatility) or in the upper left corner (in case of a rise in GDP volatility) of Figure 7.7. Only Denmark, Italy, the US and the Netherlands exhibit a significant decline in GDP standard deviation.

As far as the EMS is concerned, Figure 7.8 suggests that there is some GDP stabilization under flexible rates although the evidence is weak. The sample consists of EMS countries as well as non-EMS countries in order to distinguish EMS-specific phenomena from general tendencies in the business cycle. Figure 7.8 exhibits the standard deviation of HP-filtered GDP in the pre-1979 float and the EMS years. Indeed, the evolution of GDP standard deviation among EMS countries is heterogenous: France, Denmark, Italy and Portugal experience a significant fall in the GDP standard deviation in the post-1987 era, whereas GDP fluctuations are not significantly affected in the Netherlands, Germany, Ireland, Austria, Spain and Belgium. The distribution of countries around the 45° line does not correspond to membership or non-membership to the European System. There is no systematic link between membership to the EMS and the magnitude of business cycles.

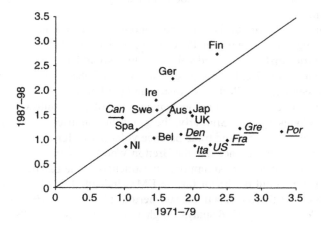

Figure 7.8 EMS – GDP volatility across exchange rate regimes.

Table 7.1 Bretton Woods System – business cycle volatility

	C		Inv		NX/GDP	
	I	II	I	II	I	II
Belgium	0.69	0.90 (+)	2.75	3.73 (+)	0.32	0.36
Denmark	1.53	1.31	4.13	4.51	0.71	0.74
France	0.76	0.79	1.60	2.83	0.45	0.37
Germany	1.56	2.96 (+)	4.06	4.19 (+)	0.45	1.39 (+)
Greece	0.84	1.12	4.95	4.39	0.52	0.80 (+)
Ireland	1.83	1.23 (−)	4.40	5.54	0.94	0.84
Italy	1.16	1.20	5.76	3.46 (−)	0.81	1.07
NL	1.91	0.87 (−)	3.08	2.07	0.49	0.55
Portugal	4.15	0.74 (−)	5.00	3.42 (−)	2.31	1.03 (−)
Spain	1.36	1.34	3.15	4.91 (+)	0.49	0.73 (+)
Austria	2.62	1.60 (−)	5.39	5.89	1.03	0.87
Finland	1.98	2.46	4.16	9.10 (+)	1.06	1.44 (+)
Sweden	1.69	1.33	1.78	6.92 (+)	0.80	0.88
UK	1.28	1.67	3.21	4.27	0.64	0.90
US	1.07	0.78 (−)	2.69	2.23	0.19	0.34 (+)
Canada	1.17	1.14	3.29	4.08 (−)	0.60	0.77
Japan	1.09	1.16	4.02	3.86	0.40	0.60 (+)

Consumption, investment and trade balance

This conclusion remains relevant when GDP components (consumption, investment and net exports to GDP) are considered. Table 7.1 displays the standard deviation of consumption (C), investment (Inv) and net exports to GDP (NX/GDP). (+) (−) indicate that the standard deviation is significantly higher (significantly lower) during the post-1987 period (period II) than in the 1960s (period I). No sign means that the standard deviation is not significantly altered by the shift to flexible exchange rates.

The evolution of the volatility of these macroeconomic aggregates is heterogeneous. Had the exchange rate system been the cause of business cycle changes, the distribution of countries that experienced volatility shift would have been similar as the one observed in Figure 7.2. For instance, consumption behavior is stabilized only in Ireland, the Netherlands, Portugal, Austria and the US while all countries experienced a sharp increase in nominal exchange rate volatility following the fall of the Bretton Woods System. Similarly, the group of countries that display significant changes in investment and trade balance volatility differ from the one on Figure 7.2. There is little evidence that the Bretton Woods System has spurred any systematic volatility shift in consumption, investment or trade balance.

A similar conclusion could be drawn for the EMS. Indeed, Table 7.2 reports standard deviations of HP-filtered data under sub-periods I (1971:1–1979:2) and II (1987:1–1998:4). Consumption (C) displays a higher variability in the EMS years in Finland and Germany while it is stabilized in Denmark, France, Greece, Ireland and Portugal, and unaffected in other EMS countries. This partition of countries does not correspond to the one displayed on Figure 7.3. Similar comments apply to investment (Inv) and net exports to GDP (NX/GDP). There is no empirical regularity among EMS countries regarding the change in the standard deviation of these quantities. This seems to indicate that fixed rates are not systematically associated with more volatile business cycles.

Table 7.2 EMS – business cycle volatility

	C		Inv		NX/GDP	
	I	II	I	II	I	II
EMS countries						
Belgium	1.37	0.91	2.08	3.75 (+)	0.63	0.36 (−)
Denmark	2.71	1.29 (−)	6.96	4.54	1.18	0.73 (−)
France	2.34	0.78 (−)	3.70	2.88	0.59	0.37 (−)
Germany	1.42	2.96 (+)	4.81	4.25	0.62	1.38 (+)
Greece	1.49	1.14 (−)	10.08	4.38 (−)	0.71	0.81
Ireland	2.46	1.22 (−)	7.26	5.43	2.31	0.83 (−)
Italy	1.23	1.17	3.51	3.42	0.90	1.07
NL	1.18	0.85	4.20	2.09 (−)	0.95	0.57 (−)
Portugal	2.62	0.74 (−)	7.42	3.45 (−)	1.83	1.05 (−)
Spain	1.02	1.34	3.50	4.91	0.67	0.73
Austria	1.96	1.60	5.02	5.91	1.17	0.89
Finland	1.68	2.52 (+)	5.22	9.31 (+)	2.04	1.44 (−)
Sweden	1.74	1.32	3.13	6.89 (+)	1.66	0.87 (−)
Non-EMS countries						
UK	2.15	1.66	2.21	4.24 (+)	0.77	0.89
US	1.80	0.77 (−)	6.57	2.20 (−)	0.52	0.33 (−)
Canada	1.10	1.11	2.98	4.03	0.90	0.77
Japan	1.86	1.17	4.53	3.85	0.77	0.60

This empirical investigation suggests that the volatility puzzle uncovered by Baxter and Stockman (1989) and Flood and Rose (1995) on the Bretton Woods System is robust to a longer data set. In addition, their findings remain relevant when one measures the impact of the EMS on business cycle characteristics. In EMS countries, the nominal and real exchange rates display a lower volatility with no corresponding counterpart in the volatility of macroeconomic fundamentals. This finding adds to the "exchange rate disconnect," that is, the discrepancy between exchange rate fluctuations and the behavior of its macroeconomic fundamentals (Obstfeld and Rogoff, 2000b).

7.4 Cross-country correlations

7.4.1 GDP comovement

Eichengreen (1994) finds an enhanced GDP comovement in the post-1972 period. Floating rates would then be associated with higher interdependence. This conclusion stems from Figure 7.9 that displays each country's correlation with its US counterpart under the Bretton Woods System (1960:1–1971:3) (on the horizontal axis) and the post-1971 era (on the vertical axis). All countries are located above the 45° line, thus suggesting a higher interdependence under the floating rates.

However, such a conclusion could be misleading since oil price changes might be at the origin of this strong comovement among industrialized countries under floating rates. In order to abstract from the effect of these world disturbances, we

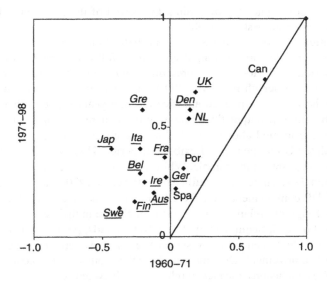

Figure 7.9 Bretton Woods – GDP comovement with the US cycle (1960–71 and 1971–98).

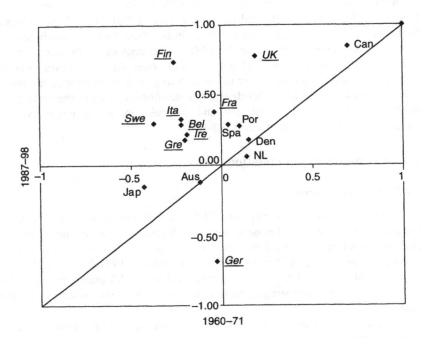

Figure 7.10 Bretton Woods – GDP comovement with the US cycle (1960–71 and 1987–98).

reexamine GDP comovement after discarding the period of the oil shocks. The flexible exchange rate regime starts in 1987.

With linear detrending, Baxter and Stockman (1989) do not uncover any systematic differences in international output correlation following the fall of the Bretton Woods period. With Hodrick and Prescott's (1997) filter, this chapter considers cycles of medium length (Canova, 1998). Figure 7.10 that reports output correlation with the US in the pegged and floating rate years suggests that the international correlation of output fluctuations actually increased: all countries, except Germany, are located above the 45° line, thereby indicating a stronger comovement with the US in the recent flexible rate period. However, this shift is not significant for all points of the sample. While all countries have suffered from an increased nominal exchange rate volatility since the early 1970s, some of them display higher GDP comovement with the US (Finland, the UK, Italy, France, Greece, Sweden, Belgium, Ireland) or no significant change in their synchronization with the US (Portugal, Spain, Denmark, the Netherlands, Austria, Japan and Canada). There is little evidence of any systematic link between exchange rate regimes and GDP comovement. Our findings show the robustness of Baxter and Stockman's (1989) conclusions: the lack of relationship between comovement and exchange rate agreements appears with an alternative filtering method and after taking into account the oil shocks.

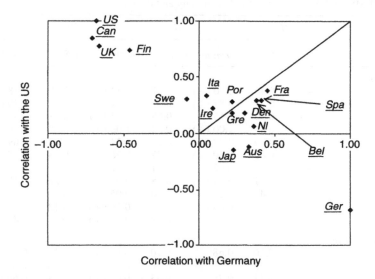

Correlation with Germany

Figure 7.11 EMS – GDP cross-country correlations (1987:1–1998:4).

Is this conclusion relevant for the EMS? In the post-1987 years, international correlations seem higher among European members than between EMS and non-EMS countries. In particular, we have isolated cross-country correlations with Germany and the US in the EMS years. The EMS has been widely described as a system dependent on the German "anchor." Thus, it seems natural to measure the business cycle synchronization of EMS partners with this country.

Figure 7.11 displays the GDP cross-country correlations during the EMS years. Correlations with the German cycle (with the US cycle) are reported on the horizontal (vertical) axis. In the post-1987 fixed rates, all EMS countries but Ireland and Portugal are located below the diagonal, thus indicating that fluctuations among EMS members have been more synchronized with the German cycle while non-EMS countries exhibit a higher comovement with the US: the correlation with the German GDP is significantly higher than the synchronization with the US cycle for Belgium, Denmark, France, the Netherlands, Spain and Austria. In contrast, we observe a more synchronized output with the US cycle for non-EMS countries (such as Sweden, the UK, Canada) or a latecomer in the European arrangement (Finland).

It is remarkable that this distribution of countries corresponds to the one observed in Figure 7.3, which displays nominal exchange rate volatility *vis-à-vis* the DM. With the exception of Ireland and Portugal, EMS countries (whose real and nominal exchange rate fluctuations were stabilized following membership to the European arrangement) exhibit a higher comovement with Germany in the post-1987 period. In contrast, with the exception of Japan, countries whose nominal exchange rate were unaffected or destabilized *vis-à-vis* the DM during the EMS years did not

Table 7.3 EMS – GDP comovement with Germany and the US

	σ_e	I		II		III	
		US	Germany	US	Germany	US	Germany
EMS countries							
Belgium	(−)	0.46	0.70 (+)	0.07	0.33 (+)	0.29	0.38 (+)
Denmark	(−)	0.79	0.87 (+)	0.54	0.54	0.18	0.30 (+)
France	(−)	0.25	0.15	−0.08	0.33 (+)	0.38	0.45 (+)
Germany		0.86	1.00 (+)	0.84	1.00 (+)	−0.68	1.00 (+)
Ireland	(−)	0.39	0.08 (−)	0.22	0.24	0.22	0.09 (−)
Italy		0.42	0.60 (+)	0.47	0.76 (+)	0.33	0.05 (−)
NL	(−)	0.50	0.62	0.81	0.82	0.06	0.36 (+)
Portugal	(−)	0.71	0.89 (+)	−0.38	−0.01 (+)	0.28	0.22
Spain	(−)	0.45	0.51	−0.30	0.05 (+)	0.29	0.41 (+)
Austria	(−)	0.43	0.68 (+)	0.20	0.56 (+)	−0.12	0.33 (+)
Finland		−0.05	0.15 (+)	−0.08	0.22 (+)	0.74	−0.46 (−)
Non-EMS countries							
Greece		0.70	0.68	0.70	0.82 (+)	0.18	0.22
Sweden		−0.35	−0.35	0.70	0.70	0.30	−0.08 (−)
UK		0.81	0.76	0.45	0.69 (+)	0.78	−0.66 (−)
US		1.00	0.86 (−)	1.00	0.84 (−)	1.00	−0.68 (−)
Canada		0.69	0.73	0.86	0.80	0.85	−0.71 (−)
Japan		0.79	0.80	0.39	0.57 (+)	−0.15	0.23 (+)

experience a more synchronized output with Germany. Greece that has not stabilized its currency against the DM is not more synchronized with the German anchor. The EMS seems to have produced a strengthening in the linkages between the participating countries, resulting in a dilution of the effect of the US business cycle in favor of a stronger effect from the German business cycle.

Finally, in order to control that the enhanced comovement observed in the EMS years is more linked to the exchange rate regime than to general tendencies in the business cycle, we report in Table 7.3 the cross-country correlations with Germany and the US in all sub-periods. For all countries, the third column (σ_e) reports the impact of behavior of the nominal exchange rate against the DM in the post-1987 era. The sign (−) indicates that the nominal exchange rate against the DM is significantly less volatile in the 1987:1–1998:4 period. No sign indicates the absence of any volatility shift in the local currency. For instance, Belgium experienced a significant stabilization in its nominal exchange rate *vis-à-vis* the German currency while the Italian lira did not exhibit any significant volatility change.[3] Columns 4–5 display the correlation with the German cycle and the US cycle in subperiod I (1971:3–1979:2). The sign (+) and the sign (−) indicate that the country is more synchronized (less synchronized) with the German cycle than with the US cycle. Columns 6–7 and 8–9 replicate the same computations for sub-periods II (1979:3–1986:4) and III (1987:1–1998:4).

The UK, Greece and Sweden have never been part of the European exchange rate arrangement. The analysis of business cycle properties in these countries allows to distinguish between the impact of the European economic integration and the consequences of the EMS. In sub-period II, British and Greek GDPs are more correlated with the German cycle while Swedish GDP is equally correlated with Germany and the US. In sub-period III, none of these countries become more correlated with Germany, thereby suggesting that the higher correlation with Germany in the post-1987 years is more linked to the EMS than to the European economic integration.

Table 7.3 shows that the enhanced comovement with the German anchor in the post-1987 period stems from the shift to pegged rates. Countries that stabilized their exchange rate against the DM display a more synchronized cycle with Germany than with the US. In contrast, all non-EMS countries (except Japan) along with Finland (a latecomer in the European arrangement) become more correlated with the US cycle in sub-period III (1987:1–1998:4) whereas, in previous sub-periods (I and II), those countries exhibit higher or equal correlation with Germany.

7.4.2 Consumption and investment international comovements

As far as the fall of the Bretton Woods System is concerned, the heterogenous behavior of cross-country consumption correlations (Figure 7.12) suggest that

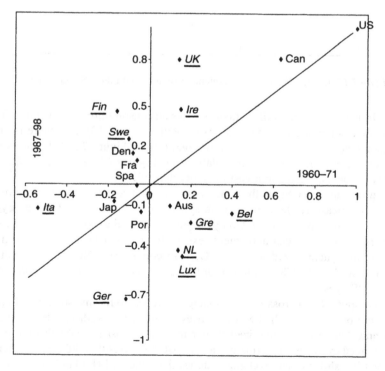

Figure 7.12 Bretton Woods – consumption correlation with the US counterpart.

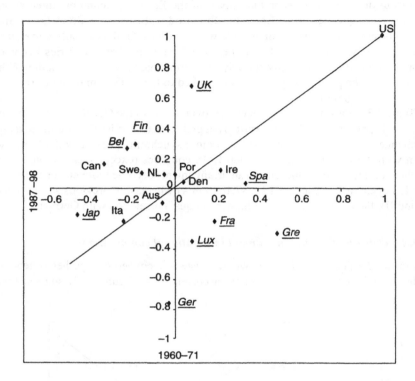

Figure 7.13 Bretton Woods – investment correlation with the US counterpart.

there is little impact of the shift to floating rates on consumption comovement. The same conclusion could be drawn for investment (Figure 7.13). For, there is little correspondence between the location of countries on Figure 7.2 that reports the evolution of nominal exchange rate volatility and Figures 7.12 and 7.13 displaying changes in consumption and investment interdependence.

In contrast, membership to the EMS seems to affect consumption comovement. Figure 7.14 measures the consumption synchronization with the German cycle (on the horizontal axis) and the US cycle (on the vertical axis) in the EMS years. Members to the European agreement, except Ireland and Denmark, are significantly more synchronized with their German counterpart. Non-EMS countries (Canada, Sweden, the UK and Japan) or latecomers (Finland) are more correlated with the US cycle.

The computation of cross-country linkages is repeated for investment on Figure 7.15. Five out of the eight EMS countries (France, the Netherlands, Portugal, Spain and Austria) that stabilized their currency against the DM display more synchronized cycles with Germany. In contrast, countries that did not experience any volatility shift in their exchange rate *vis-à-vis* the DM (Finland, Sweden, the UK and Canada) are more synchronized with the US cycle or do not exhibit

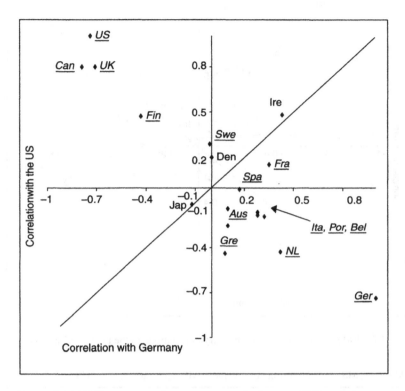

Figure 7.14 EMS – consumption comovement in the post-1987 period.

any significant correlation with either Germany or the US. Figure 7.15 suggests that the EMS has been associated with more synchronized investment cycles.

In order to check that the enhanced comovement observed in the EMS years is more linked to the exchange rate arrangement than to economic integration in Europe, Tables 7.4 and 7.5 report cross-country consumption and investment comovements for all sub-periods. As mentioned in Section 7.4.1, the behavior of correlations with the UK, Greece and Finland seems to confirm that the increased international output correlation among EMS partners is more due to EMS membership than to the European integration.

Baxter and Stockman's (1989) findings are robust. The fall of the Bretton Woods System did not generate a stronger international comovement in either GDP, consumption or investment. This evidence suggests that the exchange rate regime is neutral as far as cross-country correlations are concerned. This conclusion is not supported by European data. Indeed, EMS members that stabilized their currency against the DM experienced in the post-1987 period more synchronized cycles with the German anchor than with the US cycle.

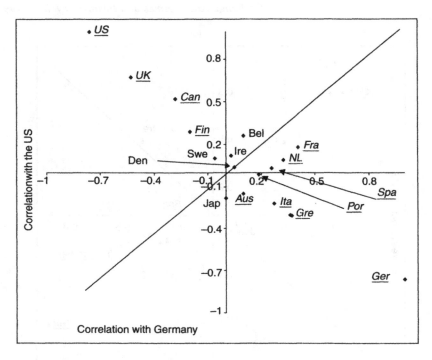

Figure 7.15 EMS – investment cross-country correlations in the post-1987 period.

Table 7.4 EMS – consumption comovement with Germany and the US

		I		II		III	
	σ_e	US	Germany	US	Germany	US	Germany
EMS countries							
Belgium	(−)	0.39	0.13 (−)	−0.08	0.56 (+)	−0.19	0.32 (+)
Denmark	(−)	0.60	0.33 (−)	0.73	0.41 (−)	0.20	0.00 (−)
France	(−)	0.16	−0.40 (−)	−0.24	0.08 (+)	0.15	0.35 (+)
Germany		0.79	1.00 (+)	0.61	1.00 (+)	−0.74	1.00 (+)
Ireland	(−)	0.63	0.47	0.45	0.80 (+)	0.48	0.43
Italy		0.18	−0.00	−0.08	0.65 (+)	−0.16	0.28 (+)
NL	(−)	0.64	0.51 (−)	0.71	0.80 (+)	−0.43	0.42 (+)
Portugal	(−)	−0.47	−0.68 (−)	−0.86	−0.38 (+)	−0.18	0.28 (+)
Spain	(−)	0.29	−0.17 (−)	−0.13	0.50 (+)	−0.01	0.17 (+)
Austria	(−)	0.25	0.22	0.02	0.03	−0.14	0.10 (+)
Finland		−0.11	−0.13	−0.06	0.24 (+)	0.47	−0.43
Non-EMS countries							
Greece		0.91	0.76 (−)	0.05	−0.13	−0.25	0.10 (+)
Sweden		−0.18	−0.27	0.08	0.48 (+)	0.29	−0.01 (−)
UK		0.40	0.36	0.41	0.79 (+)	0.80	−0.71 (−)
US		1.00	0.79 (−)	1.00	0.61 (−)	1.00	−0.74 (−)
Canada		0.34	0.19	0.56	0.75 (+)	0.80	−0.79 (−)
Japan		0.56	0.45	0.30	0.46 (+)	−0.11	−0.12

Table 7.5 EMS – investment comovement with Germany and the US

	σ_e	I US	I Germany	II US	II Germany	III US	III Germany
EMS countries							
Belgium	(−)	0.22	−0.2	0.21	0.67 (+)	0.26	0.10 (−)
Denmark	(−)	0.81	0.71	0.55	0.30	0.04	0.05
France	(−)	0.22	0.06	−0.26	0.43 (+)	0.18	0.35 (+)
Germany		0.81	1.00 (+)	0.55	1.00 (+)	−0.76	1.00 (+)
Ireland	(−)	0.84	0.82	−0.06	0.17 (+)	0.12	0.03
Italy		0.27	0.14	0.22	0.71 (+)	−0.22	0.27 (+)
NL		0.55	0.40	0.66	0.63	0.09	0.24 (+)
Portugal	(−)	0.83	0.82	−0.77	−0.07 (+)	−0.01	0.10 (+)
Spain	(−)	0.11	−0.13	−0.76	−0.02 (+)	0.03	0.13 (+)
Austria	(−)	0.43	0.53	0.35	0.59 (+)	−0.10	0.10 (+)
Finland		−0.54	−0.36 (+)	−0.59	−0.06 (+)	0.29	−0.20 (−)
Non-EMS countries							
Greece		0.78	0.91 (+)	0.44	0.59 (+)	−0.30	0.36 (+)
Sweden		−0.32	−0.02 (+)	0.26	0.44 (+)	0.10	−0.06
UK		0.43	0.19 (−)	0.42	0.46	0.67	−0.53 (−)
US		1.00	0.81 (−)	1.00	0.55 (−)	1.00	−0.76 (−)
Canada		−0.32	−0.10 (+)	0.13	0.34	0.52	−0.28 (−)
Japan		0.78	0.78	0.16	0.53	−0.18	−0.00

7.5 Conclusion

This chapter has examined international evidence on the question of whether business cycle properties of some key macroeconomic variables have changed across exchange rate regimes. While previous studies have focused on measuring the consequences of the fall of the Bretton Woods System, this chapter provides empirical evidence on the EMS case. In addition, we assess the robustness of studies on the Bretton Woods System by abstracting from the effect of the oil shocks. Finally, we have proposed a bootstrap technique to gauge the statistical significance of changes in business cycle properties observed across exchange rate regimes.

The empirical analysis seems to indicate that the consequences of exchange rate arrangements are twofold. Business cycle properties confirm that the volatility puzzle uncovered by Baxter and Stockman (1989) and Flood and Rose (1995) is robust: nominal and real exchange rate volatilities are stabilized by the fixed exchange rate regime with no corresponding changes in the variability of the macroeconomic aggregates. There is no apparent systematic relationship between the exchange rate regime and the volatility of quantities. This conclusion applies to the Bretton Woods System as well as to the European exchange rate arrangement. The next chapter gauges the ability of a two-country model to replicate this stylized fact.

The second empirical salient feature deals with interdependence. Our conclusion is consistent with Baxter and Stockman's (1989) conclusion about the lack of systematic relationship between the fall of the Bretton Woods System and international comovement. However, this feature is not a stylized fact since the analysis of EMS does not yield the same conclusion. Indeed, during the EMS period, EMS countries are more synchronized with the German cycle than with the US cycle. In that sense, since Germany can be considered as an "anchor" to participating countries, the EMS seems to favor a greater degree of synchronization among EMS countries.

Appendix A: data

All quarterly series are logged except net exports to GDP. Net exports refer to exports of goods and services minus imports of goods and services.

- Nominal exchange rates (monthly average) (1961:1–2000:1), consumer price indices (all items, base year 1990) (1961:1–1999:4) are available in the OECD Main Economic Indicators database.
- GDP and its components (private consumption, investment and net exports) come from the OECD General Economic Problem, Business Sector Data Base. Time series are available from 1960:1 to 1998:4 except for

  (i) France (1963:1–1998:4) and Portugal (1960:1–1997:4) for GDP;
  (ii) France (1963:1–1998:4), Portugal (1960:1–1997:4) and Canada (1961:1–1998:4) for private consumption, investment and net exports.

  Cross-country correlations are computed on the largest common sample. German net exports (1961:1–1998:4) stem from the OECD Main Economic Indicators database. German time series are West German aggregates. French observations were adjusted to cancel the effects of May 1968.
- The quarterly money aggregates (money + quasi money) come from the IMF *International Financial Statistics* database (1971:3–1990:4).

Table 7.6 Membership to the European arrangements

	European Union	EMS	Monetary union
Belgium	March 1957	March 1979	Qualified
Denmark	January 1973	March 1979	—
France	March 1957	March 1979	Qualified
Germany	March 1957	March 1979	Qualified
Greece	January 1981	—	Qualified
Ireland	January 1973	March 1979	Qualified
Italy	March 1957	March 1979	Qualified
NL	March 1957	March 1979	Qualified
Portugal	January 1986	April 1992	Qualified
Spain	January 1986	June 1989	Qualified
UK	January 1973	—	—
Austria	January 1995	January 1995	Qualified
Finland	January 1995	October 1996	Qualified
Sweden	January 1995	—	—

Appendix B: countries

This study documents business cycle properties of fourteen European countries (Belgium, Denmark, France, Germany,[4] Greece, Ireland, Italy,[5] the Netherlands, Portugal, Spain, the UK,[6] Austria, Finland, Sweden) and three other industrialized countries (the US, Canada and Japan). Table 7.6 summarizes the European integration process.

Notes

1 Sopraseuth (2002b) gauges the robustness of the results to alternative filtering methods.
2 This result is obtained after running ARCH tests on the residuals of the following equation:

$$\Delta x_t = a_0 + \sum_i^k a_i \Delta x_{t-i} + e_t$$

After checking that all series are $I(1)$ with ADF tests, estimates are obtained with lag k chosen to make residuals serially uncorrelated.
3 The third column of Table 7.3 (σ_e) reports the results displayed in Figure 7.3.
4 We consider only Western Germany in OECD data.
5 Italy left the EMS in September 1992 before joining again the European arrangement in November 1996.
6 The UK joined the EMS between October 1990 and September 1992.

8 A quantitative analysis of currency regimes

Luca Dedola and Sylvain Leduc

8.1 Introduction

Does the currency regime matter? The main industrial countries have experienced a wide range of exchange-rate arrangements in the last two centuries, ranging between the two polar systems of fixed and flexible exchange rates. Before the establishment in 1871 of the international gold standard, effectively a system of fixed exchange rates, the prevailing arrangement was the bimetallic system, based on the relative price of gold and silver. After the demise of the gold standard and the associated turmoil in the international financial system between the two World Wars, the Bretton Woods system was chartered in 1944. A system of fixed but adjustable exchange rates, it was abandoned in the early seventies in favor of a system of generalized floating exchange rates. In the late seventies, several European countries started the process that culminated with the launch of the euro in January 1999.

The same variety of exchange-rate regimes that we observe through time for an individual country also exists today across countries. In 1998, according to the IMF taxonomy (IMF, 1998), 66 countries unilaterally pegged either to a single or to a composite currency, 17 adhered to an exchange-rate regime with partial flexibility, and the remaining 101 followed more flexible arrangements, such as managed or independent floating. Even among the more homogeneous group of 33 OECD and newly industrialized countries, 11 were on the verge of sharing a single currency, the euro; four were pegged; and the remaining ones followed arrangements of independent and managed floating.

Against this backdrop, it is not surprising that since the early important contributions of Friedman (1953) and Mundell (1961, 1963), the above questions have ranked high in the international finance research agenda. Cooper (1999) goes as far as arguing that for many countries "the choice of exchange rate policy is probably their single most important macroeconomic policy decision."

This chapter studies the welfare effects of fixing the exchange rate from a quantitative viewpoint. We analyze a two-country equilibrium business cycle model, featuring nominal rigidities and deviations from the law of one price, due to firms pricing-to-market. In this now rather standard class of economies, real effects stem from both systematic and nonsystematic components of monetary policy. This is consistent with the consensus view that, speculative attacks aside, the exchange-rate arrangement affects real economic variables only if the latter are influenced by a systematic component of monetary policy.[1] Dedola and Leduc (2001) showed that a realistically calibrated model with such building blocks can also quantitatively account for some key stylized facts regarding the real and allocative consequences of the choice of the currency regime. In particular, the model could reproduce the findings of Baxter and Stockman (1989) and Flood and Rose (1995) that, among the statistical properties of most macroeconomic variables, only the volatility of the real and nominal exchange rates has dramatically changed after the fall of the Bretton Woods system.

We explore the welfare costs of an exchange-rate peg relative to a float, when central banks attempt to stabilize their economy by following forward-looking interest-rate rules. We find that, although the welfare differences across exchange-rate regimes are small, a flexible exchange-rate system is still preferred to a currency peg. Our result is driven by the fact that, under the flexible exchange-rate system, the central bank, via its interest-rate policy, is able to dampen the movements in output and, therefore, the volatility of employment. This does not occur under a currency peg. In this case, the central bank foregoes its interest-rate rule and sets monetary policy to keep the value of the currency fixed. Output and employment are more volatile under this regime, as a result. Since agents are risk averse, they prefer the relatively more stable employment/leisure path brought about when the currency floats.

The last step in our analysis is motivated by the observation that some specifications of the interest-rate rule may lead to monetary instability. Following a recent strand in the macroeconomic literature (e.g. Clarida *et al.*, 2000), we focus on the ability of the monetary policy rule and the exchange-rate regime to provide a credible nominal anchor and rule out bad outcomes. The idea is that the lack of credibility can result in the adoption of a monetary rule that may enable inflation expectations to become self-fulfilling (because of the indeterminacy of the steady state equilibrium). The economy may therefore fluctuate due to movements in non-fundamental shocks (or sunspots), which may reduce welfare. We show that if inflation expectations are self-fulfilling, a country would be better off by fixing its currency.

The choice of exchange-rate regimes has recently been studied by Chinn and Miller (1998) – in a flexible-price environment – and Devereux and Engel (1998) – who studied the impact of the price setting on the optimal exchange-rate regime with uncertainty arising from permanent money supply shocks. Gali and Monacelli (1999) showed that the optimal monetary policy for a small, open economy entails some management of the exchange rate. Finally, Devereux (1999) and Obstfeld and Rogoff (2000a) derive the optimal Ramsey monetary policy in tractable versions of two-country models with predetermined prices.

The remainder of the chapter is organized as follows. Section 8.2 briefly lays down the structure of the model, whose properties were fully explored in Dedola and Leduc (2001), and Section 8.3 presents the calibration. In Section 8.4, we first explore the impact of the exchange-rate regime on the volatility of macroeconomic variables. We then compute the welfare consequences of the currency regime and briefly assess the advantages of tying one's hands, via an exchange-rate peg, when monetary policy is not credible and let inflation expectations become self-fulfilling. We assess the sensitivity of our results before concluding.

8.2   The model

Building from the work of Obstfeld and Rogoff (1995) and Ohanian *et al.* (1995), we model a two-country world in which each economy is composed of two sectors: one sector produces a homogeneous good, which we assume to be identical across countries, while the other sector is specialized in the production of a set of differentiated products. Specifically, the differentiated goods sector comprises a continuum of monopolistic firms, each producing a distinct differentiated good using labor and capital. These firms, contrary to the firms in the competitive sector, face convex price-adjustment costs of the type analyzed in Rotemberg (1982a). We assume that, because of barriers to trade, monopolistic firms are able to price-discriminate across markets. The homogeneous good, which is perfectly traded in world markets, is also produced using capital and labor. Capital and labor are mobile across sectors. For simplicity, we assume that investment is made in the homogeneous good only. To generate plausible investment volatility, we postulate a cost to adjusting the amount of capital in a country, as in Baxter and Crucini (1995). We now describe the model in more detail.

8.2.1   Preferences

A representative agent inhabits each economy. The agent maximizes his expected lifetime utility as given by[2]

$$E_0 \left[\sum_{t=0}^{\infty} \beta^t U \left(C^T, C^M, \frac{M'}{P}, (1-H) \right) \right], \tag{8.1}$$

where C^T represents the agent's consumption of the homogeneous good, H represents the agent's supply of labor, M' denotes the agent's demand for nominal money balances, P is the country's price index, and C^M is an index of consumption of differentiated home and foreign goods given by

$$C^M \equiv \left(a_H \left[\int_0^1 (c(h))^\theta \, dh \right]^{\omega/\theta} + a_F \left[\int_0^1 (c(f))^\theta \, df \right]^{\omega/\theta} \right)^{1/\omega}, \tag{8.2}$$

where $c(h)$ $(c(f))$ is the agent's consumption of the home (foreign) brand $h(f)$ of the differentiated good at time t. There is a continuum of these goods, with measure one. Total consumption is defined according to a Cobb–Douglas aggregator, $C \equiv (C^T)^\gamma (C^M)^{1-\gamma}$. Preferences and consumption of the foreign representative agent, C^*, are defined in a similar way.

The demand for the brands h and f of the home and foreign differentiated goods is obtained by maximizing the differentiated good consumption index subject to expenditure:

$$c(h) = \left(\frac{p(h)}{P^H}\right)^{-1/(1-\theta)} \left(\frac{P^H}{a_H P^M}\right)^{-1/(1-\omega)} C^M, \tag{8.3}$$

$$c(f) = \left(\frac{p(f)}{P^F}\right)^{-1/(1-\theta)} \left(\frac{P^F}{a_F P^M}\right)^{-1/(1-\omega)} C^M, \tag{8.4}$$

where $p(h)(p(f))$ is the home currency price of the home-produced (foreign-produced) brand h (f) of the differentiated good.

P^M, P^H and P^F are the standard utility-based price indices:

$$P^M = \left[a_H^{1/(1-\omega)} \left(P^H\right)^{-\omega/(1-\omega)} + a_F^{1/(1-\omega)} \left(P^F\right)^{-\omega/(1-\omega)}\right]^{-(1-\omega)/\omega}, \tag{8.5}$$

$$P^H = \left[\int_0^1 p(h)^{\theta/(\theta-1)} \, dh\right]^{(\theta-1)/\theta}, \quad P^F = \left[\int_0^1 p(f)^{\theta/(\theta-1)} \, df\right]^{(\theta-1)/\theta}. \tag{8.6}$$

Finally, the overall price index is given by

$$P = \frac{(P^T)^\gamma (P^M)^{1-\gamma}}{\gamma^\gamma (1-\gamma)^{1-\gamma}}.$$

8.2.2 Production technologies

The production of the homogeneous and differentiated goods requires combining labor and capital using Cobb–Douglas production functions:

$$Y^T = A \left(K^T\right)^\rho \left(H^T\right)^{1-\rho}, \quad 0 < \rho < 1, \tag{8.7}$$

$$Y(h) = A (K(h))^\alpha (H(h))^{1-\alpha}, \quad 0 < \alpha < 1, \forall h, \tag{8.8}$$

where A represents an economy-wide, country-specific random technology shock.[3]

Capital accumulation is assumed to be carried out in the homogenous good only. In any given period, K will represent the capital stock in place in the home country. To have realistic investment flows (investment volatility tends to be too high otherwise), we follow Baxter and Crucini (1993) and assume that the law of motion of capital is subject to adjustment costs. The law of motion is described by the following equation:

$$K' = \Psi(I/K)K + (1-\delta)K, \tag{8.9}$$

where δ is the depreciation rate and $\Psi(\cdot)$ is an increasing, concave, and twice continuously differentiable function with two properties entailing no adjustment costs in steady state: $\Psi(\delta) = \delta$ and $\Psi'(\delta) = 1$.

8.2.3   The firm in the homogeneous good sector

The firm's problem is the usual one:

$$\max_{K^T,H^T} \prod^T \equiv P^T A \left(K^T \right)^{\rho} \left(H^T \right)^{1-\rho} - R^T K^T - W^T H^T, \tag{8.10}$$

where P^T, R^T, and W^T denote the nominal price of the purely tradable good, the rental rate of capital, and the nominal wage rate in the purely tradable good sector.

8.2.4   Firms in the monopolistic sector

We assume that firms in the monopolistic sector face a price-adjustment cost. When the firm decides to change the price it sets in the home (foreign) country, it must purchase an amount $\mu(h)$ $(\mu^*(h))$ of the homogeneous good. Following Hairault and Portier (1993b), the adjustment costs are given by the following quadratic functions:

$$\mu(h) = \frac{\xi}{2} \left(\frac{p_t(h)}{p_{t-1}(h)} - \pi \right)^2, \tag{8.11}$$

and

$$\mu^*(h) = \frac{\xi}{2} \left(\frac{p_t^*(h)}{p_{t-1}^*(h)} - \pi^* \right)^2. \tag{8.12}$$

Therefore, there are no costs to adjusting prices when the steady-state inflation rate π prevails. Because of this cost, a temporary decrease in the growth rate of the money supply will lead to a gradual fall in the inflation rate and to a decrease of the monopolistic good output below its steady-state value.

This quadratic adjustment cost is not amenable to standard menu cost stories, emphasizing the fixed cost of price changes. Rotemberg (1982a) rationalizes it by pointing to the adverse effects of price changes on customer–firm relationships, which increase in magnitude with the size of the price change.[4] Moreover, he shows that the implications of this setting for the aggregate dynamics of inflation are equivalent to those of the popular model of price rigidities developed by Calvo (1983) and often used in the open economy literature (e.g. in Kollmann, 2001). The quadratic cost is also consistent with the microeconomic evidence that some firms change their prices by very small amounts (Rotemberg, 1996).

The (postulated) presence of trade barriers makes it possible for firms to price-to-market, by choosing $p(h)$, the home-currency price they charge in the home market, to be different from $p(f)$, the foreign-currency price they charge for-eign consumers. Specifically, because of the presence of a price-adjustment cost, firms choose prices and inputs to maximize profits solving the following dynamic programming problem:

$$J(p_{-1}(h), p^*_{-1}(h); s) = \max_{p(h), p^*(h), K(h), H(h)} \left\{ \Delta \prod(h) + E\left[\Delta' J\left(p(h), p^*(h); s'\right)\right] \right\}$$
(8.13)

subject to (2.3) and its foreign counterpart, (2.8) and

$$\prod(h) = p(h)c(h) + ep^*(h)c^*(h) - R^M K(h) - W^M H(h) - P^T(\mu(h) + \mu^*(h)),$$
(8.14)

$$c(h) + c^*(h) \geq Y(h),$$
(8.15)

where $s \equiv (A, A^{\cdot}, g, g^*, PD^m_{t-1}, PD^{*m}_{t-1})$ denotes the aggregate state of the world in period t, with $g(g^*)$ denoting the domestic (foreign) growth rate of money and $PD^m(PD^{*m}_{t-1})$ representing the distributions of differentiated goods' prices in the domestic (foreign) economy. As markets are complete both domestically and internationally, in equilibrium Δ equals the pricing kernel for contingent claims.

8.2.5 The household

Each period the household decides how much labor to supply to the monopolistic sector, ϕH, and to the competitive sector, $(1 - \phi)H$, at the nominal wages W^M and W^T, where $0 < \phi < 1$. Similarly, the household supplies a fraction, v, of capital to the monopolistic sector and a fraction, $(1 - v)$, to the competitive sector at the nominal rental rates R^M and R^T. In addition to the factor payments, the household's wealth comprises nominal money balances M; contingent one-period nominal bonds denominated in the home currency $B(s)$ – which pay one unit of home currency if state s occurs and 0 otherwise; profits from the monopolistic firms $\int_0^1 \Pi(h) \, dh$; a governmental lump-sum tax or transfer T. The household must decide how much of its wealth to allocate to the consumption of the homogeneous and differentiated goods and how much to invest and save in the form of bonds and nominal money balances, facing the following nominal budget constraint:

$$P^T\left(C^T + I\right) + P^M C^M + \int_{s'} P_b(s', s)B(s') \, ds' + M' = \Omega$$
(8.16)

where $P_b(s', s)$ is the price of the bond contingent on the state s' occurring at time $t + 1$, given the state of the world, s, today. The agent's wealth follows the law of motion:

$$\Omega' = W^{M'}\phi' H' + W^{T'}(1 - \phi')H' + R^{M'}v'K' + R^{T'}(1 - v')K'$$
(8.17)

$$+ B(s') + M' + \int_0^1 \Pi'(h) \, dh + P^{T'}T'.$$

The household's problem can be written as the following dynamic programming problem:

$$V(\Omega; s) = \max_{C^T, C^M, B(s'), M', H, I, K', v, \phi} \left\{ U\left(C^T, C^M, \frac{M'}{P}, (1-H)\right) \right.$$

$$\left. + \beta E\left[V(\Omega'; s')\right] \right\} \tag{8.18}$$

subject to (8.16), (8.17), and the law of motion for capital given by (8.9).

8.2.6   Government

Each period the government makes a lump-sum transfer or collects a lump-sum tax (expressed in units of the tradable good) given by:

$$T = \left(\overline{M}' - \overline{M}\right).$$

The money supply evolves according to

$$\overline{M}' = (1 + g)\overline{M},$$

where the growth rate of money g will depend on the assumed monetary reaction function.

8.3   Calibration

In order to be able to solve the model we have to pick baseline values for the parameters. The top panel of Table 8.1 reports our benchmark choices, which we assume symmetric across the two countries. Several parameters' values are similar to those used in Chari *et al.* (2002), who calibrate their model to the United States and Europe. In contrast, because of data availability, we will compare our model to the G7 countries' evidence over the Bretton Woods and post-Bretton Woods periods.[5] In Section 8.4.4, we conduct some sensitivity analysis to assess the robustness of our results, under the benchmark calibration.

8.3.1   Preferences

Consider first the preference parameters. We adopt a utility function of the following form, separable between the consumption-money aggregate and leisure:

$$
U\left(C, \frac{M'}{P}, H\right) = \frac{1}{1-\eta}\left[\left(\psi\left((C^T)^\gamma (C^M)^{1-\gamma}\right)^{(\sigma-1)/\sigma}\right.\right.
$$

$$
\left.\left. + (1-\psi)\left(\frac{M'}{P}\right)^{(\sigma-1)/\sigma}\right)^{\sigma/(\sigma-1)}\right]^{1-\eta} + \upsilon\frac{(1-H)^{1-\varepsilon}}{1-\varepsilon}.
$$

(8.19)

The leisure parameters ε and υ are set so as to give an elasticity of labor supply, with marginal utility held constant, of 2 and a working time of one-quarter of the total time. We set to curvature parameter η to 2.

Following Chari *et al.* (2002), we set ψ to 0.94. The interest elasticity of money demand, σ, is known to be small but positive. We use Ireland's (1997) estimate and set it equal to 0.159. The relative share of the differentiated consumption good in steady-state consumption $(1-\gamma)$ is set to 0.58, which is the average of Rauch's (1999) estimate for differentiated products over the last three decades.[6] The discount factor β is set to 0.9901, implying a quarterly real interest rate of 1 percent.

We set θ to 6.17, yielding a value of 1.19 for the steady-state markup, equal to that estimated by Morrison (1990); this value is standard in the literature. The elasticity of substitution between monopolistic home and foreign goods is $1/(1-\omega)$; we use the estimate of Backus *et al.* (1995) and set it to 1.5. We set the parameters a_H and a_F, in the consumption aggregator – determining the steady-state monopolistic good import share – to 0.7607 and 0.2393 respectively. This corresponds to the parameters in Chari *et al.* (2002), in their high export share exercise, and is also in line with the estimates in Kollmann (2001) for the G7 countries.

8.3.2   *Production*

Consider next the technology parameters for the homogeneous and the differentiated goods. Since all the goods are traded, we used Stockman and Tesar's (1995) estimate of the labor share in the production of tradable goods and set $(1-\rho)$ and $(1-\alpha)$ to 0.61.

We set the second derivative of the capital adjustment cost function in steady state, $\phi''(\delta)$, so that the volatility of investment relative to that of output is in line with the data. Following Ireland (1997), we set the parameter of the price-adjustment cost function $\xi = 50$. Ireland shows that such a parametrization leads firms to contemporaneously erase 10 percent of the discounted gap between their current and expected future prices and the price that would be optimal in the absence of adjustment costs, a value suggested by King and Watson (1996).

8.3.3 Real shocks

We assume that the economy-wide technology shocks follow a bivariate autoregressive process:

$$z' = \lambda_z z + \epsilon',$$

where $z \equiv (z, z^*)$, $\epsilon \equiv (\epsilon, \epsilon^*)$ and λ_z is a matrix of coefficients. For our benchmark calibration, we follow Backus *et al.* (1995) and use their estimates of λ for the US and Europe:

$$\lambda_z = \begin{bmatrix} 0.906 & 0.088 \\ 0.088 & 0.906 \end{bmatrix},$$

and their values for the standard deviation and cross-correlation of the shocks (ϵ, ϵ^*), equal to 0.00852 and 0.258, respectively.

8.3.4 Monetary process

Under the flexible exchange-rate regime, we assume that the central banks follow a forward-looking Taylor-type rule, that is, a feedback rule for the nominal interest rate. Taylor (1993) argues that the US Federal Open Market Committee policy since the early 1980s has been to adjust the short-term nominal interest rate in response to deviations of inflation and the output gap from their target levels. Clarida and Gertler (1997) and Clarida *et al.* (2000), found that similar rules adequately describe the policy of most G7 and European central banks. Moreover, on theoretical grounds, several papers have shown that a feedback rule for the nominal interest rate can describe well the Ramsey monetary policy in closed economy models related to ours (see *inter alia* Carlstrom and Fuerst, 1995; Rotemberg and Woodford, 1997; King and Wolman, 1999). Finally, another strand of the literature has emphasized that an important aspect of the optimal design of interest rate rules resides in their ability to protect the economy from very bad outcomes, such as an inflation spurt like that experienced in the seventies by most industrialized countries. For instance, Clarida *et al.* (2000) in a sticky-price setting, and Christiano and Gust (1999) in a limited participation model, explore whether for some parameterizations the Taylor rule is not itself a source of welfare-reducing instability for the economy. For these reasons, we find studying the welfare consequences of abandoning such type of rules to be interesting.

We take as our benchmark the forward-looking instrument rules for the short-term interest rates estimated for the US and the other G7 countries by Clarida *et al.* (1998, 2000). Specifically, we assume that the monetary authority sets the nominal short-term interest rates according to the following feedback rule:

$$\log R_t = (1 - \alpha_R) \log \overline{R} + \alpha_R \log R_{t-1} + \alpha_\pi E_t(\widehat{\pi_{t+1}}) + \alpha_y E_t(\widehat{y_{t+1}}) + \varepsilon_{t,R},$$

where R, π, and y represent the short-term nominal interest rate, aggregate inflation, and aggregate output. As usual, $\widehat{x}$ denotes the deviation of that variable from its steady-state level. Drawing from the estimates for the US in Clarida *et al.* (2000), regarding the period 1979:3–1996:4, we set $\alpha_R = 0.79$, $\alpha_\pi = 2.15$, and $\alpha_y = 0.9$.

We set the benchmark calibration of the standard deviation of $\varepsilon_{t,R}$ to 0.005, which is a middle ground between the estimates of Ireland (1997) and those found in Angeloni and Dedola (1999). Finally, since in the model the volatility of the real exchange rate is affected by the cross-correlation of consumption, the correlation of monetary shocks across countries is set such that the model matches the empirical cross-correlation of consumption between the US and the average of the other G7 countries since 1973.

Finally, under a fixed exchange-rate regime, the central bank allows the growth rate of money to vary so that the value of the currency remains fixed.

8.4 Findings

8.4.1 A look at some business-cycle statistics

We first briefly review the impact of exchange-rate arrangements on the business cycle by focusing on volatility ratios.[7] Throughout all the exercises, we define the fixed exchange-rate regime as the one in which the foreign country (credibly) pegs its currency to that of the home country. We compute all the statistics by logging and filtering the data using the Hodrick and Prescott (1997) filter and averaging moments across 100 simulations, each running for 100 time periods each. Table 8.1 reports the ratio of standard deviations of the variables under a flexible exchange-rate regime relative to a peg, when the foreign central bank relinquishes different monetary policy rules.

In order to convey the extent of the puzzle highlighted by Stockman (1983), Mussa (1986), Baxter and Stockman (1989), and Flood and Rose (1995), Table 8.1 also reports the standard deviations of the main macroeconomic variables and exchange rates for the US and the (average of) other G7 countries. Table 8.1

Table 8.1 Volatility ratios across exchange-rate regimes

	z	π	π^*	Y	Y^*	C	C^*	I	I^*	H	H^*	NX
Data[a,b]	2.65	1.38	0.98	1.10	0.99	1.30	1.35	1.42	0.91	1.21	1.34	0.87
Model	24.05	1.07	1.14	1.13	0.87	1.17	1.27	0.88	1.12	1.29	0.78	1.58

Notes

a Series are quarterly, logged (with the exception of net exports and inflation) and passed through the HP filter.

b Data were taken from the IMF International Financial Statistics: Y is real GDP (industrial production for France); C is nominal total private consumption expenditures deflated using the GDP deflator (CPI for France); I is change in nominal stocks deflated using the GDP deflator; N is industrial employment; NX is net exports over totalsum of imports and exports; π is quarterly CPI inflation; Z is the real exchange rate *vis-à-vis* the US dollar (based on relative CPI). Home statistics refer to the US, foreign ones to averages of the other G7 countries. The Bretton Woods period is taken to run from 1957:1 to 1972:4 (or shorter subject to data availability); the Post-Bretton Woods from 1974:1 to 1997:4. Statistic value under a float over value under a peg.

clearly shows that while the real and the nominal exchange rates have become much more volatile in the post-Bretton Woods era, we do not observe a similar change in the volatility of the other macroeconomic variables reported in the table. For instance, the standard deviations of output are roughly the same under the two periods for both the US and the average of the other G7 countries. Moreover, while consumption, employment, interest rates and US investment have become more volatile since 1973, this increased volatility pales compared to the increase in the standard deviation of the nominal and real exchange rate. Finally, the standard deviation of net exports (and of foreign investment) slightly fell after the demise of Bretton Woods.

Overall, we find that our model can match the salient feature of the data qualitatively well. Comparing the ratios of volatilities of variables under either a fixed or a flexible exchange-rate regime, Table 8.1 shows that the real exchange rate is clearly the variable most affected by a change in the currency regime: Its volatility increases dramatically when the currency floats, under any type of monetary policy rules. In general, as in the data, a flexible exchange-rate regime brings about an increase in most variables' volatilities, both for the home and the foreign country, although none experiences changes in volatility as large as that of the real exchange rate. Only the volatilities of foreign output and employment and home investment slightly decrease.

However, quantitatively, on some dimensions the model is less successful. The second variable most affected by the exchange-rate regime is net exports: its standard deviation increases by about 50 percent under the float compared to that when the foreign country pegs its currency. In the model, net exports are also more volatile when the currencies float than under the fixed exchange-rate regime, whereas the opposite occurs in the data.[8]

In the following two sections, we try to understand what features of our framework are important to generate a drastic increase in the volatility of the real exchange rate, without a similar increase in that of other macroeconomic variables.

The behavior of relative prices across countries

Why are the variances of most macroeconomic series in our model, except that of the real exchange rate, unaffected by the exchange-rate regime? One immediate reason is that the change in the exchange rate system impinges mainly on the covariance between domestic and foreign relative prices. In the Appendix, we show that the variance of the real exchange rate can be written as:

$$\text{Var}(\log z) = (1 - \gamma)^2 \left[\text{Var}(\log q^*) + \text{Var}(\log q) - 2\text{Cov}(\log q^*, \log q) \right].$$

Under a flexible exchange-rate regime, the domestic and foreign relative prices are barely correlated in response to a monetary shock and perfectly correlated in response to a real shock. Since the foreign country imports the home monetary policy when it pegs its nominal exchange rate, relative prices become perfectly correlated in response to both real and monetary shocks. Therefore, the covariance

Table 8.2 Ratios of relative prices' second moments across exchange-rate regimes

	St. Dev. (q^*)	St. Dev. (q)	Cov (q^*, q)
Fix vs Float	1.08	1.14	2.03

and the correlation of relative prices increase under a fixed exchange-rate regime to such an extent that the variance of the real exchange rate is approximately zero.[9]

Table 8.2 presents the ratios of the standard deviation and the covariance of domestic and foreign relative prices under the two exchange-rate regimes. It shows that while the standard deviations of the domestic and foreign relative prices are approximately the same under the two currency regimes, the covariance between these two relative prices is two times higher when the nominal exchange rate is fixed. Therefore, because of the link between consumption and relative prices, the fact that the volatility of relative prices is barely affected by the exchange-rate system explains why consumption and output are equally volatile whether the exchange rate is fixed or not.

Local currency pricing

Here, we examine the findings of our benchmark model by varying assumptions about some of the model's features. In particular, we study the importance of the monetary rule and the market structure for the model's results. We find that while, overall, our previous findings are fairly robust to changes in systematic monetary policy, local-currency pricing (LCP) plays an important role in making some quantities less sensitive to the exchange-rate regime.

As argued earlier, the volatility of the real exchange rate does not have an impact on the volatility of quantities because of the presence of firms pricing-to-market and because of a significant share of the competitive good. Basically, the combination of pricing-to-market and price rigidity in the buyer's currency mitigates the expenditure-switching effect, since movements in nominal exchange rates do not fully pass-through to the prices consumers face. As a result, large variations in exchange rates are not necessarily associated with as large movements in consumption, output, and net exports, as when firms do net set prices in buyers' currencies. Here, we wish to shed some light on the contribution of this feature of the model, by investigating how the absence of LCP would affect the results. We report the results of these two experiments in Table 8.3.[10]

When there is no LCP, the expenditure-switching effect is magnified. First, since the exchange rate depreciated, the relative price of foreign-differentiated goods in the home country now rises. Nevertheless, home demand for these goods rises, since the monetary shock increases total domestic aggregate demand and this increase outweighs the negative impact of rising prices on demand. Similarly, since the foreign currency appreciates, home-differentiated goods are now cheaper in the foreign country. As a result foreign demand for home-differentiated goods rises. When there is no LCP, the response of expenditure on imports is much

Table 8.3 Sensitivity analysis: LCP and flexible price sector

Statistics[a]	Variations on baseline economy	
	No LCP[b] ratio	Low γ^c ratio
St. Dev.		
Y	0.99	1.08
C	1.03	1.13
I	0.86	0.89
H	1.25	1.28
NX	4.35	1.01
π	0.98	1.04
Z	18.0	24.26

Notes
a All statistics are referred to that of the home country.
b Firms are assumed to set export prices in the home currency.
c The steady-state consumption share of the homogeneous good is set
to $\gamma = 0.01$. Statistic value under a float over value under a peg.

larger than with LCP. As a result, the response of net exports of differentiated goods is about four times larger when firms do not set prices in buyers' currencies, which contributes to amplify the movements of total net exports. By reducing the volatility of net exports when the currency floats, LCP contributes in accounting for the results in Baxter and Stockman (1989). Note, however, that removing LCP does not significantly affect the volatility of the other macroeconomic variables in our simulations. The increase in the comovement of relative prices across countries, when the currency if fixed, plays the larger role for these variables.[11]

8.4.2   The long-run benefits of monetary sovereignty

In this section, we compute the welfare loss or gain for a country that decides to adopt a fixed exchange-rate regime. The stochastic structure of the economies is driven by exogenous random movements in productivity and money supply. Pegging the exchange rate amounts to changing the country's monetary process, from the forward-looking interest-rate rule, to one in which the movements in the growth rate of money are consistent with the fixed exchange rate. As a consequence, the agents' decision rules and the joint stationary distribution of all endogenous variables should change as well.

We solve for the agents' decision rules under each exchange-rate system by linearizing around the non-stochastic steady state.[12] We first simulate our two-country world economy under a flexible exchange-rate regime 1000 times for different draws of 10,000 shocks each to compute the foreign agent's expected lifetime utility under that policy. As of a given point in time, taking the values of the state variables as initial conditions, we introduce the peg in the above world economy, that is, we replace the agents' decision rules with those consistent with the new currency arrangement. Again we simulate the two economies 1000 times

Table 8.4 Welfare gains and losses accruing from a fixed exchange rate (as a percentage of steady state consumption)

	All shocks	*Real shocks*	*Monetary shocks*
Baseline model	−0.0031	−0.0010	−0.0021

for different draws of 10,000 shocks, so that they converge to the new stationary distribution, and compute the expected lifetime utility under the fixed exchange rate. Finally, to get a quantitative measure of the welfare gain/loss, we convert the difference between the two expected values into a consumption equivalent, as Lucas (1987). In particular, we find the average amount of consumption, as a percentage of its steady-state value, that the agents in the two countries under the fixed exchange-rate regime would give to be as well off as they are under the flexible one. Therefore, when this quantity has a negative sign, it means that consumers would be better off with a floating currency and should therefore be compensated under a peg.

Table 8.4 presents the results of the benchmark experiment, undertaken with the baseline calibration, in which the two countries are perfectly symmetric, with respect to parameters and shocks calibration. It is also assumed that the foreign country's shift to a peg takes place from initial conditions equal to those prevailing in the steady state. The table first shows that the welfare effects of the exchange-rate regime are small, with losses around 0.003 percentage points of foreign steady-state consumption. However, these results are sizeable relative to the usual findings in the business cycle literature. For instance, they are 10 times larger than those reported by Lucas (1987) in his exercise on the welfare benefits of eliminating business fluctuations. Our findings should not be too surprising, given the discussion of the business cycle statistics in the previous section. A change in exchange-rate regimes, in our framework, mainly affects the volatility of the real exchange rate. Therefore, the variables that are important for the welfare measure (consumption and hours worked) behave similarly under the two systems, bringing about only small changes in welfare. Nevertheless, we find that the foreign agent is better off under a flexible exchange-rate regime.

To gain some understanding of these results, we need to look at the variability of the components of the agent's welfare: consumption and leisure. Since agents are risk averse, they would prefer a regime that brings about more stable consumption and leisure paths. A quick glance at Table 8.1 shows that volatilities of foreign consumption and foreign leisure are affected differently by the exchange-rate regime. A flexible exchange-rate regime amplifies the variability of foreign consumption and lowers that of foreign hours worked. However, note that under our calibration the utility responses are mostly driven by the behavior of hours worked following a shock. This is due to the fact that the, υ, a parameter controlling the disutility of labor turns out to be relatively big (4.21) under our calibration. As a result, the foreign agent prefers the flexible exchange-rate regime mainly because it stabilizes hours worked (and therefore leisure).

The stabilization of foreign hours worked, under a flexible exchange-rate regime, is mainly due to the fact that the foreign central bank places some weight on output stability in this case. For instance, following a positive domestic productivity shock, foreign output and hours fall in the foreign country because of the presence of perfect risk sharing. The situation is however different when the foreign country lets its currency float. The foreign central bank is not passive to the fall in foreign production in this case. Because it cares about the future output gap, it wants to stimulate demand. To do so, it increases the growth rate of money. As a result of that policy, foreign hours worked falls less.

The effect of a domestic monetary shock on foreign hours worked is also amplified under fixed rates. The expansionary domestic monetary policy is exported abroad under fixed rates, which boost foreign employment, due to the presence of monopolistic competition and price rigidities. As in the case of a domestic real shock, the impact of a domestic monetary innovation is muted when the currency floats, in this case because the foreign central bank cares about inflation and decides to restrict the rate of growth of prices by conducting a relatively more restrictive policy. That policy therefore dampens the response of foreign hours worked, as a result.

8.4.3   On the advantages of tying one's hands

In the last 20 years, the focus of debates on exchange-rate systems has shifted away from traditional arguments to issues related to the credibility of monetary policy and its ability to serve as a credible constraint on the value of domestic money, the so-called nominal anchor. As convincingly argued by Mishkin (1999), this is a necessary element in successful monetary policy regimes, for at least two reasons. First, from a pure technical viewpoint, a nominal anchor provides conditions that make the price level uniquely determined, which is obviously necessary for price stability. It helps achieving this by tying down inflation expectations directly through its constraint on the value of domestic money. Moreover, a nominal anchor can be thought of more broadly as a constraint on discretionary policy that helps weaken the time-inconsistency problem so that in the long run, price stability is more likely to be achieved. The time-inconsistency problem arises because discretionary policy at each point in time can lead to very poor long-run outcomes.

A fixed exchange rate has several advantages, from the viewpoint of providing a nominal anchor.[13] First of all, it pins down the inflation rate for traded goods, and thus directly contributes to keeping inflation under control. Moreover, if it is credible (in the case of a currency board, for instance) it also anchors inflation expectations to the inflation rate in the anchor country to whose currency it is pegged. Therefore, it is not surprising that an exchange-rate peg has been used successfully to control inflation in both industrialized and emerging-market countries. In this section, we study the possibility that a country with weak monetary institutions could be made better off under a fixed exchange-rate regime, via the stabilization of inflationary expectations. We assume that weak monetary policy is embedded in an interest-rate rule under which the path to the non-stochastic steady state is not uniquely determined by initial conditions. Therefore, sudden changes in agents' expectations make the economy jump from one transitional path to another, producing fluctuations independent of those due to exogenous shocks. This occurs because the interest-rate rule dictates a weak response of the nominal interest rate to inflation expectations, which become self-fulfilling.[14]

In order to illustrate the consequences of indeterminacy and sunspot fluctuations, we computed welfare along some of the paths that are possible under the multiplicity of equilibria induced by the unstable rule. We then compared it with utility under a fixed exchange rate and the imported stable rule. We assumed that the foreign country follows an unstable forward-looking interest-rate rule, whose coefficients are $\rho_R^* = 0.68$, $\rho_\pi^* = 0.83$, and $\rho_y^* = 0.27$, while monetary policy in the anchor country is conducted according to the stable forward-looking interest-rate rule discussed in the calibration section. This unstable rule corresponds to the one estimated by Clarida *et al.* (2000) under the pre-Volcker regime. We assume that the sunspot shock, φ_t, is governed by the following distribution: $\varphi_t \sim iid N(0, \sigma_\varphi^2)$, where we choose σ_φ^2 to match the volatility of output under the flexible exchange-rate regime. We ran the same experiment as before, that is, assuming a switch to the peg as of a given point in time. However, under a float we can now arbitrarily pick an initial value for one of the controls, since the (local) multiplicity implies the presence of one more stable root in the log-linearized system. We find that the introduction of indeterminacy and sunspot fluctuations under the flexible exchange-rate regime affects welfare significantly in the foreign country. The foreign country now benefits by abandoning its unstable monetary rule: pegging the currency brings about a welfare gain of 0.01 percent of steady-state consumption.

8.4.4 Some sensitivity analysis

Finally, we assessed the importance of the initial conditions in two ways: first we examined whether the choice of the exchange-rate arrangement depends on the level of the capital stock; then we studied the case of a country with a high steady-state inflation rate that pegs to one with a low long-run inflation rate.

It may be the case that under normal circumstances, for example, with the state capital stock close to its value prevailing in steady-state, a peg is preferred to a float. However, this same choice may turn out to be a disaster under a particularly bad state of the world which depresses the level of the capital stock. A time-(in)consistency problem potentially lurks here: if preferences about the exchange-rate arrangement are dependent on state variables, they will change along with the latter, potentially resulting in welfare reversals. Hence, if agents were given the possibility to make up their mind again about a given currency regime, they could choose to renege on previous commitments. To study this possibility, we conduct experiments in which the foreign country fixes its currency when the capital stock is at different levels. We find that the transitional dynamics toward the steady state level of capital stock are not at all affected by the currency regime. As a result, our welfare findings are not sensitive to the level of the capital stock in place when the switch in regime occurs.

In the second experiment, we assumed that the foreign country had a steady-state inflation rate twice as high as that of the home country, that is, 1.24 and 0.62 percent, respectively. As of a given point in time, the higher-inflation country embarks on a fixed exchange-rate arrangement with the low-inflation one. This, therefore, implies a switch to a different steady state for the foreign country. Our calculations show that this policy is welfare-reducing for the pegging country (-0.013 percent). The benefits accruing from a lower steady-state inflation rate and a (slightly) higher capital stock are more than offset by the related costs undertaken along the transition, making the peg even less attractive. This is consistent with the findings in Moran (2000) for a closed economy: he shows that when one takes into account the costly transitional path, the welfare gains from reducing inflation result substantially smaller than those found in the literature.

8.5   Conclusion

This chapter studied the welfare effects of fixing the exchange rate in a two-country equilibrium business cycle model, featuring nominal rigidities and deviations from the law of one price due to firms pricing-to-market. Overall, we find that flexible exchange-rate regimes dominates a fixed one. By letting the currency float, the central bank can set interest rates to dampen the movements in output and, therefore, the volatility of employment. Under a fixed exchange-rate regime, the central bank must necessarily forego its stabilization policy to maintain the value of the currency, which results in more volatile output and employment. Since agents are risk averse, they prefer the relatively more stable employment/leisure path brought about when the currency floats.

The adoption of a fixed exchange-rate regime is often proposed as a means of stabilizing inflation expectations in countries in which inflation is rampant due to weak monetary institutions. If the central bank's response to increases in expected inflation is too weak it can lead to inflation being self-fulfilling and introduce sunspot fluctuations, which can result in bad economic outcomes. We showed that when this is the case, the welfare ordering can change, and a country can gain by pegging its currency to that of a country with a stable monetary policy rule.

In this chapter, we have assumed that firms and consumers face implicit barriers that makes it too costly to arbitrage the deviations from the law of one price (LOP). Recent works (Burstein *et al.*, 2000; Corsetti and Dedola, 2001) introduce distribution costs to model explicitly these costs. As shown in Corsetti *et al.* (2001), a simple model with distribution costs can generate large departures from the LOP and account for important features of the data. For instance, introducing a distribution sector can break the link between the ratio of consumptions across countries and the real exchange rate and, thus, account for the well-known (Backus and Smith, 1993) puzzle. Moreover, Corsetti and Dedola (2001) show that this goods-market segmentation has important implications for the optimal conduct of monetary policy. Understanding the quantitative implications of different monetary policies in such environments would therefore be an interesting avenue for further research.

Appendix

We focus on the equilibrium characterized by symmetry in the monopolistically competitive sector, defined as follows:[15]

- a set of decision rules for the representative household and the foreign equivalent, $C^T(\Omega; s), C^M(\Omega; s), B(\Omega; s'), M'(\Omega; s), h(\Omega; s), I(\Omega; s), K'(\Omega; s), v(\Omega; s)$, and $\phi(\Omega; s)$, solving the household's problem;
- a capital demand rule, $K(h; p_{-1}(h), p^*_{-1}(h); s)$, a labor demand rule $H(h; p_{-1}(h), p^*_{-1}(h); s)$, and pricing functions $p(h; p_{-1}(h), p^*_{-1}(h); s)$ and $p^*(h; p_{-1}(h), p^*_{-1}(h); s)$ solving the monopolistic firm's problem;
- a capital demand rule, $K^T(s)$ and a labor demand rule $H^T(s)$ solving the competitive firm's problem, taking prices, $P^T(s), W^T(s)$, and $R^T(s)$, as given;
- $p(h; p_{-1}(h), p^*_{-1}(h); s) = p(p_{-1}, p^*_{-1}; s)$ and $p^*(h; p_{-1}(h), p^*_{-1}(h); s) = p^*(p_{-1}, p^*_{-1}; s)$ for all h;
- $p(p_{-1}, p^*_{-1}; s), p^*(p_{-1}, p^*_{-1}; s), P_b(s', s), P^T(s), W^T(s), R^T(s), W^M(s)$, and $R^M(s)$ are such that the goods, money, bonds, and input markets clear.

Since the homogeneous good is perfectly traded on world markets, the law of one price holds:

$$P^T(s) = e(s)P^{*T}(s).$$

As usual, the (CPI based) real exchange rate is defined as

$$z(s) \equiv \frac{e(s)P^*(s)}{P(s)}.$$

Because of LCP, changes in the real exchange rate come from deviations from the LOP in monopolistic goods. Using the household's first-order conditions, the real exchange rate can be written as:[16]

$$z(s) = \left(\frac{P^{*M}(s)/P^{*T}(s)}{P^M(s)/P^T(s)}\right)^{1-\gamma} = \left(\frac{q^*(s)}{q(s)}\right)^{1-\gamma},$$

where, because of the Cobb–Douglas consumption aggregator

$$q(s) = \frac{1-\gamma}{\gamma}\left(\frac{C^T(s)}{C^M(s)}\right).$$

Therefore, the variance of the logarithm of $z(s)$ can be decomposed in the following way:

$$\text{Var}(\log z) = (1-\gamma)^2 \left[\text{Var}(\log q^*) + \text{Var}(\log q) - 2\text{Cov}(\log q^*, \log q)\right].$$

Notes

1 As pointed out by Stockman (1999), much of the traditional analysis of alternative exchange-rate regimes is based on models that fail to distinguish between these two components of monetary policy. A further advantage of the equilibrium approach is that it enables a more rigorous welfare analysis of the different proposed policies, by comparing the agent's expected discounted sum of utility under different monetary rules/regimes rather than comparing ad hoc loss functions.

2 In the text, a superscript prime variable will denote a time $t + 1$ variable, whereas a variable with no superscript represents a time t variable. Foreign variables will be denoted by an asterisk. A superscript T represents the perfectly competitive good, while a superscript M denotes the monopolistic sector.

3 We also examined a version of the model with sector-specific real shocks. The main findings were not affected, however, by this different stochastic structure.

4 For instance, suppose consumers have imperfect information about the distribution of prices and that this information is costly to acquire. In such an environment, firms may prefer to make frequent small price changes rather than sporadic large ones. On the one hand, a firm may be unwilling to raise its price by a large amount for fear of antagonizing consumers and inducing them to search for better price offers from its competitors. On the other hand, a firm may also be reluctant to reduce its price by a large amount in such an environment. The cost for consumers to look for better prices gives an incentive to the firm to reduce its price by a smaller amount than in a world of perfect information.

5 The G7 countries are the USA, Japan, Germany, France, the United Kingdom, Italy, and Canada.

6 In Section 8.4.2, we analyze the implications of different values of this parameter.

7 A more extensive discussion of similar results (without the presence of money-demand shocks) can be found in Dedola and Leduc (2001).

8 However, we will show next that the volatility of net exports increases much more drastically, from a fixed to a flexible exchange-rate regime, when firms do not price to market. In this sense, pricing-to-market improves the match of the model with the data.

9 The increase in the comovement of relative prices predicted by our model is consistent with the increase in the correlation of other variables under fixed rates found in Sopraseuth (2002a).

10 We only report the statistics for the home country since the impact on foreign ones is very similar.

11 We also find that the size of the sectors does not have a significant impact on the findings across regimes. We investigated this possibility by reducing γ, the share of the purely competitive, so that the size of the tradable sector is 1 percent. The results are reported in the second column of Table 8.3.

12 Since we compute the decision rules under certainty equivalence, they are unaffected by changes in second moments. However, volatility changes in the equilibrium stationary process of consumption do affect the utility function and thus welfare, since the former displays (constant) risk aversion.

13 Despite the inherent advantages of exchange-rate targeting, it is not without its serious problems as the international experience demonstrates. For a criticism of fixed exchange rates, see Obstfeld and Rogoff (1995).

14 A fixed exchange-rate regime, when combined with imperfect credibility, may leave a country vulnerable to speculative attacks. However, analyzing the consequences of imperfectly credible pegs and currency crises is beyond the scope of this chapter. The results in this section should be taken as providing upper bounds on the advantage of tying one's hands.

15 To save on notation, we do not show the conditions for the foreign country.
16 The theoretical prediction that bilateral real exchange rates should be highly correlated with cross-country consumption ratios is common to all equilibrium models, irrespective of the degree of pass-through assumed. Backus and Smith (1993) showed that this prediction hardly finds support in the data.

9 Commitment, discretion and fixed exchange rates in an open economy

Tommaso Monacelli

9.1 Introduction

The aim of this work is to provide a tractable framework for the analysis of monetary policy in a small open economy, both in terms of optimal design problem as well as of simple feedback rules.[1] The discussion is framed within the so called New Open Economy Macroeconomics (NOEM) paradigm. It draws insights from both the two streams that currently characterize such literature. The first (seminal) one dates back to the contribution by Obstfeld and Rogoff (1995) and is for the most part surveyed in Lane (2001).[2] The second stream of the NOEM literature is even more recent. In its core it emphasizes a continuity with the closed-economy New-Keynesian synthesis exemplified in the work of Rotemberg and Woodford (1999), Woodford (2003) and Clarida *et al.* (2000). There are three main features of this latter line of work, although strongly complementary to the former. The first is the adoption of the Dynamic Stochastic General Equilibrium framework as the workhorse of analysis. The second feature is the specification of the price-setting mechanism. Typically such literature makes use of a staggered price-setting structure, which allows for richer dynamic effects of monetary policy than those found in the models with one-period advanced price-setting that are common to the earlier strand. Third, and most importantly, monetary policy is modelled as endogenous, with a short-term interest rate being the instrument of that policy. This approach to the specification of monetary policy seems to accord well with the general consensus reached by roughly twenty years of VAR literature on the effects of monetary policy shocks on the business cycle.[3] In a nutshell such literature de-emphasizes the role of the unanticipated component of monetary policy as a source of business cycle fluctuations, placing instead a lot of emphasis on its systematic component. Incidentally such approach seems to accord much better with the practice of modern central banks of setting interest rates as the instruments of policy by reacting to the current state of the economy.

The open economy dimension lends itself as an ideal ground of application of such an approach. In an open economy, in fact, exchange rate regimes matter. And if indeed the specification of the monetary policy conduct is best represented in terms of systematic behavior, this holds *a fortiori* for the description of exchange rate regimes. Fixed exchange rate regimes or, alternatively, currency areas, are in fact extreme cases of pure endogeneity of monetary policy.

In this work we start by characterizing the benchmark setup, whose basic features are complete pass-through of exchange rate movements to (import) prices and perfect international risk-sharing. We then proceed by comparing a scenario in which the monetary authority can commit to a certain future course of action to another in which such commitment is unfeasible and the same monetary authority acts under discretion. At first we recover a basic (well-known) result of this framework, namely that, relative to the optimal policy under discretion, gains from commitment arise in equilibrium as an effect of the purely forward-looking nature of inflation.[4] In addition, the open economy dimension allows us to characterize the dynamic behavior of the nominal exchange rate under the alternative regimes. We show that, in such a context, the properties of the nominal exchange rate tend to mimic closely the ones of the (producer) price level. In particular, and in response to a cost-push shock, the optimal solution under commitment entails stationary exchange rate and price level, while the same is not true under the time consistent policy.

After characterizing the optimal behavior of policy, we move on to a comparison with an alternative regime, in which the authorities of the small open economy peg their currency to one of the rest of the world. We are interested in the following point. If, on the one hand, the terms of trade channel of monetary policy is enhanced by allowing the maximum exchange rate flexibility, it holds true that a regime of fixed exchange rates requires per se some type of commitment. We first show that fixed exchange rates entail the key property that characterize the optimal commitment regime, namely stationary nominal exchange rate and price level. However, under the baseline parameterization, it turns out that an exchange rate peg is dominated by the optimal time consistent policy.

We then analyze in more detail the comparison of the fixed exchange rate regime with the optimal benchmark. An exchange rate peg corresponds to the highest degree of monetary integration. Hence it reproduces the situation of a small economy relinquishing its monetary independence upon joining a currency area. We therefore explore whether the cost of relinquishing monetary independence varies with the degree of openness of the economy. One key feature of our framework is that the equilibrium volatility of international relative prices (the terms of trade) depends inversely on the degree of openness. This follows crucially from the source of deviations from purchasing power parity (PPP) in our model. Namely, the fact that preferences of the home and the foreign (world) representative consumers are asymmetric, with the latter holding only a negligible share of small economy's goods in their consumption basket. Therefore the degree of openness, from the viewpoint of the small economy, is also an inverse measure of the degree of asymmetry in preferences. It follows that the higher the degree of openness the lower the terms of trade volatility required along the equilibrium, and the lower the loss stemming from relinquishing the exchange rate as an adjustment tool.

While under our baseline parameterization the optimal time consistent policy always dominates fixed exchange rates, we show that, interestingly, the loss from relinquishing monetary independence is sensitive to two other key parameters: the relative weight attached to output gap variability in the policy authority's loss function and the elasticity of substitution between domestic and foreign goods. In particular, we analyze two deviations from the baseline case: a case in which the output gap weight is high and a case of high international elasticity of substitution. In such cases we show that, when the economy is sufficiently open, an exchange rate peg can outperform the optimal policy under discretion. We draw from this interesting conclusions for a modern version of the optimal currency area literature.

The remainder of this chapter is organized as follows. Section 9.2 contains the outline of the model. Section 9.3 describes the optimal monetary policy design problem. Section 9.4 analyzes the equilibrium dynamics implied by alternative monetary regimes and Section 9.5 concludes.

9.2   A small open economy model

The domestic (small) economy is populated by infinitely lived households, consuming Dixit–Stiglitz aggregates of domestic (C_H) and imported (C_F) goods, and by domestic firms producing a differentiated good. All goods are tradeable. In the following, lower case letters indicate log deviations from steady state and capital letters indicate levels.

Let's define C as a composite consumption index:

$$C_t = \left[(1-\gamma)^{1/\eta} C_{H,t}^{(\eta-1)/\eta} + \gamma^{1/\eta} C_{F,t}^{(\eta-1)/\eta}\right]^{\eta/(\eta-1)}, \tag{9.1}$$

with C_H and C_F being indexes of consumption of domestic and foreign goods.[5] Notice that under this specification η measures the elasticity of substitution between domestic and foreign goods. The optimal allocation of expenditures between domestic and foreign goods implies:

$$C_{H,t} = (1-\gamma)\left(\frac{P_{H,t}}{P_t}\right)^{-\eta} C_t; \qquad C_{F,t} = \gamma\left(\frac{P_{F,t}}{P_t}\right)^{-\eta} C_t, \tag{9.2}$$

where $P_t \equiv \left[(1-\gamma) P_{H,t}^{1-\eta} + \gamma P_{F,t}^{1-\eta}\right]^{1/(1-\eta)}$ is the consumer price index (CPI).

We assume the existence of complete markets for state-contingent money claims expressed in units of domestic currency. Let $h^t = \{h_0, \ldots, h_t\}$ denote the history of events up to date t, where h_t is the event realization at date t. The date 0 probability of observing history h^t is given by ψ_t. The initial state h^0 is given so that $\psi(h^0) = 1$. Henceforth, and for the sake of simplifying the notation, let's define the operator $E_t\{\cdot\} \equiv \sum_{h_{t+1}} \psi(h^{t+1}|h^t)$ as the mathematical expectation over all possible states of nature conditional on history h^t.

The problem of the domestic household is to maximize

$$E_t \sum_{t=0}^{\infty} \beta^t U(C_t, N_t),$$

subject to a sequence of budget constraints which, after considering the optimality conditions in (9.2), can be written in units of domestic currency as:

$$P_t C_t + \sum_{h_{t+1}} v_{t,t+1} B_{t+1}(h_{t+1}) = W_t N_t + B_t + \tau_t. \tag{9.3}$$

In equation (9.3) B_{t+1} is the market value (in units domestic currency) of a portfolio of state contingent securities held at the end of period t, $v_{t,t+1} \equiv v(h^{t+1}|h^t)$ is the pricing kernel of the state contingent portfolio, N is labor hours, W is the nominal wage and τ are net lump-sum transfers/taxes. After ruling out Ponzi schemes the first-order conditions of this problem can be described as follows. The efficiency condition for the consumption–leisure choice is given by

$$U_{c,t} \frac{W_t}{P_t} = -U_{n,t}, \tag{9.4}$$

where $U_{c,t}$ and $U_{n,t}$ denote the marginal utility of consumption and disutility of work respectively. The price of the state contingent asset (for any state of the world) must satisfy

$$v_{t,t+1} = \psi_{t,t+1} \frac{U_{c,t+1} P_t}{U_{c,t} P_{t+1}}, \tag{9.5}$$

where $\psi_{t,t+1} \equiv \psi(s^{t+1}|s^t)$. By assuming a separable period utility of the form

$$\frac{1}{1-\sigma} C_t^{1-\sigma} - \frac{1}{1+\varphi} N_t^{1+\varphi}$$

and recalling that the (gross) nominal interest rate can be pinned down via the arbitrage condition $R_t = \left(\sum_{s_{t+1}} v_{t,t+1}\right)^{-1}$ one can characterize the above first-order conditions in the convenient log-linearized form:

$$w_t - p_t = \sigma c_t + \varphi n_t, \tag{9.6}$$

$$c_t = E_t\{c_{t+1}\} - \frac{1}{\sigma} \left(r_t - E_t\{\pi_{t+1}\}\right). \tag{9.7}$$

In the rest of the world a representative household faces a problem identical to the one outlined above. Hence a set of analogous optimality conditions characterize the solution to the consumer's problem in the world economy. As in Gali and Monacelli (2002), however, the size of the small open economy is negligible relative to the rest of the world, an assumption that allows to treat the latter as if it was a closed economy.

Pass-through, the real exchange rate and deviations from PPP

Log-linearization of the CPI formula around the steady state yields:

$$p_t \equiv (1 - \gamma)\, p_{H,t} + \gamma\, p_{F,t}. \tag{9.8}$$

Producer inflation – defined as the rate of change in the index of domestic goods prices – and CPI-inflation are linked according to

$$\pi_t = \pi_{H,t} + \gamma\, \Delta s_t, \tag{9.9}$$

where $s_t = p_{F,t} - p_{H,t}$ denotes the (log) terms of trade, that is, the relative price of imports. The treatment of the rest of the world as an (approximately) closed economy (with goods produced in the small economy representing a negligible fraction of the world's consumption basket) implies that $P_t^* = P_{F,t}^*$, and $\pi_t^* = \pi_{F,t}^*$, for all t, that is, an equivalence between producer and CPI inflation holds in the world economy.

This allows the change in the terms of trade to be written as

$$
\begin{aligned}
\Delta s_t &= \pi_{F,t} - \pi_{H,t} \\
&= \Delta e_t + \pi_t^* - \pi_{H,t}.
\end{aligned}
$$

In this context the real exchange rate and the terms of trade are related by a simple expression:

$$
\begin{aligned}
q_t &= e_t + p_t^* - p_t \\
&= (1 - \gamma)s_t.
\end{aligned} \tag{9.10}
$$

Equation (9.10) deserves some comments. It stands clear that the source of deviation from aggregate PPP in our framework is due to the heterogeneity of consumption baskets between the small economy and the rest of the world, an effect captured by the term $(1 - \gamma)s_t$, as long as $\gamma < 1$. For $\gamma \to 1$, in fact, the two aggregate consumption baskets coincide and relative price variations are not required in equilibrium. This will become more clear when we illustrate risk sharing.

9.2.1   Producers

In the market of the domestic goods, there is a continuum of monopolistic competitive firms (owned by consumers), indexed by $i \in [0, 1]$. They operate a constant return to scale technology: $Y_t(i) = Z_t N_t(i)$, where Z is a total factor productivity shifter. Cost minimization typically leads to the following efficiency condition for the choice of labor input:

$$mc_t = (w_t - p_{H,t}) - z_t, \tag{9.11}$$

where mc indicates the real marginal cost (which is common across producers). In the following, domestic (log) productivity is assumed to follow a simple stochastic autoregressive process:

$$z_t = \rho z_{t-1} + \zeta_{z,t}, \tag{9.12}$$

where $0 \le \rho \le 1$ is a persistence parameter and $\zeta_{z,t}$ is an i.i.d shock.

Pricing of domestic goods

Domestic firms are allowed to reset their price according to a standard Calvo (1983); Yun (1996) rule, which implies receiving a price signal at a constant random rate θ. Let θ^k then be the probability that the price set at time t will still hold at time $t + k$. Firm i faces domestic and foreign demand. This kind of pricing technology leads to the following log-linear equation for newly set domestic prices:

$$p_{H,t}^{new} = (1 - \beta\theta) \sum_{k=0}^{\infty} (\beta\theta)^k E_t\{mc_{t+k} + p_{H,t+k}\}. \tag{9.13}$$

The domestic aggregate price index evolves according to:

$$P_{H,t} = \left[\theta(P_{H,t-1})^{1-\varepsilon} + (1 - \theta)(P_{H,t}^{new})^{1-\varepsilon}\right]^{1/(1-\varepsilon)}. \tag{9.14}$$

By combining (9.13) with the log-linearized version of (9.14) one can derive a typical forward-looking Phillips curve:

$$\pi_{H,t} = \beta E_t\{\pi_{H,t+1}\} + \lambda mc_t, \tag{9.15}$$

where $\lambda \equiv (1 - \theta)(1 - \beta\theta)/\theta$.

9.2.2 Risk sharing and uncovered interest parity

The existence of complete markets for nominal state contingent securities has implications for consumption risk sharing. Formally the marginal utilities of consumption must be equalized across economies in equilibrium. This implies a log-linearized condition:

$$\begin{aligned} c_t &= c_t^* + \frac{1}{\sigma} q_t \\ &= c_t^* + \frac{(1 - \gamma)}{\sigma} s_t, \end{aligned} \tag{9.16}$$

where σ is the intertemporal elasticity of substitution in consumption. Under complete international asset markets it is also possible to derive a standard log-linear version of an uncovered interest parity condition

$$r_t - r_t^* = E_t\{\Delta e_{t+1}\}. \tag{9.17}$$

It is easy to show that such an equation results from combining efficiency conditions for an optimal portfolio of bonds by both domestic and foreign residents.

230   *Tommaso Monacelli*

Labor market equilibrium and domestic real marginal cost

By combining (9.7), (9.11) and (9.16) one obtains, after aggregation, an equilibrium equation for the domestic real marginal cost (or inverse of the domestic markup), which also expresses the equilibrium in the labor market:

$$mc_t = (w_t - p_{H,t}) - z_t$$
$$= (w_t - p_t) + \gamma s_t - z_t$$
$$= \sigma y_t^* + \varphi y_t - (1 + \varphi)z_t + s_t. \tag{9.18}$$

Equation (9.18) shows that the domestic real marginal cost is increasing in domestic output (through its effect on employment and therefore the real wage) and decreasing in domestic technology (through its direct effect on labor productivity). However, open economy factors as well affect the real marginal cost: World output (through its effect on labor supply) and the terms of trade (through both its direct effect on the product wage, for any given real wage, and the indirect labor supply effect on consumption and the real wage).

9.2.3   Goods market equilibrium

It is first useful to consider log-linearized versions of the isoelastic demand functions. In particular local and foreign demand for domestic goods can be written respectively:

$$c_{H,t} = -\eta(p_{H,t} - p_t) + c_t$$
$$= \eta\gamma s_t + c_t, \tag{9.19}$$
$$c_{H,t}^* = -\eta(p_{H,t}^* - p_t^*) + c_t^*$$
$$= \eta(p_{F,t} - p_{H,t}) + c_t^*$$
$$= \eta s_t + c_t^*. \tag{9.20}$$

Finally, the demand for imports will read

$$c_{F,t} = -\eta(p_{F,t} - p_t) + c_t$$
$$= -\eta(1 - \gamma)s_t + c_t. \tag{9.21}$$

Goods market clearing implies $y_t(i) = (1 - \gamma) c_{H,t}(i) + \gamma c_{H,t}^*(i)$ for any good i, and by aggregating:

$$y_t = (1 - \gamma) c_{H,t} + \gamma c_{H,t}^*.$$

By substituting these demand functions we can rewrite the previous goods market clearing condition as

$$y_t = (1 - \gamma)c_t + \gamma c_t^* + \gamma\eta(2 - \gamma)s_t. \tag{9.22}$$

Hence one notices that, in the case of $\gamma = 0$, namely the one of a closed economy, such condition reduces simply to $y_t = c_t$, that is, to the typical resource constraint linking (in the absence of investment and capital accumulation) aggregate output to aggregate consumption.

Rearranging the previous condition by substituting (9.16) one obtains a relation between relative output and the terms of trade:

$$y_t - y_t^* = \frac{\omega_s}{\sigma} s_t,$$ (9.23)

where $\omega_s \equiv 1 + \gamma(2-\gamma)(\sigma\eta - 1) > 0$. Hence a rise of domestic output relative to foreign output requires, in equilibrium, a real depreciation (i.e. a rise of s_t). Notice also that, if $\sigma\eta > 1$,

$$\frac{\partial \omega_s}{\partial \gamma} > 0; \quad \frac{\partial \omega_s}{\partial \eta} > 0.$$ (9.24)

Hence the higher the degree of openness and the higher the elasticity of substitution between domestic and foreign goods, the smaller is the equilibrium adjustment in relative prices required to absorb a given change in relative output. Consider now a small economy joining a currency area. Such monetary arrangement implies the relinquishment of the nominal exchange rate as a macroeconomic stabilization tool. The implication of (9.24) is that such cost should be lower the more open the economy and the more substitutable her goods with the ones produced in the rest of the currency area.

Finally, it is useful to notice that, by substituting (9.16) into (9.22), the market clearing condition can in turn be written as

$$y_t = \frac{\omega_s}{(1-\gamma)} c_t + \left(1 - \frac{\omega_s}{(1-\gamma)}\right) c_t^*.$$ (9.25)

9.2.4 Policy target in the rest of the world

Let's first describe how the equilibrium looks like in the rest of the world. The equilibrium real marginal cost is given by

$$mc_t^* = (\sigma + \varphi)y_t^* - (1 + \varphi)z_t^*,$$ (9.26)

which is simply the closed economy (i.e. obtained for $\gamma = 0$) version of equation (9.18). Therefore, the natural (flexible-price) level of output easily obtains by imposing $mc_t^* = 0$ (which implies $\pi_t^* = 0$):

$$\overline{y}_t^* = \frac{(1+\varphi)}{(\sigma+\varphi)} z_t^*.$$ (9.27)

As in a canonical sticky price model with Calvo (1983) price staggering, under fully flexible prices the output gap will be completely stabilized, that is,

$$\widetilde{y}_t^* = y_t^* - \overline{y}_t^* = 0.$$ (9.28)

Throughout it will be assumed that the monetary authority in the rest of the world aims at replicating the flexible price allocation by simultaneously stabilizing inflation and the output gap. It is well known that such a policy also coincides with the first best outcome.[6]

9.2.5   *Flexible domestic prices*

Let's proceed by assuming, at first, that in the small open economy domestic producer prices are flexible. In such a case the domestic pricing equation (9.13) implies a constant markup. Therefore, it can be assumed, without loss of generality, that domestic prices remain fixed at their optimal level, as firms would have no incentive to deviate from that state of affairs. By imposing a constant markup in equation (9.18) and substituting equation (9.23) one obtains an expression for the flexible price (or natural) level of output:

$$\bar{y}_t = \left(\frac{\omega_s (1 + \varphi)}{\sigma + \varphi \omega_s} \right) z_t + \left(\frac{\sigma (1 - \omega_s)}{\sigma + \varphi \omega_s} \right) y_t^*. \tag{9.29}$$

By using equation (9.23), and noticing that

$$\bar{s}_t = \frac{\sigma}{\omega_s} (\bar{y}_t - y_t^*),$$

the nominal exchange rate can be written as

$$\bar{e}_t = \frac{\sigma}{\omega_s} (\bar{y}_t - y_t^*) \tag{9.30}$$

$$= \frac{\sigma (1 + \varphi)}{\sigma + \varphi \omega_s} (z_t - z_t^*). \tag{9.31}$$

This expression shows that, under flexible prices, a rise in domestic productivity relative to the rest of the world causes the nominal exchange rate to depreciate.

9.2.6   *The supply block*

Let's define the output gap as the percentage deviation of current output from the natural level of output, that is,

$$\tilde{y}_t \equiv y_t - \bar{y}_t. \tag{9.32}$$

Equation (9.23), in turn, implies that the output gap is proportional to the terms of trade gap:

$$\tilde{y}_t = \frac{\omega_s}{\sigma} \tilde{s}_t. \tag{9.33}$$

Therefore, the equilibrium real marginal cost (9.18) can be written after combining with (9.33) as

$$mc_t = \left(\varphi + \frac{\sigma}{\omega_s} \right) \tilde{y}_t. \tag{9.34}$$

Hence, we see that the proportionality relationship between the real marginal cost and the output gap, which is common to the prototype sticky price model with imperfectly competitive markets, survives in this open economy context. Clearly the sensitivity of the real marginal cost to movements in the output gap is affected by parameters that are typical of the open economy, namely the degree of openness γ and the elasticity of substitution between domestic and foreign goods η.

Equation (9.33) implies that the terms of trade and the output gap are strongly correlated in this context. Hence the choice of the underlying exchange rate regime, by affecting the dynamics of the terms of trade, also heavily affects the behavior of the output gap. This result, however, depends strictly on the assumption of complete exchange rate pass-through, which prevents deviations from the law of one price.[7]

By replacing (9.34) in (9.15) one obtains

$$\pi_{H,t} = \beta \ E_t \pi_{H,t+1} + \kappa_y \tilde{y}_t, \tag{9.35}$$

where $\kappa_y \equiv \lambda(\varphi + (\sigma/\omega_s))$. Hence the degree of openness affects only the slope (via its effect on ω_s) but not the specification of the Phillips curve. Notice also that this happens if and only if $\sigma\eta \neq 1$, which in turn implies that $\omega_s \neq 1$. In the empirically plausible case of $\sigma\eta > 1$, we have that a higher γ raises ω_s and hence lowers the slope of the Phillips curve. In particular, via equation (9.23) which is an alternative way of rewriting the market clearing condition, an increase in openness lowers the size of the adjustment in the terms of trade necessary to absorb a change in domestic output (relative to world output), thus dampening the impact of the latter on marginal cost and inflation. The slope of the Phillips curve is also decreasing in η, the elasticity of substitution between domestic and foreign goods. The intuition is similar. The larger such elasticity the smaller the variation in the terms of trade required to absorb a variation of domestic output relative to foreign output.

By solving (9.35) forward we obtain:

$$\pi_{H,t} = E_t \left\{ \sum_{k=0}^{\infty} \beta^k \kappa_y \tilde{y}_{t+k} \right\}, \tag{9.36}$$

which shows that domestic inflation depends on both current and expected future values of the output gap. As such inflation is a typical forward-looking variable in this context.

9.2.7 The demand block

To complete the description of the model it is useful to rewrite also the aggregate demand equations in a more compact form. By substituting (9.25) into (9.7) and making use of the definition of the output gap and of equation (9.9) we can write the following aggregate demand equation:

$$\tilde{y}_t = E_t\{\tilde{y}_{t+1}\} - \frac{\omega_s}{\sigma}(r_t - E_t\{\pi_{H,t+1}\} - \overline{rr}_t), \tag{9.37}$$

where

$$\overline{rr}_t \equiv \sigma\left(\frac{\varphi(\omega_s - 1)}{\sigma + \varphi\omega_s}\right)E_t\{\Delta y_{t+1}^*\} - \left(\frac{\sigma(1-\rho)(1+\varphi)}{\sigma + \varphi\omega_s}\right)z_t$$

is the natural real interest rate. Notice that the natural real rate depends not only on domestic productivity, but, as long as $\omega_s > 1$, also on the expected growth in world output. Besides this the effect of openness on the shape of the typical optimizing IS equation is reflected in the parameter ω_s affecting the sensitivity of the output gap to real interest rate movements.

9.2.8   The equilibrium in compact form

It is easy to rewrite the equilibrium conditions for the domestic small economy in a more compact form. By combining (9.16) and (9.22) with (9.18) one can write the following expression for the real marginal cost:

$$mc_t = \Phi s_t + (\sigma + \varphi)y_t^* - (1+\varphi)z_t, \tag{9.38}$$

where $\Phi \equiv (1 + (\varphi\omega_s/\sigma)) > 1$. By combining with (9.15) domestic inflation can be easily related to the terms of trade by the following first-order difference equation

$$\pi_{H,t} = \beta E\{\pi_{H,t+1}\} + \lambda\Phi s_t + \lambda[(\sigma + \varphi)y_t^* - (1+\varphi)z_t]. \tag{9.39}$$

Furthermore, the real version of the uncovered interest parity condition (9.17) can be written as

$$r_t - E_t\{\pi_{H,t+1}\} = rr_t^* + E_t\{s_{t+1}\} - s_t, \tag{9.40}$$

where $rr_t^* \equiv r_t^* - E_t\{\pi_{t+1}^*\}$) is the foreign real interest rate.

Hence, conditional to the definition of a monetary policy rule for the monetary authority and for any given exogenous path $\{z_t, rr_t^*, y_t^*\}$, a rational expectations equilibrium for the small open economy is a pair of processes $\{\pi_{H,t}, s_t\}_{t=0}^{\infty}$ that solves the system of equations (9.39) and (9.40).

9.3   Monetary policy, interest rate and the exchange rate

In this section we will characterize alternative monetary policy regimes for the small open economy. We will first analyze the optimal policy design problem, both when the monetary authority can commit to a certain future path of inflation and output gap (and therefore interest rates) and when such commitment is not feasible. We will then compare the outcome under the optimal policy with the one obtained when the small economy pegs its exchange rate *vis-à-vis* the rest of the world (or equivalently decides to join a currency area).

Let us first postulate that the monetary authority of the small economy tries to minimize the following loss criterion:

$$\frac{1}{2} E_0 \left\{ \sum_{j=0}^{\infty} \beta^j \left(\pi_{H,t+j}^2 + b_w \tilde{y}_{t+j}^2 \right) \right\}, \tag{9.41}$$

where b_w is the relative weight attached to output gap variability. Furthermore, as in Clarida *et al.* (2001), it is assumed that the presence of an exogenous cost-push shock u_t does not allow the monetary authority to reach the flexible price allocation, namely an equilibrium such that $\pi_{H,t} = \tilde{y}_t = 0$ for all t. The role played by such shock is crucial to generate a trade-off between the conflicting goals of stabilizing domestic inflation and the output gap. This of course is necessary to generate a nontrivial analysis of the optimal policy problem.[8]

9.3.1   Optimal policy under discretion

Let us now assume that the monetary authority cannot have access to a commitment technology and can only reoptimize period by period. In this case, and given the vector of exogenous variables $\{u_t, \overline{rr}_t, z_t^*, rr_t^*\}$, the monetary authority chooses $\pi_{H,t}$ and $\tilde{y}_{H,t}$ to

$$\max -\frac{1}{2} \left\{ \pi_{H,t}^2 + b_w \tilde{y}_t^2 \right\}, \tag{9.42}$$

subject to

$$\pi_{H,t} = F + \kappa_y \tilde{y}_t, \tag{9.43}$$

where $F \equiv \beta E_t \{\pi_{H,t+1}\} + u_t$ is a term which is taken as given by the policy authority in her maximization problem. Notice that in so doing the monetary authority recognizes that future private sector's expectations cannot be manipulated.

The first-order condition of this static problem reads:

$$\tilde{y}_t = -\Theta \pi_{H,t}, \quad \text{for all } t, \tag{9.44}$$

where $\Theta \equiv \kappa_y / b_w > 0$. This condition typically suggests that the monetary authority contracts real activity in response to a rise in inflation above the target. The parameter Θ measures the magnitude of the implied optimal adjustment of the output gap, which is increasing in the sensitivity of inflation to output gap movements κ_y, and decreasing in the preference weight attached to output gap variability. In particular, notice that

$$\frac{\partial \Theta}{\partial \gamma} < 0; \quad \frac{\partial \Theta}{\partial \eta} < 0.$$

This implies that the sensitivity of the output gap to inflation is decreasing in the degree of openness γ (for it lowers the sensitivity of the real marginal cost to the terms of trade) and decreasing in the elasticity of substitution between domestic and foreign goods η (for it lowers the adjustment in the terms of trade necessary to absorb any change in domestic output relative to world output). Hence, and in response to a rise in inflation, the monetary authority of an open economy will have to contract the output gap less relative to its closed economy counterpart. For lowering the output gap implies also an appreciation of the terms of trade, which, via (9.18), implies also a fall in the real marginal cost and a dampening of inflation. This shows that, besides the aggregate demand channel, the monetary authority of an open economy can also handle the relative price channel to inflation. It stands obvious that such channel is reinforced when the nominal exchange rate is free to float, for the exchange rate tends to compensate for the excess smoothness in the terms of trade due to the stickiness in the adjustment of nominal prices.

By substituting (9.44) into (9.15) one obtains the following second-order stochastic difference equation for the price level:

$$a\, p_{H,t} = \beta E_t\{p_{H,t+1}\} + \left(1 + \frac{\kappa_y^2}{b_w}\right) p_{H,t-1} + u_t, \tag{9.45}$$

where $a \equiv 1 + \beta + (\kappa_y^2/b_w) > 1$. The characteristic polynomial associated with the above equation is $\mu^2 - (a/\beta)\mu + (a - \beta/\beta) = 0$, whose roots are given by $\mu_{1,2} = (a/\beta)(1 \pm (a+2\beta)/a)$. For both roots lie outside the unit circle we have that under the discretionary policy the domestic price level exhibits a non-stationary dynamic.

We can then build a relationship between the dynamic of the price level and the one of the nominal exchange rate. By using equation (9.23) and (9.29), and recalling that the terms of trade (under the assumed price stability policy in the rest of the world) are given by $s_t = e_t - p_{H,t}$ we can write

$$e_t = p_{H,t} + \xi_{d,t}, \tag{9.46}$$

where

$$\xi_{d,t} \equiv -\left(\frac{\sigma \Theta w_s^{-1}}{\Theta \kappa_y + 1 - \beta\rho}\right) u_t + \left(\frac{\sigma(1+\varphi)}{\sigma + \varphi w_s}\right) z_t - \left(\frac{\sigma(\sigma + \varphi)}{\sigma + \varphi w_s}\right) y_t^*.$$

Hence, given that $\xi_{d,t}$ is composed only of exogenous stationary processes, we have the following result:

Result 1 *Under the time consistent (discretionary) policy the (producer) price level and the nominal exchange rate both exhibit a unit root.*

9.3.2 Optimal plan under commitment

In the case in which the monetary authority has the possibility of committing as of time zero, the optimal program consists of choosing a state contingent sequence

$\{\pi_{H,t}, \tilde{y}_t\}_{t=0}^{\infty}$ to maximize (9.41) subject to the sequence of constraints in (9.35) holding in every period $t + j$, $j \geq 0$.

The optimality conditions of this problem can be written as:

$$\tilde{y}_{t+j} - \tilde{y}_{t+j-1} = -\Theta \pi_{H,t+j}, \quad j > 0$$
$$\tilde{y}_t = -\Theta \pi_{H,t}, \quad j = 0. \qquad (9.47)$$

As illustrated in Clarida *et al.* (1999) and Woodford (2003), it stands clear that the optimal program under commitment entails an inertial behavior. This strategy allows the policy authority to take full advantage of the forward-looking feature of both consumers' and firms' decisions. Consider a rise in inflation due to a positive cost-push shock. Unlike the case of discretion, the Central Bank under commitment will continue to reduce the output gap beyond the impact period of the shock. If this is credible, and given the forward-looking nature of the price-setting process, anticipation of such a future path of the output gap will result in the current impact of the cost-push shock on inflation to be dampened.

By noticing that (9.47) can be interpreted as a price level targeting rule $\tilde{y}_t = -\Theta p_{H,t}$ and by substituting into (9.15) one can obtain the following second-order stochastic difference equation for the domestic price level:

$$a p_{H,t} = \beta E_t \{p_{H,t+1}\} + p_{H,t-1} + u_t. \qquad (9.48)$$

Such equation has a unique bounded solution that takes the form

$$p_{H,t} = \mu_{1,c} \, p_{H,t-1} + \left(\frac{\mu_{1,c}}{1 - \rho \beta \mu_{1,c}}\right) u_t, \qquad (9.49)$$

where

$$\mu_{1,c} \equiv \frac{a}{2}\left(1 - \sqrt{\left(1 - \frac{4\beta}{a^2}\right)}\right) < 1$$

is the stable root associated with the characteristic polynomial, and $\mu_{2,c} = \beta^{-1}\mu_{1,c}^{-1}$. Hence we see that under commitment the domestic price level must be stationary. Similarly, we can build a link between the nominal exchange rate and the price level as follows:

$$e_t = (1 + \Theta) p_{H,t} + \xi_{c,t}, \qquad (9.50)$$

where

$$\xi_{d,t} \equiv \left(\frac{\sigma(1+\varphi)}{\sigma + \varphi\omega_s}\right) z_t - \left(\frac{\sigma(\sigma+\varphi)}{\sigma + \varphi\omega_s}\right) y_t^*.$$

Hence we have the following result:

Result 2 *Under the optimal commitment policy the (producer) price level and the nominal exchange rate are both stationary.*

9.3.3   Fixed exchange rates

When the small economy pegs its exchange rate *vis-à-vis* the world economy or, alternatively, relinquishes its monetary independence by joining a currency area, the nominal exchange rate will be irrevocably fixed. In this case the interest parity condition reduces to

$$r_t = r_t^* \quad \text{for all } t$$

and the terms of trade will read

$$s_t = p_t^* - p_{H,t}$$
$$= -p_{H,t}, \tag{9.51}$$

where the second equality follows from our assumption that the monetary authority in the rest of the world pursues a price stability policy. By substituting into (9.18) and in turn into (9.15) one obtains

$$a_f\, p_{H,t} = \beta E_t\{p_{H,t+1}\} + p_{H,t-1} + u_t, \tag{9.52}$$

where $a_f \equiv 1 + \beta + \kappa_y$. This equation has a unique bounded representation of the form

$$p_{H,t} = \mu_{1,f}\, p_{H,t-1} + \left(\frac{\mu_{1,f}}{1 - \rho\beta\mu_{1,f}}\right) u_t, \tag{9.53}$$

where

$$\mu_1 \equiv \frac{a_f}{2}\left(1 - \sqrt{\left(1 - \frac{4\beta}{a_f^2}\right)}\right) < 1 \quad \text{and} \quad \mu_{2,f} = \beta^{-1}\mu_{1,f}^{-1}.$$

Hence we can state the following result:

Result 3   *In a regime of fixed exchange rates, like in the optimal commitment regime, the domestic price level must be stationary.*

9.4   Monetary regimes and equilibrium dynamics

In this section we compare the dynamics implied by the three monetary regimes in response to a cost-push shock. Before doing that let us briefly describe our baseline parameterization. We set σ equal to 1, which corresponds to a log utility specification, and η equal to 1.5. We assume $\varphi = 3$ (which implies a labor supply elasticity of $1/3$), and a value for the steady-state markup $\mu = 1.2$ (which implies that ε, the elasticity of substitution between differentiated goods, is 6). The parameter θ is set to 0.75, a value consistent with an average period of one year between price adjustments. We assume $\beta = 0.99$, which implies a riskless annual return of about 4 percent in the steady state. We assume, for simplicity, that the cost-push shock follows a simple autoregressive process with persistence parameter $\rho_u = 0.7$ and unitary standard deviation of the shock. All the previous parameters are assumed to take identical values in the small open economy and the world economy. In addition, the small economy is characterized by an openness index γ for which we assume a value of 0.4. Finally we assume that $b_w = 0.05$ as a starting baseline value. Although in the low range this is consistent with the absolute size derived in Woodford (2003), where the Central Bank's loss function is derived by means of a second-order approximation of the household's utility (so that b_w is a convolution of underlying structural parameters).[9] The sensitivity analysis on this parameter, though, will be of considerable importance.

9.4.1 Optimal policy vs time consistent

In Figure 9.1 the equilibrium response of selected variables under the optimal commitment policy is contrasted to the one under the time consistent (TC henceforth) or discretionary policy.

As expected the positive cost-push shock generates a rise in inflation and a fall in the output gap. However the implied behavior of inflation differs sharply across the two regimes. Under the TC policy inflation returns monotonically to its initial value while it displays some overshooting under the optimal policy. Under the TC policy the monetary authority cannot exploit its commitment to a certain future path for the output gap to improve the short run inflation performance, which explains the lack of persistence in the response of the output gap. The different behavior of inflation across the two regimes rationalizes the different behavior in the price level, which is stationary under the optimal program while it exhibits a unit root under the TC policy.

Under the optimal policy the response of the interest rate is much smoother than under TC. The rise in the interest rate is responsible for the initial appreciation of the nominal exchange rate, which is larger under the TC policy. However the exchange rate exhibits a sharply different dynamic under the two regimes afterwards. Namely it returns monotonically to the initial value under the optimal policy while it exhibits a unit root under the TC policy. Hence, and in response to the initial cost-push shock, the TC policy generates a permanently higher price level and depreciated nominal exchange rate.

The key factor that rationalizes this link between the price level and the nominal exchange rate is the stationarity of the terms of trade under the assumption of complete asset markets. Full risk sharing, as from equation (9.16), implies that permanent changes in relative consumption are not allowed in equilibrium in response to shocks. Hence the trade balance must always return to its steady-state value of zero.[10]

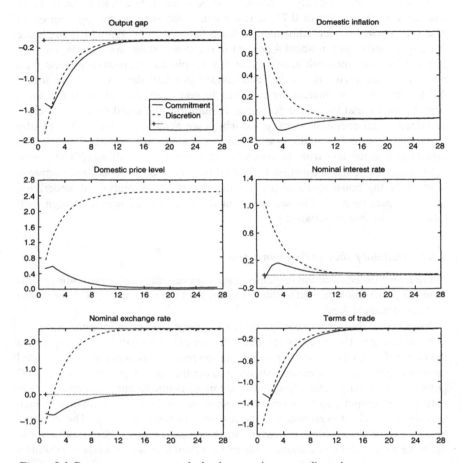

Figure 9.1 Responses to a cost-push shock: commitment vs discretion.

9.4.2   *Optimal policy vs fixed exchange rates*

What distinguishes a regime of fixed exchange rates is its nature of commitment to a certain future course of action. This raises the issue of what features such regime actually shares with the one of fully optimal commitment.

In Figure 9.2 the implied equilibrium responses of the same selected variables to a 1 percent cost-push innovation is compared to the one under fixed exchange rates.

Notice that under fixed exchange rates once again inflation rises and the output gap falls. However the response of both variables relative to the optimal policy is much more amplified under fixed exchange rates than it was the case under the TC policy. This naturally suggests that under our benchmark calibration a regime

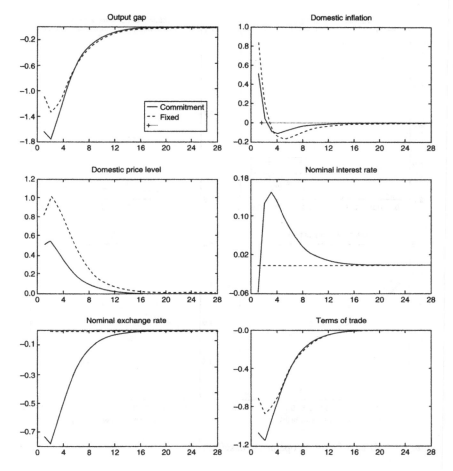

Figure 9.2 Responses to a cost-push shock: commitment vs fixed.

of fixed exchange rates implies a greater overall loss for the monetary authority of the small economy.

The distinctive feature of the fixed exchange rate regime is that it implies a stationary response of the price level. This is again a natural consequence of the stationarity of the terms of trade. By construction the response of the price level must be the mirror image of the one of the terms of trade.

The effect of varying the degree of openness

Despite the fact that stationarity of the price level is a feature that a regime of fixed exchange rates shares with the fully optimal policy the latter regime still implies large fluctuations in inflation and in the price level. In this section we show how the

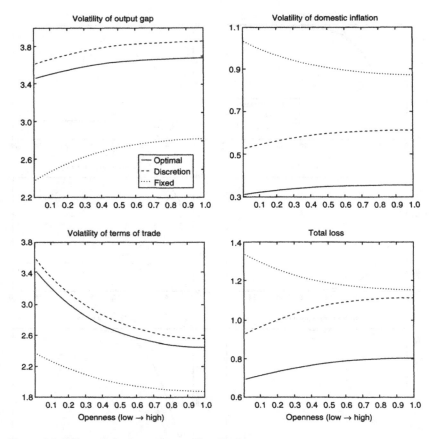

Figure 9.3 Effect of varying openness (baseline).

results are affected by one key parameter that distinguishes our analysis, namely the degree of openness. Figure 9.3 displays the effect of varying the import share γ on the volatility of the output gap, inflation and the terms of trade as well as on the total Central Bank's loss.

Notice, first, that the model implies a negative relationship between the equilibrium volatility of the terms of trade and the degree of openness. This can be clearly seen from equation (9.23). The sensitivity ω_s of relative output to the terms of trade is in fact increasing in the degree of openness. The more open the economy, the smaller is the equilibrium variation in the terms of trade necessary to absorb a required given variation in relative output. Under fixed exchange rates the volatility of the terms of trade is constantly below the one implied by the optimal policy and the TC policy. The impossibility of the nominal exchange rate to compensate for the excess smoothness in prices is responsible for this result and it is reminiscent of the widely cited empirical evidence in Mussa (1986).[11]

For any degree of openness the volatility of the output gap is larger under the TC and optimal policy than it is under fixed exchange rates. This is due to the strong link between the terms of trade and the output gap implicit in the model. As fixed exchange rates tend to dampen the volatility of the terms of trade relative to the optimal regimes this is reflected in a less volatile output gap. However fixed exchange rates imply a much larger volatility in inflation relative to the optimal regimes. This is the factor that drives the loss ranking reported in the bottom-right panel of Figure 9.3. The relatively higher volatility of inflation under fixed rates is the result of a too low volatility in the terms of trade. Hence we have the following result:

Result 4 *Relative to the optimal policies (both under commitment and discretion), fixed exchange rates tend to excessively dampen the terms of trade (and therefore the output gap) volatility and to generate too volatile inflation. This results in fixed rates delivering higher loss under our baseline parameterization.*

However, Figure 9.3 already shows that the total loss under fixed rates tend to converge quite closely to the one under TC when the degree of openness is very high, although the relative ranking is not altered. Recall that in this context the degree of openness measured by γ is also a measure of the degree of asymmetry between the domestic and the foreign consumption baskets. As $\gamma \to 1$ the two consumption baskets tend to coincide. In that limit case no relative price variation is required in equilibrium, and hence the loss from excess smoothness in the terms of trade that characterizes fixed exchange rates is minimized. Not surprisingly, then, total loss is decreasing in openness under fixed exchange rates.

High weight on the output gap Figure 9.4 displays the results of the same sensitivity analysis conducted earlier but with a change from the baseline calibration. Namely, we increase the relative weight b_w assigned to output gap volatility in the loss criterion of the Central Bank (from 0.05 to 0.2). This already implies dramatic changes in the relative ranking between TC policy and fixed exchange rates, although the value of b_w remains still in the low range from the viewpoint of the traditional literature assuming quadratic loss functions.[12]

A higher weight b_w implies more room under the optimal policy for smoothing the terms of trade (and therefore the output gap) in a way more similar to what is done under fixed exchange rates. However this tends to boost the volatility of inflation under TC. The volatility of inflation under fixed exchange rates now lies below the one under the TC policy regardless of the degree of openness. This generates a reversed ranking between TC and fixed rates, with the latter dominating the former for any degree of openness. This result can be recast in the following way:

Result 5 *When the policy weight on the output gap variability is high, fixing the exchange rate can be a good way to reduce inflation variability without trading off too much in terms of output gap volatility, a cost that must necessarily be paid under the TC policy.*

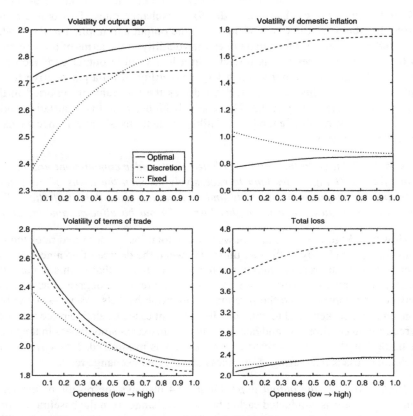

Figure 9.4 Effect of varying openness (high weight on output gap).

High elasticity of substitution between domestic and foreign goods In Figure 9.5 we conduct a final sensitivity experiment. We are still interested in analyzing the sensitivity to the degree of openness of the relative ranking between fixed exchange rates and the TC policy.

In this experiment we reduce the policy weight parameter b_w back to its original initial value ($b_w = 0.05$) and alter the baseline calibration along a different dimension, that is, the elasticity of substitution between domestic and foreign goods (from $\eta = 1.5$ to $\eta = 3$). Relative to the baseline case illustrated in Figure 9.3 this result shows that, when the elasticity of substitution is high, there exists a degree of openness for which the equilibrium total loss under fixed is smaller than the one under the TC policy. Interestingly this happens for a relatively low value of the index of openness γ. Hence, we have the following result:

Result 6 *For relatively high values of the elasticity of substitution between domestic and foreign goods (and already for a low degree of openness) a fixed exchange rate regime can dominate the optimal time consistent policy.*

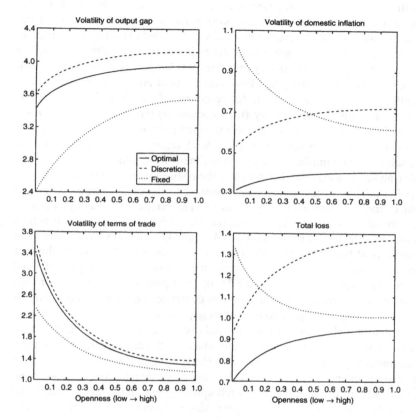

Figure 9.5 Effect of varying openness (high elasticity of substitution).

This result is driven by the large reduction in inflation volatility that higher openness brings about under fixed rates (unlike the optimal policies, see upper-right panel). It was already clear from the baseline case analyzed in Figure 9.3 that under fixed exchange rates higher openness would dampen inflation volatility. This is a direct consequence of higher openness implying smoother terms of trade and therefore more stable prices (recall that under fixed exchange rates $s_t = -p_{H,t}$). While under the baseline calibration this effect is not strong enough to switch the relative ranking between TC and fixed rates, it does deliver this result when the elasticity of substitution is high. In this case the gain of reduced inflation volatility derived from higher openness is large and allows fixed exchange rates to dominate the TC policy for low values of openness.

9.5 Conclusion

In this work, we have presented a benchmark framework for the analysis of monetary policy in an open economy. We have spelled out a dynamic model with both consumers and firms acting in an optimizing manner. The fact that inflation maintains its feature of forward-looking variable makes it an ideal starting point for the analysis of alternative monetary policy and exchange rate arrangements. We have solved the equilibrium dynamics under three alternative policy regimes: optimal policy, TC policy and fixed exchange rates. We have shown that in a baseline calibration gains from commitment arise from the possibility of affecting the expectations on the future course of variables. When commitment is not feasible a discretionary (time consistent) policy still outperforms a regime of fixed exchange rates. We have devoted particular attention to the performance of a fixed exchange rate regime. Such regime displays a fundamental pitfall, namely, that it implies an excess smoothness in the adjustment of the terms of trade (the key channel that distinguishes the open economy dimension of monetary policy). This makes it undesirable relative to the other regimes under the baseline calibration. However, a regime of fixed exchange rates displays a benefit of the optimal commitment regime that the TC policy lacks. Namely, it entails stationary price level and exchange rate. We have indeed shown that there exist combinations of the parameter values that make such benefit outweigh the cost of excess smoothness in the terms of trade thereby rendering a regime of fixed exchange rates more desirable than the TC optimal policy. This happens for high values of the elasticity substitution between domestic and foreign goods and for a high relative weight assigned to the output gap variability in the Central Bank's loss function. In such cases a regime of fixed exchange rates can be characterized as a feasible way to move the equilibrium closer to the one entailed by the optimal commitment program. This result also sheds light on a new type of trade-off that a small economy may face when choosing to participate in a currency area. Namely a trade-off between the cost of relinquishing exchange rate flexibility and the benefit of designing a monetary regime which allows to implement in practice some of the features of the optimal commitment policy.

Notes

1 This work relies heavily on previous joint work of mine with Jordi Gali whom I thank for invaluable insights. It also draws from earlier work by Clarida *et al.* (2001) who in turn draw on Gali and Monacelli (2002) in the specification of their model.
2 See, for example, Obstfeld and Rogoff (1995), Obstfeld and Rogoff (2000a), Corsetti and Pesenti (2001a), Betts and Devereux (2000) and Bachetta and Wincoop (2000). For an updated series of recent contributions see Bryan Doyle's New Open Economy Macroeconomics Homepage at http://www.geocities.com/brian_m_doyle/open.html and the Benigno–Benigno–Ghironi page on Open Economy Interest Rate Rules at http://www.geocities.com/monetaryrules/mpoe.htm
3 For an excellent contribution see Christiano *et al.* (2001).
4 Woodford (2003), Clarida *et al.* (2000).
5 Such indexes are in turn given by CES aggregators of the quantities consumed of each type of good. The optimal allocation of any given expenditure within each category of goods yields the demand functions:

$$C_{H,t}(i) = \left(\frac{P_{H,t}(i)}{P_{H,t}} \right)^{-\varepsilon} C_{H,t}; \quad C_{F,t}(i) = \left(\frac{P_{F,t}(i)}{P_{F,t}} \right)^{-\varepsilon} C_{F,t},$$

for all $i \in [0, 1]$, where $P_{H,t} \equiv (\int_0^1 P_{H,t}(i)^{1-\varepsilon}di)^{1/(1-\varepsilon)}$ and $P_{F,t} \equiv (\int_0^1 P_{F,t}(i)^{1-\varepsilon}di)^{1/(1-\varepsilon)}$ are the price indexes for domestic and imported goods respectively, both expressed in home currency. The elasticity of substitution between goods within each category is given by $\varepsilon > 1$.

6 Clarida *et al.* (1999); Goodfriend and King (2001). Woodford (2003) discusses under what conditions such a policy corresponds also to maximizing a second-order approximation of households' welfare.

7 See Monacelli (2003) for a model that allows for deviations from the law of one price.

8 The fact that this model generates no conflict between policy objectives depends crucially on the fact that the law of one price is assumed to hold throughout. In Monacelli (2003), the presence of incomplete pass-through on import prices determines endogenously a trade-off between the stabilization of domestic inflation and of the output gap.

9 The derivation, along the lines of Woodford (2003), of a tractable loss function from first principles has proved a much more difficult task in an open economy, as outlined in Benigno and Benigno (2002) and Gali and Monacelli (2002). In particular, in these models an accurate quadratic approximation of households' welfare can be obtained only under very specific assumptions on preferences and on the value of the international elasticity of substitution. The issue of computing welfare maximizing policies in fully dynamic open economy models still remains a subject of research. See Faia and Monacelli (2003) for an alternative approach based on the direct solution of the Ramsey problem and on the explicit consideration of all the distortions characterizing the equilibrium of the economy.

10 This does not imply that movements in the trade balance are not allowed in the short run. In this context, and unlike the framework of Corsetti and Pesenti (2001b), the elasticity of substitution between domestic and foreign goods can be larger than unitary and this permits movements in the trade balance around its zero steady-state value even in the case of log preferences.

11 See Monacelli (2002) for a sticky price model that is able to rationalize quantitatively the evidence of Mussa (1986), according to which, in moving from fixed to floating exchange rate regimes, industrial countries experience dramatic rises in the variability of both nominal and real exchange rates.

12 Some authors find a range $b_w \in [0, 2]$ as plausible, see, for instance, Dennis and Soderstrom (2002).

10 Price setting and optimal monetary cooperation

A New Keynesian perspective

Matthieu Darracq-Pariès

10.1 Introduction

In this chapter, we develop a simple New Keynesian framework to investigate the impact of "pricing-to-market" on optimal monetary policy. This study will highlight the importance of correctly modeling the exchange rate/international trade prices nexus as far as monetary policy is concerned. It belongs to a large strand of literature that aims at analyzing monetary policy in open economies.

On the one hand, the so-called "New Open Economy Macroeconomics" (NOEM) literature, based on Obstfeld and Rogoff's (1995) seminal paper, examines the conduct of monetary policy in a class of open economy general equilibrium models. This literature focuses in particular on the optimality of exchange rate regimes and on the welfare gains from policy coordination. Such topics have been analyzed across a large range of model specifications. It turns out that financial structure, international price setting, preference parameters and nature of shocks are key determinants. Concerning price setting schemes, part of these studies assumes that nominal prices are fixed in the producers' currency, so that prices for consumers change one-for-one in the short run with changes in the nominal exchange rate ("producer-currency-pricing," hereafter PCP). A number of recent papers are based on models in which nominal prices are set in advance in the consumers' currency. In that case, in the short run, nominal exchange rate changes do not modify the prices faced by consumers ("local-currency-pricing," hereafter LCP) assumption. Within this research agenda, some papers like Devereux and Engel (1998, 1999, 2000) or Corsetti and Pesenti (2001a) focus specifically on the connections between price setting and optimal monetary policy. The hypothesis of complete financial markets is relaxed in several papers like Obstfeld and Rogoff (2002), or Sutherland (2003) in order to analyze the welfare gains from monetary policy coordination.

On the other hand, the research program initiated by Rotemberg and Woodford (1997) led to an abundant New Keynesian literature. Whereas in NOEM models price are set on a period by period basis, leading to highly unrealistic dynamics, the staggered-price-setting model used in most of this work, has become the workhorse of monetary policy analysis in the closed economy framework. And more recently, some studies have extended the analysis to the open economy setting. Indeed, the new generation of dynamic general equilibrium models manages to mix simplicity with a rich behavioral structure. The framework we use here is closely related to those of Benigno and Benigno (2001a); Clarida *et al.* (2002) or Gali and Monacelli (2002) who study optimal monetary policy under PCP and with complete markets. Benigno (1999) introduces LCP in a New Keynesian model but he neither pursues a welfare analysis nor does he derive the optimal monetary policy. This chapter aims at filling this gap. Finally, this chapter is related to the work of Smets and Wouters (2002) on optimal monetary policy in a small open economy under LCP.

Our main objective is to study the impact of price setting on optimal monetary cooperation under "commitment" and "discretion," in a unified and simple two-country framework, featuring general preferences, both efficient and inefficient shocks and a fully fledged welfare function. But, here we do not relax the hypothesis of complete financial markets and the coordination gains are not analytically examined. We present a two-country model with imperfect competition and price rigidities in which technological shocks coexist with "cost-push" shocks. As opposed to previous studies, the purchasing power parity (PPP) does not hold here for two reasons: home bias in households' preferences and imperfect exchange rate pass-through. In our model, we explicitly use an approximation of the welfare function in order to study the features of optimal monetary cooperation. As a result, we try here to revisit and extend somewhat the results of the NOEM literature in the New Keynesian framework.

Obviously, we show that the optimal outcome depends crucially on the price setting rules and on the kind of shocks that affects the economies. When prices are sticky in the producer's currency, we revisit, in a slightly different model, the results of Benigno and Benigno (2001a) and Clarida *et al.* (2002) on optimal monetary policy and optimal exchange rate regime. With efficient shocks, pure producer price index (PPI) inflation targeting policies achieve the first best allocation. The nominal exchange rate is thus free to adjust to the required fluctuations of the terms of trade. As Friedman (1953) first advocated, it may be considered optimal to have a flexible exchange rate regime. Nevertheless, when inefficient shocks hit the economies, monetary authorities face a trade-off between the inflation rate and the output gap stabilization: It is no longer possible to reach the first best allocation. So they cooperate optimally to adjust gradually the producer price levels, the output gaps and the terms of trade. In that context, exchange rate fluctuations amplify the inflation/output gap trade-offs so that it may be optimal to limit exchange rate movements. A fixed exchange rate regime is even fully optimal under some parameter restrictions. As far as coordination gains are concerned, some non-negligible welfare improvements from cooperation are likely to exist even if shocks are efficient.

These results are not robust to modifications of the price-setting assumptions. In presence of LCP, due to the absence of direct exchange rate pass-through, monetary authorities cannot influence directly the interior terms of trade. Without home bias in national consumption, it can even be shown that terms of trade are independent from monetary policy. Consequently, no matter what kind of shocks affects the economies, monetary authorities cannot manage to completely stabilize the producer inflation rates and the output gaps: there is always a trade-off between the stabilization of import prices and producer prices. Moreover, LCP introduces in the model an additional distortion: with no preference bias, PPP does not hold and real exchange rate variations induce undesirable volatility in cross-country consumption. So monetary policies should aim at limiting such movements by targeting directly the consumer price indexes (CPI). In that case, we actually show that the credible optimal monetary coordination under LCP is a "lean against the wind" strategy that adjusts the "consumption gaps" to the consumer-price level fluctuations. Following efficient shocks, it is feasible and optimal to close the consumption gaps and to fully stabilize the CPI levels, while there still exists some fluctuations of import prices and interior producer prices. A CPI inflation targeting implements the optimal outcome. Furthermore, the predictions of the previous model about the optimal choice of an exchange rate regime are strongly modified by the assumption of LCP. The failure of the law of one price creates new incentives for monetary authorities to control exchange rate fluctuations. We prove that the case for fixing the nominal exchange rate is stronger under LCP: without preference bias, the optimal solution implies a fixed exchange rate regime, independent of the nature of the shocks under a particular combination of parameters, and when shocks are efficient. This need for some kind of exchange rate arrangement gives us the intuition that cooperation gains are likely to arise more easily under LCP.

The chapter is structured as follows. Section 10.2 presents a derivation of the core model. Section 10.3 solves the equilibrium under flexible price, under PCP and under LCP. Section 10.4 derives the optimal monetary cooperation under "commitment" and "discretion," and presents the consequences in terms of optimal exchange rate regime. Some intuitions are given on the potential cooperative gains in Section 10.5.

10.2   The core model

The New Keynesian models that are abundantly used in the literature are quite simple to derive and present relevant microeconomic foundations. They bring new perspectives in the field of monetary policy analysis due to their treatment of anticipations and the possibility to pursue welfare analysis.

The world economy consists of two symmetric countries, Home and Foreign. In each country, there is a continuum of differentiated goods indexed on [0,1]. The number of households is proportional to the number of firms. Consumers receive utility from consumption, real money holdings and disutility from labor. They are identical to each other in the sense that they share the same intertemporal elasticity of substitution and the same elasticity of labor supply with respect to the real wage. But, in each country, they have biased preferences towards locally produced goods. Household behavior consists in an intertemporal smoothing of consumption, an arbitrage between labor and consumption and a money demand. Financial markets are complete both domestically and internationally. In that context, we show that households are identical with respect to their consumption and labor supply choices. On the labor market, wages are fully flexible.

10.2.1 Consumer's program

At time t, the utility function of a generic domestic consumer h belonging to country H is

$$U_t^h = E_t \sum_{s \geq t} \beta^{s-t} \left(U(C_{t+s}^h) + N \left(\frac{M(h)_{t+s}}{P_{t+s}} \right) - V(L_{t+s}^h) \right).$$

Households obtain utility from consumption of an aggregate index and the liquidity services of holding money $M(h)_{t+s}/P_{t+s}$, while receiving disutility from labor L_{t+s}^h.

Markets are complete both at international and domestic level. Each period, consumers can trade freely within a complete set of Arrow–Debreu securities. For each state of nature, there is a contingent one period nominal bond. Let $Q(s^{t+1}/s^{\rightarrow t})$ denote the price of this bond at date t, and $B_t^h(s^{t+1})$ the number of units bought by consumer h. The probability that the state of nature s^{t+1} occurs, knowing the past history of shocks until date t, is $\mu(s^{t+1}/s^{\rightarrow t})$.

Each household h maximizes its utility function under the following budgetary constraint:

$$\sum_{s^{t+1}} \frac{Q(s^{t+1}/s^{\rightarrow t}) B_t^h(s^{t+1})}{P_t} + \frac{M_t^h}{P_t} = \frac{B_t^h(s^t)}{P_t} + \frac{M_{t-1}^h}{P_t} + \frac{W_t^h L_t^h}{P_t} + \frac{\pi_t^h}{P_t} - C_t^h,$$

$$(10.1)$$

where W_t^h is the wage, π_t^h represents the nominal profits from the firm owned by consumer h.

The first-order conditions corresponding to the quantity of contingent bonds are

$$\forall s^{t+1} \quad Q(s^{t+1}/s^{\rightarrow t}) = \beta \mu(s^{t+1}/s^{\rightarrow t}) \frac{U_C(C_{t+1}^h(s^{t+1}))}{U_C(C_t^h)} \frac{P_t}{P_{t+1}(s^{t+1})}. \quad (10.2)$$

A portfolio consisting in one unit of each elementary security has the same value as a one-period bond, so

$$\sum_{s^{t+1}} Q(s^{t+1}/s^{\rightarrow t}) = \frac{1}{1+i_t}.$$

Equations (10.1) and (10.2) lead to the well-known Euler equation, reflecting the intertemporal consumption-smoothing behavior of households:

$$U_C(C_t^h) = (1+i_t)\beta E_t \left(U_C(C_{t+1}^h) \frac{P_t}{P_{t+1}} \right).$$

We can show that, as financial markets are complete domestically, marginal utilities of consumption are equalized across households, as are the consumption levels since the utility function chosen here is additively separable.

Moreover, as in Erceg *et al.* (2000), each household is a monopoly supplier of a differentiated labor service. For sake of simplicity, we assume that she sells her services to a perfectly competitive firm which transforms it into an aggregate labor input using the following technology:

$$L_t = \left[\int_0^1 L_t^{h(\varepsilon_w - 1)/\varepsilon_w} \, dh \right]^{\varepsilon_w/(\varepsilon_w - 1)}.$$

The household faces a labor demand curve with constant elasticity of substitution:

$$L_t^h = \left(\frac{W_t^h}{W_t} \right)^{-\varepsilon_w} L_t,$$

where $W_t = \left(\int_0^1 W_t^{h 1 - \varepsilon_w} \, dh \right)^{1/(1 - \varepsilon_w)}$ is the aggregate wage rate. The first-order condition associated with wage setting is

$$\frac{\varepsilon_w}{\varepsilon_w - 1} V_L(L_t^h) = U_C(C_t) \frac{W_t^h}{P_t}.$$

The real wage is equal to a constant markup over the marginal rate of substitution between consumption and labor. Because of wage flexibility, the households will all set the same wage and offer the same quantity of labor:[1]

$$L_t^h = L_t \text{ and } W_t^h = W_t \quad \forall h \in [0, 1], \ \forall t.$$

Finally, the demand for real money holdings is:

$$N_M \left(\frac{M_t^h}{P_t} \right) = U_C(C_t) \frac{i_t}{1 + i_t}.$$

The marginal rate of substitution between money and consumption is equal to the opportunity cost of holding it. In our framework, we do not describe monetary policy in terms of money supply strategy. For example, if the behavior of monetary authorities consists in an interest rate reaction function, we can neglect the money demand relations, assuming that money supply automatically adjusts to clear the money market. In the rest of the chapter, we will not mention the monetary aggregates anymore.

10.2.2   *Optimal risk sharing*

In addition to the completeness of domestic markets, we also assume that financial markets are complete internationally. Households in both countries are allowed to trade in the contingent one-period nominal bonds denominated in the home currency. This leads to the following risk sharing condition:[2]

$$\frac{U_C(C_t^*)}{U_C(C_t)} = \kappa \frac{S_t P_t^*}{P_t}, \tag{10.3}$$

where S_t is the nominal exchange rate, and κ is a constant depending on initial conditions (here normalized to 1). Equation (10.3) is derived from the set of optimality conditions that characterize the optimal allocation of wealth among state-contingent securities.

When markets are complete, it is useless to evaluate the current account path in order to determine the relative consumption dynamics. Consumption levels in both countries differ only to the extent that the real exchange rate deviates from PPP. In our model, those deviations are allowed by two assumptions. The first one is the preference bias for locally produced goods, implying that real exchange rate depends on terms of trade. The second one is the possibility that prices might not be denominated in the producer currency, which, combined with sticky prices, generates failures of the law of one price.

Moreover, Equation (10.3) ensures that in the model, consumption levels and the real exchange rate are stationary variables. Hence, should we consider stationary shocks, it would be relevant to analyze the model's properties in the neighborhood of a well-defined steady state.

10.2.3   Demands for differentiated goods

Consumers prefer locally produced goods. This composition bias in the household preferences determines the degree of openness at steady state. The aggregate consumption indexes are defined as follows:

$$C = \left[n^{1/\xi} C_H^{(\xi-1)/\xi} + (1-n)^{1/\xi} C_F^{(\xi-1)/\xi} \right]^{\xi/(\xi-1)},$$

$$C^* = \left[(1-n)^{1/\xi} C_H^{*(\xi-1)/\xi} + n^{1/\xi} C_F^{*(\xi-1)/\xi} \right]^{\xi/(\xi-1)}, \quad \xi > 1.$$

C_H and C_F are consumption subindexes of the continuum of differentiated goods produced respectively in country H and F. ξ is the elasticity of substitution between bundles C_H and C_F. Notice that when $n = 0.5$, the preference bias in national consumption disappears. The elementary differentiated goods are imperfect substitutes with elasticity of substitution denoted ε.

$$C_H = \left[\int_0^1 c(h)^{(\varepsilon-1)/\varepsilon} dh \right]^{\varepsilon/(\varepsilon-1)}, \quad C_F = \left[\int_0^1 c(f)^{(\varepsilon-1)/\varepsilon} df \right]^{\varepsilon/(\varepsilon-1)},$$

$$C_H^* = \left[\int_0^1 c^*(h)^{(\varepsilon-1)/\varepsilon} dh \right]^{\varepsilon/(\varepsilon-1)}, \quad C_F^* = \left[\int_0^1 c^*(f)^{(\varepsilon-1)/\varepsilon} df \right]^{\varepsilon/(\varepsilon-1)}.$$

In order to keep the derivation of the core model independent from the price setting assumptions, we do not make here any hypothesis concerning the linkages between the price of local sales and foreign sales. So for a domestic product h, we denote $p(h)$ its price on the local market and $p^*(h)$ its price on the foreign import market.

The consumption-based price indexes associated are defined as

$$P = \left[n P_H^{1-\xi} + (1-n) P_F^{1-\xi} \right]^{1/(1-\xi)},$$

$$P^* = \left[(1-n) P_H^{*1-\xi} + n P_F^{*1-\xi} \right]^{1/(1-\xi)}$$

with

$$P_H = \left[\int_0^1 p(h)^{1-\varepsilon}\,dh \right]^{1/(1-\varepsilon)}, \quad P_F = \left[\int_0^1 p(f)^{1-\varepsilon}\,df \right]^{1/(1-\varepsilon)},$$

$$P_H^* = \left[\int_0^1 p^*(h)^{1-\varepsilon}\,dh \right]^{1/(1-\varepsilon)}, \quad P_F^* = \left[\int_0^1 p^*(f)^{1-\varepsilon}\,df \right]^{1/(1-\varepsilon)}.$$

Each household allocates consumption across the differentiated goods as follows:

$$\forall h \in [0,1] \quad c(h) = \left(\frac{p(h)}{P_H} \right)^{-\varepsilon} C_H, \quad c^*(h) = \left(\frac{p^*(h)}{P_H^*} \right)^{-\varepsilon} C_H^*,$$

$$\forall f \in [0,1] \quad c(f) = \left(\frac{p(f)}{P_F} \right)^{-\varepsilon} C_F, \quad c^*(f) = \left(\frac{p^*(f)}{P_F^*} \right)^{-\varepsilon} C_F^*$$

and

$$C_H = n \left(\frac{P_H}{P} \right)^{-\xi} C, \qquad C_H^* = (1-n) \left(\frac{P_H^*}{P^*} \right)^{-\xi} C^*,$$

$$C_F = (1-n) \left(\frac{P_F}{P} \right)^{-\xi} C, \quad C_F^* = n \left(\frac{P_F^*}{P^*} \right)^{-\xi} C^*.$$

Each producer faces the aggregate local and foreign demand given by

$$\forall h \in [0,1] \quad Y_H^d(h) = \left(\frac{p(h)}{P_H} \right)^{-\varepsilon} \left(\frac{P_H}{P} \right)^{-\xi} nC,$$

$$Y_H^{d*}(h) = \left(\frac{p^*(h)}{P_H^*} \right)^{-\varepsilon} \left(\frac{P_H^*}{P^*} \right)^{-\xi} (1-n)C^*,$$

$$\forall f \in [0,1] \quad Y_F^d(f) = \left(\frac{p(f)}{P_F} \right)^{-\varepsilon} \left(\frac{P_F}{P} \right)^{-\xi} (1-n)C,$$

$$Y_F^{d*}(f) = \left(\frac{p^*(f)}{P_F^*} \right)^{-\varepsilon} \left(\frac{P_F^*}{P^*} \right)^{-\xi} nC^*.$$

10.2.4 Technology and market clearing conditions

On the supply side, goods are produced with a technology that is linear in labor input as follows:

$$\forall h \in [0,1], \quad Y_t(h) = AL_t(h) \quad \text{and} \quad \forall f \in [0,1], \quad Y_t^*(f) = A^* L_t^*(f),$$

where A and A^* are exogenous technology parameters.

Each firm sells its products in the local market and in the foreign market. We denote $Y_H(h)$ and $Y_H^*(h)$ (respectively $Y_F^*(f)$ and $Y_F(f)$) the local and foreign sales of domestic producer h (respectively foreign producer f) and we define $L_H(h)$ and $L_H^*(h)$ (respectively $L_F^*(f)$ and $L_F(f)$) the corresponding labor demand.

Aggregate productions are obtained using the CES aggregator $\int_0^1 \cdot^{(\varepsilon-1)/\varepsilon} dz^{\varepsilon/(\varepsilon-1)}$ and labor demands are given by the following relations:

$$Y_{H,t} = \frac{A_t L_{H,t}}{V_{H,t}}, \quad Y_{H,t}^* = \frac{A_t L_{H,t}^*}{V_{H,t}^*},$$

$$Y_{F,t} = \frac{A_t^* L_{F,t}}{V_{F,t}}, \quad Y_{F,t}^* = \frac{A_t^* L_{F,t}^*}{V_{F,t}^*},$$

where

$$V_{H,t} = \int_0^1 \left(\frac{p_t(h)}{P_{H,t}} \right)^{-\varepsilon} dh, \tag{10.4}$$

$$V_{H,t}^* = \int_0^1 \left(\frac{p_t^*(h)}{P_{H,t}^*} \right)^{-\varepsilon} dh, \tag{10.5}$$

$$V_{F,t} = \int_0^1 \left(\frac{p_t(f)}{P_{F,t}} \right)^{-\varepsilon} df, \tag{10.6}$$

$$V_{F,t}^* = \int_0^1 \left(\frac{p_t^*(f)}{P_{F,t}^*} \right)^{-\varepsilon} df. \tag{10.7}$$

The $V_{\bullet,t}$ and $V_{\bullet,t}^*$ terms illustrate the dispersion of interior production prices and export prices for both countries. Total output and labor are denoted Y and L in country H, Y^* and L^* in country F. Market clearing conditions on good markets are given by

$$Y = \left(\frac{P_H}{P} \right)^{-\xi} nC + \left(\frac{P_H^*}{P^*} \right)^{-\xi} (1-n)C^*,$$

$$Y^* = \left(\frac{P_F}{P} \right)^{-\xi} (1-n)C + \left(\frac{P_F^*}{P^*} \right)^{-\xi} nC^*.$$

So far, no assumption has been made about the international price-setting. In order to keep general the core model derivation, several relative price indicators are worth noting. $chger_{h,t} = S_t P^*_{H,t}/P_{H,t}$ and $chger_{f,t} = P_{F,t}/S_t P^*_{F,t}$ represent the aggregate relative margins on exports for producers in country H and F, respectively. If there is some form of international price discrimination, those ratios capture the relative profitability of foreign sales compared with the local ones. $T = P_F/P_H$ and $T^* = P^*_F/P^*_H$, denote the interior terms of trade and measure the competitiveness of local producers against import competitors.

10.2.5 Log-linearization of the core model

The deterministic steady state, around which we linearize the model, is associated with the case where all shocks are held at their unconditional mean. There is no inflation and no exchange rate depreciation. All price levels are equalized. In that context, PPP does hold and all macroeconomic aggregates are the same across countries.

We use identical utility function for all households in the world economy, given by

$$U^h_t = E_t \sum_{s \geq t} \beta^{s-t} \left(\frac{C^{1-\sigma}_{t+s}}{1-\sigma} + \chi \log \frac{M_{t+s}}{P_{t+s}} - K \frac{L^{1+\varphi}_{t+s}}{1+\phi} \right).$$

In what follows, lower case letters stand for the logarithmic deviation from steady state.

First-order conditions describing the household's behavior become

- Euler equations

$$c_t = E_t(c_{t+1}) - \frac{1}{\sigma}(i_t - E_t(\pi_{t+1})), \tag{10.8}$$

$$c^*_t = E_t(c^*_{t+1}) - \frac{1}{\sigma}(i^*_t - E_t(\pi^*_{t+1})). \tag{10.9}$$

- Wage equations

$$w_t - p_t = \phi l_t + \sigma c_t, \tag{10.10}$$

$$w^*_t - p^*_t = \phi l^*_t + \sigma c^*_t. \tag{10.11}$$

The optimal risk sharing condition can be written as

$$\sigma c_t - \sigma c^*_t = chger_t = s_t + p^*_t - p. \tag{10.12}$$

Using equations (10.8), (10.9) and (10.12), it is easy to see that uncovered interest rate parity holds, independently from the specified price-setting rules:

$$E_t \Delta s_{t+1} = i_t - i^*_t,$$

good markets clearing conditions lead to the following relations:

$$y_t + y_t^* = c_t + c_t^*, \tag{10.13}$$

$$y_t - y_t^* = Z(t_t + t_t^*) + (2n - 1)\frac{chger_h - chger_f}{2\sigma} \tag{10.14}$$

with $Z = 2n(1 - n)\xi + (2n - 1)^2/2\sigma$. The real exchange rate is a function of the relative export margins and the interior terms of trade:

$$chger_t = (2n - 1)\frac{t_t + t_t^*}{2} + \frac{chger_h - chger_f}{2}. \tag{10.15}$$

A first-order approximation of the production functions leads to

$$y_t = a_t + l_t \quad \text{and} \quad y_t^* = a_t^* + l_t^*. \tag{10.16}$$

The $V_{\bullet,t}$ and $V_{\bullet,t}^*$ terms in equations (10.4)–(10.7) are constant up to a first order (see Erceg *et al.*, 2000).

From now on, we just need the pricing equations of firms to close the model. In the next section, the required supply curves will be derived using two polar assumptions on the international price-setting.

10.3   Equilibrium

10.3.1   *The flexible price equilibrium*

Not only can the economies be affected by various "efficient" shocks like techno-logical shocks, but it is also possible to introduce inefficient shocks that lead to a short run inflation/output gap trade-off for the conduct of monetary policy. In our model, we might rationalize those shocks as markup fluctuations in the labor market (due to wage rigidity for example) or as markup fluctuations in the good markets (following fiscal modifications).

Nevertheless, when prices are fully flexible, only efficient shocks – which means shocks that do not introduce new distortions – are relevant. Thus, in order to derive the flexible price allocation, markups in the good markets as well as in the labor market are assumed to be constant. By doing so, we do not want the natural level of output to reflect variations in the degree of efficiency of the economies. This property is all the more appropriate since we could treat changes in the wage markup as standing for wage rigidity.

In the absence of price stickiness, firms set prices equal to a constant markup over marginal cost. Moreover, as the demand elasticity is the same for local sales and exports, firms have no incentive to discriminate and the law of one price holds.

The flexible allocation is therefore strictly independent from the price setting rules.

$$\forall z \in [0, 1] \quad p^*(z)S = p(z), \quad P_F^* S = P_F, \quad P_H^* S = P_H.$$

Consequently, interior terms of trade are equalized across countries and relative export margins remain constant:

$$T = T^*,$$

$$chger_h = chger_f = 1.$$

Because of the home bias, PPP does not hold

$$\frac{SP^*}{P} = \left(\frac{nT^{1-\xi} + 1 - n}{n + (1 - n)T^{1-\xi}} \right)^{1/(1-\xi)}.$$

Therefore, with the law of one price, equations (10.14) and (10.15) are considerably simplified: the real exchange rate and relative output are only related to the terms of trade by the following relations:

$$chger_t = (2n - 1)t_t, \tag{10.17}$$

$$y_t - y_t^* = 2Zt_t. \tag{10.18}$$

In order to close the model, we need to derive the aggregate price-setting equations. Firms are identical and wages are flexible. So all producer prices are equalized and the aggregated index is given by

$$P_{H,t} = \frac{\varepsilon}{(\varepsilon - 1)(1 - \tau)} \frac{W_t}{A_t},$$

$$P_{F,t}^* = \frac{\varepsilon}{(\varepsilon - 1)(1 - \tau^*)} \frac{W_t^*}{A_t^*},$$

where τ (respectively τ^*) denotes a tax on the Home (respectively Foreign) firm's revenue. In deviation from its steady state value, those conditions state that real marginal costs are equal to zero:

$$w_t - p_{H,t} = a_t \quad \text{and} \quad w_t^* - p_{F,t}^* = a_t^* \tag{10.19}$$

Finally, as money policy is neutral on the flexible price allocation, the model is closed without specifying the monetary policies.

The sticky price supply curves depend on the flexible price equilibrium. So it is convenient to indicate with a "—" over a variable a flexible price allocation. Moreover, since the model is easily solved in terms of world aggregate and cross-country difference, defined for any variable X as $X^W = (X + X^*)/2$ and $X^R = (X - X^*)/2$, respectively. Finally, we assume that technological shocks are drawn from the following stochastic processes $a_t = \rho_a a_{t-1} + \varepsilon_t^a$ and $a_t^* = \rho_a a_{t-1}^* + \varepsilon_t^{a*}$.

Using equations (10.8)–(10.12), (10.13), (10.16)–(10.19), we obtain the following reduced form:

World aggregate output: $\bar{y}_t^W = \dfrac{1+\phi}{\sigma+\phi} a_t^W$

Cross-country output: $\bar{y}_t^R = \dfrac{(1+\phi)Z}{1/2+Z\phi} a_t^R$

World aggregate consumption: $\bar{c}_t^W = \dfrac{1+\phi}{\sigma+\phi} a_t^W$

Cross-country consumption: $\bar{c}_t^R = \dfrac{(n-1/2)(1+\phi)}{\sigma(1/2+Z\phi)} a_t^R$

Terms of trade: $\bar{t}_t = \dfrac{1+\phi}{1/2+Z\phi} a_t^R$

World interest rate: $\bar{r}_t^W = \sigma \, \underset{t}{E}(\Delta \bar{c}_{t+1}^W)$

Cross-country interest rate: $\bar{r}^R = \sigma \, \underset{t}{E}(\Delta \bar{c}_{t+1}^R)$.

10.3.2 The PCP model equilibrium

The New Keynesian Phillips curves

Under PCP, firms are monopolistic suppliers who set their price in the national currency. In this context, the law of one price holds: there is no sticky import price behavior and the supply side of the model consists of two Phillips curves.

Firms are monopolistic competitors, produce differentiated products and set prices on a staggered basis *à la* Calvo (1983). In each period, a firm h (respectively f) faces a constant probability $1 - \alpha_H$, (respectively $1 - \alpha_F^*$), of being able to re-optimize its nominal price. This probability is independent across firms and time in the same country. The average duration of a rigidity period is $1/(1 - \alpha_H)$ (respectively $1/(1 - \alpha_F^*)$). If a firm cannot re-optimize its price, the price evolves according to the following simple rule: $P_t(z) = P_{t-1}(z)$. Therefore, the firm h chooses $\tilde{P}_t(h)$ to maximize its intertemporal profit

$$\underset{t}{E} \sum_{j=0}^{\infty} \alpha_H^j \, \Xi_{t,t+j} Y_{t+j}^d(h)[(1-\tau)\tilde{P}_t(h) - MC_{t+j} P_{H,t+j}],$$

where

$$\Xi_{t,t+j} = \beta^j \frac{U_C(C_{t+j}) P_t}{U_C(C_t) P_{t+j}}$$

is the marginal value of one unit of money to the household. $MC_{t+j} = W_{t+j}/P_{H,t+j} A_{t+j}$ is the real marginal cost. τ is a tax on firm's revenue. Due to our assumptions on the labor market, the real marginal cost is identical across producers. In our model, all firms that can re-optimize their price at time t choose the same level (see Woodford, 1999a, for example).

The first-order condition associated with the firm's choice of $\tilde{P}_t(h)$ is

$$
E_t \sum_{j=0}^{\infty} \alpha_H^j \, \Xi_{t,t+j} Y_{t+j}^d \, P_{H,t+j} \left[(1-\tau) \frac{\tilde{P}_t(h)}{P_{H,t+j}} - \frac{\varepsilon}{\varepsilon-1} MC_{t+j} \right] = 0.
$$

(10.20)

When the probability of being able to change prices tends towards unity, equation (10.20) implies that the firm sets its price equal to a constant markup, $\varepsilon/(\varepsilon-1)(1-\tau)$ over marginal cost as in the flexible price model. Otherwise, the firm's markup equals a weighted average of marginal costs over time.

Only a fraction $(1-\alpha_H)$ of producers in country H can re-optimize its price, each period. So the aggregate PPI is given by

$$
P_{H,t}^{1-\varepsilon} = \alpha_H (P_{H,t-1})^{1-\varepsilon} + (1-\alpha_H) \tilde{P}_t^{1-\varepsilon}(h).
$$

(10.21)

Equations analogous to (10.20) and (10.21) hold for foreign producers.

Notice that in the sticky-price equilibrium, the economies are also hit by cost-push shocks following the stochastic processes $u_t = \rho_u u_{t-1} + \varepsilon_t^u$ and $u_t^* = \rho_u u_{t-1}^* + \varepsilon_t^u$. The stochastic processes present a same autoregressive coefficient in order to keep the derivation of the optimal policy under commitment tractable. In the presentation of the model, those shocks originate from fiscal innovations. However, it would have been possible to rationalize the "cost-push" shocks as wage markup variations.

When linearizing the first-order condition (10.20), we obtain the following relation:

$$
\tilde{p}_t(h) = \sum_{j=1}^{\infty} (\beta\alpha_H)^j \, E_t(\pi_{H,t+j}) + (1-\beta\alpha_H) \sum_{j=0}^{\infty} (\beta\alpha_H)^j \, E_t(mc_{t+j} + u_{t+j}),
$$

(10.22)

where π_H is the PPI inflation rate. Moreover, equation (10.21) becomes

$$
\pi_{H,t} = \left(\frac{1-\alpha_H}{\alpha_H} \right) \tilde{p}_t(h).
$$

(10.23)

Combining equations (10.22) and (10.23), we derive the so-called New Keynesian Phillips curve:

$$
\pi_{H,t} = \beta \, E_t \pi_{H,t+1} + \lambda_H mc_t + u_{H,t},
$$

where

$$
\lambda_H = \frac{(1-\alpha_H)(1-\beta\alpha_H)}{\alpha_H}
$$

and

$$mc_t = w_t - p_{H,t} - a_t. \tag{10.24}$$

The same relation holds for country F, that is

$$\pi^*_{F,t} = \beta^* \underset{t}{E} \pi^*_{F,t+1} + \lambda^*_F mc^*_t + u^*_{F,t},$$

where

$$\lambda^*_F = \frac{(1 - \alpha^*_F)(1 - \beta\alpha^*_F)}{\alpha^*_F}$$

and

$$mc^*_t = w^*_t - p^*_{F,t} - a^*_t. \tag{10.25}$$

The cost-push shocks that affect directly the inflation rates are defined as $u^*_{F,t} = \lambda^*_F u^*_t$ and $u_{H,t} = \lambda_H u_t$.

Reduced form of the PCP model

A hat over a variable indicates the absolute deviation from its flexible price value. For example, $\hat{y}^W = y^W - \bar{y}^W$ is the world output gap.

After some algebra, the model collapses to a reduced form consisting in an aggregate demand equation, the uncovered interest rate parity, two Phillips curves and the relation defining the terms of trade. Besides, the marginal costs can be expressed easily in terms of the aggregate output gap and the terms of trade misalignments, using equations (10.10)–(10.12), (10.13), (10.16)–(10.18), (10.24), (10.25) in deviation from the flexible price allocation:

$$\sigma \underset{t}{E} (\hat{y}^W_{t+1} - \hat{y}^W_t) = \frac{i_t + i^*_t}{2} - \bar{r}^W_t - \underset{t}{E} \pi^W_{t+1}, \tag{10.26}$$

$$\underset{t}{E} \Delta s_{t+1} = i_t - i^*_t, \tag{10.27}$$

$$\pi_{H,t} = \beta \underset{t}{E} \pi_{H,t+1} + \lambda_H \left[(\sigma + \phi) \hat{y}^W_t + (1/2 + \phi Z) \hat{t} \right] + u_{H,t}, \tag{10.28}$$

$$\pi^*_{F,t} = \beta \underset{t}{E} \pi^*_{F,t+1} + \lambda^*_F \left[(\sigma + \phi) \hat{y}^W_t - (1/2 + \phi Z) \hat{t} \right] + u^*_{F,t}, \tag{10.29}$$

$$\hat{t}_t = \hat{t}_{t-1} + \Delta s_t + \pi^*_{F,t} - \pi_{H,t} - \Delta \bar{t}_t, \tag{10.30}$$

$$\pi_t = n\pi_{H,t} + (1 - n)(\Delta s_t + \pi^*_{F,t}), \tag{10.31}$$

$$\pi^*_t = (1 - n)(\pi_{H,t} - \Delta s_t) + n\pi^*_{F,t}. \tag{10.32}$$

In this reduced form, all state variables are written in deviation from its flexible-price path and real shocks are introduced in the model through the natural interest rate in equation (10.26) and through the flexible-price path of terms of trade in equation (10.30). Output gap is obviously a familiar notion in applied economics. The terms of trade misalignments may deserve much more attention. Consider a positive productivity shock in country H, in a flexible economy. Excess supply in this country would call for a decrease in the relative price of local products. However, due to price stickiness, relative producer prices cannot adjust freely to mimic the flexible economy path unless the nominal exchange rate closes the gap. As prices are rigid in the producer currency, exchange rate pass-through to the terms of trade is high and some kind of flexibility seems appropriate to accommodate real shocks. We will come back to this issue later.

Moreover, terms of trade misalignments drive the wedge between the inflation rates in both countries. They enter the aggregate supply equations through two different channels. First, workers negotiate real wages measured with CPI whereas the producer price inflation rate depends on real wages measured with PPI. So when the price of foreign goods increases, workers want higher salaries to compensate for lower real income, which pushes up local producer prices. Second, the expenditure-switching effect reflects the fact that an increase in the price of goods produced in one country relative to goods produced in the other boosts the demand for goods produced in the latter and hours worked by residents. They ask for higher wages so that producer inflation increases in this country. Notice that the introduction of home bias in the model does not modify the structure of the reduced form under PCP. It just magnifies the expenditure-switching effect through the impact of terms of trade on relative consumption.

10.3.3   The LCP model equilibrium

We change in this section the price-setting rule on international markets. Firms denominate their foreign sales in the local currency. So, due to some kind of nominal rigidity in export markets, the law of one price does not hold anymore. It is the simplest way to introduce "pricing-to-market" into the model. Without this rigidity, it is not optimal for monopolistic firms to set different prices on local and foreign market since the elasticity of demand is the same at home and abroad.

In our model, we consider only traded goods. It would have been possible to introduce non-traded goods as a source of deviation from PPP. But our assumption that export prices are set in the consumer currency seems to be consistent with empirical studies.[3] Those papers show in particular that real exchange rate fluctuations are mainly caused by international market segmentation.

The supply curves

Now, each firm faces two distinct probabilities of being able to re-optimize its price for local sales and for sales in the foreign market. We denote α_H the probability prevailing in the local market (respectively α_F^* for producers of country F) and α_H^* the probability prevailing in the export market (respectively α_F for producers of country F). As highlighted by Smets and Wouters (2002), the degree of price rigidity affecting the import goods is likely to be very close to the one concerning domestic sales of locally produced goods. Therefore, we believe that the assumption consisting in $\alpha_F^* = \alpha_H^*$ and $\alpha_F = \alpha_H$ might be justified in the LCP model.

First-order conditions concerning the firm h become

$$E_t \sum_{j=0}^{\infty} \alpha_H^j \, \Xi_{t,t+j} Y_{H,t+j}^d P_{H,t+j} \left[(1-\tau) \frac{\tilde{P}_{H,t}(h)}{P_{H,t+j}} - \frac{\varepsilon}{\varepsilon - 1} MC_{t+j} \right] = 0,$$

$$E_t \sum_{j=0}^{\infty} (\alpha_H^*)^j \, \Xi_{t,t+j} Y_{H,t+j}^{d*} P_{H,t+j} \left[(1-\tau) \frac{\tilde{P}_{H,t+j}^*(h)}{P_{H,t+j}^*} \frac{S_{t+j} P_{H,t+j}^*}{P_{H,t+j}} - \frac{\varepsilon}{\varepsilon - 1} MC_{t+j} \right] = 0,$$

where MC_{t+j} is the real marginal cost deflated by interior-production-price index. As seen before, the dynamics of price indexes are:

$$P_{H,t}^{1-\varepsilon} = \alpha_H (P_{H,t-1})^{1-\varepsilon} + (1 - \alpha_H) \tilde{P}_t^{1-\varepsilon}(h),$$

$$P_{H,t}^{*1-\varepsilon} = \alpha_H^* (P_{H,t-1}^*)^{1-\varepsilon} + (1 - \alpha_H^*) \tilde{P}_t^{*1-\varepsilon}(h).$$

Analogous conditions for country F are inferred by symmetry. Following the steps of the previous case, the log-linearized aggregate supply curves are modified:

$$\pi_{H,t} = \beta \, E_t \, \pi_{H,t+1} + \lambda_H mc_t + u_{H,t},$$

$$\pi_{H,t}^* = \beta \, E_t \, \pi_{H,t+1}^* + \lambda_H^* (mc_t - chger_h) + u_{H,t}^*,$$

$$\pi_{F,t}^* = \beta \, E_t \, \pi_{F,t+1}^* + \lambda_F^* mc_t^* + u_{F,t}^*,$$

$$\pi_{F,t} = \beta \, E_t \, \pi_{F,t+1} + \lambda_F (mc_t^* - chger_f) + u_{F,t}.$$

The cost-push shocks, here again, are defined as $u_{H,t} = \lambda_H u_t$, $u_{H,t}^* = \lambda_H^* u_t$, $u_{F,t}^* = \lambda_F^* u_t^*$ and $u_{F,t} = \lambda_F u_t$. Notice that our hypothesis on the rigidity coefficients imposes $\lambda_H = \lambda_F$ and $\lambda_H^* = \lambda_F^*$.

Reduced form of the LCP model

As we have already done for the PCP model, it is possible to considerably simplify the model. The number of state variables has increased: in addition to the aggregate output gap, the deviations from the law of one price imply that from now on, relative export margins must be taken into account and the interior terms of trade are not equalized across countries anymore. Using equations (10.10)–(10.12), (10.13)–(10.16), (10.24), (10.25), the real marginal costs can be expressed in terms of the state variables:

$$\sigma \, \underset{t}{E}(\hat{y}_{t+1}^W - \hat{y}_t^W) = \frac{i_t + i_t^*}{2} - \bar{r}_t^W - \underset{t}{E} \pi_{t+1}^W,$$

$$\underset{t}{E} \Delta s_{t+1} = i_t - i_t^*,$$

$$\pi_{H,t} = \beta \, \underset{t}{E} \pi_{H,t+1} + \lambda_H mc_t + u_{H,t}, \tag{10.33}$$

$$\pi_{H,t}^* = \beta \, \underset{t}{E} \pi_{H,t+1}^* + \lambda_H^*(mc_t - chger_{h,t}) + u_{H,t}^*, \tag{10.34}$$

$$mc_t = (\sigma + \phi)\hat{y}_t^W + \left(\frac{1}{2} + \phi Z\right)\left(\frac{\hat{i}_t + \hat{i}_t^*}{2}\right) + (2n - 1)\left(\frac{\hat{i}_t^* - \hat{i}_t}{4}\right)$$

$$+ \frac{(2n - 1)}{4\sigma}\phi(chger_{h,t} - chger_{f,t}) + \frac{chger_{h,t}}{2}, \tag{10.35}$$

$$\pi_{F,t}^* = \beta \, \underset{t}{E} \pi_{F,t+1}^* + \lambda_F^* mc_t^* + u_{F,t}^*, \tag{10.36}$$

$$\pi_{F,t} = \beta \, \underset{t}{E} \pi_{F,t+1} + \lambda_F(mc_t^* - chger_{f,t}) + u_{F,t}, \tag{10.37}$$

$$mc_t^* = (\sigma + \phi)\hat{y}_t^W - \left(\frac{1}{2} + \phi Z\right)\left(\frac{\hat{i}_t + \hat{i}_t^*}{2}\right) + (2n - 1)\left(\frac{\hat{i}_t^* - \hat{i}_t}{4}\right)$$

$$- \frac{(2n - 1)}{4\sigma}\phi(chger_{h,t} - chger_{f,t}) + \frac{chger_{f,t}}{2}, \tag{10.38}$$

$$\hat{i}_t = \hat{i}_{t-1} + \pi_{F,t} - \pi_{H,t} - \Delta \bar{i}_t, \tag{10.39}$$

$$\hat{i}_t^* = \hat{i}_{t-1}^* + \pi_{F,t}^* - \pi_{H,t}^* - \Delta \bar{i}_t, \tag{10.40}$$

$$chger_{h,t} = chger_{h,t-1} + \Delta s_t + \pi_{H,t}^* - \pi_{H,t}, \tag{10.41}$$

$$chger_{f,t} = chger_{f,t-1} + \pi_{F,t} - \Delta s_t - \pi_{F,t}^*, \tag{10.42}$$

$$\pi_t = n\pi_{H,t} + (1 - n)\pi_{F,t},$$

$$\pi_t^* = n\pi_{F,t}^* + (1 - n)\pi_{H,t}^*.$$

The LCP hypothesis introduces two additional distortions in the model. First of all, the nominal exchange rate does not directly affect the interior terms of trade. Thus, the expenditure-switching role of exchange rate is dampened by the stickiness of import prices. Interior terms of trade are almost immune to monetary policy. However, the exchange rate instantaneously modifies the relative export margins of producers, which induces some second round effects on inflation rates. This transmission mechanism conveys a second source of distortion. The variability of relative export margins implies some undesirable fluctuations of the real exchange rate. Under PCP, the real exchange rate moves in line with the terms of trade when there is a home bias in national consumption. Under LCP, there is an additional source of deviation from PPP. This further deteriorates the international consumption risk sharing. Unlike the previous model, it turns out that the LCP model is significantly modified by the preference bias hypothesis. In particular, it changes the qualitative impact of interior terms of trade and relative export margins on real marginal costs. As a result, it may be helpful to restrain the analysis to a case without any home bias.

No home bias in national consumption

We examine here the LCP model without preference bias (i.e. $n = 0.5$). This assumption allows to derive a highly tractable reduced form for the LCP model:

$$\sigma \, \underset{t}{E}(\hat{y}^W_{t+1} - \hat{y}^W_t) = \frac{i_t + i^*_t}{2} - \bar{r}^W_t - \underset{t}{E}\pi^W_{t+1}, \tag{10.43}$$

$$\underset{t}{E}\Delta s_{t+1} = i_t - i^*_t, \tag{10.44}$$

$$\pi_t = \beta \underset{t}{E}\pi_{t+1} + \lambda_H\left[(\sigma + \phi)\hat{y}^W_t + \tfrac{1}{2}chger\right] + \bar{u}_t, \tag{10.45}$$

$$\pi^*_t = \beta \underset{t}{E}\pi^*_{t+1} + \lambda^*_F\left[(\sigma + \phi)\hat{y}^W_t - \tfrac{1}{2}chger\right] + \bar{u}^*_t, \tag{10.46}$$

$$chger_t = chger_{t-1} + \Delta s_t + \pi^*_t - \pi_t. \tag{10.47}$$

The cost-push shocks that affect the consumer-price inflation rates are given by $\bar{u}_t = \lambda_H(u_t + u^*_t)$ and $\bar{u}^*_t = \lambda^*_F(u_t + u^*_t)$.

Under this restriction, the only state variables of the model are the world output gap, the real exchange rate and the CPI inflation rates. Given the aggregate output gap, interior terms of trade misalignments have no impact on CPI, but they still push away import prices from interior producer prices. Under LCP, there is no direct pass-through of nominal exchange rate to interior terms of trade. The immediate transmission mechanism of exchange rate relies on its impact on relative export margins and on the real exchange rate. Precisely, it is now the real exchange rate that pushes the inflation rates in opposite directions through the modified aggregate supply curves. This canonical representation of the economy under LCP will be useful in drawing the intuition about the properties of the optimal policy. Since the real exchange rate determines cross-country consumption, we can already notice that, compared to the PCP model reduced form, CPI inflation rates and consumption gaps replace PPI inflation rates and output gaps as the fundamental state variables driving the economy. This might influence the choice of targets for monetary policy.

10.4 Optimal monetary cooperation

Our approach is mainly illustrative. The influence of price setting on optimal monetary policy is studied through highly stylized models. Nonetheless, the results we obtain are interesting and can be qualitatively extended to more general setting. Our main contribution here is to examine in a unified framework the optimal monetary cooperation, under PCP versus LCP, under efficient versus inefficient shocks, under "commitment" versus "discretion." Two papers are closely related to our analysis. Clarida *et al.* (2002) studied the welfare gains from international cooperation under PCP within a slightly different model. Smets and Wouters (2002) give some results about optimal monetary policy in a small open economy with imperfect exchange rate pass-through. But here, we propose a unified treatment of a large range of issues. More precisely, in this section, it is shown that international price-setting matters as far as the choice of the price index to target and the optimal exchange rate regime are concerned.

10.4.1   Optimal policy under commitment

PCP model

If monetary authorities accept to cooperate, they will maximize the unconditional expectation of the average of household utility functions. Since the consumption levels and working hours are equalized across households, the global welfare function is given by

$$W = E_0 \sum_{t=0}^{\infty} \beta^t \omega_t,$$

where

$$\omega_t = \frac{U(C_t) + U(C_t^*)}{2} - \frac{V(L_t) + V(L_t^*)}{2}.$$

In this specification, the utility gains, derived from the liquidity service of holding money, has been assumed to be very small. We then take a second-order approximation of this welfare function around a steady state in which a taxation subsidy completely offsets the monopolistic distortions in both countries. In this context, there is no first-order distortion and the flexible price allocation is the first best solution.

So, as it is shown in Appendix A.1, the welfare function is such that

$$W = -\frac{1}{2} U_C \bar{C} E_0 \sum_{t=0}^{\infty} \beta^t \Lambda_t, \tag{10.48}$$

where

$$\Lambda_t = (\sigma + \phi)(\hat{y}_t^W)^2 + Z \left(\frac{1}{2} + \phi Z \right) \hat{t}_t^2 + \frac{\varepsilon}{2\lambda_H} \pi_{H,t}^2 + \frac{\varepsilon}{2\lambda_F^*} (\pi_{F,t}^*)^2. \tag{10.49}$$

This expression of the aggregate welfare function is to be related to what Benigno and Benigno (2001a) and Clarida *et al.* (2002) obtain. When $n = 0.5$, we find the same approximated welfare function. Our main contribution here is to extend the model to the case of home bias in national consumption in order to introduce more realistic openness ratios. Under PCP, this assumption increases the distortions associated with terms of trade misalignments: terms of trade affect relative output both through the traditional expenditure switching effect and through its impact on relative consumption (see the risk sharing condition (10.3)). The social cost of those deviations is analogous to what we would have found in a model without preference bias and with higher intratemporal elasticity of substitution. In that sense, the fundamental channels through which terms of trade affect the welfare function are not qualitatively modified by the home bias hypothesis: terms of trade misalignments are costly due to its impact on relative output gap and on relative labor supply. World output gap fluctuations affect welfare both through the consumption and the labor supply channels. The distortions associated with price rigidities are captured by the inflation rate variances whose weights are functions of relative size of countries, degrees of rigidity and markup on product markets.

Result 1 states the form of the optimal monetary policy under commitment. Monetary authorities maximize the households' intertemporal welfare under the structural equations describing the functioning of the economy. After some algebra, two relations, linking the state variables of the model, represent the optimal policies.

Result 1 Under PCP, the optimal policies are determined by the following equations

$$\varepsilon \, \pi_{H,t} = -\hat{y}_t + \hat{y}_{t-1} \quad \text{and} \quad \varepsilon \, \pi_{F,t}^* = -\hat{y}_t^* + \hat{y}_{t-1}^*. \tag{10.50}$$

Proof See Appendix B.1. □

The optimal strategies are strictly analogous to the closed-economy results presented by Clarida *et al.* (1999) and Woodford (1999b). Indeed, monetary authorities only target interior objectives: the PPI and the output gap. From equation (10.50), we see that it is optimal to adjust the producer price level to the national output gap. In the event of upward inflationary pressures, for example, policymakers commit to pursue a "lean against the wind policy" and decrease the output gap. Notice however that this equivalence to the closed economy optimal policy does not mean that international linkages are neutral on the optimal policy design. Even if policymakers try to manipulate interior state variables as they would do in a closed economy context, they need of course to take into account the international spillovers in order to implement the optimal allocation. We will make this point clearer in the next section when deriving the "discretionary" optimal cooperation.

The main feature of the optimal monetary policies will crucially depend on the kind of shocks affecting the economy. Under efficient shocks, producer price inflation rates and output gaps move in the same direction. There is no monetary policy trade-off in stabilizing both objectives. After a positive technological shock, potential output increases, output gap becomes negative and inflation slows down. A monetary easing may reduce the slack and push the inflation up. The associated depreciation of the nominal exchange rate passes through relative producer prices and is likely to offset the terms of trade misalignments. These elements give the intuition of the following corollary.

Corollary 1   *Under PCP and following efficient shocks, the optimal cooperative policy achieves the flexible price allocation: there is no volatility of inflation and output gaps are closed. In that case, pure inflation targeting policies implement the optimal solution.*

Proof   Replace in (10.28) and (10.29) the inflation rates using (10.50) and the terms of trade using (10.18).   □

With cost-push shocks, monetary authorities face a trade-off between stabilizing the output gap or the inflation rate. A markup shift or an increase in wages pushes the output gap and the producer inflation rate in opposite directions whereas a monetary innovation induces a co-movement of both variables. There is a policy dilemma. A monetary tightening would reduce inflation at a cost of depressed output gap. A monetary easing would sustain demand but increase inflation. In that context, the nominal exchange rate does not seem to be very useful. Due to its expenditure switching effect, exchange rate fluctuations impact relative output gaps, which may reinforce the monetary transmission mechanism and may even aggravate the existing inflation/output gap trade-off. We will come back on this point later. The following corollary summarizes the properties of the optimal policy in presence of inefficient shocks.

Corollary 2   *Under PCP and following inefficient shocks, the monetary author-ities face an inflation/output gap trade-off so that, in the optimal cooperative solution, the producer inflation rates are state contingent and it is no longer possible to fully stabilize the economies.*

Finally, it is worth emphasizing an important feature of "commitment" in the design of the optimal policy. Monetary authorities target the level of producer prices and commit to bring it back to the steady-state path after transitory shocks.

Corollary 3   *Provided shocks are drawn from stationary distributions, prices and nominal exchange rate are stationary variables under optimal monetary cooperation with commitment.*

Summing up, the properties of the optimal plan clearly indicate that mone-tary authorities must target PPI inflation rates under PCP. Pure inflation targeting strategies are required when shocks are efficient. Otherwise, more flexible rules are preferable. The commitment solution exhibits inertia and is history-dependent in order to affect in a credible way the expectations of the private sector on the future path of inflation. Those results are already found in the literature but our contribution here is to be able to draw a clear comparison with the LCP case in a simple and unified framework.

LCP model

Appendix A.2 derives the welfare approximation under LCP. Equation (10.49) is modified in the following way:

$$
\Lambda_t = (\sigma + \phi)(\hat{y}_t^W)^2 + n(1-n)\,\xi\left(\frac{\hat{t}_t^2 + \hat{t}_t^{*2}}{2}\right) + \sigma(\hat{c}_t^R)^2 + \phi(\hat{y}_t^R)^2
$$

$$
+ \frac{\varepsilon}{2}\left(n\frac{\pi_{H,t}^2}{\lambda_H} + (1-n)\frac{(\pi_{H,t}^*)^2}{\lambda_H^*}\right) + \frac{\varepsilon}{2}\left(n\frac{(\pi_{F,t}^*)^2}{\lambda_F^*} + (1-n)\frac{\pi_{F,t}^2}{\lambda_F}\right).
$$

$$(10.51)$$

To grasp the intuition behind the objective function under LCP, let us consider the case of no preference bias ($n = 0.5$). Λ_t is then given by

$$
\Lambda_t = (\sigma + \phi)(\hat{y}_t^W)^2 + \frac{\xi}{4}\left(\frac{\hat{t}_t^2 + \hat{t}_t^{*2}}{2}\right) + \phi\frac{\xi^2}{4}\left(\frac{\hat{t}_t + \hat{t}_t^*}{2}\right)^2
$$

$$
+ \frac{(chger_t)^2}{4\sigma} + \frac{\varepsilon}{4}\left(\frac{\pi_{H,t}^2}{\lambda_H} + \frac{(\pi_{H,t}^*)^2}{\lambda_H^*}\right) + \frac{\varepsilon}{4}\left(\frac{(\pi_{F,t}^*)^2}{\lambda_F^*} + \frac{\pi_{F,t}^2}{\lambda_F}\right).
$$

Compared to the PCP model, two additional distortions enter the welfare function approximation: the costs associated with import prices stickiness and the welfare loss due to the failure of the law of one price. The former effect works through the variability of import price inflation rates. Concerning the latter, even without home bias, PPP does not hold so that real exchange rate fluctuations induce some undesirable volatility of cross-country consumption and deteriorate the international risk sharing. Besides, notice that the relative cost of import price and production price rigidities depends on the stationary openness ratio and on the relative degree of stickiness.

The first property of the optimal stabilization plan, which contrasts crucially with the PCP case, is summarized in the following result.

Result 2 Under LCP, the optimal cooperative policy cannot achieve the first best allocation. The optimal plan always requires adjusting gradually the price levels and the nominal exchange rate.

Independently from the kind of shock affecting the economies, monetary authorities face new trade-offs. Under LCP, it is impossible to stabilize both import price and interior production price without destabilizing the relative consumption gap and the relative output gap. From equations (10.33) to (10.38), we see that the difference between import price and interior price inflation rate depends only on interior terms of trade and relative export margins. Since there is no immediate exchange rate pass-through to the relative price of home and foreign goods, it seems that the most effective way of moving the relative inflation rates is to affect the export margins using the nominal exchange rate. But, by doing so, real exchange fluctuates and relative consumption suffers from undesirable variability.

In order to gain a better intuition on the optimal monetary cooperation when prices are denominated in the consumer currency, assume that $n = 0.5$. In that context, the real exchange rate moves only to the extent that there are some deviations from the law of one price.

Result 3   Under "local-currency-pricing" and without preference bias, the interior terms of trade are independent from monetary policy.

Proof   Substract equation (10.33) to (10.36), (10.34) to (10.37) and replace the inflation rate differentials by the interior terms of trade using equations (10.39) and (10.40). Furthermore, making use of $\hat{t}_t - \hat{t}_t^* = chger_{h,t} + chger_{f,t}$, one easily obtains two relations linking the interior terms of trade gaps to exogenous shocks.   □

In that case, it becomes clear that monetary policy cannot stabilize both the interior producer price and the import price. Independently from the kind of shock hitting the economy, Result 3 shows that the difference between the two inflation rates are unaffected by monetary policy. Since monetary policy has no control over interior terms of trade, the loss function is reduced to

$$\Lambda_t = (\sigma+\phi)(\hat{c}_t^W)^2 + \frac{(chger_t)^2}{4\sigma} + \frac{\varepsilon}{4\lambda_H}(\pi_{H,t}^2 + \pi_{F,t}^2) + \frac{\varepsilon}{4\lambda_F^*}((\pi_{H,t}^*)^2 + (\pi_{F,t}^*)^2).$$

We see that monetary authorities penalize the interior producer price inflation rate and the import price inflation rate with a consumption-based weight structure since we made the hypothesis of the same degree of rigidity within each country (i.e. $\lambda_H = \lambda_F$ and $\lambda_H^* = \lambda_F^*$). As the real exchange rate is directly connected to the consumption through the optimal risk sharing condition, it seems that they cannot do better than stabilizing the CPI inflation rates and the consumption gaps. This intuition is confirmed by the following result.

Result 4   Without preference bias, the optimal cooperative policies under LCP is given by

$$\varepsilon\,\pi_t = -\hat{c}_t + \hat{c}_{t-1} \quad \text{and} \quad \varepsilon\,\pi_t^* = -\hat{c}_t^* + \hat{c}_{t-1}^*. \tag{10.52}$$

Proof   See Appendix B.3.   □

Whereas, under PCP, monetary authorities adjust the producer price inflation rate in response to output gap fluctuations, when prices are set in the consumer currency, it is optimal to adjust the consumer price level to changes in the cross-country consumption gap. We have already seen that monetary policy has no impact on inflation differential between import price and producer price and cannot alleviate the distortions associated with terms of trade misalignment. Consequently, monetary stabilization works only on global consumption gap (equal to the aggregate output gap), the real exchange rate and the CPI inflation rates.

As in the PCP case, the optimal policy under commitment targets the levels of nominal exchange rate and CPI. All prices are therefore stationary when shocks are drawn from stationary distributions.

Corollary 4 *Following efficient shocks and without preference bias, the optimal solution under LCP consists of completely stabilizing the consumer price levels and closing the consumption gaps. Pure CPI inflation targeting implements the optimal policy.*

Proof Replace the CPI inflation rates in (10.45) and (10.46) using (10.52) and the real exchange rate using (10.12). This shows obviously that consumption gaps are systematically closed. □

Following efficient shocks, the optimal plan succeeds in eradicating the social costs of deviations from the natural level of aggregate output gap and failures of PPP. Consumption gaps are closed, consumer price levels remain constant and exchange rate is fixed. However, as we have already mentioned, there still exists a trade-off between import price and producer price stabilization.

10.4.2 *Optimal discretionary policy*

In this section, we focus on the case in which monetary authorities cooperate but lack a commitment technology that would allow them to choose credibly, once for all, an optimal state-contingent plan. Since they are unable to influence current expectations on future consumption and inflation, they have to take those expectations as given. Accordingly, the optimal outcome maximizes each period Λ_t under the behavioral equations, assuming that the expectations are exogenous.

PCP model

The following result provides the expression of the optimal policies in the discretionary case. Discretion changes the difference rules for $\hat{y}_t$ under commitment into a level rule, but the optimal strategy is qualitatively the same. Monetary authorities pursue a "lean against the wind" policy, contracting the output gap in the event of inflationary pressures and sustaining demand when inflation slows down.

Result 5 Optimal cooperative policies in the PCP model are given by

$$\varepsilon \pi_{H,t} = -\hat{y}_t \quad \text{and} \quad \varepsilon \pi_{F,t}^* = -\hat{y}_t^*.$$

Proof The derivation of optimal policies is similar to what is done in Appendix B.1, replacing $\Delta\mu$ by μ in the first-order conditions relative to the inflation rates. □

In the discretionary case, it is possible to show that the optimal outcome can be implemented by Taylor's (1993) style reaction functions.

Corollary 5 *Under PCP, the optimal policies in the cooperative equilibrium can be written as Taylor rules, which are linear in the domestic and foreign PPI inflation rates.*

$$i_t = \bar{r}_t + (1-n)\, \underset{t}{E}\, \Delta \bar{i}_{t+1} + \omega_1\, \underset{t}{E}\, \pi_{H,t+1} + \omega_2\, \underset{t}{E}\, \pi^*_{F,t+1},$$

$$i^*_t = \bar{r}^*_t - (1-n)\, \underset{t}{E}\, \Delta \bar{i}_{t+1} + \omega_2\, \underset{t}{E}\, \pi_{H,t+1} + \omega_1\, \underset{t}{E}\, \pi^*_{F,t+1},$$

where

$$\omega_1 = 1 + \frac{\varepsilon(1-\rho_u)}{2\rho_u}\left(\sigma + \frac{1}{2Z}\right)$$

and

$$\omega_2 = \frac{\varepsilon(1-\rho_u)}{2\rho_u}\left(\sigma - \frac{1}{2Z}\right).$$

Proof The proof is quite straightforward: introducing the equations of Result 5 into the aggregate supply curves and solving forward the first difference equations shows that the inflation rates are linear combinations of the cost-push shocks. Therefore, we know that

$$\underset{t}{E}\, \pi_{\bullet,t+1} = \rho_u \pi_{\bullet,t} \quad \text{and} \quad \underset{t}{E}\, \hat{y}^\bullet_{t+1} = \rho_u \hat{y}^\bullet_t.$$

Once you have expressed the expected nominal exchange rate changes as a function of the inflation rates using equation (10.30), make use of (10.26) and (10.27) to obtain the Taylor rules of Corollary 3. □

Monetary authorities adjust the nominal interest rates in response to the expected PPI inflation rates in both countries. But notice that the reaction functions verify the Taylor principle: the coefficient of expected domestic inflation rate is bigger than one ($\omega_1 > 1$). This property ensures that the equilibrium is determinate. Clarida *et al.* (2002) obtained the same result in the case of an unitary intratemporal elasticity of substitution and without home bias.

LCP model without preference bias

As in the commitment case, the following result shows that the optimal policies target consumption-based aggregates: the monetary cooperation requires adjusting the CPI inflation rate to the level of the consumption gap. Here again, discretion implies a level rule on the consumption gap.

Result 6 Optimal cooperative policies in the LCP model and without preference bias are given by

$$\varepsilon \pi_t = -\hat{c}_t \quad \text{and} \quad \varepsilon \pi_t^* = -\hat{c}_t^*.$$

Proof The derivation of optimal policies is similar to what is done in Appendix B.3, replacing $\Delta\mu$ by μ in the first-order conditions relative to the inflation rates. □

The discretionary case is very useful to illustrate the differences of the optimal policies between PCP and LCP. Corollary 6 derives the interest rate reaction functions underlying the optimal monetary cooperation.

Corollary 6 *Under LCP, the optimal policy links the nominal interest rate to the domestic consumer-price inflation rate*

$$i_t = \bar{r}_t + \omega_3 \, \underset{t}{E} \, \pi_{t+1},$$

$$i_t^* = \bar{r}_t^* + \omega_3 \, \underset{t}{E} \, \pi_{t+1}^*$$

with

$$\omega_3 = 1 + \frac{(1 - \rho_u)}{\rho_u}\sigma\varepsilon.$$

Proof As for the proof of Corollary 6, introducing the equations of Result 6 into the aggregate supply curves and solving forward the first difference equations shows that the inflation rates are linear combinations of the cost-push shocks. Therefore, $E_t \pi_{t+1}^{\bullet} = \rho_u \pi_t^{\bullet}$ and $E_t \hat{c}_{t+1}^{\bullet} = \rho_u \hat{c}_t^{\bullet}$. Once again, we express the expected nominal exchange rate changes as a function of the inflation rates using equation (10.47) under LCP and make use of equations (10.44) and (10.43) to obtain the reaction functions. □

Under LCP, monetary authorities pursue "traditional" Taylor rules: the nominal interest rate overreacts to domestic expected CPI inflation rate. As in the PCP case, the reaction function incorporates both domestic and foreign inflation rates but here with a consumption-based structure. Consequently, the only information concerning foreign prices, relevant for domestic interest rate policy is included in the CPI. Under PCP, both producer price inflation rates had to be examined to move nominal interest rates.

10.4.3 *Optimal exchange rate regime*

As far as optimal exchange rate regime is concerned, price-setting assumption is likely to completely reverse the conclusions. Depending on the kind of shocks hitting the economies, policy prescriptions turn out to be very different. In this section, results obtained by Devereux and Engel (1998, 1999, 2000) are partly revisited and extended to the case of cost-push shocks. Our main contribution here is to derive results on exchange rate regime optimality based on a fully fledged welfare approximation in order to highlight the importance of international price setting.

In this section, we study the optimality of exchange rate regimes under PCP and under LCP without preference bias.

PCP model

Following efficient shocks, the optimal policy replicates the flexible price allocation. Therefore, as the inflation rates are equal to zero and the "terms of trade gap" is closed, equation (10.30) shows that the nominal exchange rate has to adjust to the required terms of trade path under flexible prices. This property seems to plead in favor of a flexible exchange rate regime when real shocks prevail. The intuition behind this result lies simply in the expenditure-switching role of nominal exchange rate under PCP. Assume that monetary policies succeed in fully stabilizing the producer price inflation rates. Without exchange rate adjustment, the terms of trade would not move and a misalignment would appear. Hopefully, nominal exchange rate fluctuations allow to mimic the flexible-price path of terms of trade while inflation rates equal zero. However, in presence of inefficient shocks, the associated inflation/output gap trade-off does not allow to fully stabilize the economies. The optimal monetary cooperation targets the producer price levels and the nominal exchange rate. A fixed exchange rate regime might even be optimal as the following result states.

Result 7   Under PCP and following efficient shocks, it is optimal to let the exchange rate freely adjust to the efficient fluctuations of international relative prices. But, following inefficient shocks, an exchange rate management is needed and it is optimal to fix it when $\varepsilon = 2Z$.

Proof   Combining equations (10.50) and (10.30) from the PCP model, it is easy to show that the inflation rate differential realizes exactly the required terms of trade adjustment if $\varepsilon = 2Z$, thus leaving no role for exchange rate variations.   □

Concerning inefficient shocks, the preceding result becomes more intuitive when considering the terms of trade equation. We see that there is no need for a nominal exchange rate adjustment under the optimal plan if the inflation rate differential provides the required terms of trade path. This happens when $\varepsilon = 2Z$. In the general case, exchange rate fluctuations amplify the inflation/output gap trade-off induced by cost-push shocks. That is why full flexibility may not be optimal.

LCP model without preference bias

Under LCP, the law of one price does not hold and the expenditure-switching role of exchange rate is muted. Therefore, it may seem quite appropriate to limit exchange rate variations in order to minimize the welfare costs associated with these distortions, since those fluctuations do not seem to provide some compensating gains in terms of stabilization. This property is likely to prevail independently from the originating shocks. The following result shows that a fixed exchange rate regime is optimal under certain conditions.

Result 8 Under LCP and with $n = 0.5$, the optimal cooperative policy imposes a fixed exchange rate regime if either shocks are efficient or $\varepsilon\sigma = 1$.

Proof Following efficient shocks, the optimal policy fully stabilizes the consumer-price levels and closes the consumption gaps. Using equations (10.12), we see that the real exchange rate remains constant. So equation (10.47) implies that the nominal exchange rate is fixed. Otherwise, reminding that the purchasing power parity holds in the flexible equilibrium without preference bias, we make use of equation (10.52) to show that the optimal real exchange rate variations are matched by the inflation rate differential if $\varepsilon\sigma = 1$. □

Under LCP, the optimal policies target CPI inflation rates and consumption gaps. Recall that real exchange rate drives the relative consumption gap, it then seems clear that the more effective monetary authorities will be in stabilizing their objectives, the less necessary nominal exchange rate changes. Following efficient shocks and without home bias, CPI are constant and consumption gaps are closed. Fixing exchange rate is obviously optimal. In presence of cost-push shocks, it may happen that the relative CPI inflation rate paths exactly provide the required adjustment of real exchange rate. It is the case when $\varepsilon\sigma = 1$.

10.5 Cooperation gains and implementation of the optimal policy

Quantifying the cooperation gains is clearly beyond the scope of the chapter. Our main objective is to highlight the feature of the optimal monetary cooperation under different price-setting schemes. But the general framework developed here enables us to revisit some interesting results found in the literature. We even intend to suggest the intuition of what our model would say about the welfare gains from cooperation under LCP. The approach is illustrative and further work would be needed to derive formal results. Moreover, the literature has emphasized the relevance of financial structure as far as cooperation gains are concerned (see Benigno, 2001; Devereux, 2001; Sutherland, 2003), but we abstract from that point in the following discussion and keep the hypothesis of financial markets completeness.

In the model developed in this chapter, we propose both a micro-founded model and a welfare criterion based directly on consumers' utility. This approach is then consistent with the NOEM literature. Obstfeld and Rogoff (2002) suggested that the potential gains from monetary coordination are zero with complete markets, and negligible with incomplete markets. However, those papers are mostly based on static models, in which prices are pre-set one period in advance and shocks are efficient. In the dynamic "New Keynesian" framework, the cooperation gains are examined in a model where efficient shocks coexist with inefficient supply shocks, where we allow for incomplete pass-through and for a non-unitary intratemporal elasticity of substitution which turns out to affect critically the normative conclusions of the previous works.

Therefore, the absence of cooperative gains is only validated in some special cases. As Benigno and Benigno (2001a) emphasized, when prices are denominated in the producer currency, the cooperative optimal plan leads to the same allocation as the Nash equilibrium, following efficient shocks and with $2Z = 1$ or $\sigma = 1/2Z$. Clarida *et al.* (2002) end up with the same conclusion in a model without home bias and with unitary intratemporal elasticity of substitution. Note that the marginal cost, when $\sigma = 1/2Z$, is only a function of domestic output gap so that there is no interdependence. The producer inflation rates and the output gaps dynamics in each country mirror their closed economy equivalents. Clarida *et al.* (2002) even extend the analysis to the case of inefficient shocks. We can review their argument in our framework and show that when $2Z = 1$ and $\sigma = 1$, there is still no gain from any cooperation.

In general, however, the gains are likely to be all the more substantial as inefficient shocks hit the economies or as exchange rate "pass-through" is incomplete. A typical example of monetary cooperation is a fixed exchange rate system. Under such a monetary arrangement, policymakers leave their complete monetary independence to ensure a fixed parity. We have already seen that in presence of cost-push shocks and under LCP, some kind of exchange rate management is required. This gives us the intuition that potential cooperative gains are more likely to arise in that context. The perceived trade-offs might be more favorable at the central-planner level. Under LCP in particular, independent monetary policies would lead to further deviations from the law of one price without yielding compensating gains.

As far as the policy implementation is concerned, Benigno and Benigno (2001a) give an interesting result that can be easily extended to our framework. Under PCP, they show that it is possible to replicate the optimal outcome by assigning to decentralized monetary authorities some well-defined "flexible" inflation targeting strategies: each policymaker commits to a loss function penalizing for the deviation of the producer inflation rate from target and for changes in the output gap. However, such a result does not seem to hold under LCP. It must be impossible to implement the optimal solution by targeting internal variables and without some kind of exchange rate arrangement.

10.6   Conclusion

The main result of this chapter is that the international optimal monetary cooperation depends crucially on the way prices are set. We show that the introduction of "pricing-to-market" changes previous results found in the literature.

- Under LCP and without preference bias, monetary authorities should target the CPI. A pure CPI inflation targeting strategy implements the optimal outcome when shocks are efficient. An analogous result holds under PCP concerning the optimality of PPI inflation targeting.

- The optimal discretionary policy can be implemented by Taylor style reaction functions. Under LCP and without preference bias, the monetary authority adjusts the national nominal interest rate to domestic expected CPI inflation rate with semi-elasticity above one. Under PCP, nominal interest rate is a function of both domestic and foreign PPI inflation rate with a weight higher than one on domestic inflation.

- A fixed exchange rate regime may be optimal under LCP in order to alleviate distortions associated with failures of the law of one price. Under PCP, a flexible exchange rate regime is optimal following efficient shocks. However, the presence of cost-push shocks implies some kind of exchange rate management.

- Finally, as far as potential gains from coordination are concerned, we develop here the intuition that such gains are more likely to arise in model incorporating cost-push shocks and incomplete exchange rate pass-through.

Our analysis reveals the lack of robustness of results about optimal monetary policy in open economies and the importance of correctly modeling the international price-setting. In particular, further work should be done concerning the assessment of cooperative gains under LCP and toward more empirically based models.

Appendix A: approximation of the welfare function

A.1 The PCP case

In this appendix, we derive in detail the second-order approximation of the welfare function in the PCP case (see Woodford, 1999a). It is mostly for technical convenience that we focus here on this price-setting. Indeed, the expansion of the welfare function under the LCP hypothesis is globally similar to the following one but the calculations are a little more complicated.

The aggregate welfare is given by

$$W = \underset{0}{E} \sum_{t=0}^{\infty} \beta^t \omega_t,$$ (10.53)

where

$$\omega_t = \frac{U(C_t) + U(C_t^*)}{2} - \frac{V(L_t) + V(L_t^*)}{2}.$$

The steady state is fully symmetric: all shocks are normalized to one (i.e. $A = A^* = 1$), price levels and macro aggregates are equalized across countries. Next, we assume that a subsidy completely offsets the monopolistic distortions so that, in each country, $V_L(\bar{L}) = U_C(\bar{C})$ and $\bar{Y} = \bar{C} = \bar{L}$.

Finally, in order to keep the calculations tractable, we restrict here to technological shocks. Notice of course that only efficient shocks matter for the derivation of the welfare approximation. We define $\hat{X}_t = (X_t - \bar{X})/\bar{X}$ and $\tilde{x}_t = \log(X_t/\bar{X})$.

First, we take a second-order expansion of the welfare component based on consumption. We have also neglected terms independent of monetary policy.

$$
\begin{aligned}
\frac{U(C_t) + U(C_t^*)}{2} &= \frac{1}{2} U_c \bar{C} \left(\hat{C}_t + \hat{C}_t^* - \sigma \frac{\hat{C}_t^2}{2} - \sigma \frac{\hat{C}_t^{*2}}{2} \right) + t.i.p. + o(\|\xi\|^3), \\
&= \frac{1}{2} U_c \bar{C} \left(\tilde{c}_t + \tilde{c}_t^* + (1 - \sigma) \left(\frac{\tilde{c}_t^2}{2} + \frac{\tilde{c}_t^{*2}}{2} \right) \right) + t.i.p. + o(\|\xi\|^3), \\
&= U_c \bar{C} \left(\tilde{c}_t^W + (1 - \sigma) \left(\frac{\tilde{c}_t^{W2}}{2} + \frac{\tilde{c}_t^{R2}}{2} \right) \right) + t.i.p. + o(\|\xi\|^3).
\end{aligned}
$$

$$(10.54)$$

Regarding the labor component, as before, we obtain

$$
\frac{V(L_t) + V(L_t^*)}{2} = V_L \bar{L} \left(\hat{L}_t^W + \phi \left(\frac{\hat{L}_t^W}{2} + \frac{\hat{L}_t^R}{2} \right) \right) + t.i.p. + o\left(\|\xi\|^3 \right).
$$

$$(10.55)$$

Remember that

$$
L_t = \frac{Y_t}{A_t} \int_0^1 \left(\frac{P_t(h)}{P_t} \right)^{-\varepsilon} dh.
$$

We now need the following lemma to pursue the derivation.

Lemma 7

$$
\tilde{v}_t \equiv \log \left(\int_0^1 \left(\frac{P_t(h)}{P_{H,t}} \right)^{-\varepsilon} dh \right)
$$

$$(10.56)$$

is a second-order term and we have

$$
\tilde{v}_t = \frac{\varepsilon}{2} \int_0^1 (p_t(h) - p_{H,t})^2 dh + o(\|\xi\|^3) \equiv \frac{\varepsilon}{2} v_p^2 + o(\|\xi\|^3).
$$

Proof See Woodford (1999a) or Gali and Monacelli (2002). □

We can now proceed to the expansion of $\hat{L}_t^W$

$$
\hat{L}_t^W = \frac{\tilde{v}_t + \tilde{v}_t^*}{2} + \tilde{c}_t^W + \frac{\tilde{c}_t^{W2} + \tilde{c}_t^{R2}}{2} + n(1-n)\xi \tilde{\imath}_t^2 - \frac{1}{2}\tilde{a}_t \tilde{y}_t
$$
$$
- \frac{1}{2}\tilde{a}_t^* \tilde{y}_t^* + t.i.p. + o(\|\xi\|^3),
$$
$$
= \frac{\tilde{v}_t + \tilde{v}_t^*}{2} + \tilde{c}_t^W + \frac{\tilde{c}_t^{W2} + \tilde{c}_t^{R2}}{2} + n(1-n)\xi \tilde{\imath}_t^2 - \tilde{a}_t^W \tilde{y}_t^W
$$
$$
- \tilde{a}_t^R \tilde{y}_t^R + t.i.p. + o(\|\xi\|^3). \tag{10.57}
$$

Moreover,

$$
\hat{L}_t^{W2} = \tilde{l}_t^{W2} + o(\|\xi\|^3) = (\tilde{y}_t^W - a_t^W)^2 + o(\|\xi\|^3) \tag{10.58}
$$

and

$$
\hat{L}_t^{R2} = \tilde{l}_t^{R2} + o(\|\xi\|^3) = (\tilde{y}_t^R - a_t^R)^2 + o(\|\xi\|^3). \tag{10.59}
$$

Replacing (10.54), (10.55), (10.57), 10.58 and (10.59) into (10.53) leads to

$$
\omega_t \approx -\frac{U_C \bar{C}}{2}\left[(\sigma + \phi)\tilde{y}_t^{W2} + \sigma \tilde{c}_t^{R2} + \phi \tilde{y}_t^{R2} + n(1-n)\xi \tilde{\imath}_t^2 \right.
$$
$$
\left. - 2(1+\phi)a_t^W \tilde{c}_t^W - 2(1+\phi)a_t^R \tilde{y}_t^R \right]
$$
$$
- \frac{U_C \bar{C}}{2}[\tilde{v}_t + \tilde{v}_t^*] + t.i.p. + o(\|\xi\|^3).
$$

In order to express the welfare function in terms of cross-country variables, we use

$$
(1+\phi)a_t^R \tilde{y}_t^R = \frac{\phi Z(1+\phi)}{1/2 + \phi Z}a_t^R \tilde{y}_t^R + \frac{(n-1/2)(1+\phi)}{1/2 + \phi Z}a_t^R \tilde{c}_t^R
$$
$$
+ \frac{n(1-n)\xi(1+\phi)}{1/2 + \phi Z}a_t^R \tilde{\imath}_t^R.
$$

Therefore,

$$
\omega_t = -\frac{U_C \bar{C}}{2}\left[(\sigma + \phi)\hat{y}_t^{W2} + \sigma \hat{c}_t^{R2} + \phi \hat{y}_t^{R2} + n(1-n)\xi \tilde{\imath}_t^2 + \tilde{v}_t + \tilde{v}_t^* \right]
$$
$$
+ t.i.p. + o(\|\xi\|^3).
$$

A second result can be used here to introduce the inflation rates in the aggregate welfare.

280   *Matthieu Darracq-Pariès*

Lemma 8   *The variables are related to the producer-price inflation rate through the following equation:*

$$\sum_{t=0}^{\infty} \beta^t v_{p,t}^2 = \frac{\alpha_H}{(1-\alpha_H)(1-\beta\alpha_H)} \sum_{t=0}^{\infty} \beta^t \pi_{H,t}^2.$$

Proof   See Woodford (1999a). □

Using this, the aggregate welfare approximation is immediately given by

$$W = -\frac{1}{2} U_C \bar{C} \, E_0 \sum_{t=0}^{\infty} \beta^t \Lambda_t,$$

where

$$\Lambda_t = (\sigma + \phi)(\hat{y}_t^W)^2 + n(1-n)\,\xi\,\hat{t}_t^2 + \sigma(\hat{c}_t^R)^2 + \phi\,(\hat{y}_t^R)^2 + \frac{\varepsilon}{2}\frac{\pi_{H,t}^2}{\lambda_H} + \frac{\varepsilon}{2}\frac{(\pi_{F,t}^*)^2}{\lambda_F^*}. \tag{10.60}$$

A.2   The LCP case

The derivation is basically the same. The main difference is the expansion of $\hat{L}^W$. Due to nominal rigidities on the import markets, there are now two interior terms of trade and four indicators of "price dispersion" ($\tilde{v}_{H,t}, \tilde{v}_{H,t}^*, \tilde{v}_{F,t}^*, \tilde{v}_{F,t}$). Equation (10.57) becomes

$$\hat{L}_t^W = \tilde{c}_t^W + \frac{\tilde{c}_t^{W2} + \tilde{c}_t^{R2}}{2} + n(1-n)\xi\left(\frac{\tilde{t}_t^2 + \tilde{t}_t^{*2}}{2}\right) - \tilde{a}_t^W \tilde{y}_t^W - \tilde{a}_t^R \tilde{y}_t^R$$

$$+ \frac{n\tilde{v}_{H,t} + (1-n)\tilde{v}_{F,t}}{2} + \frac{n\tilde{v}_{F,t}^* + (1-n)\tilde{v}_{H,t}^*}{2} + t.i.p. + o(\|\xi\|^3).$$

Using the following decomposition

$$(1+\phi)a_t^R \tilde{y}_t^R = \frac{\phi Z(1+\phi)}{1/2 + \phi Z} a_t^R \tilde{y}_t^R + \frac{(n-1/2)(1+\phi)}{1/2+\phi Z} a_t^R \tilde{c}_t^R$$

$$+ \frac{n(1-n)\xi(1+\phi)}{1/2+\phi Z} a_t^R \left(\frac{\tilde{t}_t^R + \tilde{t}_t^{*R}}{2}\right).$$

(10.60) is replaced by

$$\Lambda_t = (\sigma + \phi)(\hat{y}_t^W)^2 + n(1-n)\xi\left(\frac{\hat{t}_t^2 + \hat{t}_t^{*2}}{2}\right) + \sigma(\hat{c}_t^R)^2 + \phi(\hat{y}_t^R)^2$$

$$+ n\frac{\varepsilon}{2}\frac{\pi_{H,t}^2}{\lambda_H} + (1-n)\frac{\varepsilon}{2}\frac{\pi_{F,t}^2}{\lambda_H} + n\frac{\varepsilon}{2}\frac{(\pi_{F,t}^*)^2}{\lambda_F^*} + (1-n)\frac{\varepsilon}{2}\frac{(\pi_{H,t}^*)^2}{\lambda_F^*}.$$

Appendix B: derivation of the optimal policy under commitment

B.1   The PCP case

Under PCP, the derivation of the optimal policy is easier because of the restricted number of state variables. The welfare function (10.48) has to be maximized under only two constraints: domestic and foreign Phillips curves. Equation (10.30) determines residually the exchange rate, while the aggregate demand equations give the optimal paths of nominal interest rates. We use the Lagrangian method and denote μ and μ' the associated multipliers.[4]

The first-order conditions with respect to $\hat{y}^W$, $\hat{\imath}$, π_H and $\hat{y}^W$ are given by

$$2Z\hat{\imath}_t = \mu_t^* - \mu_t,$$

$$\hat{y}_t^W = -\frac{\mu_t + \mu_t^*}{2},$$

$$\varepsilon\pi_{H,t} = \mu_t - \mu_{t-1},$$

$$\varepsilon\pi_{F,t}^* = \mu_t^* - \mu_{t-1}^*.$$

Using (10.50), it is possible to show that the optimal plan is characterized by the two following equations:

$$\varepsilon\pi_{H,t} = -\hat{y}_t + \hat{y}_{t-1}$$

and

$$\varepsilon\pi_{F,t}^* = -\hat{y}_t^* + \hat{y}_{t-1}^*.$$

B.2   The LCP case

The optimal monetary cooperation under commitment is derived by maximizing the welfare function (10.51) under the structural equilibrium conditions (10.33), (10.34), (10.36), (10.37), (10.41), (10.42), (10.39) and (10.40). The interest rates are then determined by the aggregate demand equations.

Here again, the optimal plan can be described using the intertemporal Lagrangian method with multipliers μ_H, μ_H^*, μ_F^* and μ_F associated with the aggregate supply equations,[5] v and v^* with the terms of trade equations, θ and θ^* with the relative export margin equations. The first-order necessary conditions with respect to the inflation rates are

$$n\varepsilon\pi_{H,t} = \Delta\mu_{H,t} + \lambda_H v_t + \lambda_H \theta_t, \tag{10.61}$$

$$(1-n)\varepsilon\pi_{H,t}^* = \Delta\mu_{H,t}^* + \lambda_H^* v_t^* - \lambda_H^* \theta_t, \tag{10.62}$$

$$n\varepsilon\pi_{F,t}^* = \Delta\mu_{F,t}^* - \lambda_F^* v_t^* + \lambda_F^* \theta_t^*, \tag{10.63}$$

$$(1-n)\varepsilon\pi_{F,t} = \Delta\mu_{F,t} - \lambda_F v_t - \lambda_F \theta_t^*. \tag{10.64}$$

After some algebra, those corresponding to the world output gap and the interior terms of trade, lead to

$$2\hat{y}_t^W = -\mu_{H,t} - \mu_{H,t}^* - \mu_{F,t}^* - \mu_{F,t}, \tag{10.65}$$

$$2\hat{y}_t^R = -\mu_{H,t} - \mu_{H,t}^* + \mu_{F,t}^* + \mu_{F,t} + \frac{2}{1/2 + \phi Z}\left(v_t^W - \beta \underset{t}{E} v_{t+1}^W\right), \tag{10.66}$$

$$n(1-n)\xi\hat{t}_t^R + (n-1/2)\hat{y}_t^W = \hat{v}_t^R - \beta \underset{t}{E} \hat{v}_{t+1}^R. \tag{10.67}$$

Finally, the conditions associated with the relative export margins and the nominal exchange rate imply that

$$\frac{\mu_{H,t} + \mu_{F,t}^* - \mu_{H,t}^* - \mu_{F,t}}{2} = \theta_t^W - \beta \underset{t}{E} \theta_{t+1}^W, \tag{10.68}$$

$$\frac{\hat{c}_t^R}{2} = \frac{\mu_{F,t}^* + \mu_{H,t}^* - \mu_{F,t} - \mu_{H,t}}{4} - \frac{(n-1/2)\phi}{\sigma(1/2 + \phi Z)}\left(v_t^W - \beta \underset{t}{E} v_{t+1}^W\right), \tag{10.69}$$

$$\theta_t = \theta_t^*.$$

B.3   The special case

We assume now that $n = 0.5$, and we use the fact that $\lambda_H = \lambda_F$ and $\lambda_H^* = \lambda_F^*$. From (10.61) – (10.64), we get

$$\varepsilon\pi_t^* = \Delta(\mu_{H,t}^* + \mu_{F,t}^*)$$

and

$$\varepsilon\pi_t = \Delta(\mu_{H,t} + \mu_{F,t}).$$

Moreover, we deduce from (10.69) and (10.65) that

$$\hat{c}_t^* = -\mu_{H,t}^* - \mu_{F,t}^* \tag{10.70}$$

and

$$\hat{c}_t = -\mu_{H,t} - \mu_{F,t}. \tag{10.71}$$

By combining (10.70) and (10.71), we obtain two relations between the consumer-price inflation rates and the consumption gaps:

$$\varepsilon\pi_t = -\hat{c}_t + \hat{c}_{t-1},$$

$$\varepsilon\pi_t^* = -\hat{c}_t^* + \hat{c}_{t-1}^*.$$

Notes

1 Clarida *et al.* (2002) make the same assumption.
2 A full derivation of this result can be found in Chari *et al.* (2002).
3 Chari *et al.* (2002) and Engel (2002) among others.
4 In fact, those multipliers denote the Lagrangian multipliers, respectively, multiplied by the rigidity coefficients λ_H and λ_F^*.
5 Here again, those multipliers denote the Lagrangian multipliers, respectively, multiplied by the rigidity coefficients.

Bibliography

Ambler, S. (2002) Nominal wage rigidity as a Nash equilibrium. Draft, CIRPEE, UQAM.

Ambler, S. and Phaneuf, L. (1994) Modèles du cycle economique et marché du travail. *Revue Economique*, 45: 1065–1078.

Ambler, S., Guay, A., and Phaneuf, L. (2001) Labor market frictions and endogenous business cycle propagation. Draft, CREFE, UQAM.

Andolfatto, D. and Gomme, P. (2000) Monetary policy regimes and beliefs. Working Paper 9905R, Federal Reserve Bank of Cleveland.

Andrade, P., Bruneau, C., and Gregoir, S. (2001) Testing for the cointegration rank when some cointegrating directions are changing. Mimeo, CREST and THEMA.

Angeloni, I. and Dedola, L. (1999) From the ERM to the euro: new evidence on economic and policy convergence among EU countries. Working Paper 4, European Central Bank.

Artis, M. and Taylor, M. (1994) The stabilizing effect of the ERM on exchange rates and interest rates. *IMF Staff Papers*, 41(1): 125–148.

Artis, M. and Zhang, W. (1999) Further evidence on the international business cycle and the ERM: is there a European business cycle? *Oxford University Press*, 51: 120–132.

Auray, S., Collard, F., and Fève, P. (2000) Habit persistence and beliefs: lessons for the effects of monetary policy. Miméo, GREMAQ.

Bachetta, P. and Wincoop, E. (2000) Does exchange rate stability increase trade and welfare? *American Economic Review*, 90: 1093–1109.

Backus, D. and Smith, G. W. (1993) Consumption and real exchange rates in dynamic economies with non-traded goods. *Journal of International Economics*, 35: 297–316.

Backus, D., Kehoe, P., and Kydland, F. (1992) International real business cycles. *Journal of Political Economy*, 100(4): 745–775.

Backus, D., Kehoe, P., and Kydland, F. (1994) Dynamics of the trade balance and the terms of trade: The j-curve?. *American Economic Review*, 84(1): 84–103.

Backus, D., Kehoe, P., and Kydland, F. (1995) International business cycles: theory versus evidence. In Cooley, T., editor, *Frontiers of Business Cycle Research*, Princeton, NJ: Princeton University Press.

Balassa, B. (1964) The purchasing power parity doctrine: a reappraisal. *Journal of Political Economy*, 72: 584–596.

Baxter, M. and Crucini, M. (1993) Explaining saving investment correlation. *American Economic Review*, 83: 416–435.

Baxter, M. and Crucini, M. (1995) Business cycle and the asset structure of foreign trade. *International Economic Review*, 36(4): 821–854.

Baxter, M. and Stockman, A. (1989) Business cycles and the exchange rate system: some international evidence. *Journal of Monetary Economics*, 23: 377–401.

Beaudry, P. and Devereux, M. (1995) Money and the real exchange rate with sticky prices and increasing returns. *Carnegie Rochester Conference Series on Public Policy*, 43: 55–101.

Beaudry, P. and Guay, A. (1996) What do interest rates reveal about the functioning of real business cycle models? *Journal of Economic Dynamics and Control*, 20: 1661–1682.

Benhabib, J., Schmitt-Grohé, J. S., and Uribe, M. (2002) Chaotic interest rate rules. *American Economic Review*, 92: 72–78.

Benigno, G. (1999) Real exchange rate persistence and monetary policy rules. Mimeo, Bank of England.

Benigno, P. (2001) Price stability with imperfect financial integration. CEPR Discussion Paper 2854.

Benigno, G. and Benigno, P. (2001a) Implementing monetary cooperation through inflation targeting. CEPR Discussion Paper 3226.

Benigno, G. and Benigno, P. (2001b) Monetary policy rules and the exchange rate. CEPR Discussion Paper 2807.

Benigno, G. and Benigno, P. (2002) Price stability in open economies. *Review of Economic Studies*, forthcoming.

Bergin, P. R. and Feenstra, R. C. (2000) Staggered prices setting, translog preferences and endogenous persistence. *Journal of Monetary Economics*, 45: 657–680.

Bergin, P. R. and Feenstra, R. C. (2001) Pricing to market, staggered contracts and real exchange rate persistence. *Journal of International Economics*, 54: 333–359.

Betts, C. and Devereux, M. (1996) The exchange rate in a model of pricing-to-market. *European Economic Review*, 96(29): 1007–1021.

Betts, C. and Devereux, M. (2000) Exchange rate dynamics in a model of pricing-to-market. *Journal of International Economics*, 50(1): 215–244.

Blanchard, O. (1985) Debt, deficits and finite horizons. *Journal of Political Economy*, 93: 223–247.

Blanchard, O. and Kahn, C. (1980) The solution of linear difference models under rational expectations. *Econometrica*, 48(5): 666–689.

Blanchard, O. and Kiyotaki, N. (1987) Monopolistic competition and the effect of aggregate demand. *American Economic Review*, 77(4): 647–666.

Blanchard, O. and Quah, D. (1989) The dynamic effects of aggregate demand and supply disturbances. *American Economic Review*, 79(4): 655–673.

Boldrin, M., Christiano, L., and Fisher, J. (2001) Habit persistence, assets returns and the business cycle. *American Economic Review*, 91: 149–166.

Bonser-Neal, C., Vance Roley, V., and Sellon, G. (1998) Monetary policy actions, intervention, and exchange rates : a reexamination of the empirical relationships using federal funds rate target data. *Journal of Business*, 71(2): 147–177.

Boothe, P. and Glassman, D. (1987) Statistical distribution of exchange rates: some empirical evidence. *Journal of International Economics*, 22: 297–319.

Bordes, C., Girardin, E., and Marimoutou, V. (1996) Le nouveau sme est-il plus asymétrique que l'ancien? *Economie et Prévision*, 123–124(2–3): 175–188.

Branson, W. H. and Henderson, D. W. (1985) The specification and influence of asset markets. In Jones, R. W. and Kenen, P. B., editors, *Handbook of International Economics*, pp. 749–805, New York: Elsevier Science Publisher.

Braun, P., Constantidines, G., and Ferson, W. E. (1993) Time nonseparability in aggregate consumption. *European Economic Review*, 37: 897–920.

Burstein, A. T., Neves, J. C., and Rebelo, S. (2000) Distribution costs and real exchange rate dynamics during exchange-rate-based-stabilizations. NBER Working Paper 7862.

Calvo, G. (1983) Staggered prices in a utility-maximizing framework. *Journal of Monetary Economics*, 12: 383–398.

Campbell, J. Y. (1994) Inspecting the mechanism : an analytical approach to the stochastic growth model. *Journal of Monetary Economics*, 33: 463–506.

Campbell, J. and Cochrane, J. (1999) By force of habit: a consumption–based explanation of aggregate stock market behavior. *Journal of Political Economy*, 107: 205–251.

Canova, F. (1998) Detrending and business cycle facts. *Journal of Monetary Economics*, 41: 475–512.

Caporale, G. and Pittis, N. (1995) Nominal exchange rate regimes and the stochastic behavior of real variables. *Journal of International Money and Finance*, 14(3): 395–415.

Cardia, E. (1991) The dynamics of a small open economy in response to monetary, fiscal and productivity shocks. *Journal of Monetary Economics*, 28: 411–434.

Cardia, E. (1995) The effects of fiscal policies in a general equilibrium model with nominal wage contracts. *Economics Letters*, 49: 69–75.

Carlstrom, C. and Fuerst, T. (1995) Interest rate rules vs. money growth rules: a welfare comparison in a cash-in-advance economy. *Journal of Monetary Economics*, 36: 247–267.

Cavallo, M. and Ghironi, F. (2002) Net foreign assets and the exchange rate: redux revived. *Journal of Monetary Economics*, 49: 1057–1097.

Chari, V., Kehoe, P., and McGrattan, E. (2002) Can sticky price models generate volatile and persistent real exchange rates? *Review of Economic Studies*, 69(3): 533–563.

Chinn, D. and Miller, P. J. (1998) Fixed vs. floating exchange rates: a dynamic general equilibrium analysis. *European Economic Review*, 42: 1221–1249.

Cho, J. O. and Phaneuf, L. (1993) A business cycle model with nominal wage contracts and government. Working Paper 6, CREFE, UQAM.

Chow, G. C. and Lin, A.-L. (1976) Best linear unbiased estimation of missing observation in an economic time series. *Journal of the American Statistical Association*, 71: 719–721.

Christiano, L. (1991) Modeling the liquidity effect of a money shock. *Federal Reserve Bank of Minneapolis Quarterly Review*, 15(1): 3–34.

Christiano, L. and Eichenbaum, M. (1992a) Liquidity effects and the monetary transmission mechanism. *American Economic Review*, 82(2): 346–353.

Christiano, L. and Eichenbaum, M. (1992b) Some empirical evidence on the liquidity effect. In Cukierman, Z., Hercowitz, Z., and Leiderman, L., editors, *Political Economy, Growth and Business Cycle*, Cambridge, MA: MIT Press.

Christiano, L. and Gust, C. (1999) Taylor rules in a limited participation model. *De Economist*, 147(4): 437–460.

Christiano, L., Eichenbaum, M., and Evans, C. (1997) Sticky price and limited participation models of money: a comparison. *European Economic Review*, 41: 1201–1249.

Christiano, L., Eichenbaum, M., and Evans, C. (2001) Monetary policy shocks: what have we learned and to what end? In Taylor, J. and Woodford, M., editors, *Handbook of Macroeconomics*, Amsterdam: Elsevier North Holland.

Clarida, R. and Gali, J. (1994) Sources of real exchange rate fluctuations: how important are nominal shocks? *Carnegie Rochester Conference Series on Public Policy*, 41: 1–56.

Clarida, R. and Gertler, M. (1997) How the bundesbank conducts monetary policy. In Romer, C. D. and Romer, D. H., editors, *Reducing Inflation: Motivation and Strategy*, pp. 363–406, Chicago: University of Chicago Press.

Clarida, R., Gali, J., and Gertler, M. (1998) Monetary policy rule in practice: some international evidence. *European Economic Review*, 42: 1033–1067.

Clarida, R., Gali, J., and Gertler, M. (1999) The science of monetary policy: a new keynesian perspective. *Journal of Economic Literature*, 37: 1661–1707.

Clarida, R., Gali, J., and Gertler, M. (2000) Monetary policy rules and macroeconomic stability: evidence and some theory. *Quarterly Journal of Economics*, 105(1): 147–180.

Clarida, R., Gali, J., and Gertler, M. (2001) Optimal monetary policy in open vs. closed economies: an integrated approach. *American Economic Review*, 91(2): 248–252.

Clarida, R., Gali, J., and Gertler, M. (2002) A simple framework for international monetary policy analysis. *Journal of Monetary Economics*, 49(5): 879–904.

Cole, H. and Obstfeld, M. (1991) Commodity trade and international risk sharing. *Journal of Monetary Economics*, 28: 3–24.

Cole, H. and Ohanian, L. (1999) A neoclassical analysis of Britain's interwar depression. Miméo, Federal Reserve Bank of Minneapolis.

Constantidines, G. (1990) Habit formation: a resolution of the equity premium puzzle. *Journal of Political Economy*, 98: 519–543.

Constantidines, G. and Ferson, W. E. (1991) Habit persistence and durability in aggregate consumption. *Journal of Financial Economics*, 29: 199–240.

Cooley, T. and Hansen, G. (1989) The inflation tax in a real business cycle model. *American Economic Review*, 79: 733–748.

Cooley, T. and Hansen, G. (1995) Money and the business cycle. In Cooley, T., editor, *Frontiers of Business Cycle Research*, chapter 7. Princeton, NJ: Princeton University Press.

Cooper, R. N. (1999) Exchange rate choices. Discussion Paper 1877, Harvard University.

Corsetti, G. and Dedola, L. (2001) Macroeconomics of price discrimination. Mimeo, Yale University and Bank of Italy.

Corsetti, G. and Pesenti, P. (2001a) International dimensions of optimal monetary policy. NBER Working Paper 8230.

Corsetti, G. and Pesenti, P. (2001b) Welfare and macroeoconomic interdependence. *Quarterly Journal of Economics*, 116: 421–446.

Corsetti, G., Dedola, L., and Leduc, S. (2001) Consumption and real exchange rates with goods and asset markets frictions. Mimeo.

Deaton, A. (1992) *Understanding Consumption*. New York: Oxford University Press.

Dedola, L. and Leduc, S. (2001) Why is the business cycle behavior of fundamentals alike across exchange rate regimes? *International Journal of Finance and Economics*, 6(4): 401–419.

Dennis, R. and Soderstrom, U. (2002) How important is precommitment for monetary policy? Working Paper 139, Federal Reserve Bank of San Francisco.

Devereux, M. (1999) A simple general equilibrium analysis of the trade off between fixed and floating exchange rates. Manuscript, University of British Columbia.

Devereux, M. (2001) International financial markets and the exchange rate: re-evaluating the case for flexible exchange rate. Unpublished manuscript.

Devereux, M. (2003) A tale of two currencies : the Asian crisis and the exchange rate regimes of Hong Kong and Singapore. *Review of International Economics*, 11: 38–54.

Devereux, M. and Engel, C. (1998) Fixed versus floating exchange rates: how price setting affects the optimal choice of exchange-rate regime. NBER Working Paper 6867.

Devereux, M. and Engel, C. (1999) The optimal choice of exchange rate regime: price-setting rules and internationalized production. NBER Working Paper 6992.

Devereux, M. and Engel, C. (2000) Monetary policy in the open economy revisited: Price setting and exchange rate flexibility. NBER Working Paper 7665.

Dib, A. and Phaneuf, L. (1998) Two-dimensional labor supply models and money. Draft, CREFE, UQAM.

Dornbusch, R. (1976) Expectations and exchange rate dynamics. *Journal of Political Economy*, 84: 1161–1176.

Dornbusch, R. and Fischer, S. (1980) Exchange rates and the current account. *American Economic Review*, 70: 960–971.

Eichenbaum, M. and Evans, C. (1995) Some empirical evidence on the effect of shocks to monetary policy on exchange rates. *Quarterly Journal of Economics*, 110: 975–1009.

Eichengreen, B. (1994) History of the international monetary system: implications for research in international macroeoconomics and finance. In Van Der Ploeg, F., editor, *Handbook of International Macroeoconomics*, pp. 153–191, Oxford: Blackwell.

Elliot, G., Rothenberg, T. J., and Stock, J. H. (1996) Efficient tests for an autoregressive unit root. *Econometrica*, 64: 813–836.

Engel, C. (1996) A model of foreign exchange rate indetermination. NBER Working Paper 5766.

Engel, C. (1999) Accounting for US real exchange rate changes. *Journal of Political Economy*, 107(3): 507–538.

Engel, C. (2002) Expenditure switching and exchange rate policy. NBER Working Paper 9016.

Engle, R. (1982) Autoregressive conditional heteroscedasticity with estimates of the variance of United Kingdom inflation. *Econometrica*, 49: 987–1007.

Engle, R. and Granger, C. (1987) Cointegration and error correction: representation, estimation and testing. *Econometrica*, 55(2): 251–276.

Erceg, C., Henderson, D. W., and Levine, A. (2000) Optimal monetary policy with staggered wage and price contracts. *Journal of Monetary Economics*, 46: 281–313.

Faia, E. and Monacelli, T. (2003) Ramsey monetary policy and international relative prices. Mimeo, IGIER Bocconi and Universitat Pompeu Fabra.

Fairise, X. and Langot, F. (1995) A RBC model for explaining cyclical labor market features. In Hénin, P. Y., editor, *Advances in Business Cycle Research*, Berlin: Springer Verlag.

Farmer, R. (1993) *The Macroeconomics of Self-fulfilling Prophecies*. Cambridge, MA: MIT Press.

Faust, J. and Rogers, J. (2000) Monetary policy's role in exchange rate behavior. Board of Governors of the Federal Reserve System – International Finance Discussion Paper 652.

Feenstra, R. C. (1994) New product varieties and the measurement of international prices. *American Economic Review*, 84: 157–177.

Feldstein, M. and Horioka, C. (1980) Domestic saving and internal capital flows. *Economic Journal*, 90: 314–329.

Fleming, J. (1962) Domestic financial policies under fixed and floating exchange rates. *IMF Staff Papers*.

Flood, R. and Rose, A. (1995) Fixing exchange rates: a virtual quest for fundamentals. *Journal of Monetary Economics*, 36: 3–37.

Frenkel, J. and Razin, A. (1987) *Fiscal Policies and the World Economy: An Intertemporal Approach*. Cambridge: MIT Press.

Friedman, M. (1953) The case for flexible exchange rates. In Friedman, M., editor, *Essays in Positive Economics*, Chicago, IL: University of Chicago Press.

Froot, K. and Rogoff, K. (1995) Perspectives on PPP and long-run real exchange rates. In Grossman, G. and Rogoff, K., editors, *The Handbook of International Economics*, Chapter 32, pp. 1647–1687, Amsterdam: North Holland.

Fuerst, T. (1992) Liquidity, loanable funds, and real activity. *Journal of Monetary Economics*, 29: 3–24.

Fuller, W. A. (1976) *Introduction to Statistical Time Series*. New-York, NY: Wiley.

Gagnon, J. (1996) Net foreign assets and equilibrium exchange rates: panel evidence. International Finance Discussion Paper 574, Federal Reserve Board of Governors.

Gali, J. and Monacelli, T. (1999) Optimal policy and exchange rate volatility in a small open economy. Manuscript.

Gali, J. and Monacelli, T. (2002) Monetary policy and exchange rate volatility in a small open economy. NBER Working Paper 8905.

Gavin, W. and Kydland, F. (1999) Endogenous money supply and the business cycle. *Review of Economic Dynamics*, 2: 347–369.

Ghironi, F. (2000) Macroeconomic interdependence under incomplete markets. Working Paper 471, Boston College.

Giavazzi, F. and Wysploz, C. (1984) The real exchange rate, the current account and the speed of adjustment. In Bilson, J. and Marston, R. C., editors, *Exchange Rate Theory and Practice*, Chicago: University of Chicago Press.

Goodfriend, M. and King, R. (1997) The new neoclassical synthesis and the role of monetary policy. In Bernanke, B. and Rotemberg, J., editors, *NBER Macroeconomics Annual*, pp. 231–283, Cambridge: MIT Press.

Goodfriend, M. and King, R. G. (2001) The case for price stability. In Garcia-Herrero, T., editor, *Why Price Stability*, European Central Bank.

Gregory, A. W., Nason, J. M., and Watt, D. G. (1996) Testing for structural breaks in cointegrated relationship. *Journal of Econometrics*, 71: 321–341.

Gros, D. and Thygesen, N. (1998) *European Monetary Integration*. Reading, MA: Addison Wesley Longman, 2nd edition.

Hairault, J. and Portier, F. (1993a) Money, new Keynesian macroeconomics and the business cycle. *European Economic Review*, 37: 1533–1568.

Hairault, J. and Portier, F. (1993b) Monnaie et inflation dans un modèle de cycles réels. *Recherches Economiques de Louvain*, 59(4): 427–461.

Hairault, J., Patureau, L., and Sopraseuth, T. (2001) The exchange rate disconnect puzzle: a reappraisal. *Journal of International Money and Finance*, forthcoming.

Hansen, B. E. (1992) Test for parameters instability with I(1) processes. *Journal of Business and Economics Statistics*, 10: 321–335.

Hansen, G. (1985) Indivisible labor and the business cycle. *Journal of Monetary Economics*, 16(3): 309–327.

Hau, H. (2000) Exchange rate determination under factor price rigidities. *Journal of International Economics*, 50(2): 421–447.

Hau, H. and Rey, H. (2003) Exchange rates, equity prices and capital flows. CEPR Discussion Paper 3735.

Hodrick, R. and Prescott, E. (1997) Post war US business cycles: an empirical investigation. *Journal of Money, Credit and Banking*, 29: 1–16.

Huang, K. and Liu, Z. (2002) Staggered contracts and business cycle persistence. *Journal of Monetary Economics*, 49: 405–433.

Hummels, D. (1999) Toward a geography of trade costs. Manuscript, University of Chicago.

International Monetary Fund (1998) *International Financial Statistics*.

Ireland, P. (1997) A small, structural, quarterly model for monetary policy evaluation. *Carnegie Rochester Conference Series on Public Policy*, 47: 83–108.

Johansen, S. (1988) Statistical analysis of cointegration vectors. *Journal of Economic Dynamics and Control*, 12: 231–254.

Johansen, S. (1991) Estimation and hypothesis testing of cointegration vectors in gaussian vector autoregressive models. *Econometrica*, 59: 1551–1580.

Juster, F. T. and Stafford, M. W. (1991) The allocation of time: empirical findings, behavioral models, and problems of measurement. *Journal of Economic Literature*, 29: 471–522.

Kalyvitis, S. and Michaelides, A. (2001) New evidence on the effects of US monetary policy on exchange rates. *Economics Letters*, 71(2): 255–263.

Kim, S. and Roubini, N. (2000) Exchange rate anomalies in the industrial countries: a solution with a structural VAR approach. *Journal of Monetary Economics*, 45: 561–586.

Kimball, M. (1995a) The dynamic implications of the quantitative neo-monetarist model. *Journal of Money, Credit and Banking*, 27: 1241–1277.

Kimball, M. S. (1995b) The quantitative analytics of the basic neomonetarist model. *Journal of Money, Credit and Banking*, 27: 1241–1277.

King, R. and Watson, M. (1996) Money, prices, interest rates and the business cycle. *Review of Economics and Statistics*, 78(1): 35–53.

King, R. and Wolman, A. (1999) What should the monetary authority do when prices are sticky? In Taylor, J. B., editor, *Monetary Policy Rules*, Chicago, IL: University of Chicago Press.

King, R. G., Plosser, C. I., and Rebelo, S. T. (1987) Production, growth and business cycle: Technical Appendix. Working Paper, University of Rochester.

King, R., Plosser, C., and Rebelo, S. (1988) Production, growth and business cycles I: The basic neoclassical model. *Journal of Monetary Economics*, 21(2–3): 196–232.

Kollmann, R. (2001) The exchange rate in a dynamic-optimizing current account model with nominal rigidities: a quantitative investigation. *Journal of International Economics*, 55: 243–262.

Kollmann, R. (2002) Monetary policy rules in the open economy: effects on welfare and business cycles. *Journal of Monetary Economics*, 49: 989–1015.

Kraay, A., Loayza, N., Servén, L., and Ventura, J. (2000) Country portfolios. NBER Working Paper 7795.

Kwiatkowski, D., Phillips, P. C. B., Schmidt, P., and Shin, Y. (1992) Testing the null hypothesis of stationarity against the alternative of a unit root. How sure are we that economic time series have a unit root? *Journal of Econometrics*, 54: 159–178.

Kydland, F. and Prescott, E. (1982) Time to build and aggregate fluctuations. *Econometrica*, 50: 1345–1370.

Lane, P. (2001) The new open economy macroeconomics: a survey. *Journal of International Economics*, 54: 235–266.

Lane, P. R. and Milesi-Ferretti, G. M. (2000) The transfer problem revisited: net foreign assets and long-run real exchange rates. CEPR Discussion Paper 2511.

Lane, P. R. and Milesi-Ferretti, G. M. (2002a) External wealth, the trade balance, and the real exchange rate. *European Economic Review*, 46: 1049–1071.

Lane, P. R. and Milesi-Ferretti, G. M. (2002b) Long-term capital movements. In Bernanke, B. and Rogoff, K., editors, *NBER Macroeconomics Annual 2001*, Cambridge: MIT Press.

Leonard, G. and Stockman, A. C. (2002) Current accounts and exchange rates: a new look at the evidence. *Review of International Economics*, 10: 483–496.

Lettau, M. and Uhlig, H. (1995) Can habit formation be reconciled with business cycles facts? Mimeo, Center for Economic Research, Tilburg University. *Review of Economic Dynamics*, 3: 79–99.

Long, J. and Plosser, E. (1983) Real business cycles. *Journal of Political Economy*, 91: 39–69.

Lucas, R. (1987) *Models of Business Cycles*. Oxford: Basil Blackwell.

Lucas, R. (1990) Liquidity and interest rate. *Journal of Economic Theory*, 50: 237–264.

Lütkepohl, H. (1991) *Introduction to Multiple Time Series Analysis*. Berlin: Springer-Verlag.

Meese, R. and Rogoff, K. (1983) Empirical exchange rate models of the seventies: do they fit out of the sample? *Journal of International Economics*, 14: 3–24.

Mendoza, E. (1991) Real business cycles in a small open economy. *American Economic Review*, 81(4): 797–818.

Mishkin, F. (1999) International experiences with different monetary policy regimes. *Journal of Monetary Economics*, 43: 579–605.

Monacelli, T. (2002) Into the mussa puzzle: monetary policy regimes and the real exchange rate in a small open economy. *Journal of International Economics*, forthcoming.

Monacelli, T. (2003) Monetary policy in a low pass-through environment. IGIER Working Paper 228.

Moran, K. (2000) *Essays in Monetary Economics and Monetary Policy*. PhD thesis, University of Rochester.

Morrison, C. (1990) Market power, economic profitability and productivity growth measurement: an integrated structural approach. NBER Working Paper 3355.

Mundell, R. (1961) A theory of optimum currency area. *American Economic Review*, 51: 657–665.

Mundell, R. (1963) Capital mobility and stabilization policy under fixed and flexible exchange rates. *Canadian Journal of Economics and Political Science*, 29: 475–485.

Mussa, M. (1986) Nominal exchange rate regimes and the behavior of real exchange rates: evidence and implications. *Carnegie-Rochester Conference Series on Public Policy*, 25: 117–213.

Naik, N. and Moore, M. (1996) Habit formation and intertemporal substitution in individual food consumption. *The Review of Economics and Statistics*, 78(2): 321–328.

Obstfeld, M. and Rogoff, K. (1983) Speculative hyperinflations in maximizing models: can we rule them out? *Journal of Political Economy*, 91: 675–687.

Obstfeld, M. and Rogoff, K. (1995) Exchange rate dynamics redux. *Journal of Political Economy*, 103(3): 624–660.

Obstfeld, M. and Rogoff, K. (1996) *Foundations of International Macroeoconomics*, Cambridge: MIT Press.

Obstfeld, M. and Rogoff, K. (2000a) New directions for stochastic open economy models. *Journal of International Economics*, 50: 117–153.

Obstfeld, M. and Rogoff, K. (2000b) The six major puzzles in international macroeconomics: is there a common cause? In Bernanke, B. and Rogoff, K., editors, *NBER Macroeconomic Annual 2000*, pp. 339–390, Cambridge: MIT Press.

Obstfeld, M. and Rogoff, K. (2001) Perspectives on OECD, economic integration: implications for US current account adjustment. In *Global Economic Integration: Opportunities and Challenges*, pp. 169–208, Federal Reserve Bank of Kansas City.

Obstfeld, M. and Rogoff, K. (2002) Global implications of self-oriented national monetary rules. *Quarterly Journal of Economics*, 117: 503–536.

Obstfeld, M. and Stockman, A. (1985) Exchange rate dynamics. In Jones, R. W. and Kenen, P. B., editors, *Handbook of International Economics*, pp. 917–977, Amsterdam: Elsevier Science Publisher.

Ohanian, L. E., Stockman, A. C., and Kilian, L. (1995) The effects of real and monetary shocks in a business cycle model with some sticky prices. *Journal of Money, Credit, and Banking*, 27: 1209–1234.

Perron, P. and Ng, S. (1996) Useful modifications to some unit root tests with dependent errors and their local asymptotic properties. *Review of Economic Studies*, 63: 435–463.

Prescott, E. C. (1986) Theory ahead of business cycle measurement. *Federal Reserve Bank of Minneapolis Quarterly Review*, 10: 9–22.

Rauch, J. (1999) Networks versus markets in international trade. *Journal of International Economics*, 48: 7–35.

Rebelo, S. T. and Végh, C. (1995) Real effects of exchange rate based stabilization: an analysis of competing theories. In Bernanke, B. S. and Rotemberg, J. J., editors, *NBER Macroeconomic Annual 1995*, MA: MIT Press.

Rogoff, K. (1996) The purchasing power parity puzzle. *Journal of Economic Literature*, 34: 647–668.

Rotemberg, J. (1982a) Monopolistic price adjustment and aggregate output. *Review of Economic Studies*, 158: 517–531.

Rotemberg, J. (1982b) Sticky prices in the United States. *Journal of Political Economy*, 90: 1187–2111.

Rotemberg, J. (1996) Prices, output, and hours: an empirical analysis based on a sticky price model. *Journal of Monetary Economics*, 37: 505–533.

Rotemberg, J. and Woodford, M. (1997) An optimization-based econometric framework for the evaluation of monetary policy. In *NBER Macroeconomics Annual*, number 233, pp. 297–344. NBER.

Rotemberg, J. and Woodford, M. (1999) Interest-rate rules in an estimated sticky price model. In Taylor, J. B., editor, *Monetary Policy Rules*, number 6618. Chicago, IL: University of Chicago Press.

Samuelson, P. (1964) Theoretical notes on trade problems. *Review on Economics and Statistics*, 46: 145–164.

Sarno, L. (2001) Toward a new paradigm in open economy modeling: where do we stand? *Federal Reserve Bank of Saint Louis Review*, pp. 21–36.

Schlagenhauf, D. and Wrase, J. (1995) Liquidity and real activity in a simple open-economy model. *Journal of Monetary Economics*, 35(3): 431–461.

Schmitt-Grohé, S. and Uribe, M. (2003) Closing small open economy models. *Journal of International Economics*, forthcoming.

Senhadji, A. (1995) Adjustment of investment to external shocks in a small open economy under perfect and imperfect financial structures. Draft, Washington University.

Shiells, C. R., Stern, R. M., and Deardoff, A. V. (1986) Estimates of the elasticities of substitution between imports and home goods for the United States. *Weltwirtschaftliches Archiv*, 122(3): 497–519.

Sims, C. and Zha, T. (1998) Does monetary policy generate recessions. Atlanta Federal Reserve Bank Working Paper 98-12.

Smets, F. and Wouters, R. (2002) Openness, imperfect exchange rate pass-through and monetary policy. *Journal of Monetary Economics*, 49: 947–981.

Sopraseuth, T. (2002a) Exchange rate regimes and international business cycles: some empirical evidence from the Bretton Woods system and the EMS. In Hairalt, J. O. and Sopraseuth, T., editors, *Exchange Rate Dynamics*, London: Routledge.

Sopraseuth, T. (2002b) Fluctuations et régimes de change. *Annales d'Economie et Statistiques*, 66.

Stockman, A. (1983) Real exchange rates and the alternative exchange rate systems. *Journal of International Money and Finance*, 2(2): 147–166.

Stockman, A. and Tesar, L. (1995) Tastes and technology in a two-country model of the business cycle: explaining international comovements. *American Economic Review*, 85(1): 168–185.

Stockman, A. C. (1988) Real exchange rates variability under pegged and floating nominal exchange rate systems: an equilibrium theory. *Carnergie-Rochester Conference Series on Public Policy*, 29: 259–294.

Stockman, A. C. (1999) Choosing an exchange rate system. *Journal of Banking and Finance*, 23(10): 1483–1498.

Sutherland, A. (2003) International monetary coordination and financial market integration. Manuscript, University of Saint Andrews and CEPR.

Taylor, J. (1980) Aggregate dynamics and staggered contracts. *Journal of Political Economy*, 88(1): 1–23.

Taylor, J. (1993) Discretion vs. policy rules in practice. *Carnegie-Rochester Conference Series on Public Policy*, 39: 195–214.

Tille, C. (2000) Is the integration of world asset markets necessarily beneficial in the presence of monetary shocks? Staff Report 114, Federal Reserve Bank of New York.

Uctum, M. (1999) European integration and asymmetry in the EMS. *Journal of International Money and Finance*, 18(5): 769–798.

Uzawa, H. (1968) Time preference, the consumption function and optimum asset holdings. In Wolfe, J. N., editor, *Value, Capital and Growth: Papers in Honor of Sir John Hicks*, Edinburgh: Edinburg University Press.

Warne, A. (1993) A common trends model: identification, estimation and inference. Institute for International Economic Studies' Seminar Paper (555).

Warnock, F. E. (1998) Idiosyncratic tastes in a two-country optimizing model: implications of a standard presumption. International Finance Discussion Paper (1998-631), Federal Reserve Board.

Weil, P. (1989) Overlapping families of infinitely-lived agents. *Journal of Public Economics*, 38: 183–198.

Woodford, M. (1999a) Inflation stabilization and welfare. Mimeo, Princeton University.

Woodford, M. (1999b) Optimal monetary policy intertia. NBER Working Paper 7261.

Woodford, M. (2003) *Interest and Prices. Foundations of a Theory of Monetary Policy*. Princeton, NJ: Princeton University Press.

Yun, T. (1996) Monetary policy, nominal price rigidity, and business cycles. *Journal of Monetary Economics*, 37: 345–370.

Index